Towards Peoples' Histories in Pakistan

Critical Perspectives in South Asian History

Critical Perspectives in South Asian History publishes innovative scholarship on South Asian pasts that will be widely accessible to a broad scholarly audience. Titles in the series interrogate existing themes and periodisations as well as open up new areas of inquiry by welcoming a range of disciplinary and theoretical perspectives within a historical argument. The series focuses on three broad scholarly developments: a growing engagement with the public life of South Asian History, a conceptual shift from South Asia being the 'object' of study to becoming the generator or driving force behind new and distinctive research, and a concerted effort to study hitherto obscured regions, peoples, methods and sources that point to a reframing of the current boundaries in South Asian history. This series invites new works that creatively engage with public debates about the past, draws attention to the distinctiveness of different South Asian contexts, integrate South Asia within global histories and draw upon South Asian material. Welcoming South Asian Histories from the ancient world to the modern day, this series looks to bring scholarship on South Asia from different parts of the world in closer conversation and showcase the range and variety of new research in the field.

Published

Forms of the Left in Postcolonial South Asia, Sanjukta Sunderason & Lotte Hoek (eds)

Political Imaginaries in Twentieth-Century India, Mrinalini Sinha & Manu Goswami (eds)

Workplace Relations in Colonial Bengal, Anna Sailer

The Emergence of Brand-Name Capitalism in Late Colonial India, Douglas E. Haynes

The YMCA in Late Colonial India: Modernization, Philanthropy and American Soft Power in South India, Harald Fischer-Tine

Towards Peoples' Histories in Pakistan

(In)audible Voices, Forgotten Pasts

Edited by
Asad Ali and Kamran Asdar Ali

B L O O M S B U R Y
NEW DELHI • LONDON • OXFORD • NEW YORK • SYDNEY

BLOOMSBURY INDIA
Bloomsbury Publishing India Pvt. Ltd
Second Floor, LSC Building No. 4, DDA Complex, Pocket C–6&7,
Vasant Kunj, New Delhi 110070

BLOOMSBURY, BLOOMSBURY ACADEMIC INDIA and the Diana logo are trademarks of Bloomsbury Publishing Plc

First published in India 2023
First published in Great Britain 2023

Series design by Jade Barnett

Cover image © Bani Abidi, Jerry Fernandes – 7:45 pm, 21st August 2008, Ramadan. Karachi from Karachi Series I. Courtesy the artist

This edition published with permission from Bloomsbury Publishing Plc, 50 Bedford Square, London, WC1B3DP, UK

A catalogue record for this book is available from the British Library.
A catalog record for this book is available from the Library of Congress.

ISBN: 978-93-54357-91-6

Series: Critical Perspectives in South Asian History

Typeset by Newgen KnowledgeWorks Pvt. Ltd., Chennai, India
Printed and bound in India by Replika Press

To find out more about our authors and books visit www.bloomsbury.com and sign up for our newsletters

To our mothers, Zahida Sultana and Nur-un-Nehar Asdar, whose senses of the past fueled their hopes for the future

Contents

Figures

Acknowledgments

The authors want to thank the contributors to this volume for working with us with patience and perseverance. We would like to thank Kiran Ahmed, Noman Baig, Abdul Aijaz, Ilyas Chatta, Maira Hayat, and Vazira Zamindar for their support and conversations during the shaping of this project and to Bani Abidi for the cover image. Special thanks to our friends and colleagues Iftikhar Dadi and Anita Mir, who were a source of intellectual inspiration and encouragement throughout. Our sincere appreciation to the reviewers and editors at Bloomsbury, especially Maddie Holder, who early on saw promise in our volume, and Abigail Lane, who guided us during the entire process. In the end our profound sense of gratitude to our respective families.

Introduction

Asad Ali and Kamran Asdar Ali

History writing in Pakistan has for the most part been the writing of Pakistani History. As if the nation-state is the only subject of history—the only horizon of possible futures. These works concerned with high politics, of governments and regimes, of military coups and constitutional arrangements, regional tensions, and "insurgencies," the state of the economy and the economy of the state, the relationship of religion, politics, and the country's ideology continue with a long-standing tradition of History as the history of the nation-state. In "*Towards Peoples' Histories* in *Pakistan*" (rather than "A People's History *of* Pakistan") we seek to shift away from the singularity of the nation-state and offer a collection of essays that attempt other histories—ones that not only complicate nationalist historiography, from alternate perspectives that have often been ignored and erased, but are also attentive to other historical sensibilities and modalities of historical temporality, where temporality, as David Scott succinctly puts it, is "the lived experience of time passing—the social relation, more precisely, between past (the time of memory), present (the time of conscious awareness), and future (the time of anticipation)" (2014: 1).

The dominance of nationalism, and nationalist history, has often led to the mobilization and positioning of "people's history" in oppositional terms, as an alternative history. For example, Howard Zinn's influential *A People's History of the USA* sought to challenge the exclusions of triumphant nationalist historiography by attending to class conflicts, racial injustices, and gender inequalities. His attention to the multiplicity of social groups and their aspirations, desires, and conflicts was salutary in foregrounding erased histories and struggles and turning both "history" and "people" away from nationalist appropriations. As such, it was a counter narrative but one that, in the US case, followed a conventional chronology: "1492–present" (Zinn 2005). While complicating the putative basis of the "nation" and its progressivist erasure of violence, Zinn nonetheless retained the "nation-state" as the object of history as well as a conception of time, as sequential and linear that undergirds conventional historicism and historiography. Yet as Prasenjit Duara argued a generation ago, we have to "rescue history from the nation" (Duara 1995: 3) and we would add, by invoking Walter Benjamin, the unorthodox Marxist literary critic and cultural theorist, that we need to rescue history from "homogeneous, empty time" (Benjamin 2006: 395) (of which more below). The task was, as Duara formulated it, to decouple the "deep, tenacious and … repressive connection between history and the nation" while at the same time he acknowledged that it was, as yet, impossible to radically displace the nation as the locus of history" (Duara 1995: 4). In this volume, through a focus on peoples' histories we attempt this displacement while remaining attentive to the ways in which nationalist and peoples' histories can be imbricated and entangled.

In formulating this task, we conceive peoples' histories in the plural in contrast to, "the people," with a definite article, which assumes a known object and invokes a singular collectivity (Bosteels 2016; Olsen 2016). "Peoples" in the plural is suggestive of discrete and multiply differentiated groups and the plurality of life and therefore of histories, rather than History. It is, however, in the movement between existing peoples in their concrete actuality and plurality, and the abstract modern form of an imagined undifferentiated collectivity, "the people," that possibilities as well as tensions arise and closures accrue. Nationalism is one, intrinsically impossible attempt, to resolve this tension—one that emerges from the political potentialities of the peoples in their multiplicity and diversity being constrained within a singular community of identity and sentiment. Nonetheless, for us, a peoples' histories approach emphasizes how peoples in their variety and heterogeneity make history, not just of their differing accounts of themselves but also of their differing experiences of time, of the relations between past, present, and future, which is crucial to their historical consciousness. A peoples' histories perspective therefore necessarily grates against the compulsions that promote the nation as the singular subject of history.

In *Silencing the Past* (1995) the anthropologist, Michel-Rolph Trouillot, examines how power and representation are constitutive of what we understand to be history, and its concomitant silences. He points to how people are constantly making history in myriad ways but that these often remain ignored or unregistered by the academic profession. In saying "yet the fact that history is produced outside of academia is largely ignored in theories of history" (21), Trouillot forces us to think about the active production of history, between what happened and what is said to have happened. How history is recorded, produced, and engaged with is a crucial concern. In addition to revisiting the history of particular moments in Pakistan's past, we remain interested in the trajectories, archives, methodologies, processes, and eventual representation of the past. History writing, or historiography, far from being a neutral and scholarly enterprise based on positivist conceptions of evidence and objectivity that depicts itself as a transparent medium of understanding what the past is, on the contrary, as Duara argued, best understood as a discourse that enables "historical players (including historians) to deploy its resources to occlude, repress, appropriate and sometimes, negotiate with other modes of depicting the past, and thus, the present and the future" (5).

A peoples' histories perspective is necessarily attentive to other forms of social and political collectivity through which lives are lived, desires formed, aspirations articulated, struggles undertaken, and histories made. At the same time, the particular discursive configuration of nation and history has material effects in the world, both in how we understand and do history and how it governs people's lives. Therefore, this volume of peoples' histories in Pakistan works both against and in relation to the nation-state and its attendant history/historicism.

Time/History/Nation

The year 2022 marked Pakistan's seventy-fifth year. This co-incidence of a standardized quantitative measure with a collectivity, the nation, expresses the conjuncture of a particular conception of temporality, modern linear time, and but one form of collectivity, whereby diverse peoples occupying some 340,500 square miles (Pakistan) are reduced to a singular "nation." Seventy-five years marks the nation in history, and history, as the history of the nation-state. By "co-incidence," we do not mean a random, unrelated happenstance, but the elective affinity between a conception of temporality, one that undergirds modern history, and the nation as the singular subject of history. This concept of temporality, where time is understood as discrete, successive, and linear is what Walter Benjamin (1892–1940) in his last published work—the thesis "On the Concept of History," a critique of a theory of history (historicism) which had already become the predominant way of relating to the past—referred to as "homogeneous, empty time."[1]

Homogeneous, empty time is a conception of time emptied of the rhythms, cycles, ritual repetitions, traditions, and memories that gave the experience of time cultural meaning: the movement away from lived qualitative time into time as an abstract quantitative measure, marked by the development of clocks, elaborated in relation to an emergent capitalist economy and conceptualized through the development of Newtonian mechanics (Hunt 2008; Thompson 1991). It was this novel conception of time that, as the intellectual historian Reinhart Koselleck has shown, colonized and transformed traditional conceptions of *historia*, where the past, as a repository of experiences, was still meaningful and instructive to the present. But the "temporalization of history" through the new developments in the modern discipline of history enabled the transformation of *historia* from a domain of similarity, a repository of wisdom and exemplary actions into a domain of knowledge, of truths about actions, events, and processes that may explain the current structures and shape of the present, and as patterns are discerned and processes identified, also predictive of the future (Koselleck 2004: chapter 2). The past was no longer a "space of experience" but an arena where explanations of the present could be sought. But in so doing the past was unjoined from the present except through this passage of chronological time, so much so that the past is considered over with and dead.

Historicism is predicated on a series of assumptions, borrowed from the natural sciences, in which the past is temporally dislocated and sequestered from the present; the present can be understood as brought about by a causal sequence of events, of cause and effect, which the historian can reconstruct through an objective analysis of the evidence, usually written documents. This positivist idea of history as a means to

[1] The most used English translation of title and content, one that remains widely cited, is "Theses on the Philosophy of History" in Hannah Arendt (ed.) *Illuminations* (1992) and is widely referred to as "Theses on History." A more recent and increasingly cited translation, one used here, is entitled, "On the Concept of History," (H. Eiland and M. W. Jennings (eds.) *Selected Writings Volume 4: 1938–40* (Cambridge, MA: Harvard University Press, 2006), 389–400). Benjamin's article is now often referred to as the "Theses on the Concept of History."

the past, and of the relation of past and present, is determined by a causally connected series, which not only purports to describe the past "as it really was" but also identifies patterns and processes that enable predictions, and subsequently logics and teleologies of progress and development. This allowed, as Koselleck noted, the future as the place where science and reason could coalesce so that utopias could be imagined—that the future as it became more unknown, in that it was less and less reiterative of the past, was also, paradoxically, more plannable (Koselleck 2004: 39).

Historicism organized the investigation of the past as a site of knowledge and objective truths and in so doing was instrumental to an associated philosophy of history, where history orients itself as much to the future, as the place where a telos identified in the past will be realized. This was most fully elaborated by Hegel and inherited, albeit with critically informed revisions, by Marx into a materialist and dialectical history.[2] While the telos of history has variously been reason, freedom, humanity's self-realization—and usually some combination of these—the principal sociological forms in which they have been located, from the late nineteenth century on, has either been through national or class solidarities. Histories organized around nation and class have tended to be reductionist although the theoretical and analytical power of these two traditions is widely discrepant. Nationalist or nationally inspired histories, under the guise of positivist history (in its better versions) or through explicit ideologically informed histories (in its cruder variants), have sought either to describe the development of a nation's history or to cultivate national identity. Marxist-inspired approaches, however, by shifting the historical lens from the nation-state to the dominated, in what can be collectively described as "histories from below," have been immensely productive.[3] Thus it might not altogether be unsurprising that one of the most influential analyses of nationalism, albeit a highly sympathetic one, by Benedict Anderson (originally published in 1983) was produced by a scholar engaged with Marxist thought, who while noting how scholars were puzzled by nationalism's "philosophical poverty," also argued that the phenomena of nationalism had been largely disregarded by Marxism. That is, Marxist theorists, with a focus on class as the determinative dynamic of history, considered nationalism as either "anomalous" or even as "pathological."

Anderson sought rather to explain the cultural power of nationalism, its ability to generate affective attachments, and to do so he in part turned to another unorthodox Marxist, Walter Benjamin, who had, facing the successes of fascism, been critical of mainstream Marxism's inability to adequately analyze or comprehend this phenomenon. Crucial for Anderson is Benjamin's articulation of "homogeneous

[2] Traverso (2011, 2016) notes that there is more than one conception of history in Marx and that the dominant teleological and positivist version especially prominent in scientific Marxism can no longer be sustained, but there is also a dialectical and anti-positivist dimension of history that continues to be productive.

[3] In Pakistan, for example, the critique of nationalist history, of its errors, omissions, and distortions especially through state ideological apparatuses such as the national curriculum, text books, and the teaching of history has been referred to by the historian K. K. Aziz as "the murder of history" (1993). However, this critique, while important, is one mounted within the positivist tradition of historicism, in that it amounts to a critique of the failure to be properly objective and rigorous in the evaluation and use of evidence and factuality rather than to a critique of nationalist history.

empty time," which in Anderson's account is indicative of transformations in the "modes of apprehension" that were critical for the flourishing of the various modalities of print capitalism such as novels and newspapers that allowed one to imagine oneself as part of, and simultaneously with, a wider contemporary society. However, Anderson ignores Benjamin's fundamentally radical critique of "homogenous, empty time" and its corollary, historicism.[4] In using "homogeneous, empty time" as a sociological reality, Anderson effectively inhabits and reproduces historicisms' methodological assumption into a sociological explanation (see also Lynn Hunt 2008). That is, the concept of "homogenous, empty time" emerges from the transformation of social practices, particularly of the workplace, brought about by a mercantile and subsequently a capitalist economy. But to assume that it becomes the *only* conception of time, one that structures the only relation to the past, is to assume too much.[5] While it may have become hegemonic in our understanding of history/historicism—it remains but one way of relating to the past. Benjamin sought to recuperate and activate other forms of consciousness and relations to the past in order to enable a historically informed politics, and a politically informed historical practice, one that reanimates and reconnects the past to the present in a qualitatively lived experience of history. In Benjamin's life this task was even more urgent as history was predominately history written by the victors who erased the defeated and vanquished from history and in so doing rendered the present as "natural" or "necessary" rather than the outcome of political contestations and struggles. For Benjamin, therefore, the historian was a crucial political actor who intervened to break the continuums imposed by dominant historiographic traditions by "cast[ing] a new eye on the past and save the 'history of the vanquished' from oblivion" (Moses 1989: 11).[6]

Benjamin wrote his reflections on history in 1940 under extraordinary circumstances, when fascism was ascendant, when communism, in Stalin's USSR, had stymied socialism's promise, and with the Soviet-Nazi pact had betrayed the working classes and oppressed. In short, the prospects for a radical politics of emancipation, equality, and social justice never seemed so bleak. However, as he reminds us in the eighth thesis what seemed extraordinary for some was a persistent condition for the majority: "The tradition of the oppressed teaches us that the 'state of emergency' in which we live is not the exception but the rule" (Benjamin 2006: 392). A radical

4 Benjamin's "Theses" are opaque, partly because of his preferred aphoristic style and partly because they are the condensed poetic expression of his lifelong philosophical thinking on the intersection of politics, theology, and temporality. The "Theses" were not intended for publication as Benjamin recognized that "that would throw wide open the doors to enthusiastic incomprehension" (Lowy 2016: 17). The theses have occasioned extensive commentary. See Lowy (2016) for a brief contextual overview and a very useful exegesis and Eiland and Jennings's biography on Benjamin that discusses the context of the writing of the theses (2014: 647–76). Benjamin's poetic sensibility, incorporation of Jewish theological themes, and innovative style made his thought and writing, as many commentators have noted, *sui generis*.

5 Even the form of novel and newspaper that Anderson emphasized as crucial to the experience of simultaneity "was not necessarily an experience of temporal homogeneity; the present was shot through with past and future in novel and newspaper alike" (Burges and Elias 2016: 9–10).

6 See Moses (1989) and Brown (2001) for two instructive reflections and explications. For Benjamin the critique of historicism was a critical political task in enabling a redemptive politics, "not only of revolutionary politics but of everyday politics" (Brown: 157).

critique of the premises underlying historicism, such as the notion of progress which had become "common sense" and disabled critique needed to be dispensed with, so that neither the future as some promised utopia to which we are progressing, either in liberal or Marxist versions, nor the periodization of time which demarcated past from present could be the basis of critical understanding of a liberatory or redemptive politics (Brown 2001; Moses 1989; Traverso 2016). In the sixth thesis Benjamin argues, the critical task of the historian is not some description of the past, in "the way it really was"—but to reconnect the potentiality of the past, which is never quite dead, to the living, otherwise the dead too will be lost to the enemy.

> The only historian capable of fanning the spark of hope in the past is the one who is firmly convinced that *even the dead* will not be safe from the enemy, if he is victorious. And this enemy has never ceased to be victorious. (Benjamin 2006: 391, emphasis in original)

The Benjaminian imperative and impulse toward history outside of historicism in its nationalist, liberal, or Marxist forms through recognition of past struggles reconnects the dead to the living, dispenses with temporality as homogenous and empty, and instead brings the past into the present, where the example of the past is grasped to reignite struggles in the present, and where the present in so doing is capable of fulfilling and redeeming that past.[7] The historian in the present by recuperating histories of the oppressed and vanquished, of those written out, seeks to reclaim these histories for a politics in the present, to disavow what Benjamin termed "leftist melancholy" for that is to be beholden to a conception of time, history, and a telos rather than to struggle in the present.[8] In the wake of the ruins of postsocialist and postcolonial futures, David Scott has suggested that only by breaking with such ontologies of time can the future once again be opened as "undecidable and with heterogenous possibilities" (2014: 10).

Histories beyond the Nation

Within South Asian studies, one major intervention that reoriented history away from colonial and nationalist perspectives and toward peoples' histories was subaltern studies. This trend in Indian historiography was linked to the emergence

7 For Benjamin the authority of a living tradition had been sundered by the immense transformations brought about by the forces unleashed by "capitalism" but the past, in images, memories, objects, writings, sayings, and ways of doing nonetheless carried a potentiality and a force, and an attendant claim, into the present. Hannah Arendt suggests that Benjamin discovered the power of this fragmented past, in its citability and transmissibility—in place of authority to unsettle the present (1992: 43).

8 As Wendy Brown notes, Benjamin coined the term "left melancholy" in his criticism of revolutionaries who were "attached more to a particular analysis or ideal—even to the failure of that ideal—than to seizing possibilities for radical change in the present" (Brown 1999: 20). Enzo Traverso, however, while noting this negative aspect of melancholia in Benjamin, also points to the productive aspect of melancholy, which despite itself brings the past into the present (2016: 45–8).

of postcolonial studies as a valid space for critique and introspection about the histories of the non-West. Subaltern studies opened up the methodological arena of reading archives against the grain and paying attention to silences to bring forward subaltern voices. These interventions made it possible for many scholars to not only deconstruct nationalist narrative (influenced as this move was by Hayden White's insistence on form, narrative, and trope), but also question the "West" as the harbinger of all history.

While this paradigmatic shift in Indian historiography inspired new scholarship in Indian history and more widely, such as in Latin America, it has not, however, generated more than cursory engagement in Pakistan. It is beyond our capacity to review all the developments in South Asian historiography since the 1980s except to note that the emphasis on social history, subaltern studies, critical histories of colonialism—engendered by discourse analysis—as well as critical explorations of Indian capitalism, reflections on history itself and much besides have, as yet, not really left a significant mark on Pakistani historians. Very little attention has been paid to alternative social and political imaginaries and struggles, or methodologically to the "small voices of history" (Guha 1996) that could illuminate history from the ground up.

In recent years, however, there has been theoretically engaging and methodologically innovative work that has in important ways shifted attention away from the teleological Muslim nationalism that informs nationalist historiography.[9] Spurred by these developments, this book seeks to build on and extend this shift and suggest that, to this end, recent Palestinian scholarship is instructive. After years of writing within an overly charged nationalist framework, some Palestinian scholars have broken away and are writing histories of the everyday, of ordinary life and mundane practices.[10] We seek to encourage similar moves where long-neglected topics and themes can be brought in to broaden the scope of our understanding of society and culture in Pakistan. Nonetheless, it also remains vital to contest the various forms of national amnesia in Pakistan, which has taken many forms. From memory lapses (on the struggles of the Bengali and Baluch people) to a general silence on gendered violence, both during the 1947 Partition of British India and during 1971. The general point we make in this text is about recording the history of those who are inaudible in the grand narratives of national history through a methodology that incorporates a heterogeneity of ideas, images, and genres of writings. We would argue, where more formal archives are absent, then silences may be replaced through a close reading of fiction or other forms of representation. Further, we foreground the fragmentary, constructed, and contested nature of history writing so that the essays in this volume are neither tied

[9] To name but a few, works by Vazira Zamindar (*The Long Partition*), William Glover (*Making Lahore Modern*), Aamir Mufti (*Enlightenment in the Colony: The Jewish Question and the Crisis of Post-Colonial Culture*), Iftikhar Dadi (*Modernism and the Art of Muslim South Asia*), Farina Mir (*The Social Space of Language: Vernacular Culture in British Colonial Punjab*), and Ali Raza (*Revolutionary Pasts: Communist Internationalism in Colonial India*) stand out as doing exciting work on the region and country.

[10] See, for example, Salim Tamari, *Mountain against the Sea: Essays on Palestinian Society and Culture* (Berkeley: University of California Press, 2008).

to one methodology nor to a singular perspective. We hope that the essays reflect a sensibility that allows space for unruly and contradictory voices, open to both diverse perspectives and genres of writing, in order to enable multiple renderings of the past, and of ways of recounting those pasts.

Left Histories and the Question of "Progress"

In the "Theses" Benjamin's reflections on and critique of the idea of progress tethered to "homogeneous, empty time" was in no small part directed at those on the Left who subscribed to the notion of a telos to history—in short to the entirety of the Marxist tradition—although he directed his most acute comments to German and European social democrats. In the thirteenth thesis he says, "The concept of mankind's historical progress cannot be sundered from the concept of its progression through a homogenous, empty time. A critique of the concept of such a progression must underlie any criticism on the concept of progress itself"(2006: 394–5). This critique of progress is most vividly depicted in the famous ninth thesis where he describes, through a painting by Paul Klee, the angel of history whose back is to the future, his eyes directed at the past, seeing only the wreckage of the past as it accumulates but which he is helpless to prevent as a storm, which is called progress, propels him into the future and leaves catastrophe in its wake. History absent a telos removes the concept of progress from masking and subsuming the violence, inequities, and injustices of the past, and allows us to see the "storm." The idea of change as progress, as David Scott notes, "not only has a formal built-in rhythm of movement and alteration but also a built-in *vector* of moral direction" (Scott 2014: 5). Although the collapse of communism and retreat of socialist discourse since the 1990s has opened up the problem of teleology, the label "progressive" by the Left is still widely held. Insofar as the Left considers itself such because of its commitments to social justice, economic and social equality, and emancipation from precarity and servitude, then the term "progressive" can be considered shorthand for these principles. But we must disconnect the concept from temporality if we are to retain the term "progress" as a political and ethical orientation.

The essays in the first part of the book, on histories of working-class, communist activists and Left-wing political workers, together introduce us to an unrecognized and particularly underwritten history in Pakistan's context. They rely on oral history, memoirs, memories, and archives of leftist publications to reconstruct the past. The essays (and photo essay) help document and reframe social and cultural history by presenting other possible imaginations that were available for the country during the early decades of its existence. Yet they also remind us of the periodic arrests of activists and political victimization: lay-offs of workers were the state's response as people struggled for their rights and civic freedoms.

Enzo Traverso (2016) has suggested that many of those who work on the history of the Left do not explore a far and unknown past, but rather in many instances have lived and experienced the past they write about (as have several contributors to this volume). It is a history that is part of the lived memory of the writers themselves.

Their personal knowledge of the actors they are writing about at times complicates the distinctions between history and memory, as their work balances between the process of writing history and their own memories. This process of being part of the world that one describes is perhaps, not all that surprisingly, reflected in the essays—given that the majority of contributors are historically minded anthropologists, sociologists, and political scientists, rather than traditional historians who usually seek greater distance from their own immediate experience.

An example of this process is present in Kamran Asdar Ali's contribution to this volume where he traces the history of working-class politics in Karachi (the major industrial hub of the country) during what he refers to as the "long 1960s." Partly informed by his own memory as a student member of Left formations he focuses on archival material and oral histories, to raise questions on memory and history writing. The essay provides a narrative that traces the history of the progressive/labor movement and its links to the evolving political alternatives within Pakistan, after the banning of the Communist Party (1954) and subsequent to the martial law imposed in 1958, when formal politics was also restricted. Anushay Malik and Hassan Javid's essay deepens our understanding of this period. Through a "life writing" approach they examine the decline of the Left movement in Pakistan, as refracted through the experiences of activist B. M. Kutty, by focusing on the effects of three major turning points, namely the immediate aftermath of Partition in 1947, the war with India in 1965, and the liberation war in Bangladesh in 1971. Malik and Javid argue that the postcolonial state's drive to centralize power deepened ethnic and regional cleavages, bringing together diverse actors who laid the organizational foundations for the progressive movement in Pakistan. Like Ali, they detail how ideological differences within the nascent movement fractured its cohesion, and how state repression was successful in undermining progressive organizations while also casting their demands as being "seditious."

Despite state repression of Left cadres and political formations in Pakistan, there has always been a tradition of contesting state-sponsored narratives and ideology. Mahvish Ahmad, Hashim bin Rashid, and Ahmad Salim's contribution, in the shape of a photo essay, tells a story of Left-wing papers like *Surkh Parcham*, the organ of the banned Communist Party. The covers of a range of progressive and nationalistic magazines tell a broader story of the Left, not only the ability to publish and propagate ideas under regimes of strict state sponsored censorship, but also of how many of the political and editorial collectives behind this combination of publications politically differed from one another. Yet, simultaneously, the disjointed constellation of prints shed light on the vast and rich intellectual and political paper production that has always been a mainstay of the many lefts in Pakistan and survive as a central part of the country's cultural and political history. Almost all the publications featured in this photo essay were banned at some point, while others—like *Jabal*, issued as the organ of the armed Balochistan People's Liberation Front in the 1970s—were never legal to begin with. The authors argue that the building of alternative networks by these "little magazines" did far more than circumvent censorship, they also made possible the articulation and circulation of noncanonical political ideas and vocabularies that contested nation-state linked histories.

Nationalism's Many Violences

Recuperating leftist histories, of struggles for other possible presents and futures that have been repressed, is crucial if we are to stimulate alternative political imaginaries. But perhaps the most obvious erasures in the telling of Pakistan's national history is the state-sponsored violence against regional, ethnic, and political opponents that have been marked as enemies of the state. In terms of sheer scale and significance for Pakistan as an entity is the history of atrocities committed in East Pakistan in 1971, which has been mostly erased from national memory. What primarily passes as the history of 1971—never a part of the educational curriculum—is the constant retelling of one version of history that is present in the popular press and in published biographies by primarily ex-high-ranking army officers seeking to absolve themselves of any responsibility in the events that led to the breakup of the country. Such histories, by and large, remain apologies for the violence that the Pakistani military unleashed against Bengali citizens.

This erasure of violence is explored in Nayanika Mookherjee's essay that details the active forgetting, repression, and silencing of rape as an instrument of terror and war during the West Pakistani military's attempt to suppress a history of East Pakistani grievances and a nascent Bangladeshi nationalism. In Pakistan's official history this violence unleashed on its own citizens is still justified to maintain the nation's integrity. The path taken did not save the country from the ensuing death, destruction, and subsequent division. To be clear, for the most part, this is a period that has been systematically erased from national discourse and popular memory. Mookherjee's essay is, hence, an important corrective and reminder that raises issues of justice, forgiveness, and reparations that need to be faced rather than forgotten.

With Dina Siddiqi's essay we shift from post-1971 Pakistan to how the history of a unified Pakistan is a problem for the emerging nationalist historiography of Bangladesh. Through the figure and experiences of Biharis, who were collectively deemed to have been collaborators of the Pakistan Army and were now stranded in Bangladesh while awaiting "repatriation" to Pakistan, she examines, from the other side to Mookherjee, a history that "has been rendered unspeakable." The Biharis, once citizens, became stateless in Bangladesh (until 2003), and for a long time Pakistani governments refused to take them. Stranded in camps and caught between national and international legal regulations and the machinations of political regimes they inhabited an anomalous position of being neither citizens nor refugees. The Biharis' history in East Pakistan and their experiences in Bangladesh puncture nationalist narratives of a Bengali nation. As such, along with Partition, they prove a reminder of a history that proves awkward for Bengali nationalist history which demands their erasure. Siddiqi concludes that calls to make nationalism more inclusive are insufficient and that we need to "'denationalize' the writing of history—to move away from statist and teleological versions of history in order to address the incongruous and that which has been rendered 'unspeakable' through nationalist myth making."

Naila Mahmood's essay mirrors the issue of statelessness and citizen rights in detailing the experience of Bengalis in post-1971 Pakistan. For many years before and after its independence, Bangladesh suffered disasters such as floods, cyclones, and droughts and a severe famine in 1974. These events intensified the effects of the colossal economic damage caused by the war, severely affecting industrial workers, small peasants, agricultural laborers, and rural communities. The dire situation in Bangladesh during the 1970s led many poor Bangladeshis to illegally migrate to India and also to Pakistan. Hence, despite the memory of the war and its atrocities, many in Bangladesh illegally crossed dangerous borders in the 1970s and 1980s to arrive in a less-than-hospitable Pakistan; incidentally this indicates how nationalist imaginaries can be trumped by economic compulsions. Like the Biharis stranded in Bangladesh these Bengali migrants remain undocumented, legible to the Pakistani state only as "illegals." By focusing on oral narratives, Mahmood documents how Bengali women workers in Karachi, due to their class, language, and appearance, became easy targets of discrimination and ridicule. Bengali women faced unique and difficult challenges—besides the ethnic and class prejudices suffered by all Bengali migrants, they also had to endure and navigate patriarchy and gender discrimination.

Alternate Registers/Other Histories

The case of Baluchistan raises similar concerns over nationalist history and its various omissions and erasures. The ongoing insurgency in Baluchistan is a struggle that is ignored by most in the country.[11] As the writer Asif Farrukhi described, in a trenchantly incisive essay, Baluchistan continues to burn despite being '*na deeda aur na shunida*' (unseen and unheard, perhaps unrecognized), not that the embers had ever cooled down from earlier conflicts and oppression.[12] It is indeed a story that needs to be reconfigured by bringing together its various parts.

Balochistan and Balochis do, however, figure in the national imaginary as violent male subjects. Rather than accounts of political marginalization, economic exploitation, and military violence against the Baloch, Adeem Suhail, in his essay argues that the figuration of the Baloch as violent is a constitutive aspect of processes of archivization. The archives, in the broadest sense of the term, enable certain kinds of actions, usually attached to the notion of gendered male violence, through which the Baloch enter the historical record. Thus the Baloch, posited as "violent subjects," are subjected to state violence and they in turn produce counternarratives of heroic and violent resistance. As against this statist, gendered nationalist archive and discourse, and its mirroring, Suhail utilizes Gyanendra Pandey's notion of "unarchived histories"—that is, not

[11] Since Pakistan's independence, there have been five uprisings against the state in Baluchistan, in 1948, 1958–60, the mid-1960s, a major insurgency between 1973 and 1977, and a low-level insurgency that began in the early 2000s and is still going on. Today, killings and disappearances of Baluch political activists are commonplace. For the insurgency of the 1970s, see Selig Harrison, *In Afghanistan's Shadow: Baluch Nationalism and Soviet Temptations* (Washington, DC: Carnegie Endowment, 1981).

[12] Asif Farrukhi, "Muzahimat Ki Darsiyat," in Afzal Murad (trans. and ed.), *Injeer Kay Phool* (Balochistan Kay Afsaney) (Karachi: Scheherazade Publications, 2005), 161–80.

only those histories that have been actively forgotten by the processes of inclusion and exclusion attendant to any discursive formation but also those that are considered too "trifling" to enter the historical register (Pandey 2014).[13] By privileging the voices of two Balochi women, Suhail not only critiques the masculinist aspects inherent in all nationalist discourses but also puts forward the argument (as many essays in this volume do) for a new attempt to remember and recuperate that which always remains partial and fragmentary. It is akin to, as the historian Joan Scott reminds us, an archaeological reconstruction of a pot from shards and pieces found in a dig (Scott 2011: 11–13).

The essays in this volume lead to a broader discussion on the relation between documents and history. As De Certeau has argued, history is primarily historiography, a form of writing about the past, based on documents, or other forms of writing that have existed (De Certeau 1988). For Benjamin too, the history of the oppressed, whether it remained unwritten because of active erasure, or could not be written because of the lack of documents and archives, required a different sense of what might constitute archive and history, to "brush history against the grain" (Benjamin 2006: 392). As against the documentary records and their forms of transmission Benjamin, in his wider work, emphasizes memories, images, cultural artifacts, historical products, social practices, stories, and archival fragments through which the past resides in tradition, culture, practice, memory—alternative modes of transmission that can challenge the written historiography of the dominant, and of the state. Given that the production of documents is one of the principal activities of a state and the relative paucity of documents written by the oppressed, historians in postcolonial societies (and elsewhere) have in the past few decades developed new innovative means to write history and, perhaps also ought to consider, ways other than writing, to think more expansively about history (Palmié and Charles Stewart 2016).

In Pakistan we need not only to find traces of these histories in various archives and writings, but also to develop methodologies that incorporate a diversity of ideas, images, and genres of representation. Further, where more formal archives are absent the silences of the traditional archive may be replaced through a close reading of fiction or other forms of representation. Kasmani's essay evocatively mobilizes poetic and sonic registers to "critique, interrupt, and refuse a for-granted continuity of the present." He examines how these registers produce lyrical affects and forms of "unstraight" and/or "queer" narratives and belongings. Kasmani juxtaposes two scenes of queerness, the poetry of the gay Pakistani-American poet Iftikhar Naseem and Shi'i-religious lyric from the shrine of Sehwan Sharif, in Sindh, that enable other inhabitances of temporality and forms of historical consciousness—one's that depart from the constraints of historicism. Although Kasmani does not invoke Benjamin, the echo of Benjamin is in his work, as it is in many of the contributions to this volume. This Benjaminian impulse without Benjamin is testimony to how many

[13] Pandey, in turn, borrows the term "unarchived" from Derrida (Derrida 1996) and redeploys it in order to consider how the trifling "attitudes and actions that are so utterly ordinary and routinized as to be taken as being 'always so'" ; and consequently are unmarked, unremarked and unhistorical is one aspect of the unarchived (Pandey 2014: 7).

of his insights have been independently developed by scholars in postwar forms of history, in Western and postcolonial states as they sought to overcome the limitations of historicism both in terms of the subjects of history and the traditional archives upon which it relied.

Amen Jaffer's essay also explores how alternative forms of historical imaginings and temporality are formed through social practices in Sufi shrines, in this case the relatively minor and unknown shrine of Khawaja Bihari in Lahore. Such "wayside shrines," he suggests, often act as spaces of refuge and possibility detached from the dominant narratives and temporalities of the "modern." Practices of storytelling that weave between personal biographies, the prosaic and miraculous activities of Sufi saints, allow for the making of contemplative sensibilities, morally instructive practices and forms of solidarity that can be politically mobilized to challenge state authority.

Storytelling through performance modes at important ritual and celebratory occasions has, as Claire Pamment describes in her contribution, long been the preserve of transgender persons in South Asia. Pamment examines this practice and way of life that has long been considered marginal and, more recently, as "backward" and disreputable. Consequently, the inclusion of transgenders as citizens by the Pakistani courts is seen as a sign of national inclusion and progress. But rather than mapping transgender through this linear historical temporality—one that both invokes progress and correlatively the past as a site of loss and absence—Pamment, invoking Anjali Arondekar's critique of the recuperative impulse, urges instead moving "beyond the grammars of failure of loss and toward an archival poetics of ordinary surplus" or "abundance." The excerpts from a collaborative performance piece, *Teesri Dhun* (The Third Tune) is both a compelling example of irreverent play with pious homilies and a questioning of liberatory narratives of progress. Here too then the fragments from the past, whether in cultural memory and/or embodied performances, rather than a stimulus of melancholic feelings of loss, from some supposed totality, is a catalyst for the constitution of joy, abundance, and solidarities in the present and future.

Politics and "the people"

The question of who constitute "the people," conceptually and in practice, has always been a complicated one. In modern political thought "the people," from social contract theory on, have been the source of sovereignty and democratic legitimacy. But in addition to the people as sovereign, a second aspect, deriving from Roman history, is the idea of the common people (*populus*, usually the *plebs*), and thirdly, from romantic thought, the conception of the people as the nation (Canovan 2005).[14] There is then, as Canovan remarks of the concept, a "range of meanings and internal tensions that give the notion both its rhetorical usefulness and its conceptual obscurity" (39). On the one hand, an abstract political concept of "the people," and on the other a range

[14] Although as Canovan carefully notes, "the plebian *populus* was a defined class of citizens ... the English 'common people' would include all the lower orders" (2005: 12).

of actually existing peoples in various societies and histories. It is the interaction between these political conceptions and social groupings of various peoples through which a singular conception of "the people" is delimited in any given sociopolitical order. As such there are powerful tendencies to posit a particular grouping, whether class, nation, or some other particular category, to stand for the whole. Through the interplay of political concepts and actual social entities, of different articulations of the social and the political, various configurations of the people are possible—but these all necessarily entail exclusions. The contributors to a recent volume, from within political philosophy, who sought to reflect on the valence and mobilization of this concept in contemporary times, argued that while the category, as with all categories, has limits and exclusions, this should not render the category as "practically inoperative" but rather to recognize that the political and social "divisions and exclusions that keep the people from ever being one are very much part and parcel of the category's uncanny political efficacy" (Bosteels 2016: 4). They argue that rather than "the people" it is vital to consider peoples in the plural. In this volume we have sought not only to attend to the specific histories of particular peoples but also to explore mobilizations of the political category of "the people" in various ways. Thus while being attentive to the rhetorical invocations of "the people" in the singular, both Akhtar's and Iqtidar's essays attend to the manner of exclusions they generate.

Akhtar traces the political imaginaries and reflections of political activists on the Left who, inspired, by socialism and communist discourses were inculcated as revolutionary subjects. They expected the "idealized trinity" of students, workers, and peasants to usher in a social and political revolution. The failure of the revolution to materialize, however, while indicative of limitations in orthodox leftist discourse and its interpreters, did not, however, leave these political workers as either cynical or nostalgic; that is, on the one hand rejecting the possibility of radical transformation and, on the other, attaching to and persisting with a form of political thought and action that was found inadequate or irrelevant. On the contrary, their continued political work and reflections, while remaining couched in Marxism, at the same time questioned the old certainties. This enabled them to expand and broaden their thought and action in relation to ongoing conditions. Akhtar sensitively traces this movement that both relies on somewhat simplified political categories and imaginaries to enable political action and the social complexities and divisions in Pakistani society.

Humeira Iqtidar reflects on a different kind of exclusion—of how particular peoples are included but also marginalized through liberal political rationality—in particular, how liberal discourses of tolerance and intolerance enable exclusion and violence. While having the people as the source of popular sovereignty and legitimate democracy theoretically entails their inclusion as individual citizens, liberalism and democracy have not always been aligned as the conjunction of liberal-democracy would suggest. On the contrary, liberalism as a political technology of government has been more than amenable to enabling various exclusions, historically with, as she says, the "working classes, women, religious minorities and racialized others."[15] Through a

[15] In the Pakistani context, see Asad Ahmed's account of how the Ahmadiyya were excluded from Muslim identity and community through liberal legalism (Ahmed 2010).

micro-study of an event, of interreligious violence in a Lahori neighborhood, Iqtidar examines the interplay of political and social understandings of "the people." She argues that liberalism's focus on the individual, and its discourse of tolerance, as an individual virtue to manage differences deflects from ongoing economic, social, and political processes through which difference is both produced and lived with, albeit through other registers of social practice.

From a micro-study of a violent event we shift, with Farida Shaheed's essay, to reflections on the women's movements response to Zia-ul-Haq's systemic violence against women. Shaheed's essay shows the manner in which Islam, under General Zia, was mobilized in a state-led political project of cultural hegemony, to reduce, marginalize, and diminish the capacity of women as political subjects. Under Zia, a particularly patriarchic and religious conception of the people was propagated. Shaheed reflects on how a handful of women activists, who were and continue to be routinely dismissed as "western" and "anti-national," were nonetheless effective in contesting Zia's program. The inability to roll back all of the discriminatory legislation or to radically transform societal attitudes on gender has led some to label the women's movement a "failure." But Shaheed argues that the modalities and practices of activism itself challenged the production of cultural hegemony in demonstrating the capacity, actions, and desires of women who, through reclaiming public space, disrupted patriarchy and in responding to rules of exclusion produced new kinds of arguments that exceeded the mere assertion of rights. As such the women's movement, with their everyday tactics of mobilization, disruption, and engagement—in spite of their limited numbers—brought women's issues, differences, and thought to public and political prominence. In so doing they not only effectively challenged but countered Zia's attempt at cultural hegemony.

Crucial to women's mobilization was a sense of anger and outrage at Zia's policies, of emotional solidarities forged among diverse and stratified groups of women as they struggled, over decades, to reassert their political and legal rights. In the "Theses" Walter Benjamin locates emotion as central to politics for it is through emotions that values and aspirations are transformed into political action, both in pursuit of ideals and against adversaries. One commentator, Werner Hamacher, argues that in the "Theses" Benjamin uncovers "the temporal structure of the political affect" (2001: 161). By this he means that past political actions and struggles hold an affective potentiality that can be recognized and reactivated in the present, thereby forging a connection to a past moment that animates present political struggles. In his recognition of political emotion, as with so much else, Benjamin brushed against the grain. Hamacher comments, "The fact that *pathemata*, affects, passions, were already to a large extent discredited within political theory during Benjamin's times must have been attributed by him to the disappearance of their genuine political dimension" (ibid.). It is only recently that this exclusion of emotion from politics has been challenged by scholars in a variety of disciplines, and Asad Ali's contribution explores the "genuine political dimension" of emotions among Pakistan People's Party (PPP) workers who were politicized in the election campaign of 1970. His essay seeks to relocate the place of political emotion in the politics of the oppressed. In the PPP case emotions generated by emancipatory struggles and demands for equality came to be invested in, channeled through, and embodied by Zulfikar Ali Bhutto. Ali's essay seeks to shift the usual understanding of an emotional politics, which focuses on Bhutto's charisma, in order to retrieve the politics in emotion that emerged from the aspirations, activism, and struggles of ordinary people and political workers as they coalesced in a political movement.

It is time then to shift our gaze from the nation and its historiography and attend to multiple histories from the ground up, to rescue history from the nation—and time from History—for histories. As against concepts of progression and progress that enable nationalist, ideological, and even "emancipatory" violence on varied peoples, we seek to reorient and expand the conception and practice of history, and of other forms of relating to the past. This, we suggest, will enable a renewed emphasis on the qualitative lived heterogeneous time of peoples in their multiplicity, variety, struggles, and self-conception.

Our approach then is fragmentary, episodic, even at times conflictual, for this reproduces the experiences of social division and difference. Unharnessed from the determinations imposed by a historical object such as the nation or revolution, a peoples' histories perspective does not therefore have any methodological imperatives to a spurious comprehensiveness. There is no need to chronologically divide and link successive periods and eras but rather to weave in, out, and through such histories. We hope that this volume, with its possibilities and problems, will stimulate a productive conversation, encourage others to critically engage with its themes, enable more robust historical thinking, and generate a re-envisioning of the potentiality of the past and the obligations it confers.

Bibliography

Ahmed, Asad A. 2010. "The Paradoxes of Ahmadiyya Identity: The Legal Appropriation of Muslimness and the Construction of Ahmadiyya Difference," in N. Khan (ed.), *Beyond Crisis: A Critical Second Look at Pakistan*. New Delhi: Routledge, 273–314.

Anderson, Benedict. 1991. *Imagined Communities: Reflections on the Origins and Spread of Nationalism*. London: Verso.

Arendt, Hannah. 1992. "Introduction: Walter Benjamin 1892–1940," in Hannah Arendt (ed.), *Illuminations*. London: Fontana Press, 7–58.

Aziz, Khursheed K. 1993. *The Murder of History in Pakistan*. Lahore: Sang-e-Meel.

Benjamin, Walter. 1992. "Theses on the Philosophy of History," in Hannah Arendt (ed.), *Illuminations*. London: Fontana Press, 245–55.

Benjamin, Walter. 2006. "On the Concept of History," in Howard Eiland and Michael W. Jennings (eds.), *Walter Benjamin: Selected Writings Volume 4, 1938–40*. Cambridge, MA: Belknap Press of Harvard University Press, 389–400.

Bosteels, Bruno. 2016. "Introduction: This People Which Is Not One," in A. Badiou, J. Butler, G. Didi-Huberman, S. Khiari, J. Rancière, and P. Bourdieu, *What Is a People?* New York: Columbia University Press, 1–20.

Brown, Wendy. 2001. "Specters and Angels: Benjamin and Derrida," in *Politics Out of History*. Princeton, NJ: Princeton University Press, 138–73.

Brown, Wendy. 1999. "Resisting Left Melancholy." *Boundary 2* 26 (3): 19–27.

Burges, J., and A. J. Elias. 2016. "Time Studies Today," in *Time*. New York: New York University Press, 1–27.
Canovan, Margaret. 2005. *The People*. Cambridge: Polity.
Certeau, Michel de. 1988. *The Writing of History*. New York: Columbia University Press.
Derrida, Jacques. 1996. *Archive Fever: A Freudian Impression*. Chicago: University of Chicago Press.
Duara, Prasenjit. 1995. *Rescuing History from the Nation: Questioning Narratives of Modern China*. Chicago: University of Chicago Press.
Eiland, Howard, and Michael W. Jennings. 2014. *Walter Benjamin: A Critical Life*. Cambridge, MA: Belknap Press of Harvard University Press.
Farrukhi, Asif. 2005. "Muzahimat Ki Darsiyat," in Afzal Murad (trans. and ed.), *Injeer Kay Phool* (Balochistan Kay Afsaney). Karachi: Scheherazade Publications Karachi, 161–80.
Gilmartin, David. 1988. *Empire and Islam: Punjab and the Making of Pakistan*. Berkeley: University of California Press.
Guha, Ranajit. 1996. "The Small Voice of History," in *Subaltern Studies* 9. Delhi: Oxford University Press, 1–12.
Hamacher, Werner. 2001. "'NOW': Walter Benjamin on Historical Time," in Heidrun Friese (ed.), *The Moment: Time and Rupture in Modern Thought*. Liverpool: Liverpool University Press, 161–96.
Harrison, Selig. 1981. *In Afghanistan's Shadow: Baluch Nationalism and Soviet Temptations*. Washington: Carnegie Endowment.
Hartog, Francois. 2015. *Regimes of Historicity: Presentism and the Experience of Time*. New York: Columbia University Press.
Hunt, Lynn. 2008. *Measuring Time, Making History*. New edition [online]. Budapest: Central European University Press (generated 12 January 2023). Available online: http://books.openedition.org/ceup/810. ISBN: 9786155211485.
Jalal, Ayesha. 1985. *The Sole Spokesman: Jinnah, the Muslim League and the Demand for Pakistan*. Cambridge: Cambridge University Press.
Kosselleck, Reinhart. 2004. *Futures Past: On the Semantics of Historical Time*. New York: Columbia University Press.
Lowy, Michael. 2016. *Fire Alarm: Reading Walter Benjamin's "On the Concept of History."* London: Verso.
Manto, Sadat H. 1990. "Jaib-e-Kafan" (The Shroud's Pocket), in *Manto Nama* Lahore: Sang-e-Meel Press, 221–9.
Moses, Stephane. 1989. "The Theological-Political Model of History in the Thought of Walter Benjamin." *History and Memory* 1 (2) (Fall–Winter): 5–33.
Olsen, Kevin. 2016. "Conclusion: Fragile Collectivities, Imagined Sovereignties," in A. Badiou, J. Butler, G. Didi-Huberman, S. Khiari, J. Rancière, and P. Bourdieu. *What Is a People?* New York: Columbia University Press, 107–31.
Palmié, Stephan, and Charles Stewart. 2016. "Introduction: For an Anthropology of History." *HAU: Journal of Ethnographic Theory* 6 (1): 207–36.
Pandey, Gyanendra. 2014. *Unarchived Histories: The "Mad" and the "Trifling" in the Colonial and Postcolonial World*. New York: Routledge.
Scott, David. 2014. *Omens of Adversity: Tragedy, Time, Memory, Justice*. Durham, NC: Duke University Press.
Scott, Joan W. 2011. *The Fantasy of Feminist History*. Durham, NC: Duke University Press.
Thompson, Edward P. 1991. *Customs in Common*. London: Merlin Press.
Traverso, Enzo. 2016. *Left-Wing Melancholia*. New York: Columbia University Press.

Traverso, Enzo. 2011. "Marx, History, and Historians: A Relationship in Need of Reinvention," *Actuel Marx* 2 (50): 153–65. DOI: 10.3917/amx.050.0153. https://www.cairn-int.info/journal-actuel-marx-2011-2-page-153.htm.
Trouillot, Michel-Rolph. 1995. *Silencing the Past*. Boston: Beacon Press.
Zinn, Howard. 2005. *A People's History of the United States: 1492–Present*. New York: Harper Perennial Modern Classics.

Part One

Recalling "Progressive" Histories

1

The Left and Its Legacies: The Long 1960s in Pakistan

Kamran Asdar Ali

In officially sanctioned Pakistani nationalist historiography, the scholarly preoccupation remains linked to the narrative surrounding the creation of a unified nation (in Pakistan's case, the unified Muslim nation) by giving the diversity of national life scant attention. In addition to the focus on Muslim nationalism, other narratives are rehearsed as political histories that create predictive lenses for the present. A popular story about early postindependence history retells the history of Muslim nationalism and its logical continuation in the late 1940s' Objective Resolution for an Islamic State, but then culminates in the 1980s and General Zia-ul-Haq's (1977–88) era of Islamization and the proliferation of Islamist politics. There are other such histories that circulate around elite personalities, be they past presidents, prime ministers, or martial law administrators.

Yet Pakistan's early history has been one of contestation and conflict around questions of national self-determination of various ethnic groups, while the promised or imagined religious (Muslim) cohesiveness and national belonging have been difficult to achieve. Within this context, as much as the new country was formed on an ideological platform of Muslim nationalism in South Asia, the shape of its future culture, polity, and forms of governance initially remained an open question. As the historical moment produced discussions on the future of the new state, one major vision was that of the Communist Party of Pakistan (CPP) and its small number of cadres. Hence, class along with ethnicity and national rights remain relevant categories as one attempts to, as I propose to do in this essay, write a history of the Pakistani Left.

Not to belabor the point, but in his examination of another South Asian event of the early twentieth century, Shahid Amin (1995: 3) reminds us how nationalist master narratives can induce selective national amnesia in relation to events that fit awkwardly into neatly woven patterns.[1] Similarly, few in Pakistan even remember the series of events that shaped Left and labor politics in many cases during the 1950s and 1960s. The mostly unwritten history of such struggles is connected to their unremembered status in the national psyche. For example, it is almost forgotten how

[1] The Chauri Chaura incident took place in February 1922. The major incident was the burning of a police station by a politicized and angry mob.

the long military rule in the 1950s and 1960s, with deep links to industrial and feudal interests, led to a popular mobilization that demanded democratic reform, economic redistribution, social justice, and rights for ethnic minorities. Indeed, the results of the 1970 elections—with nationalist parties winning in Baluchistan, North-West Frontier Province (NWFP),[2] and East Bengal—is interpreted by some as an important juncture in Pakistan's history in which there was a popular consensus to resolve the nationalities question.

In this essay I retrace the early history of the Communist and Left movement in Pakistan while specially focusing on the history of working-class politics in Karachi (the major industrial hub of the country) during, what I refer to as, the long 1960s.[3] Working with archival material and oral histories, the essay seeks to raise questions on memory and history writing that this volume (and several of the included essays) is itself engaged with. In the subsequent sections I will briefly provide a narrative that traces the history of the progressive/labor movement and its links to the evolving political alternatives within Pakistan after the banning of the CPP (1954) and subsequent to the martial law imposed in 1958, when formal politics was also restricted. Addressing this challenge, in an earlier published book (Ali 2015) I focused on communist and working-class history from 1947 to 1972. If the late 1940s are considered the founding moment of communism in the country (along with the independence of Pakistan itself), linked as the period was to the international consolidation of communism in Eastern Europe and the victory of Maoism in China, then the 1960s were surely its zenith, as urban-based working-class and student movements destabilized the status quo. I place the current essay as continuum with my former work. This path, in addition to documenting the period, enables me to reframe Pakistan's social and cultural history by presenting other possible imaginations for Pakistan's future that were available during the formative period and sensitive to an approach that is open to a diversity of voices (points of view), to multiple renderings of the past (including state violence and repression), and to counter-memories that challenge the more established histories, even of the Left.

In providing this narrative, we need to be mindful that the leadership within progressive forces (including CPP) were sincere, thoughtful, and in solidarity with those who are considered to be the downtrodden and the marginalized within Pakistani society. Their commitment made possible a different trajectory of politics among the urban working class, peasants, students, middle-class intellectuals, artists and literary personalities that grew to sometimes challenge the status quo and demand changes in governance structure during Pakistan's short history. There was a transformational hope in the proclamations and a learning from history, a memory of the past (albeit a Marxist vision of history) that informed most of the leaders and workers of the movement to imagine a more socially just and egalitarian future. I however, also remain sensitive to other voices in the process of writing this history as attention needs to be paid to those perspectives from within the Left cadres itself that could update us about

[2] The province has been renamed Khyber Pakhtunkhawa (KPK) in recent years.

[3] It is formulated as a period that links the political changes in the 1960s, which have an organic link to the preceding decade and carry on into the next.

those not in the leadership, who with all the uncertainties in their lives, struggled to create opportunities to lead meaningful existences.

Detailing this history, I borrow from Lauren Berlant's (2011) suggestion that we now live in a "presentist" time and have almost extinguished the history of a Marxist past. A history and memory that was necessarily oriented toward the future. As Enzo Traverso (2016) argues (albeit from mostly a European perspective), 1989 also became a "spiritual roofless" moment as previously there may have been a more general understanding regarding past attempts to transform or interpret the world. Rather than succumb to the inevitability of the neoliberal present, as today new avenues are sought for socially just futures, Traverso maintains that there needs to be a critical reengagement with past histories of struggle. He calls for us to critically rethink socialist and progressive histories while it is being erased from collective memory. As much as the First World War birthed the twentieth century, the events of 1917 shaped hope and utopia for millions around the globe, including the then colonized world. The Russian Revolution (with all its tragedies and subsequent failures) and its emancipatory impulses were integral to the history of the past century. Traverso claims that we now enter our new century without that history of hope, utopia, and transformation. He reminds us, for example, how during the student- and workers-led movements in many parts of the world in the 1960s—the anti-war movement in the United States, student protests in France, the Mexico City student movement, and the Prague Spring in Czechoslovakia (to name a few)—there were utopian strains where history and memory were not about a cult (or being commodified), but rather mobilized to be incorporated into these struggles; Auschwitz informed the anticolonial commitment of many French intellectuals (Traverso 2016).[4]

I partially follow Traverso's argument to make a related assertion in order to reiterate that the history of either communism or the progressive movement in Pakistan is part of a forgotten past at best and can be considered as discarded "debris" at its worst (see Stoler 2008). It will hence question the assumption of an inevitable history of progress and redemption (in a Benjaminian sense, also see the introduction to this volume), in order to critique the universalistic tendencies embedded in Left politics itself. As suggested above, in a postcolonial and post-Empire register, researchers could reframe the present outside teleological certainties of progressive histories and perhaps productively use concepts such as "debris" and "ruin" to understand the multiple forms—along with the concomitant contradictions and uncertainties—in which the past continues and impinges on the present in dynamic and unpredictable ways.[5]

New Beginnings

The CPP was formed a few months after British India separated into two countries as the Communist Party of India (CPI) also divided into two constitutive parts during its second Congress in February–March of 1948. Syed Sajjad Zaheer was elected the

[4] Enzo Traverso, *Left Wing Melancholia* (New York: Columbia University Press, 2016).
[5] Also see the discussion on Walter Benjamin in this volume's introduction.

general secretary as he had opted to go to Pakistan. It was also initially decided that the East Bengal party would continue to be guided by the West Bengal Communist Party and retain its link to CPI, hence it was only the West Pakistan Party that would constitute an entirely separate entity.

Like Zaheer, CPP's leadership, generally arrived from India, was not familiar with the cultural and political landscape of the country and many belonged to the North Indian *ashraf*, a highly educated and self-conscious Muslim elite, personally steeped in the comportment, culture, and aesthetics of North Indian *adab* in its many connotations and meanings—as literary genre, concept, and personal quality (Metcalf 1984). Yet these very same people were also dedicated to establishing a future socialist society that was committed to democratic values, distribution of wealth, and putting an end to exploitation of the oppressed. They brought with them a vision of an anticipatory politics that argued for a future that would be more egalitarian and more liberating than that being offered by the dominant political forces. These men (and they were mostly men) had grown up influenced by the lessons of the Soviet October Revolution of 1917 and had similar utopian visions of delivering happiness to humankind in South Asia (Pakistan) by transforming nature to ensure material needs and by struggling against individualism and exploitation to guarantee social justice (Stites 1989). These dreams and ideals, along with a commitment to the anti-colonial struggle, were at the core of the communist movement in British India that they brought with them to the newly formed state after 1947.

Within this context, the CPP started work in an international climate in which the Pakistani state became enmeshed in Cold War politics soon after its independence. The British and US intelligence agencies worked closely with the higher echelons of the Pakistani state to curtail the "communist threat." In the 1950s, this relationship intensified and Pakistan's political and military leadership took the country into US-sponsored anti-communist treaties such as SEATO and CENTO (Gardezi and Rashid 1983),[6] leading to severe repression of the Communist Party and its eventual banning in 1954.

The Pakistan Trade Union Federation (PTUF) was the most important link that the Communist Party had with the working class. By 1948–9, approximately 150 unions were distinctly placed in two camps; the PTUF was led by leaders close to members of the Communist Party and was the continuation of the former Communist-supported All India Trade Union Congress (AITUC). The other major (non-communist) group of unions was the Pakistan Federation of Labor (West Pakistan) and the All Pakistan Trade Union Federation (East Pakistan), which merged by 1949 to become the All Pakistan Federation of Labor (APFL). Indeed, in 1947 Pakistan was primarily a rural

[6] From the late 1940s and for most of the 1950s, defense accounted for almost 50 percent of the total state expenditure. There were visits to Pakistan by US naval ships in 1948, and in May 1948 the US War Assets Administration gave a credit of 10 million dollars to the Pakistani Ministry of Finance to purchase US surplus military hardware. In May–June 1950, Prime Minister Liaquat Ali Khan made an official trip to the United States, spurning an offer from the Soviet Union. The following July, Pakistan entered the IMF and subsequently received several grants and loans from the US government and from the World Bank. To manage this developing aid and military relationship, the Ford Foundation stepped in to train local administrators, social scientists, and military officers.

country with majority of its 80 million inhabitants in both wings earning their living through agriculture. Less than 1 percent of its population were involved in wage labor that included working in factories, mines, railroad transport, and tea plantations. The country inherited only 9 percent of the total industrial establishment of British India. The lack of industrial capital was mirrored by the weakness of organized industrial labor and the peasantry (Shaheed 1983).

In its initial period of existence, the nascent Pakistan government followed an import substitution model to rapidly industrialize the economy. The state also relied heavily on agricultural exports, specifically East Pakistani jute, to subsidize industrial development in West Pakistan (Papenek 1967). The state promoted industrialization by providing soft loans and tax holidays and by setting up the Pakistan Industrial Credit and Investment Corporation in the late 1940s with assistance from the World Bank and foreign capital. Due to early lack of response from the local merchant capital, the state also formed the Pakistan Industrial Development Corporation (PIDC) through which it initiated industrial projects that were then transferred to the private sector at bargain prices.[7] The first phase of private industrialization occurred after the Korean War, when the profits gained by Pakistani traders were channeled into industrial investment. For example, special areas were developed in Karachi: the Sindh Industrial Trading Estate (SITE) and Landhi–Korangi industrial area, and land was sold to construct factories at extremely generous rates. With the state's role in setting up industries, the bureaucracy became intrinsically involved in the control of this industrial expansion. For example, 774 new industries were established in Karachi between 1947 and 1955, representing almost 50 percent of all industrialization in Pakistan (Salar 1986)). State agencies directly financed the industrial concerns or participated in legislating laws to favor this growth. On the one hand, the collusion of the bureaucracy and the industrialist was manifested in facilitating the finances for expansion of industrial groups that were controlled by different families (e.g., Adamjee, Dawood, Saigol, Isphahani, Valika). On the other hand, this alliance kept the wage rates down and ensured industrial peace by suppressing the working class.

Although the unionized strength of workers was very small, by the early 1950s the PTUF along with its communist allies was active in bringing like-minded groups of intellectuals, peasants, and workers together to demand higher wages, shorter working hours, land reforms, the repeal of the Public Safety Acts, and also to condemn the government of Pakistan for its cooperation with the Anglo-American bloc.[8] It set out demands that included Pakistan's immediately establishing a friendly relationship with the Soviet Union and Communist China, support for the Soviet Union policy of banning the use of atomic weapons and resigning from the British Commonwealth. In communiques, PTUF argued that a large portion of the country's budget was being spent on defense-related expenditure and not on enhancing workers' wages or providing them with better housing, free education, and quality health care.[9] All these

7 See National Archives, USA 890-D.053/2.252, Foreign Service Dispatch, February 2, 1952, PIDC.

8 See *The Status of Organized Labor in Pakistan*, OIR Report # 5286.

9 See London, TNO/PRO DO 142/160, "Weekly Report, Deputy High Commissioner, Lahore," May 10, 1950.

demands were to be fulfilled by abolishing landlordism and feudalism and distributing the seized land among the tillers. The big industries were to be nationalized and foreign capital was to be taken over by the state without any compensation. The path to this transformation was the formation of strong and fighting unions and their preparation for the final struggle, the general strike to move forward a vigorous campaign to gain victory.[10]

Hence and despite Karachi, as in other places in Pakistan, having lost a large number of militant and organized cadres (mostly Hindu) from the trade unions due to Partition, still retained a diversified labor movement that included unions among bidi workers, tram workers, railway workers, and hotel workers.[11] Most of these unions had communist influences. Being the major port in West Pakistan, the Karachi Port Trust (KPT) had the highest number of employed dock workers, and Mohammad Sharaf Ali, a member of the party who had migrated from India, was elected its general secretary.[12] Due to CPP's post-Calcutta Congress immediate political position that the post-independence moment was a time of generalized insurrection to move to the next stage of social evolution, there was a constant call on cadres and workers to involve themselves in strikes, sit downs, and work place agitation. Hence, under Sharaf Ali's general leadership communist unions in Karachi moved the workers forward toward a more militant struggle; the CPP pushed a politics of agitation on all fronts. So, if the Port Trust workers struck on one day, the postal workers would bring out a procession the following week or the Public Works Department (PWD) workers would hold a hunger strike a few days later. In Karachi alone, Communist Party fellow travelers and sympathizers in the autumn of 1951 organized strikes by the employees of Hotel Metropole, one of the most posh hotels in the city, by the transport workers union, at the Pakistan Tobacco Company and in the oil companies—Burmah Shell, Standard Vacuum, and Caltex.[13]

The government was ever more vigilant in Karachi, the capital, against any kind of threat to the law-and-order situation and responded with widespread arrests.[14] It used the Public Safety Act and other draconian measures from the colonial era to harass Communist Party workers and sympathetic trade unionists. Important members of CPP's central committee were periodically put in jail and communist publications were routinely banned or confiscated. By all accounts the government was firmly in control of the situation and used a law-and-order pretext to take vigorous action against any political threat from the Left.

It is within the parameters of such political processes that we should place the most blatant attack on the CPP when on March 9, 1951, the government of Pakistan

[10] See *The Status of Organized Labor in Pakistan*.

[11] See London, TNO/PRO 890D.06/1–852. Also see "American Embassy, Karachi Despatch 742," January 8, 1952.

[12] Sharaf Ali was also the secretary of the Karachi District Organizing Committee of the CPP and a member of the Provincial Organizing Committee. He was originally from Allahabad in Uttar Pradesh, India.

[13] See PRO 890D.06/1–852, "American Embassy, Karachi Despatch 742," January 8, 1952.

[14] PRO DO 142/160, "Pakistan Labour Review, Report by Labour Advisor to the High Commissioner, Karachi," April 8, 1949.

brought charges of sedition and of plotting a military coup against certain leaders of its own military (see Zaheer 1998) and against members of the Central Committee of the CPP, Sajjad Zaheer (general secretary) and Mohammad Ata.[15] This event in Pakistan's history now known as the Rawalpindi Conspiracy Case is based on a crucial meeting in Rawalpindi at the residence of a senior member of the Pakistan Army, Major General Akbar Khan on February 23, 1951. Following the charges there were widespread arrests and a blanket clampdown on the Communist Party's activities, and by the summer of 1951, although it had not been declared illegal, most of its first and second tiers of leadership were in jail, the party had been linked to a case of high treason, and many fellow travelers had left the popular front organizations due to the state's repression. The authorities had also seized party documents and now had a more thorough knowledge of the party's inner workings than ever before (see Anwer Ali 1952). The conspiracy case gave the government a conduit to publicly revile the party as anti-state and anti-Islam and increased its future vulnerability due to the added information that the police and intelligence services had about its workings.

The entire process crippled the movement and demoralized numerous cadres. The communist movement in Pakistan, nascent as it was, did not recover from this suppression for years.[16] There was no doubt that in the aftermath of the Rawalpindi Conspiracy Case there was general disillusionment and disarray among the members and cadres of the CPP. Once the party was officially banned in the summer of 1954 after the dismantling of the United Front government in East Bengal,[17] there was a new wave of political suppression along with arrests of the remaining active cadres. The party had to move its work underground and function in various mass fronts (whether in student groups, labor fronts, or peasant organizations) in different parts of the country without a centralized structure guiding them. Further, by 1954, the CPP-supported Pakistan Trade Union Federation (PTUF) had also been weakened and many had joined the state-sponsored All Pakistan Confederation of Labour (APCOL) as that was the only vehicle to conduct trade union politics in the country.

Yet, despite state-sponsored repressive measures, worker unrest increased. The deteriorating social and economic conditions of the working class and the disparity in income levels that were becoming evident in the Pakistan of the 1950s gave rise to several labor strikes. According to estimates, between 1954 and 1957 there were more than 250 strikes in Karachi alone in which more than 200,000 workers were involved (Salar 1986). However, labor was periodically warned by government functionaries throughout the 1950s not to hamper the industrialization process with strikes and upheavals. The emerging state structure subordinated labor organizations by sponsoring, as mentioned above, anti-communist trade unions (APCOL) by banning Left and popular trade unions, and passing draconian labor laws that effectively

15 Zaheer and Ata were arrested a few weeks later.

16 A discussion of these arrests and attacks on the CPI in the post- Conspiracy era can be found in PRO DO 35.2591, Report on the Communist Activity in Pakistan.

17 Under the pretext of the law-and-order situation, the state dismissed the elected government on May 30, 1954, only a few months after it was elected in to power. Governor's direct rule was imposed and Iskander Mirza, the defense secretary (and later president), was sent as the governor to "control" the situation.

prevented collective bargaining or the right to strike (Shaheed 1983: 272).[18] Finally, the Martial Law in 1958 eventually made it more difficult to organize labor on a radical trade union platform.

The 1950s

In order to offer a more personal rendering of the communist movement in the 1950s, let me introduce Hasan Nasir, one of the major figures of the movement of the period, who died in government custody in 1960.[19] Hasan Nasir arrived in Karachi during the summer months of 1948. The city was then the first capital of Pakistan and was undergoing rapid social and cultural change. The city's population was around 450,000 in 1947; Sindhi was spoken by 60 percent of the inhabitants and 51 percent of those were Hindus, while 42 percent were Muslims. By 1951, with the influx of almost 600,000 "refugees" from India, the entire demographics of the city had changed. It had become a predominantly Urdu-speaking city with a majority of them being Muslims.

Hasan Nasir was born in 1928 into a middle-class *Shia* Muslim family in the principality of Hyderabad in British India. It is possible that after the Calcutta Congress, the party had directed him, like many Muslim comrades in India, to go to Pakistan and help the newly appointed secretary general of CPP, Sajjad Zaheer, in his work. From his arrival in Pakistan onward Hasan Nasir became a member of the CPP and was one of the first few full-timers in the Karachi district organizing committee. By 1949 he was also one of the members from Sind on the central committee of the CPP. Nasir was just twenty years old and had become active in the inner circle, working with the trade union movement, the progressive writers, and also overseeing the distribution of *Naya Zamana*, the party periodical. After coming to Pakistan, he was first arrested after the Rawalpindi Conspiracy Case, but was released within a year. He spent part of his detention in 1951–2 in the Lahore Fort. He was picked up again in 1954 when the Communist Party was eventually banned and he was exiled from the country, most probably spending this time in India. He came back to Pakistan in 1955. There may have been a few more arrests in the 1950s during which time he was in Karachi Central Jail, but he was arrested for the final time in August 1960 after evading arrest and surviving mostly underground since October 1958 when martial law was declared in the entire country by General Mohammad Ayub Khan.[20]

[18] In my interviews with trade union workers, they remembered how radical workers and those desiring to form unions were either harassed, beaten by local thugs hired by the industrialists, or dismissed from work on one pretext or another. With rampant unemployment and a surplus of labor many workers desisted from joining unions due to the fear of such reprisals.

[19] The official version was that Hasan Nasir had committed suicide by hanging himself with a pyjama string on November 13, 1960. This version has been vigorously contested by his comrades and family and the death has been attributed to state torture while in custody.

[20] Ayub was the first Pakistani head of the army and he was appointed in 1950. Between the years 1950 and 1958 he had become an influential figure at the highest level in the corridors of power and was also one of the major architects of Pakistan's close relationship with the United States at the height of the Cold War.

Due to his many stints in prison, Nasir was well aware of how the state reacted by arresting political workers in moments of national crisis. He also understood how the law could be manipulated in order to equip the security services with the tools to harass their political opponents. Even as early as 1949, in a CPP district organizing committee report, Hasan Nasir (under the pseudonym Ghaznavi) discussed how the police relied on informants to arrest and interrogate party sympathizers in order to reach the central leadership. Armed searches, interrogation techniques (that combined bribing, coaxing, and cajoling with severe torture), and constant surveillance and harassment of family members created a sense of fear among the workers who were close to the party or were linked to one of the affiliated trade unions (Anwer Ali 1952: 149–52). As mentioned above, these patterns continued throughout the 1950s as scores of political workers—many belonging to the Communist Party, the trade union movement, or progressive political alliances—were taken to police stations, jails, lockups, and prisons under the Public Safety Act or the Security Act of Pakistan.[21] Among all these sites of interrogation and detention, the most dreaded space was the Lahore Fort, where Hasan was found dead in November of 1960.

Hasan Nasir's death is commemorated by the Left in Pakistan even today. Especially in the first decade or two following his death, which were characterized by political turmoil and social movements, his life and death became a symbol of protest and resistance to the military regimes and oppressive governments. There is hardly a memoir of a leftist leader of a certain generation in Pakistan that does not mention his first or last meeting with Hasan Nasir, an association that gives legitimacy to the leader's own credentials as a selfless worker for the cause.[22] Yet despite this commemoration in Pakistan there is very little known about his personal or political life. Similarly, his early life remains somewhat shrouded in mystery (much like the name of his house in Hyderabad, *Dhoop Chaon*, meaning Sun and Shade or Light and Shadows). It is possible that as a young man in Hyderabad, he may have been influenced by the Telangana peasant movement in south India and joined the communist movement as a student. It is also possible that he may have moved to Bombay to work with the party in the trade union movement from where he was asked to come to Pakistan. We get fragments of anecdotes from memoirs or newspaper columns written much after his death in custody. One source that does share much about the life and times of Hasan Nasir during his Karachi days, and hence gives us a glimpse of Left politics from a more non-elite perspective, is the interview by Mohammad Ali Malabari, a trade union worker, who in the 1950s was a member of the Communist Party of Pakistan. This interview from the 1960s (Malabari 2008) helps us get to know Mohammad Ali himself who, as a *beedi* (rolled tobacco) worker from the Indian province of Karnataka, came to Karachi a couple of years prior to the country's independence in 1947. He had traveled to Karachi after working in Bombay

[21] The Public Safety Act was a continuation of early colonial era rules and was used widely in preemptive arrests of political opponents (especially communists) in the late 1940s by the government of Pakistan. The Security Act of Pakistan was introduced in 1952 giving the federal government the right to review every three months without judicial intervention and prolong the preventive detention of a suspect.

[22] Almost all progressive poets have written poems celebrating Nasir's sacrifice, and in 2010, for the first time Pakistan's state television, PTV, organized a talk show about Hasan Nasir.

and Lyallpur, where he got involved in working-class politics through Sikh comrades and eventually joined CPP in the late 1940s. Soon after Partition, Karachi was teeming with people from different parts of India and the working class itself was divided in terms of which Indian province people had come from: United Provinces, Central Provinces, Hyderabad, Bihar, Kerala, Karnataka, and so on. Prior to1947, most of the local workers in different trade unions were either Hindu (they had a large presence in the municipal corporation), from Marathi or Gujrati background or Makrani Baluch (Karachi Port Trust). The Urdu-speaking workers (immigrants) from North India mostly arrived in the city after the country was formed. Mohammad Ali talks about this group as coming from small towns and rural parts of India where they did not have any experience of working in factories or of working-class politics. Acknowledging how people like Hasan Nasir tried to regroup a movement that had become devastated due to Partition, Mohammad Ali in his interview says:

> Due to the creation of Pakistan, Hindu comrades had to leave and it would take time for Muslim workers to take their place. The partition violence was used in such a way that those Hindu workers who did not want to leave the country, their lives were threatened and religious hatred increased to such an extent that they would have to accept marginalized lives in the new country. In Karachi's established proletariats, the majority was Hindu and when they left it was not only that the workers were gone, but the entire trade union movement (which had Hindu leaders) was destroyed.

Hence the challenge in the early years was to reconnect with the new laborers and bring them into the fold of class-based politics, where the tendency among the newcomers from India was more toward regional and ethnic solidarity. As mentioned above, although Karachi was not a very industrialized city (like Bombay, Calcutta, or Ahmedabad in undivided India), the Communist Party had roots in different working groups, such as the Port Trust workers, postal workers, tramway company, Burmah Shell, and the *beedi* (rolled tobacco) workers union (these unions were affiliated with the CPI before Partition). Most of the *beedi* workers were from South India and lived in a part of the city called Soldier Bazaar. In those days, due to the concentration of these workers, the area was also called Stalingrad. Mohammad Ali being a trained *beedi* worker from before also being from South India found a place among those already living in Soldier Bazaar.

The interview is given in a form of homage and is almost hagiographic in its presentation. However, it also gives us a sense of deep respect and friendship toward Nasir. He speaks about first meeting Hasan Nasir in 1948–9 when he used to come to Mohammad Ali's living quarters to give study lessons on Marxism to the workers. Later he remained close to him and spent many years under his tutelage. There are passages about both of them spending the entire night walking around different parts of Karachi and also ending up in the newly constructed upper-middle-class neighborhoods of PECHS (Pakistan Employees Cooperative Housing Society) with their large bungalows and manicured lawns.[23] Through Mohammad Ali's rendition we

[23] Also see Qurutal Ain Hyder's novella, *Housing Society*, in *A Season of Betrayals* (a short story and two novellas), 1999, which reveals a similar sense of the city.

get a spatial understanding of Karachi in the 1950s and how it was fast becoming a hierarchically class-based society. During one such long walk (after the banning of the CPP in 1954), Mohammad Ali discusses how he shared his own apprehensions about continuing his political/trade union work and his desire to migrate to the Arab Gulf states as opportunities were opening up there for workers in the construction sector and the oil refineries. He shares that Hasan Nasir would admonish him and say that workers have no land, their land is where they have work and where they conduct their working-class politics. According to Mohammad Ali, Nasir would say how he was exiled to India (1954–5), but came back. His family's lands and riches could not keep him there. Neither could the party (CPI), nor could his family who had spoken to them about him remaining in India. The question he raised was why did he not stay there? His answer was that his struggle was in Karachi; the labourers he had lived with, learnt from, and taught socialism to, were in Karachi. Not in India. He would occasionally say to Mohammad Ali, seeking to persuade him not to leave Karachi for Dubai, "I will stay here, so will you. Our graves will be made in this land" (Malabari 2008: 303).

In the subsequent portions of the interview, Mohammad Ali mentions that Nasir was a quiet and serious in temperament about the task he had dedicated himself to, the building of a proletarian party. Nasir's ten years or so in Karachi were lived mostly underground, constantly hiding from the security services. Mohammad Ali remembers Hasan Nasir as having no permanent home and his eating and sleeping habits being irregular: "He would eat the simplest of street food and sleep wherever he could get some space, on a park bench, on the Party office's floor,[24] or in a worker's living quarters" (Malabari 2008: 291–312).[25]

During his imprisonment in the early 1950s, Nasir was popular among the prisoners and even among the prison staff. In the interview Mohammad Ali Malabari remembers that when he himself was arrested in the early 1950s and sent to Karachi Central Jail, the other nonpolitical prisoners, on hearing he was Hasan Nasir's friend, started paying him additional respect (ibid.), Even the guards would take care of him and the officers would not ask him to do manual labor as they knew Hasan Nasir had taught him how to resist such orders as political prisoners had to be treated differently from common criminals. However, being in a police lockup or in Karachi's Central Jail may have been different from being in the Lahore Fort,[26] the seat of power of the dreaded CID and Intelligence Bureau of the time. Where Hasan Nasir could resist the demands of the jail authorities, in the Lahore Fort such demands could be taken as resistance that more torture could tame and discipline. Or perhaps Hasan Nasir remained silent,

[24] The CPP had an office near the Lighthouse Cinema near the Municipal Building on Bundar Road (now M. A. Jinnah Road) in Karachi.

[25] Mohammad Ali reports from a few eyewitness accounts of Nasir's days before he was arrested for the last time that he was constantly followed and it was becoming very dangerous for him to even visit close relatives or friends who as a routine would provide him with shelter and food. He found for the last time Hasan Nasir lying in a city park a month before his arrest; Nasir had not eaten for a few days and asked for monetary assistance from Mohammad Ali. ("Ek Mazdoor Sathi Ki Yadein," 291–312).

[26] The circumstances of Nasir's arrest are attributed to people within communist movement who may have informed the police of his whereabouts. This is a larger discussion outside the purview of this essay.

not offering to speak and provide a confession. The response to this silence is at times the increase in the intensity of torture. Silence in this case, however, is the absence of confession and a narrative that is meaningful language, as the prisoner does make audible noises due to pain and agony. Did his silence require an intensification of violence on Nasir's body by the state structure in order to tame through torture and interrogation the "disorder" residing in his specific body and through the exercise of this material power eventually seek to spread fear over a larger population? (Feldman 1991). Perhaps Nasir's death, a loss for his comrades and family, also became the limit of the interrogation itself—the speaking body with a possible confession was no more.

Formal Politics and the Left

I detoured into Hasan Nasir's brief life history to offer a more personalized glimpse on the working of the communist cadres in the Karachi of the 1950s. It was also during the aftermath of CPP's official ban in 1954, individual and now underground CPP leaders entered into alliances with emerging political formations and political parties that were nationalist, secular, and anti-imperialist in orientation. Many joined the Awami League, a political party led by the peasant leader Maulana Abdul Hameed Bhashani and Huseyn Shaheed Suhrawardy, a democratic and secular politician. While the Awami League had its base in East Bengal, in the West, Mian Iftikharuddin (a politician and publisher of progressive newspapers) and his Azad Party took the initiative of inviting various regional and nationalist groups to form a new party, which was opposed to the centralizing tendencies of the Pakistan government and also had an anti-imperialist and pro-worker politics.

In October 1955, prior to the passing of the new constitution in 1956, the government had created two provinces, East and West Pakistan (this was called the One Unit system). The process was perceived as a counterbalance to the political and population strength in East Pakistan where the majority were Bangla-speaking. However, this was at the cost of denying the ethnically and linguistically diverse population of West Pakistan their right to self-determination. The regional linguistic and cultural groups, such as the Sindhis, Pashtuns, and Baluch, were vehemently opposed to their loss of provincial autonomy.[27] So the secular but nationalist leadership of these provinces, which at times consisted of tribal chiefs and big landholders, and who had been denied the political space to form their own provincial governments, were seen as allies by the progressive elements and the scattered ex-Communist Party cadres. Iftikharuddin was successful in bringing these groups and parties together in a coalition, the Pakistan National Party (PNP), in 1956.[28]

[27] The One Unit administration was put in place to ostensibly solve the government's problem of governing parts of Pakistan that were thousand miles apart. The program merged the four provinces of West Pakistan to bring it into numerical parity with East Pakistan. West Pakistan's capital was in Lahore and East Pakistan's in Dhaka (then spelled Dacca).

[28] In addition to the Azad Party, there was Ghaffar Khan's Khudai Khimatgar Movement (his brother, Dr. Khan Saheb was also incidentally the governor of West Pakistan during this time), G. M. Syed's Sind Awami Mahaz, Prince Karim's Ustman Gal (People's Party, Baluchistan), and also from Baluchistan Samad Achakzai's Waroor Pakhtoon (Pakhtoon Brotherhood). Later this group reached

During this same period Huseyn Shaheed Suhrawardy of the Awami League became the prime minister of Pakistan (in office, September 1956–October 1957) and in a policy decision favored the Anglo-French position during the Suez crisis in 1956. This led to division and protest within the party and Bhashani and his faction left the Awami League. This breakaway group aligned with the PNP and in July 1957, the National Awami Party (NAP) was formed as a secular nationalist party with a progressive manifesto. Bhashani was elected the central president, the Pashtun leader Ghaffar Khan as the president of West Pakistan, and Mahmud ul Haq Usmani, a Karachi-based politician, as the general secretary.

One of the main objectives of the newly formed party was the undoing of the One Unit. Despite their subservience (and they did not have many options in formal politics as the Communist Party was officially banned), the Left worked toward retaining the party's unity as it was committed to the ideals of regional and cultural autonomy in the face of the state-sponsored Muslim nationalist (one people, Islam, Urdu) ideology. Further, groups representing various regions within the NAP agreed with the Left's anti-imperialist position and on the question of agrarian reform. So there was a pragmatic agreement to continue to work within the framework of the party, albeit the Left was seldom in a position of power or authority.[29] Yet, more seasoned Communist Party workers like Mohammad Ali Malabari along with the leftist elements in these various parties felt sidelined by the dominance of regional leaders (mostly large landholders). For example, in his above-cited interview, Mohammad Ali also comments on this process by saying,

> After the country gained independence we were tied to the *nawabs* who were not part of the government. For example, Mian Iftikharuddin[30] and his Azad Party, then we joined Awami League, from where we entered NAP, which also was a party of those with means. It had *khans* from NWFP, *sardars* from Baluchistan, landlords from Punjab and *waderas* from Sindh. There were bourgeois of all kinds, and lastly there were communist … we would run the trade union and do the office work. Those amongst us who were educated, those were better off communists they would recite ghazals (poetry) in gatherings. When such people went to jail, even there they would get an orderly … so there were two classes of communists, those who were first class and then rest of us. (Malabari 2008: 251–2)

This encapsulates a sense of betrayal that many sincere workers felt toward their own leaders in the progressive movement during the first two decades after Pakistan's independence. This resentment also reflects the political crisis that had engulfed

out to Gantantari Dal (People's Party) in East Pakistan, which also joined the party. See Ayesha Jalal, *The State of Martial Rule* (Cambridge: Cambridge University Press, 1990), 233.

29 In contrast to the ambivalent relationship of the CPP in the late 1940s (see Ali, *Communism in Pakistan*), now the Left was forced to enter into an alliance with the same elite leadership of tribal chiefs and large landowners for its own political survival.

30 Mian Iftikharuddin (1907–1962), left-wing politician and publisher of progressive newspapers, came from a wealthy land-owning class.

Pakistan since the early part of the 1950s, which culminated in the dissolution of the constituent assembly by the governor general Ghulam Mohammad in October 1954. Between 1954 and 1958, Pakistan saw the changing of prime ministers at regular intervals. Despite the constitution and the nonrepresentativeness of the assembly, the promised and necessary elections were continuously postponed. With high food costs, a political system that was bordering on the farcical and the increasing dissatisfaction among the population, an election and a legitimately elected civilian government may have been the only way out of the social and political impasse. Instead, in October 1958, as mentioned above, General Ayub Khan took power through a military coup, the constitution was suspended, all political parties were banned, and the elections were indefinitely postponed. Due to the Pakistan Army's close alliance with the United States, Pakistan subsequently served on the frontlines of the US anti-communist policy in the region (Jalal 1990: Ch. 5; McGrath 1996: Chs. 4 and 5). The major change in the political atmosphere renewed the fear of being arrested among activists in the trade union movement and in Left politics, forcing them to go underground. The 1958 martial law intensified the state's clampdown on political activities leading to arrests and harassment of leftist political workers and leaders.

To take an example, there was a work stoppage at the Adamjee Jute Mills in East Bengal on February 9, 1959. This was due to some worker grievances against the management. Although foreign observers thought of the strike as not having been instigated by radical trade unionists, the Martial Law authorities clamped down hard and used the pretext to severely punish those it thought of as "ring leaders." They were given five to six years in jail along with five lashes. Strikes were banned under the new regime and any kind of work stoppage (or political activity) was thought of as a threat by the government. Soon after, in March 1959, the Minister for Health and Social Welfare Lt. General Burki announced the government's new labor policy,[31] which was more favorable to the management and sought a restricted collective bargaining arrangement. For the regime, when the workers became restive, in Burki's own words, it needed to "sort the bastards out."[32] No wonder this is the same period in which Hasan Nasir was arrested, tortured, and died in police custody. This was one of the most difficult times for the underground communist movement and many cadres left politics, others signed pardons to be released from prison, and yet others revealed names of comrades under duress to achieve leniency.

[31] Industrial Disputes Act of 1947 under which most labor laws were functioning until the time was repealed and reenacted under the rubric of Industrial Dispute Ordinance. The ordinance brought more industries under the essential services banner prohibiting the formation of unions there. Strikes were made illegal and the registration of unions was made difficult. To safeguard against contravening ILO conventions, a system of conciliation and mediation was devised. Conciliation officers were government functionaries that referred unsettled disputes to industrial courts for mediation where the process could take months to settle. The idea was to move labor grievances from the streets to the courts and boardrooms under the watchful eye of state functionaries.

[32] See PRO, FO371/14477. Confidential Memos from Office of the British High Commissioner New Delhi, February 21, 1959, and March 1, 1959.

The Left Splits

By the early 1960s the various groups of the Left had also started to feel the impact of the Sino-Soviet split within international communism.[33] In Pakistan some of these international differences were played out in terms of factional rivalries, while others took the form of tangential arguments on the nature of the martial law regime. As the government's relationship with China improved, especially in the aftermath of the Sino-Indian war (1962) when Britain and the United States supported India and Ayub felt vulnerable against its larger neighbor, the pro-China Left elements started becoming more restrained in their critique of the government. For example, the Ayub martial law in 1960 had instituted an indirect system of elections which would elect 80,000 individuals who, in turn, would serve as Basic Democrats and work in municipalities at the local level; they would also serve as an electoral college to elect the president of the country. Some in the Left argued that the Basic Democracy system was similar to the Russian soviets at the time of the 1917 revolution (Naqvi 1989).[34] To take another concrete example of this tendency, within most Left formations, but especially in Punjab, in Sind, and in Karachi, there were serious discussions on whether the Ayub regime should be considered as representative of the progressive (national as opposed to comprador) bourgeoisie. Hence, at one level there was a radicalization of politics with anti-martial law demonstrations by students (Leghari 1979; Naqvi 1989),[35] yet there were also tendencies within the Left that wanted a more accommodating relationship with the Ayub regime.

There were other differences on the issue of the Indo-Pakistan War in 1965 in which some leftists took an openly anti-India stance as China was supportive of Pakistan during the war. These and many other disagreements (some basically related to personalities and mere factionalism) led to the fracturing of the underground party and to the proliferation of Maoist groups, first in Punjab (under the veteran trade unionist C. R. Aslam) and then in Karachi (under Tufail Abbas). The Sind provincial committee that considered itself the center of the Communist Party in Pakistan formally split in 1966 into pro-Soviet and pro-Chinese factions. Tufail Abbas, who was based in Karachi, who controlled the progressive labor union in PIA, the national airline, started leading the underground pro-Peking faction.

The reverberations of this split were then felt in the NAP, which had gone through internal discussions on a range of issues right from the beginning of its formation. For example, in 1957–8, there already were debates on whether the NAP should dissolve because of disagreement as to whether the party should incline toward a class-based

[33] Although there were latent tensions between the Soviet Union and the People's Republic of China during Stalin's lifetime (the peasant model of revolution in contrast to the urban insurrectionary model), these became more open after Stalin's death in 1953. Krushchev and Mao differed on many issues, including the argument for "peaceful coexistence" with capitalist countries that Mao accused the Soviets of following.

[34] The Chinese premier Chou en Lai was reported to have said that the Basic Democracy system was close to the Chinese system. Naqvi, 'Communist Party', 34–5.

[35] These demonstrations were spontaneous and the Left groups had little to do with them (Leghari 1979: 95–100; Naqvi 1989: 32–9).

politics or whether it should favor a nationalist position representing smaller ethnic groups. Other discussions were held on whether the NAP should participate in the anticipated 1959 elections[36] prior to the dissolution of the One Unit system, and in the early 1960s there were arguments about whether the party should join other political groups to create a larger party to campaign for the restoration of democracy during Ayub's martial law. There were also major differences on choosing the nominee to stand against Ayub Khan for the combined opposition during the 1965 elections.[37]

These differences, personality clashes, and the rising tide of Maoist radicalism, against the more established elite leaders within the NAP, led to a break in the party by 1967–8. One group was favored by the pro-Chinese Left and represented by Maulana Bhashani, and the other was linked to the pro-Soviet Left and was led by Mahmud Ali Kasuri and then by the nationalist Pashtun leader, Khan Abdul Wali Khan, the son of Ghaffar Khan. In the late 1960s a breakaway faction of the NAP (led by Mohammad Ishaq in Punjab and Afzal Bangash in NWFP) formed the Mazdoor Kisan Party (The Worker Peasant Party).

The 1960s

General Ayub Khan's rule (1958–69) was also an era of unprecedented growth in the wealth and holdings of Pakistan's major industrial houses. They moved into banking and insurance, which supplied them with the funds for further expansion. Pakistan's growth was heralded by economists from the United States as a model for the rest of the third world and as a premier example of "free enterprise." Gustav Papanek, the head of the Harvard Advisory Group to Pakistan, would affectionately call Pakistan's state-sponsored bourgeoisie "robber barons" and argued that the rising social and economic inequality contributed to the economy's growth and would eventually lead to the improvement in the living conditions of the lower income groups (Ali 1983: 69). Irrespective of Papanek's "rosy" predictions, all through the 1960s retrenchment and dismissals were common tools for disciplining workers. An outburst of workers' accumulated frustrations was evident in the March 1963 demonstration in the Sind Industrial Trading Estate (SITE) area under the Mazdoor Rabita committee (workers coordinating committee) (Naqvi 2003). The strikes led to police firing on demonstrating laborers, and several people were killed. This incident led to an increased radicalization among the workers which was in turn

[36] The elections were canceled by the military regime.

[37] Many felt that the candidate should be General Azam Khan, a retired general who was very popular and had democratic credentials. However, Bhashani convinced the entire opposition to favor Fatima Jinnah, Jinnah's younger sister. There is some speculation that she was the weaker candidate and Bhashani pushed her candidacy because he wanted Ayub, who was favored by the Chinese, to win. The various Left factions acted differently during the elections, some favoring Ayub Khan (C. R. Aslam), some opposing him completely (the pro-Moscow Group), and others were more ambivalent about Ayub Khan and yet opposed him (Major Ishaq). See, Mohammad Ishaq, *National Awami Party ke Androoni Ikhtalafat Androoni Jad o Jahad* (National Awami Party's Internal Differences and Struggles) (Lahore: Pakistan Printing Works, 1966), 3–4, and Leghari, "The Socialist Movement," 108–12.

subdued by mass arrests of the mill-level leadership. Industrialists taking note of the state response continued with their policy of dismissals and retrenchment. Usman Baluch, a trade union leader, who lived through this and later labor struggles, represented the situation by stating that "the bureaucracy through the labour courts, the industrialists through their jobbers, masters and paid strong men and the police through violent suppression of demonstrations worked in unison to suppress the labour movement."[38]

The heavy reliance on foreign capital for the industrialization process faced a major setback when after the 1965 war with India, World Bank funds were cut off and then resumed at much lower levels. As the entire structure was built on a large inflow of foreign capital, the growth began to sputter. Bad harvests in 1965 and 1966, and the demand of the East Pakistani middle classes for a more equitable share of the spoils of development, created a major political turmoil in the country (Alavi 1983; Amjad 1983). Ayub Khan's much heralded "decade of development" hence came to an abrupt end when, in 1968–9, students, intellectuals, the urban poor, and the working classes participated in a massive civil disobedience movement. Spearheaded by the PPP in the West and the Awami League in the Eastern province, this movement was not only against the political bankruptcy of the Ayub regime but also a protest against the deteriorating economic conditions and the increasing inequality in the distribution of wealth (see Ali 1970; Amjad 1983; Burki 1988).

The economist Rahman Sohban in an article from 1969 comments on the initial urban nature of the anti-Ayub unrest. He argues that this was due to the resentment against the suppression of civic freedoms and the barriers placed on political expression. Further, according to him, it was because of the social inequality prevalent in urban areas where the top 5 percent of the population earned 26 percent of the income and the bottom 50 percent earned a mere 21 percent in all of Pakistan. Sobhan argues that the social effect these income gaps had on the livelihoods of students, shop assistants, clerks, and low-level office workers (not to mention industrial workers) created conditions for them to protest against the Ayub regime. The regime was also not supported by the majority of the population consisting of urban poor and peasants, as along with the erosion of liberties there was no material improvement in people's lives either. Both social equality/justice and civil liberties had been casualties during Ayub's "decade of progress."

The article further discusses the call for economic and political autonomy by the Bengali middle class from the centralizing and controlling state in West Pakistan. This sentiment was radicalized by the demands of the students linked to the peasants and industrial workers in East Pakistan who were in turn joined by the urban poor, most of whom were surviving on less than one rupee a day, while many were surviving on even less. Sobhan, in a sensitive passage, argues that to understand the anti-Ayub demonstrations especially in East Pakistan in the late 1960s we need to appreciate that it was not only the students and factory workers, but as in any such occasions, the urban poor, the unemployed, the casual laborers, "street urchins," pick pockets,

[38] Interview with Usman Baluch, who was president of Mutahida Mazdoor Federation in 1972 and one of the major leaders of the labor movement (Karachi, Summer 1998).

beggars, vendors, and others who live in hovels and pavements and who are considered the most marginalized in any society participated in the protests (Subhan 1969).[39]

Uncertain Futures

After decades of state repression, Ayub's departure (1969) brought a new energy into the labor movement. Taking advantage of the clauses introduced through new labor ordinances by the newly instituted military junta of General Yahya Khan (1969–71) for registration and constituting collective bargaining agents, moribund and underground unions started coming to life. New alliances were made as communist groups and student activists assisted the working-class leadership in reorganizing their trade unions. Before long, in response to the sustained repression of its leaders, an alternate leadership started taking hold in many trade unions. Following the lead of the Bengali working-class and peasant leader Maulana Abdul Hamid Bhashani,[40] the labor groups, now under a more radicalized leadership, took to demonstrating at particular industries (*gherao*, lit: encircling). Using these new tactics, the workers started to demand bonuses, better working conditions, and back pay and in some cases protested against the dismissal of their comrades. Despite the friction within and between the leftist groups in Pakistan, it was clear that in the prevailing international atmosphere and the political realties within Pakistan, the Maoist groups with more radical anti-imperialist slogans (anti-Americanism and support for the people of Vietnam), their anti-India stand and call for active (and armed) struggle became more popular among the youth and the students.

Returning to the voice of another working-class activist, like Mohammad Ali, in conclusion, let me share a lengthy abstract from Aziz ul Hasan, who during the 1960s and early 1970s matured into a major figure in the labor struggle in Karachi. Aziz ul Hasan was born in India and like Mohammad Ali Malabari migrated to Pakistan. Aziz ul Hasan came to Pakistan as a young boy in the late 1940s. In his interview with me he shared that he lost his parents when he was a school age boy and his brother started working soon after his parent's death after completing his tenth grade to support his family. His brother then got a job in the national airline, PIA, where he became close to Tufail Abbas, who was the leader of the PIA workers union and also led the underground Karachi-based pro-Peking communist group. He himself started to work in a textile mill in 1968. Given below are excerpts from his interview:

> *In those days there was no labour policy and the management would have its own union through which it controlled the workers; they were called pocket unions. I started to work with other comrades to create a union of our own. Noticing my*

[39] To read a more recent analysis of the protests in 1969 that emphasizes the participation of the urban poor, see Nusrat Sabina Chowdhury, "Dhaka 1969," *Economic and Political Weekly* 56 (44) (2021): 47–52.

[40] Maulana Bhashani was a leader of one section of the National Awami Party (NAP), which was pro-Peking in orientation.

activities I was given harsh duty hours. I used to work as an operator in the nylon department; they would put me with four others so that they could keep an eye on me. It was a time of much labour oppression and people were harassed and beaten up by the goons who worked for the company if you raised a voice against the management.

The movement against Ayub Khan had started and people were on the streets demanding their rights. During this phase the National Awami Party [NAP] leader, Maulana Bhashani came to Landhi and spoke to the workers. This created a lot of enthusiasm among all of us. As Ayub left office a new martial law regime came into power, promising nation-wide elections. There was a new labour policy that allowed for all of us to become active and we pushed for a referendum to choose a new collective bargaining agent at Dawood Mills. We worked hard and were successful in winning the referendum.

Ironically as we won the referendum, Tufail Abbas's[41] *group lost the union election at Pakistan International Airlines (PIA). The Jamaa't*[42] *won there. The reason was simple, there had not been elections at PIA before and Tufail Abbas had continued to have a union there partially through management support … . We were upset at him not winning as we had become close to his party, but were not surprised. We also had a number of National Student Federation (NSF) students come visit us in the industrial area. These were selfless students and the workers gave them a lot of respect. These middle-class educated young people would eat and sleep with us and also help us in writing our pamphlets, give speeches, prepare banners or accompany us to write slogans on the walls (chalking) late at night.*

In early 1970s we created a charter of demands for the workers in our factory. Once when we were demonstrating, it must be April of 1970, for back pay or reinstatement of dismissed labourers, the police came and charged on us with batons. There were arrests and some who were arrested were taken to the factory owner's personal office, stripped naked and beaten with canes. We were told that the owner would himself pay the police a sum of money for each lash. I too was picked up and taken to the police station where they took all my clothes off and severely beat me. I can still recall the names of my torturers. They taunted me of being a communist involved in creating a Red Guard and kept on accusing me of being part of the bloody revolution my seniors were plotting. After days of daily torture I could not even lie on my back or walk for a while.

We were then put in a lock-up and several cases under martial law regulations were brought against us. I still remember we were presented in a martial law summary court in front of military judges. They convicted us in all cases. I was in the Karachi Central Jail. I was released on bail around the time Bhutto came into power. [43]

41 Tufail Abbas also headed the pro-China underground communist group in Karachi.

42 Jamaa't Islami is a major Islamic-oriented political party.

43 Interview with Aziz ul Hasan (Karachi, Summer 1998), who was one of the main labor leaders during the October 1972 labor movement in Landhi–Korangi, Karachi.

In the early 1970s Aziz ul Hasan participated in one of the most protracted labor struggles in Pakistan's history. Starting in the late 1960s, this movement, as mentioned above, was pivotal in shaping the transition from military rule to democratic forms of governance. After the liberation of Bangladesh (1971), Zulfikar Ali Bhutto's Pakistan People's Party (PPP) had itself come to power through the overwhelming support of the working class, students, and radical Left groups—the key participants in this movement. It is indeed ironic and also revealing of Bhutto's politics that the PPP was later instrumental in suppressing the workers' struggle (Ali 2015; Shaheed 2007).

In its effort to reestablish state authority after the debacle in Bangladesh, the Bhutto government not only crushed the radicalized movement but also sought to reconfigure the working class according to its own vision of clienteist politics. There was also severe repression, in the shape of arrests and dismissals, of any dissenting voice from within the working class (however, see Asad Ali in this volume for another perspective on Bhutto's politics). The collapse of the textile industry in the mid-1970s led to a large-scale dislocation of textile workers. The immigration of Pakistani labor to the oil-rich Arab Gulf states subsequently brought a qualitative change in the labor movement. Bhutto's government, inclusive of its populist rhetoric and genuine attempts to institute reform in Pakistan's cultural and political life, continued to harass and persecute any and all political opponents within and outside the party, from the left and the right of the political spectrum. One of the most egregious acts was the dismissal of Baluchistan's NAP government in 1973 on the pretext that it was receiving arms shipments from Iraq and was involved in a conspiracy with the Soviet Union and Iraq to break up Pakistan and Iran. This dismissal led to the protest resignation of the NAP–JUI (Jamaat-i-Ulema, Islam) coalition government in the NWFP. On a more serious note, this act led to a popular armed insurgency in Baluchistan that was brutally crushed by the PPP government. Bhutto gave the Pakistan military free rein in that province enabling the military to return to public life after its defeat in East Pakistan and the creation of Bangladesh. Through a coup in 1977, this invigorated military forced Bhutto out of power. In an ongoing saga of deprivation, Bhutto's overthrow by another military regime intensified brutality against labor organizations and the emphasis on religious identity during General Zia-ul-Haq's tenure (1977–88). The untold history of that period needs a detailed discussion, however, a rendition of the Left and nationalistic politics of the 1970s to 1990s is provided by Aasim Sajjad and Hassan Javid and Anushay Malik in this volume.

Conclusion

Laurent Berlant's book *Cruel Optimism* (2011) helps us understand some of the political and economic issues pertaining to contemporary Pakistan (and elsewhere). Berlant argues that, at least in the West, a sense of economic precarity has penetrated the lives of those who previously had aspirations of upward mobility. This contemporary global moment has intensified long-term patterns of economic disenfranchisement, Berlant suggests, by the shrinkage of the welfare state, the privatization of publicly held utilities, the increase in pension insecurities, and the flexible regimes of capital that are based on contractual relationships between owners and workers rather than long-term job security. It has further led to the erosion of unions, which gave hope of upward mobility to the working class. Similarly, in Pakistan, the current economic model, and its reliance on foreign capital and loans from international financial institutions, somewhat follows Berlant's argument. The privatization of large state-owned industries has also meant a lack of job security, an increase in contract labor, high rates of unemployment in the formal sector, flexible manufacturing regimes and the dominance of informal/service sector work, creating new challenges for those involved in organizing industrial workers. In the rural areas, unfavorable and changing land tenancy laws, the failure to distribute agricultural land, and the impact of climate change have led to continuous migration patterns to the cities or, for those who are lucky, to the Gulf Arab States. Further, inflationary pressures leading to food insecurity, lack of growth in the industrial sector, and an anemic private investment rate are bound to create further social conflict. It should not surprise us if, like Berlant argues, risk, uncertainty, and precarity have become constitutive social experiences for many in Pakistan.

The current moment allows me to take the reader to the essay's main concern. As I suggested above, this essay is part of an attempt to see what is tenacious in the residues and how there are emergent and resurgent histories embedded in the "ruins" of the past. In this work I have remained influenced by the lingering concerns about social and economic inequity so courageously emphasized by generations of Left-leaning activists in Pakistan. Hence the essay ends with a voice (Aziz ul Hasan) that gives us a sense of the personal and collective struggles for a socially just future, an aspiration for common liberation, yet remains critical of the leadership of the progressive movement similar to that of Mohammad Ali Malabari. It also reminds us of the sacrifice that working-class cadres gave for their ideology and politics (Hasan Nasir among scores of others). Returning to Enzo Traverso's (2106) call for us to critically rethink socialist and progressive histories while it is being erased from collective memory, I would argue such histories may enable us to trace the dynamic forms in which people in present times, amid all the debris and destruction, create opportunities to build new social relations and a politics of combination and engagement. This essay, like most attempts at history writing, is partly about the present and hopes to encourage further scholarship that shows how historically situated processes (in grounded social, political, and cultural situations) may continue to inform us.

Bibliography

Alavi, Hamza. 1983. "Class and State," in H. Gardezi and J. Rashid (eds.), *Pakistan: The Roots of Dictatorship*. London: Zed Press, 40–93.

Ali, Kamran Asdar. 2015. *Communism in Pakistan*. London: I.B. Tauris.

Ali, Mian Anwer. 1952. *The Communist Party of West Pakistan in Action*. Lahore: Government Printing Press.

Ali, Tariq. 1970. *Pakistan Military Rule or People's Power*. New York: W. Morrow.
Ali, Tariq. 1983. *Can Pakistan Survive?* London: Penguin Books.
Amin, Shahid. 1995. *Event, Metaphor, Memory: Chauri Chaura, 1922–1992.* Berkeley: University of California Press.
Amjad, Ali. 2001. *Labour Legislation and Trade Unionism in India and Pakistan.* Karachi: Oxford University Press.
Amjad, Rashid. 1983. "Industrial Concentration and Economic Power," in H. Gardezi and J. Rashid (eds.), *Pakistan: The Roots of Dictatorship*. London: Zed Press, 228–69.
Berlant, Laurent. 2011. *Cruel Optimism*. Durham, NC: Duke University Press.
Burki, Shahid Javed. 1988. *Pakistan Under Bhutto*. London: Macmillan.
Chowdhury, Nusrat Sabina. 2021. "Dhaka 1969." *Economic and Political Weekly* 56 (44): 47–52.
Feldman, Allen. 1991. *Formations of Violence*. Chicago: University of Chicago Press.
Hyder, Qurutal A. 1999. "Housing Society," in C. M. Naim (ed. and trans.), *A Season of Betrayals: A Short Story and Two Novellas*. New Delhi: Kali Press for Women.
Ishaq, Mohammad. 1966. *National Awami Party ke Androoni Ikhtalafat-Androoni Jad o Jahad* (National Awami Party's Internal Differences and Struggles). Lahore: Pakistan Printing Works.
Jalal, Ayesha. 1990. *The State of Martial Rule*. Cambridge: Cambridge University Press.
Leghari, Iqbal. 1979. "The Socialist Movement in Pakistan: An Historical Survey." Unpublished PhD dissertation. Montreal Laval University.
McGrath, Allen. 1996. *The Destruction of Pakistan's Democracy*. Karachi: Oxford University Press.
Malabari, Mohammad Ali. [1975] 2008. "Ek Mazdoor Sathi Ki Yadein," in Major Mohammad Ishaq (ed.), *Hasan Nasir Ki Shahadat* (Hasan Nasir's Matyrdom). Multan: Ishaq Academy, 251–312.
Metcalf, Barbara. 1984. *Moral Conduct and Authority*. Berkeley: University of California Press.
Naqvi, Jamal. 1989. *Communist Party of Pakistan mai Nazariati Kash Makash ki Mukhtasar Tarikh* (A Short History of the Ideological Struggle in the Communist Party of Pakistan). Karachi: Maktaba-e-Roshan Khyal.
Naqvi, Nayab. 2003. *Yakam March 1963 Ki Mazdoor Tehreek: Aik Pas Manzar* (The Labor Struggle of 1 March 1963: A Perspective). Karachi: PILER and Pakistan Study Center, University of Karachi.
Papanek, Gustav F. 1967. *Pakistan's Development*. Cambridge, MA: Harvard University Press.
Rashid, Jamil, and Hasan Gardezi. 1983. "Independent Pakistan: Its Political Economy," in Hasan Gardezi and Jamil Rashid (eds.), *Pakistan: The Roots of Dictatorship*. London: Zed Press, 4–19.
Salar, Fasihuddin. 1986. "The Working Class Movement in Pakistan." Unpublished manuscript.
Shaheed, Z. A. 1983. "Role of the Government in the Development of the Labour Movement," in H. Gardezi and J. Rashid (eds.), *Pakistan: The Roots of Dictatorship*. London: Zed Press, 270–90.
Stites, Richard. 1989. *Revolutionary Dreams*. New York: Oxford University Press.
Stoler, Ann. 2008. "Imperial Debris: Reflections on Ruins and Ruination." *Cultural Anthropology* 23 (2): 191–219.

Subhan, Rehman. 1969. "The Economic Causes of the Current Crisis," *Pakistan Left Review* (2). Reprinted in Nadir Cheema and Stephen Lyon (eds.), *Pakistan Left Review: Then and Now*. Karachi: Oxford University Press, 2022.

Traverso, Enzo. 2016. *Left Wing Melancholia*. New York: Columbia University Press.

Zaheer, Hasan. 1998. *The Times and Trial of the Rawalpindi Conspiracy Case*. Karachi: Oxford University Press.

2

South Asia's Partitions and the Limiting of Progressive Possibilities in Pakistan

Anushay Malik and Hassan Javid

Just two years after Pakistan came into existence, a nineteen-year-old college student studying in Madras boarded a train to Bombay and traveled from there to Karachi. A stranger in a strange land, the young man—named Biyyothil Mohyuddin Kutty (B. M. Kutty)—nonetheless chose to stay on in Pakistan, leaving behind a life and family in his home state of Kerala. Why did Kutty move to Pakistan? An article that appeared in *The Hindu* in 2015 answered this question by assuming "he was inspired by the idea of Pakistan during the 1940s" (Bhattacherjee 2015). However, Kutty's autobiography tells a different story: noting how his parents struggled to pay his college fees, Kutty felt an increasing despondency at the prospect of leading the thoroughly conventional life that was expected of him. "I had so many dreams and desires, but no way of seeing any of them realized," he writes, and the spur-of-the-moment decision he took to travel to Bombay and then to Karachi in the summer of 1949 emerged out of a wish to run away and chart an alternative course for his life (Kutty 2012: 40).[1] Reading his autobiography, Kutty's desire to find love and to pursue adventure jump out in the first few chapters, but it merits asking if this would even be possible, especially after the violence of Partition produced dynamics of state power and control that imposed new limits on imagination and identity. Clearly, to the officers who would arrest Kutty a decade later, convinced that he had come to Pakistan as a trained spy for India, being a South Indian limited who Kutty could be.

By the time B. M. Kutty passed away in Karachi in 2019, he had long been an important trade unionist and prominent figure in Pakistan's progressive circles. From fighting for the rights of workers, ranging from Beedi-makers and cargo-loaders in the 1950s, to working alongside Mir Ghaus Buksh Bizenjo (who he refers to as Mir Saheb) in Balochistan in the early 1970s, to becoming involved with Pakistan's anti-dictatorship Movement for the Restoration of Democracy (MRD) during the 1980s, Kutty's triumphs and defeats mirror, in many ways, the fortunes of the progressive movement in Pakistan more generally. This essay argues that the decline of the progressive movement in Pakistan can be best explained with reference to several

[1] This essay makes use of the Urdu edition of Kutty's autobiography. All translations to English are our own.

mutually imbricated processes that limited who Pakistanis could be, and what they could demand, from the very beginning of the country's existence. Using a life-writing approach we focus on three major turning points; namely the years immediately following Partition in 1947, the war with India in 1965, and the liberation war in Bangladesh in 1971. These three turning points had the combined effect of deepening ethnic and regional cleavages within Pakistan that generated forms of resistance tying different progressive actors together. In 1947, 1965, and again in 1971 the postcolonial state's drive to centralize power, a tendency bequeathed to it by the Raj, legitimized and justified in terms of the perceived security threat from India was enacted and overseen by a predominantly Punjabi establishment commanding the heights of the country's military and bureaucratic institutions. This provided opportunities to forge networks of solidarity and lay the organizational foundations for the progressive movement in Pakistan, but it also prompted the state to engage in increasing amounts of repression that were relatively successful in undermining and delegitimizing opposition to the political status quo while simultaneously casting progressive demands for regional autonomy—and the progressive movement more generally—as seditious. The essay further argues that these processes of centralization and repression continued throughout the 1970s and 1980s, ultimately coinciding with broader processes of neoliberal capitalist transformation that further eroded the ability of Pakistan's working classes to engage in collective political action.

In this essay, our methodological choice to focus on one individual and the story of his life that emerges from his autobiography, as well as the biography of his close comrade and one-time Balochistan governor Mir Ghaus Baksh Bizenjo (Bizenjo 2009), is rooted in a desire to highlight histories that look beyond the categorization and assumed chronology in a state archive. This is important because it allows for insight into what self-described progressives and leftists were doing, what motivated them, and, crucially for this essay, what limited their politics over time. It does not claim to be the complete story by any means, but it does provide important insights about how the progressive movement in Pakistan declined by looking at what it meant to some of the people who lived it. We make no attempt to write a complete life history of Kutty, but focus instead on the turning points, the junctures at which major changes took place. In other words, we use the life of this one individual and his closeness to progressive and labor politics to help illuminate some of the factors contributing to the decline of the progressive movement in Pakistan.

Focusing on B. M. Kutty's life also provides an insight into the diversity of experiences and, indeed, aspirations that characterized the lives of activists and others who saw Pakistan, at least in its initial decades, as a project replete with possibilities for the attainment of progressive goals. While dominant, exclusionary nationalist narratives in Pakistan have defined citizenship by emphasizing Islam as the dominant organizing principle of public life, and have encouraged subordination to a security state whose contours are defined by the interests of the military establishment and its allies from among the country's propertied classes, Kutty embodied the kind of life and principles that did not fit within this official orthodoxy. His story, with all its complexity, is a potent reminder of all that is often erased from the mainstream narration of history in Pakistan.

The essay begins with an account of B. M. Kutty's decision to move to Pakistan and the ways in which increasingly formalized and institutionalized notions of citizenship shaped his own experiences as both a migrant and an activist in a context where the state sought to control and limit the space for ideological and political diversity. This is followed by a discussion of the Rawalpindi Conspiracy Case and the East Pakistan elections of 1954, and how both these events solidified the connection between progressive activists and those working to secure greater rights and representation from the state, a moment that not only generated networks of solidarity and support but also induced official anxieties about the threats posed by "regionalism" and communism to the established political order. The next section of the essay discusses the events of 1965 and 1971, showing how the war with India and the creation of Bangladesh exposed rifts within the progressive movement in Pakistan, weakening it even as the state continued to centralize power and use repression to curtail the emergence of alternative narratives and types of politics. The essay then discusses the 1970s and 1980s, as viewed through Kutty's eyes, and highlights how the PPP (Pakistan People's Party) government under Bhutto continued to reinforce the state's tendency toward centralizing power and repressing those that opposed it, creating new challenges for a progressive movement that, while a part of the MRD, was ultimately relegated to being a relatively marginal force in Pakistani politics by the end of the 1980s. The essay then concludes with an account of how broader changes in the economy have served to further undermine the progressive cause.

The Problem with the Question: "Why Did Kutty Choose to Come to Pakistan"?

In one review of B. M. Kutty's autobiography, the writer asks, "One often wondered how a leftist Malayali ended up in Pakistan" (Bansal 2011: 236). This was a question that Kutty was asked often and comes up in almost every one of the several accounts of his life. The problem with the question, however, is that it assumes that there was a clear idea of who a Pakistani was in the 1940s and that Kutty did not fit within it. "Leftist" and "Malayali" were both categories that already existed within the borders of Pakistan, as Kutty's autobiography makes very clear, but over time, the space for diversity and divergent political opinion became increasingly narrow.

The official limits imposed on identity by the Pakistani state were produced through both administrative and ideological mechanisms. In the very early years after Partition, it was relatively easy for people to travel across the border between India and Pakistan because passports and visa requirements were simply not enforced. By 1951, the introduction of the Pakistan Citizenship Act effectively ended the free movement of people across the border. While the actual implementation of citizenship acts on both sides of the border was initially uncertain and slow, in part due to how criteria for citizenship were sometimes debated and contested by minorities and other marginalized groups from below (Chatterji 2012), the move to formally establish a territorial basis for inclusion within the nation, with all of its attendant ideological baggage, helped to sharpen the divide between Pakistan and India while also providing the pretext for some of the state's earliest attempts to centralize power and expand its capacity to regulate and control the population; indeed Pakistan's first personal ID cards were introduced in 1950 to document the arrival of refugees and migrants from India. However, the clear line between a Pakistani and Indian citizen was not always visible immediately after Partition, a point Kutty himself makes when he describes why he chose to go on to Karachi from Bombay in 1949. Kutty's decision was based in part on the absence of any need for passports or other documentation to travel to Pakistan, but was also informed by the presence of older connections that transcended the borders of the newly formed South Asian states; when Kutty arrived in Karachi, he was able to receive support and assistance from a significant Malayali population that had long been resident in the city and who, along with other people from South India, worked as journalists, set up restaurants, and sold *paan* and *beedis*. Over time, as the border between Pakistan and India became firmer and visa restrictions were put in place, many members of this community chose to leave Pakistan, either going to India or traveling to find work in the Gulf. A few remained, often because they had small children or "Pakistani" spouses (Kutty 2012: 40).

The imposition of these new administrative restrictions was accompanied by a parallel process through which the state sought to limit and control the ideological contours of politics and contestation in Pakistan. The early 1950s witnessed crackdowns on leftist students, workers, and activists, something that Kutty would experience firsthand. Kutty had been involved with Left-wing politics as a high school student in Kerala and describes how, when he was even younger, he attended a school where many of the Muslim students had pasted pictures of Muhammad Ali Jinnah in the corners of their notebooks. This is perhaps not surprising, as social histories of Partition tell us that freedom, Partition, and independence meant different things to different groups (Khan 2008), and Kutty himself acknowledges that his parents actively supported the Muslim League despite being from Kerala and choosing to remain there after Partition. Once in Pakistan, Kutty interacted with fellow South Indians who came from a variety of different political backgrounds and as he traveled between Karachi and Lahore, he began to make connections with people who were part of the many fronts of the Communist Party.

The story of leftists in Pakistan's early years has received a considerable degree of scholarly attention in recent years that has detailed the ways in which, very early on, the Pakistani state actively sought to cultivate a relationship with the United States, offering to provide the latter with ideological support in the fight against communism in exchange for security cooperation and military and economic assistance (Ali 2015; Saif 2010). The enthusiasm with which Pakistan sought to place itself firmly on the side of the United States during the Cold War, formalized through membership in forums like the now-defunct CEATO and SENTO, meant that domestically, there was official support for the doctrine of anti-communism and the vigorous persecution of individuals and organizations associated with Left-wing politics. More significantly, just as debates over citizenship provided a pretext for expanding and institutionalizing the regulatory power of the state, attacks on Left-wing politics created an opportunity for the state to begin defining Pakistan and its identity in relatively narrow religious and territorial terms, eschewing the possibility of a more pluralistic, inclusive, and redistributive approach to politics that would have challenged the authority of entrenched state and propertied elites. Events like the infamous Rawalpindi Conspiracy Case in 1951, in which military officers were accused of planning a coup against the government, led to the arrest of dozens of prominent Left-wing activists alleged to have links with the coup plotters, and fed into official narratives about the dangers posed by communism. However, it is perhaps not coincidental that these measures also had the effect of preventing progressive activists from mobilizing for provincial elections, essentially stopping them from becoming more prominent in mainstream politics (Malik 2013). Similar repressive measures were also launched against activists in East Pakistan who, by campaigning for greater recognition and representation, problematized the national narrative being pushed forward by the state. Indeed, matters came to a head very early on in 1954 when the Constituent Assembly, the body tasked with drafting Pakistan's constitution, was dissolved and replaced after it suggested a formula for power sharing that would have given East Pakistan a majority in Parliament in line with its population. Anxieties about communism and "regionalism," often cast in terms of national security and "unity," loomed large in the state's political calculus precisely because of the threats they allegedly posed to the established order, and the state's repressive response sought to undermine progressive movements by both reducing their organizational capacity and emphasizing an ideological narrative that posited Islam as a source of national cohesion against the dangers of ethnic identity and regionalism. These anxieties, and the state's increasing use of religion as a criterion for determining patriotic citizenship, were neatly encapsulated in the remarks of the police officers who arrested Kutty in 1959, telling him, "You have come [from India] on a mission to spy on Pakistan. You are not a Muslim. You have just been trained to act like one" (Kutty 2012: 149).

Unlike many of his peers, Kutty himself was not actually arrested until the beginning of General Ayub Khan's military regime in 1959, but repressive as that regime was, its inception did not necessarily mark the beginning of a new political era or process. While there is often a tendency to periodize history in a way that sees transitions from one leader to another or from one regime to another as being moments of tremendous rupture and discontinuity, Kutty's story highlights, perhaps unintentionally, how the beginning of military rule in Pakistan was really a continuation of the process through which state power was becoming more centralized at the expense of the provinces. Nowhere was this more evident than in what happened in East Pakistan during the 1954 provincial elections when the United Front defeated the Muslim League. The United Front's success embodied the fears the military-bureaucratic establishment had regarding the potential for provincial politics to disturb the existing order, but as Layli Uddin persuasively argues in a recent piece on these events, this perceived threat was connected to the power of labor in specific locations within present-day Bangladesh, which were, in turn, connected to networks of organization and solidarity that predated Partition. As Layli Uddin shows, workers' riots at this time could not be understood by a communal lens alone and that even in the "full flush of rage" individuals in the crowd saved certain employees and supervisors while attacking others, decisions that were rooted in the multiple identities of labor and contextually located moral economies (Uddin 2020: 645). For the central state in Pakistan, the victory of the United Front, while fueling fears about provincial politics, was also seen as creating an environment in which Left-wing movements and activists, such as striking workers, who were invariably viewed by the state as troublemakers and even "traitors," would only be emboldened. Regionalism and communism were thus intertwined in the official imagination.

In his autobiography, Kutty discusses the events of 1954, something that is therefore important because it gives one indication of how this turning point was perceived by some progressive groups within West Pakistan, particularly those who would go on to ally with Maulana Bhashani (who was part of the United or Jugto Front in the 1954 election) as part of the National Awami Party. Before this alliance emerged, the "regional nationalist groups" in Pakistan had already come together to form the Pakistan National Party. The significance of this lay in how it represented an acknowledgment, on the part of progressives, that the state was unlikely to make any concessions to demands for greater provincial autonomy and representation. The Language Riots of 1952 had already made this obvious, but it was transformed into political fact with the imposition of governor's rule in East Pakistan in 1954. As mentioned previously, the wave of repression unleashed after the Rawalpindi Conspiracy Case in 1951 and the subsequent banning of the Communist Party in 1954 also made it clear that the state had little tolerance for Left-wing activism and ideology. Yet, this did not necessarily mean that the regionalists and leftists were two distinct groups, or that either label effectively captured the spectrum of internal opinion. Indeed, as the example of Kutty's friend and collaborator Mir Buksh Bizenjo showed, being Left-leaning and supporting self-determination was as much an anti-colonial position as it was a theoretical position derived from socialism.

As such, when speaking of the events of 1954, it is notable that Kutty highlights the colonial background of Iskander Mirza, the official who put governor's rule in place in East Pakistan. Kutty describes the victory of the United Front as a victory of leftists that was disliked by a corrupt Muslim League threatened by the former's revolutionary potential (Kutty 2012: 97). Mirza, on the other hand, is represented in Kutty's text as colonial rule personified in the administrative structure of the state. This is clearly intentional because right before the discussion of 1954, Kutty provides a detailed account of a visit to Lahore by members of the Left-wing People's Progressive Party of British Guiana who had won an election there. Nor is it a coincidence, in our reading, that he quotes from a speech given at this gathering in Lahore where statements were made about the inevitable end of the British Empire. Against this background, it is important to note that progressives like Kutty in West Pakistan explicitly saw the Muslim League and its actions as a continuation of colonial rule:

> A civil employee of the British period, Major General Iskander Mirza was made the governor of East Pakistan. Within 6 years of Independence, he trampled the wishes of the people. (2012: 99)

The depiction of the Muslim League, bureaucrats, and the Pakistani state more generally as part of a hopelessly corrupt colonial formation lay at the heart of the logic that saw regionalists and progressives align with each other in the earliest years of Pakistan's existence. The view that emerged in this period was one that saw the state of Pakistan as something that was not worth protecting, not least of all because it had demonstrated a vicious resistance to the possibility of any kind of change that threatened entrenched, elite interests. Even so, as Kutty suggests, the intent on the part of progressives was to make the state something new, something pro-people, something closer to what they had imagined a postcolonial state would be emerging from the ashes of colonialism. This was very obvious to the military establishment as well which set about, very explicitly, to control the threat of any such revolutionary insurrection by launching a sustained propaganda campaign against "regionalists" as being a threat to the "integrity of Pakistan" (a phrase that was regularly thrown around in the press) and, on the administrative level, by putting in place legal measures like the One Unit scheme of 1955, which sought to negate any numerical advantage East Pakistan might have had in legislative and other administrative matters (Afzal 1986: 243).

Friendships and the Progressive Networks of the 1960s

It is with this context in mind that we come back to Kutty's life as he narrates it. From the outset, it may seem strange that a person like Kutty could come to the areas that were Pakistan and end up being involved in Balochistan's politics to the extent where he served as personal secretary to Mir Buksh Bizenjo. However, if we center Kutty's story as one voice among many that sought to challenge power and demand its redistribution, his choice to side with Bizenjo in Balochistan makes perfect sense.

In Kutty's introduction to Bizenjo's biography he explains how he got involved in Balochistan's politics and how he first met Mir Saheb at a house they regularly frequented. The house belonged to Mahmudul Huq Usmani who was then the secretary general of Pakistan Awami League's Karachi chapter and would later become an important figure in the National Awami Party. These regular visits were interrupted when Kutty was arrested in 1959, but his time in jail served to bring him even closer to what was happening in Balochistan because he spent quite some time in Jail with Agha Abdul Karim of Kalat from whom he learnt about politics and political leaders in the province. For skeptical readers, this—a chance meeting in prison—might seem to be a little far-fetched, but students of progressive movements in Pakistan might recognize how chance meetings in prison between leftist friends were relatively frequent precisely because so many of them were arrested in the 1950s and 1960s. Indeed, after Kutty was released from jail in 1961, he connected dock workers in Karachi with Hashmat Warsi, an experienced trade unionist he had befriended in prison, who then helped them form a union of their own (Kutty 2012: 203).

By the time Kutty became involved in Balochistan's politics, he had been connected to political networks of progressives in Kerala, Lahore, and Karachi. For Kutty, this involvement in politics, and the cultivation of friendships and networks in progressive circles, was simply part of what he viewed as being the struggle for a better world. However, this is also precisely what led the state to view Kutty as a potential spy and conspirator working to undermine the territorial integrity of Pakistan, providing the pretext for his arrest.

Kutty's life and friendships in the 1960s also provide an important insight into how the war of 1965 was experienced on the ground, particularly by minorities in precarious positions. In 1965, Kutty traveled to Lahore and stayed with a friend named Pritam. From the time his train neared Lahore he described the fear that the rest of the passengers felt as Indian airplanes flying overhead became visible. He discusses the fear in the air and the exaggerated declarations of love for country that he witnessed during his time in Lahore. He went to Pritam's house and as Lahore was experiencing a blackout with no electricity, he and Pritam went to sit outside. One of Pritam's neighbors saw them while passing by and yelled out, "Look at that Hindu thug Pritam, he is giving the Indians signals from his torchlight!" (Kutty 2012: 219). Kutty was very worried, but his friend showed no reaction. Pritam had friends in his neighborhood and knew that nobody would believe a man who, it was well known, had been hostile toward him for some time. While Pritam presumably emerged from this incident relatively unscathed it is worth wondering how many people in that position could have been confident of such support from their neighbors? What happened when such support did not exist? The 1965 war served to reinforce official narratives about citizenship and belonging in Pakistan, reaffirming the state's official emphasis on an Islamic identity juxtaposed against an eternally antagonistic Hindu and Indian "Other," and the political environment in 1965 more generally was one in which voicing opposition to the government, and particularly the military, potentially came at very high cost (Malik 2020).

In addition to raising the cost of political action, the war of 1965 also divided the progressive movement in Pakistan. The National Awami Party had already split along pro-China and pro-Russia lines that had less to do with the splits in international communism and more to do with the political divisions engendered by the war (Ali 2011; Ahmed 2010). Kutty describes this when he discusses how many Punjabis became pro-China, while many East Pakistanis became pro-Russia. This may have been because many progressives in West Pakistan supported the Ayub regime's close relationship with China, while their counterparts in East Pakistan did the opposite because they were opposed to both the Ayub regime and the 1965 war. Reality, as Kutty himself acknowledges (Kutty 2012: 233–4), was a bit more complicated than this, with division and debates among progressives in both East and West Pakistan. However, for the purposes of the argument presented here, the key point is that in the context of a war that reinforced official narratives about the state, identity, and citizenship, the events of 1965 generated a significant split within the progressive movement in an inversion of the process that had brought progressives from both parts of the country together a decade earlier in 1954.

This is important because even though progressives, students, and the working classes would join forces to bring Ayub Khan's regime to an end in 1969, deep differences remained beneath the surface. The economic strain of the war and rising inequality contributed to popular dissatisfaction with the Ayub regime, and this was amplified by the terms of the Tashkent Declaration, the ceasefire that brought an end to the war, which was seen by many, including some progressives in West Pakistan, as an unnecessarily generous capitulation to India. This tells us that even though the movement against Ayub Khan in 1969 may have seemed like a moment of power and unity of leftist forces across the country, the reasons for which people came out on the street were not the same in different parts of Pakistan. For progressive groups within what was then East Pakistan, who had wished for an end to the war from the very beginning, and for whom the Ayub regime embodied the marginalization and exploitation they had experienced since Partition, rage at Tashkent was not a contributory factor.

This vision of an ostensibly united progressive front among students, for instance, comes across in descriptions of 1969. Students were described as burning effigies of Ayub and breaking into bookstores to burn his newly released autobiography *Friends not Masters*, something that they were doing in "both wings of the country" (Ziring 1971). However, it was specifically people in East Pakistan who had been referred to in that book as racially inferior to West Pakistanis and so this coming together in this moment needs to be seen as very much temporary and part of a longer process by which progressive groups had become increasingly divided on the issue of whether a collective, inclusive solution was even possible without a radical rethinking of how the state functioned and how power was divided between the provinces. Thinking about a progressive movement that was based on demanding greater economic and political redistribution of power was increasingly impossible without thinking about the redistribution of power between the center and the provinces.

Soon after Operation Searchlight was launched in March 1971, Kutty found himself traveling outside Pakistan. He had been unable to find employment and one of his wife's relatives, who was working in a hosiery manufacturing business, wanted help with a series of trips he was planning to take to find new markets for his goods. One of his destinations was Budapest, and it was there that Kutty met a group of Bangladeshis who he knew from before because they had been part of the National Awami Party. They had met last before the 1970 elections and were all very happy to see one another. They told Kutty how, after the Pakistan Army attacked Dhaka, they had managed to escape to Calcutta, where they would be returning after a conference that they were in Budapest to attend. They had given up on Pakistan and said that the demand for provincial autonomy was now only a dream (Kutty 2012: 248). This incident is instructive for several reasons. First, it shows how even though bonds of camaraderie may have existed across East and West Pakistan NAP members, the large physical distance between the two meant that their interactions had always been relatively infrequent, as evinced by how long it had been since Kutty had last seen his friends. Second, Kutty's conversation with his friends showed how the experiences and inspirations of progressives in East and West Pakistan had grown ever more divergent from each other. The latter's dislike of Ayub Khan, the way they were treated by the military-bureaucratic establishment since 1947, and the experiences of 1971 meant that the critique of the West Pakistani state and the bases of its power were substantially different from what the progressive group, ostensibly under the same party name in West Pakistan, felt and articulated. When Bangladesh came into being in 1971, it spelt the definitive end of any hope that the progressives, mainly allied with the NAP, had of causing any substantial change in the status quo or of effectively challenging those who held the reins of power in West Pakistan. This was not only because of the loss of networks of support and solidarity, and an entire tradition of radical politics now associated with Bangladesh, but also because of the apparent inability of progressives to effectively critique and counter state power in Pakistan.

Provincialism and Progressives in B. M. Kutty's Politics, 1970s–1980s

One of B. M. Kutty's greatest skills was his ability to write well in English. After the elections of 1970, it was this that reportedly prompted Bizenjo to ask Kutty to draft his press statements in English and was what led to Kutty spending more time working for him (Bizenjo 2009). In 1972, Bizenjo asked him to come to Quetta to work with him as part of the NAP coalition government that had been elected to power in the province. This government would last less than a year and was dissolved by Zulfikar Ali Bhutto who, as chief artial law administrator and subsequently as prime minister, continued with the process of centralizing state power and limiting the room for any kind of progressive politics to function (Ali 2005; Jones 2003). In February 1973, after the dismissal of the Balochistan government, Kutty would again find himself behind bars, and in 1975 the NAP was banned. It was not until later, when Kutty was visiting his ailing father in Kerala that he came across a newspaper article running the headlines that Bhutto had been arrested and thrown in jail by the army.

Reading the history of Pakistan through Kutty's narrative, in his autobiography and Bizenjo's biography, the PPP is barely visible. This, we would argue, is deliberate and is the direct result of Kutty's closeness to Balochistan and Bizenjo, as well as his explicit belief in the idea that there could not be any radical or progressive politics in Pakistan without the devolution of power from the central government. When Kutty discusses the PPP victory, he does so by stressing that Bhutto came to power as the Chief Martial Law Administrator (CMLA). When he brings up 1971, he is clear about the position of the PPP, and explicitly states that it was one of the groups that was clearly among Yahya Khan's favorites. For him, the decline of progressive politics and the denial of sovereignty and autonomy to the provinces are both part of the same process.

General Zia-ul-Haq took power in 1977 after a coup that resulted in the arrest and subsequent execution of Zufiqar Ali Bhutto in 1979. By 1981, a resistance movement emerged that called itself the Movement for the Restoration of Democracy (MRD) and comprised political parties including the PPP, the ANP, and others. Many leftists and progressives were also part of the MRD and it was while participating in the activities of this movement that Kutty found himself imprisoned once more for four months in 1983.[2] However, for Kutty it was significant that the MRD's platform explicitly linked a progressive agenda to provincial autonomy. He describes how Bizenjo launched

2 As Kutty describes it, the Karachi Central Jail at the time was a hotbed of political activity—home to over five hundred political prisoners from across the political spectrum. According to Kutty, the presence of so many activists and leaders, as well as a sympathetic jail administration, meant that the Karachi Central Jail essentially became home to the MRD's steering committee, with the linkages formed between groups and individuals in jail helping to further the movement's agenda across the rest of Pakistan.

a five-year campaign for greater rights to be given to the provinces, producing a Declaration on the Autonomy of Federating Units on August 2, 1986 (Bizenjo 2009: 13). This resolution is described by Kutty as the "Historic Lahore Declaration" and so evokes a sense of something similar to the mood of the more famous one in 1940 (ibid.). This resolution was signed by the leadership of the MRD, and it imagined a form of provincial autonomy in which the central government only had control over defense, foreign affairs, currency, and communications. This was not, of course, implemented, but the key factor was that this was a cause that had been taken up by the groups that had previously been part of the NAP. For them, being in opposition and pushing for radical change in Pakistan necessarily meant demanding provincial autonomy.

In many ways, however, this was perhaps too little, too late. When the Zia regime came to an end, it was not due to the results of a popular movement, as had been the case with Ayub Khan, but because of the former's death in a plane crash that has long been the subject of much speculation and conspiratorial thinking. As has been argued in this essay, the decline of the progressive movement in Pakistan can be attributed to a longer process by which progressive ideas, activists, and organizations were targeted and delegitimized, partly due to the ideological vagaries of Cold War politics, but also due to the way in which progressive ideas came to be inextricably linked, both in the eyes of the state and through the networks of activists, to the "regional" and ethnic question in Pakistan. The state's concerted attempts to use repression and ideology to counter these threats, in the name of national security, met with some success, but the split between East and West Pakistani progressives generated by the wars of 1965 and 1971 also served to weaken and diminish the progressive movement. After 1971, the ostensibly leftist PPP government engaged in a strategy of coopting elements of the progressive movement while simultaneously continuing with the postcolonial state's imperative to centralize power, generating yet more friction with Pakistan's smaller provinces, and ensuring that the "regional" question continued to be framed in terms of threats to Pakistan's integrity and security. By the time the Zia regime was in power, the progressive movement in Pakistan, riven with sectarian splits and shattered by repression, could do little more than play a marginal role within the broader platform of the MRD, a conglomeration of larger mainstream parties that were willing to accommodate progressive ideas without necessarily delivering on them.

Bizenjo passed away in 1989 and soon after, Kutty started working for the Pakistan Institute of Labour Education and Research (PILER), an organization that was the brainchild of Karamat Ali, a progressive who had been closely associated with both the NAP and the MRD. The work Kutty did with PILER represented a significant shift from the kind of political work he had previously done with various parties and with Bizenjo, but it was nonetheless progressive work clearly aimed at supporting both organized and unorganized labor movements in Pakistan. The work that PILER has done in documenting this history is also worthy of mention, and their collection of short life histories of prominent labor leaders is just one of the many ways in which this organization remains connected to its more political roots. However, if we were to look around at the groups of people who were part of Pakistan's progressive movements, we would find that by the late 1980s and early 1990s, many of them would, like Kutty, be involved with organizations like PILER, working outside of the formal political space that had previously been occupied by the parties and movements of an earlier period. These are clearly forms of organization and mobilization with much more limited radical potential but also represent the kinds of formations that emerge in situations where the space for political action has been severely circumscribed.

The broader political landscape of Pakistan in the 1990s and 2000s was also markedly different from that which had characterized the first decades of independence, even if contemporary political outcomes continued to bear the imprint of events from that time. For one, the nature of Pakistan's economy had changed tremendously. In 1947, Pakistan was an overwhelmingly agrarian country with small pockets of urbanization and, crucially, industry in cities like Lahore and Karachi. Particularly in a context where the first two decades after independence were characterized by economic planning that emphasized the need for rapid, state-led industrialization, it could be argued that workers in strategic sectors, particularly those like the railways, which had a long tradition of organization and mobilization, could play a particularly disruptive political role. This might account for both their capacity to mobilize, limited as it may have been, as well as the way in which they were viewed as a threat by the state in the 1950s and 1960s. In the 1970s, however, significant sections of the working classes were coopted into networks of state patronage through public sector employment, and the subsequent initiation of donor-driven neoliberal market reforms in the late 1980s and 1990s served to change the nature of work and employment in Pakistan, exposing the working classes in rural and urban Pakistan to increased exploitation and precarity at the hands of largely unregulated domestic and foreign capital, even as provisions for welfare and social security were systematically eroded (Candland 2007; Munir et al. 2015). In a context where the progressive movement has already been weakened by the processes described above, and the very idiom of progressive politics is absent from mainstream political discourse, the spaces within which the working classes and other marginalized groups can come together and organize for collective political action remain fragmented and limited.

Conclusion

As B. M. Kutty recounts in his autobiography, the idea of Pakistan was, for some, associated with the hope that independence and a new postcolonial future would be characterized by a politics predicated on equality and inclusiveness. Yet, very soon after independence, it became clear that the state would operate in a manner not dissimilar to the Raj that had preceded it, centralizing control and curbing dissent in the interest of maintaining the dominance of entrenched elites. The progressive movements that arose in response to this, some of which themselves had antecedents in the colonial period, coalesced around demands for greater representation and autonomy for Pakistan's ethnic minorities, and for a politics that put the collective good before private interests. In the context of the Cold War, however, and an emerging state narrative that privileged religion as a source of national unity and cohesion, demands for recognition and redistribution were seen as suspect and consequently met with repression through administrative and ideological mechanisms. While progressives and "regionalists" found common cause in their opposition to the state and benefitted from the emergence of networks of support and solidarity that cut across Pakistan, their ability to withstand the state was severely circumscribed by differences that emerged between different tendencies in the movement during the war against India in 1965 and emergence of an independent Bangladesh in 1971. At the same time, these wars served to both strengthen the state and heighten its anxieties, further associating progressive movements with threats to national security, and contributing to their delegitimization as seditious and unacceptable. Weakened by splits, the decline of the progressive movement thus went hand in hand with the development of an exclusionary national imaginary that prioritized security and unity at the expense of inclusivity and pluralism.

Bibliography

Afzal, Muhammad Rafique. 1986. *Political Parties in Pakistan: 1947–1958*. Islamabad: National Institute of Historical & Cultural Research.

Ahmed, Ishtiaq. 2010. "The Rise and Fall of the Left and the Maoist Movements in Pakistan." *India Quarterly: A Journal of International Affairs* 45 (3): 251–65.

Ali, Kamran Asdar. 2005. "The Strength of the Street Meets the Strength of the State: The 1972 Labor Struggle in Karachi." *International Journal of Middle East Studies* 37 (1): 83–107.

Ali, Kamran Asdar. 2011. "Communists in a Muslim Land: Cultural Debates in Pakistan's Early Years." *Modern Asian Studies* 45 (3): 501–34.

Ali, Kamran Asdar. 2015. *Surkh Salam: Communist Politics and Class Activism in Pakistan, 1947–1972*. Karachi: Oxford University Press.

Bansal, Alok. 2011. "Review of *Sixty Years in Self Exile: No Regrets: A Political Autobiography*." *Indian Foreign Affairs Journal* 6 (2): 236–8. https://www.jstor.org/stable/45340890.

Bhattacherjee, Kallol. 2015. "A Mapila in Karachi Remembers His Roots." *The Hindu* (November 8). https://www.thehindu.com/todays-paper/tp-national/a-mapilla-in-karachi-remembers-his-roots/article7856681.ece.

Bizenjo, Mir Ghaus Buksh. 2009. *In Search of Solutions: An Autobiography of Mir Ghaus Baksh Bizenjo*, B. M. Kutty (ed.). Karachi: Pakistan Study Centre, University of Karachi.

Candland, Christopher. 2007. *Labor, Democratization and Development in India and Pakistan*. London: Routledge.

Chatterji, Joya. 2012. "South Asian Histories of Citizenship, 1946–1970." *Historical Journal* 55 (4): 1049–71.

Jones, Philip. 2003. *The Pakistan People's Party: Rise to Power*. Karachi: Oxford University Press.

Khan, Yasmin. 2008. *The Great Partition: The Making of India and Pakistan*. New Haven, CT: Yale University Press.

Kutty, Biyyothil Mohyuddin. 2012. *Khud Ikhtiar Kardah Jila Watni: Siyasi Jad-o-Juhd ke 62 Saal*. Lahore: Jumhoori Publications.

Malik, Anushay. 2013. "Alternative Politics and Dominant Narratives: Communists and the Pakistani State in the Early 1950s." *South Asian History and Culture* 4 (4): 520–37.

Malik, Anushay. 2020. "Narrating Christians in Pakistan through Times of War and Conflict." *South Asia: Journal of South Asian Studies* 43 (1): 68–83.
Munir, Kamal Ahmad, Natalya Naqvi, and Adaner Usmani. 2015. "The Abject Condition of Labor in Pakistan." *International Labor and Working-Class History* 87: 174–83.
Saif, Lubna. 2010. *Authoritarianism and Underdevelopment in Pakistan 1947–1958: The Role of Punjab*. Karachi: Oxford University Press.
Uddin, Layli. 2020. "'Enemy Agents at Work': A Microhistory of the 1954 Adamjee and Karnaphuli Riots in East Pakistan." *Modern Asian Studies* 55 (2): 629–64.
Ziring, Lawrence. 1971. *The Ayub Khan Era: Politics in Pakistan, 1958–1969*. New York: Syracuse University Press.

3

On Progressive Papers in Pakistan

Mahvish Ahmad, Hashim bin Rashid, and Ahmad Salim

In 1972, when the Communist Party of Pakistan (CPP) officially established *Surkh Parcham* or Red Flag, as its party organ, it was impossible to find anyone willing to publish and distribute copies. With the CPP banned since 1954 and unable to operate, the CPP Central Committee could not secure a "Certificate of Declaration for the Publication of Newspaper/Magazine etc."—or what in everyday parlance is merely referred to as a "declaration"—which would allow access to formal printing presses and distribution networks. Like other banned publications, the CPP found another way: They wrote *Surkh Parcham* by hand, prepared stencil copies of their write-ups, covered it with ink, and printed multiple copies by themselves. The CPP rank-and-file was then enrolled into the role of distributor, receiving 15–20 copies, which they were tasked with delivering to members and sympathizers. One of these distributors was a young, eighteen-year-old Ahmad Salim, one of the coauthors of this contribution, whose early politicization as a communist was bound up in distributing *Surkh Parcham*. He eventually joined its editorial board. The CPP found a way to build alternative infrastructures that allowed them to curate, print, and distribute a communist line on Pakistani politics, often directly targeting sitting regimes, their imperial backers, and powerful feudal, capitalist interests, despite attempts by this assemblage of power brokers to shut them down. In turn, these networks became a means through which its political workers could be trained. As many old Communists like to tell their younger counterparts, the underground distribution of illegal prints instilled in them a discipline that is lost on today's leftists.

This photo essay tells a story of Left-wing papers like *Surkh Parcham*. It does not claim that only Left prints were banned; several magazines published by the political right, like Jamaat-e-Islami, have been subject to similar kinds of censorship. Nor does the choice of prints in this essay claim to represent what constitutes Left politics in Pakistan, or try to homogenize this definition: publications from the Pashtun, Sindhi, Gilgiti, Balti, or other minoritized lefts around the country, as well as feminist and agrarian movements, have not received the attention they deserve. Many of the political and editorial collectives behind this combination of prints were also at loggerheads with one another. Some were closely aligned with Zulfikar Ali Bhutto, for instance, while others took the side of the National Awami Party (NAP), which Bhutto famously banned and whose leaders he arrested and tried in the Hyderabad Conspiracy Case.

Nevertheless, this disjointed constellation of prints sheds light on the vast and rich, intellectual, and political paper production that has always been a mainstay of Pakistan's plural lefts, which despite censorship and repression backed up by Cold War–era anti-Communist funding has survived as a record of marginal and dissident voices in the country's cultural and political history. Almost all the prints featured in this photo essay were banned at some point in their tenure, while others—like *Jabal*, issued as an organ of the armed Balochistan People's Liberation Front in the 1970s—were illegal to begin with. Despite the pressures they faced, the collectives responsible for these prints found creative ways to circumvent censorship. While publications like *Surkh Parcham* or *Jabal* had to rely on independent, parallel print and distribution networks, others like *Al Fatah* and *Meyār*—both banned under Zia—would buy up "declarations" of legal magazines every time they were banned, and then continue to print their content under new titles, often including a logo of the original journal at the bottom to indicate that they were still around despite Zia's attempt to repress their publications.

The building of alternative infrastructures by these "little magazines" did far more than circumvent censorship, they also made possible the articulation and circulation of counter-hegemonic and noncanonical political ideas and vocabularies, that reimagined ideas of history, territory, and subjectivity. For instance, in a study of the Mazdoor Kissan Party (MKP) Circular, Sara Kazmi (2021) shows how Malik Agha Sahotra, a central leader in MKP Punjab, analyzed "how the exclusions of caste and indigeneity were articulated within a section of the Pakistani Left" on the pages of the Circular. Similarly, in her study of *Jabal*, another coauthor of this article, Mahvish Ahmad joins Mir Mohammad Ali Talpur (2021) to investigate how the Balochistan People's Liberation Front articulated alternative ideas of Third World internationalism to that pursued by postcolonial states, one that advocated for a direct link between struggles rather than governments. Even today such magazines continue to circulate marginalized ideas of who constitutes the central political subject of Pakistani progressive politics. For instance, on the November 2021 cover of *Sangat*, which continues to be printed out of Quetta under the editorial leadership of Dr. Shah Mohammad Marri, we find an image of the *machere* or fisherfolks of the Indian Ocean coast in southern Balochistan, who are presented as a central, laboring figure affected and displaced by the China–Pakistan Economic Corridor, and as a key figure of resistance against military-directed, accumulation by dispossession in Gwadar. As this essay went to press, thousands of Gwadar's fishermen have organized under the auspices of Haq Do Tehreek to directly confront the securitization and displacement of their lives and livelihoods in the fast-developing port city.

Finally, the magazines were sites of cultural experimentation. As both Saadia Toor (2011) and Kamran Asdar Ali (2015) remind us, debates on what should constitute Pakistan's cultures were a key site of political contestation. Magazines such as *Sawera*, *Lail-o-Nihār*, and *Meyār* and the writers and editors behind them—like Faiz Ahmed Faiz, Sibte Hassan, Fehmida Riaz, and Mehmood Shaam—are known as much for their Left and progressive politics as their literary pursuits, both of which they saw as intimately intertwined. Magazines that came from some of Pakistan's more peripheralized geographies, such as Balochistan, would go further, by mixing the languages that they printed in, recognizing the multiplicity of Pakistan's languages and cultural expressions.

Today, for instance, *Sangat*'s editor Dr. Shah Mohammad Marri says that the magazine prints articles not just in Urdu, but also in Balochi, Brahui, and Farsi.[1]

Most of the issues featured in this contribution are available in the 40,000-strong collection held by Ahmad Salim at his South Asian Research and Resource Centre (SARRC), housed in a building donated to him by a scholar of Urdu literature, Dr. Humaira Ishfaq and her husband Qaiser Abbas, outside of Islamabad. Our decision to center prints available at SARRC is an acknowledgment of Ahmad Salim's forty-year long effort to archive the material legacies of the Pakistani Left, and the arduous and at times dangerous labor that has gone into this project. It has been no easy task for Ahmad Salim to keep these papers safe and secure. It required him cajoling comrades and friends to hand over old copies of radical journals to him for safe-keeping, rather than throwing them out or burning them. At one point, he thought entering into a collaboration with the International Institute of Social History in Amsterdam might help keep these papers secure, only to discover that this meant that important documents of the Pakistani Left were being shipped abroad, making them functionally inaccessible to the many scholars and activists who live in Pakistan (he discontinued the collaboration). When he found out that many old books had been sold to street sellers, he started visiting these make-shift shops to buy up old copies, only to have his doctor tell him that he had a "book dust allergy" and was putting his health at risk. Rather than stop the work, he decided to continue it, wearing a mask and gloves. Ahmad Salim's archival labor mirrors the work of the editors and writers whose work he has preserved. Like them, the histories he has secured face repression and neglect. His work reminds us of the vibrant, counter-hegemonic politics that has always been a part of Pakistan's history, despite active attempts to obscure and erase them in national history books. We hope that this contribution can serve as a reminder to scholars of the Pakistani Left; a reminder that much work remains to be done. The materials that make our research possible remain fragmented and scattered, and our accessibility to them depends on the deep commitment of people like Ahmad Salim.

Surkh Parcham | Red Flag

Surkh Parcham or Red Flag was the official organ of the CPP. With the party established in Pakistan in 1948, *Surkh Parcham*'s formal establishment in 1972 was preceded by a series of CPP pamphlets, circulars, and other papers without formal titles. Indeed, this initial, untitled period of publications could be understood as the first phase of publishing by the CPP, though copies of earlier prints produced by the party are hard to locate. In this earlier phase, the responsibility for CPP publications sat with Sibte Hassan (1916–1984), a member of the CPP, the Progressive Writers Association (PWA), and a journalist who went on to work for progressive publications like *Imroze*, *The Pakistan Times*, and *Lail-o-Nihār*. In turn, Hameed Akhtar (1924–2011)—also a member of the

[1] With thanks to Dr. Shah Mohammad Marri, the current editor of *Sangat*, for providing additional information on this magazine in its post-1990s iteration.

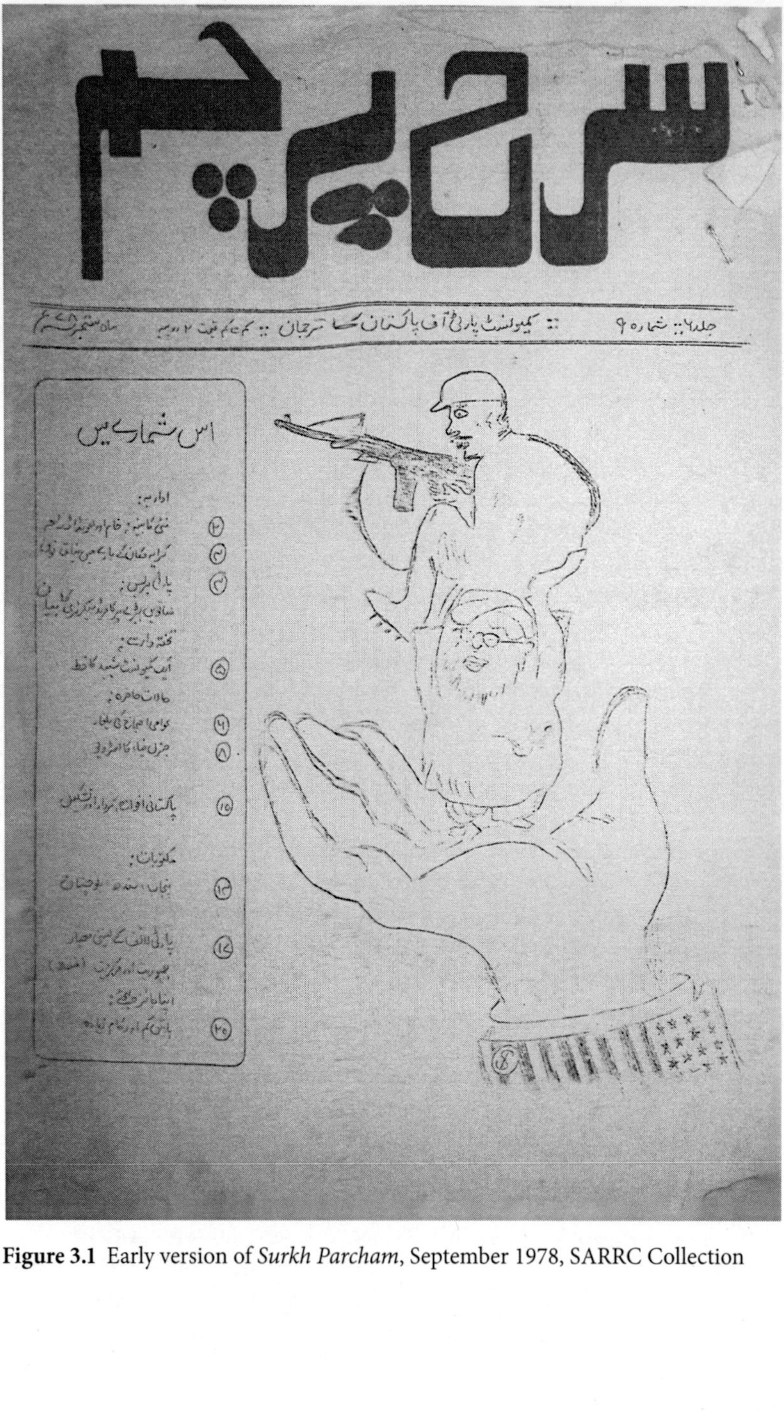

Figure 3.1 Early version of *Surkh Parcham*, September 1978, SARRC Collection

CPP and the secretary general at one point of the PWA—was responsible for printing. In this first phase, anti-Communist policies by the government—culminating in the 1954 ban of the CPP—meant that various party prints were repeatedly seized and declared illegal, forcing CPP print and distribution to take place underground and in secret. To circumvent bans, the CPP tried to publish its content in legalized magazines, but remained under heavy surveillance.

In 1972, in what could be understood as the second phase of CPP publications, the party formally began to publish regularly, giving its organ the name, *Surkh Parcham*. However, like its predecessors, *Surkh Parcham* was declared illegal, meaning it had to continue to operate surreptitiously and underground. As a result, *Surkh Parcham* was written by hand and prepared with a stencil that was then run through a cyclostyle machine. It was not possible to print large runs of the organ in a formal printing press. This also meant that neither its editorial board nor its writers were publicly known. Though the CPP's Central Committee made formal decisions about the content of *Surkh Parcham*, including who would pen what article, poem, or translation, all editors and authors were identified on its pages with pseudonyms denoting either collectives—like "Rashid Group" or "Jamia Karachi"—or individuals, like "Khurshid." Nevertheless, knowledge of the CPP itself means that we know about some of the writers. For example, Ahmad Salim worked as a volunteer translator with *Surkh Parcham* in his capacity as a member of the CPP. He would regularly translate poetry from Pashto, Punjabi, and Sindhi into Urdu for the organ. Up until the late 1980s and early 1990s—with the fall of the Soviet Union—possessing copies of *Surkh Parcham* was extremely dangerous and those caught with copies ran the risk of being prosecuted for treason.

By the early 1990s, *Surkh Parcham* entered its third phase: It went from underground to overground, and by the early 2000s started publicly printing the name of the CPP general secretary as the editor of the magazine. No longer forced to operate underground, it is now published at a legal printing press and comes out as a formal magazine.

Sangat | Comrade

Sangat, the word used for "comrade" or "friend" in Balochi and Sindhi, was established in 1972 out of Quetta, Balochistan, as a magazine aligned with NAP. NAP had just won the province's first democratic elections in the 1970 election. *Sangat* did not last too long, and the team managed to publish just seven or eight issues, under the editorship of Bizen Bizenjo (the son of NAP leader, Ghaus Bakhsh Bizenjo) and with the involvement of Communists like Rauf Warsi (a member of the banned CPP who, like other underground Communists, chose NAP as a front organization). It stopped publishing when NAP was banned in 1973 under Prime Minister Zulfikar Ali Bhutto; its leaders were arrested in 1975 as part of the Hyderabad Conspiracy Case. As a magazine closely aligned with NAP, it was heavily sympathetic to the party central to its founding. With NAP declaring itself a socialist party that propagated a multinationalist and multilingual dispensation—it famously brought together Pakistan's minoritized nationalities especially Pashtun, Baloch, and Bengali political figures—*Sangat* also reflected this party line. Ahmad Salim was a member of NAP in

Figure 3.2 Front cover of *Sangat* from 1998 entitled 'Bolshevik Revolution'

these days and regularly wrote diary entries from Lahore that were published in the pages of *Sangat*.

Sangat was shut down in 1973. Though it resumed publication for a short period in the 1970s, it was only properly relaunched in the 1990s. At this point, the Quetta-based Communist, public intellectual, and resident pharmacist Dr. Shah Mohammad

Marri shifted out of his role as a writer with *Nokeen Daur*, or New Age, another Quetta-based magazine, and decided to buy up the "declaration" for *Sangat*. He believed that the magazine's title, *Sangat*, was well-suited to his vision, which aimed to recirculate a more grounded vocabulary for Marxist politics within Balochistan. Today, *Sangat* is published under the larger Sangat Academy of Sciences, run by Dr. Marri out of Quetta. The Academy also prints other books and organizes study circles and debates. Since Dr. Marri took over *Sangat* has been published regularly, every month, and celebrated its twenty-fifth year anniversary in 2021. Circulating as an important, Communist magazine among Baloch communities—at one point being sent to Baloch diaspora not just within Pakistan and in places like Malir, Lyaari, and interior Sindh, but also further afield, in the Gulf—the magazine publishes in multiple languages including Balochi, Urdu, and Farsi.

Jabal | Mountain

Published between 1973 and 1977 by a group of urban Marxist-Leninists allied with the Balochistan People's Liberation Front (BPLF) in the 1970s, *Jabal* was an underground and banned pamphlet published in English and Urdu. *Jabal*, which meant mountain in Balochi and Sindhi, was a homage to the northeastern mountain tracts where the BPLF were in armed confrontation with the government, protesting the dismissal of a democratically elected provincial government in Balochistan. Just two years after Bangladesh's liberation, Bhutto launched a military operation in Balochistan after accusing NAP leaders of sedition.

In at least fourteen issues published over three years, *Jabal*'s editors, writers, and allies surreptitiously curated, printed, and distributed alternative histories, news and information, critiques of the regime and its policies, and strategic and tactical analyses of the operation. Published entries included original writings and translated or republished texts from other national liberation and revolutionary movements from around the world. In its first editorial, *Jabal's* creators stated that they wanted to help readers "overcome" the "lies and distortions spewed out daily by the … regime" and to "lay the basis for the unity of all oppressed nationalities, democratic and progressive forces in Pakistan" and around the world for the purposes of reimagining the postcolonial state. The articles on its pages propagated a series of radical ideas about how to organize collective life in Pakistan. For instance, *Jabal* spoke often about the importance of multinationalism, the recognition of Pakistan's multiple nationalities and languages, and the importance of establishing a Communist society in order to make space for this kind of political dispensation. Similarly, *Jabal* criticized state-to-state diplomatic relations that worked to undermine minoritized communities, for instance criticizing the recruitment of mercenaries from the Indian Coast to serve in the Omani Army to suppress the Dhofar Rebellion.

As a bulletin written in English and Urdu, *Jabal* was not meant for Baloch members of the movement against military operations, a significant portion of whom were unable to read and write, and many of whom did not speak English or Urdu. Instead, through close coordination between the BPLF leadership and the

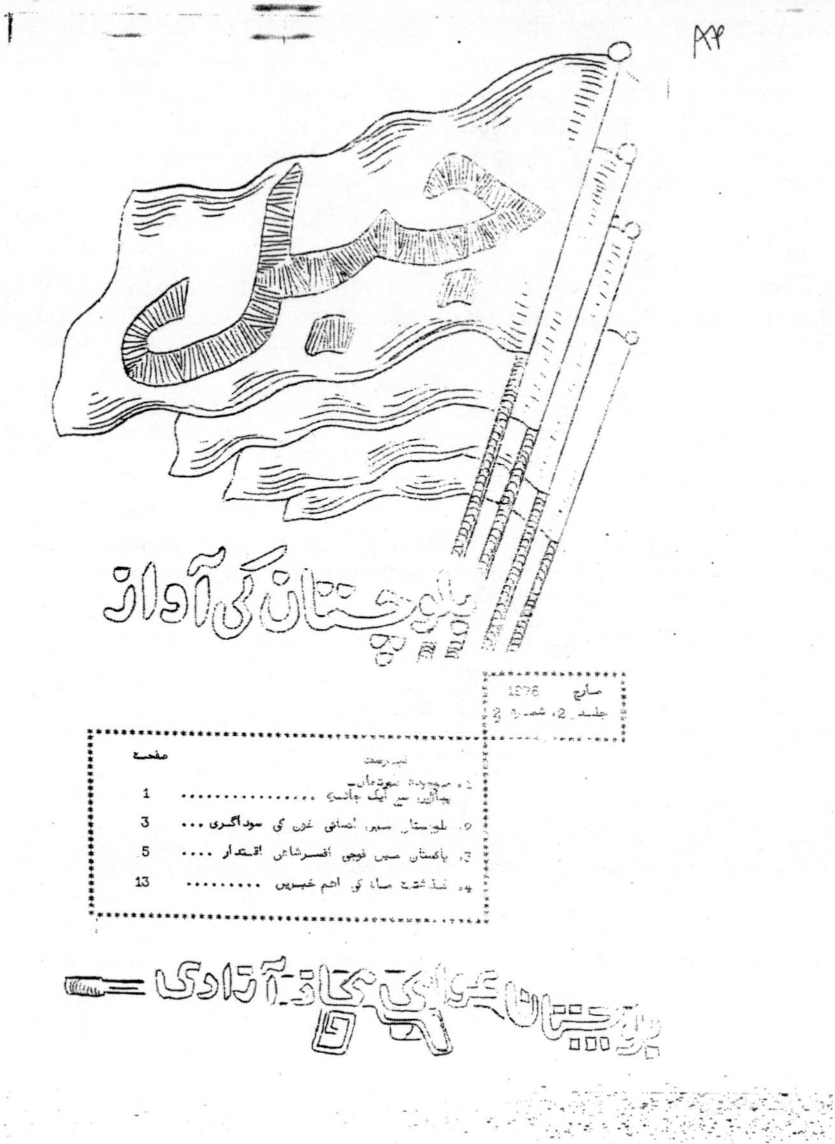

Figure 3.3 An Urdu edition of *Jabal* from March, 1978. One of the articles is entitled "The Trade in Human Blood in Balochistan." Private collection. Some issues also available at SARRC

editorial collective, it served as a vehicle to forge solidarity with struggles around Pakistan and the world.[2]

Lail-o-Nihār | Night and Day

Lail-o-Nihār or Night and Day was a literary and political weekly published by Progressive Papers Limited (PPL), a progressive printing press that also brought out the English Daily *Pakistan Times* and the Urdu daily *Imroze*. It was published under the chief editor Faiz Ahmad Faiz, and included as its executive editor another member of the CPP and PWA, Sibte Hassan. The broader PPL included major and famous figures of the mainstream Pakistani Left, including Mian Iftikharuddin and Ahmad Nadeem Qasmi. Known for both high-quality political and literary writing, as well as its CPP line, *Lail-o-Nihār* remains one of the most important legacies of progressive print in Pakistan today.

On April 18, 1959, Ayub Khan's military regime famously surrounded the offices of the PPL, with the explicit purpose of arresting and replacing key Left leaders within the press. As a result of the takeover, editors and writers like Sibte Hassan, Mazhar Ali Khan, and Ahmad Nadeem Qasmi—who at the time was leading *Imroze* and regularly wrote for *Lail-o-Nihār*—resigned in protest from their positions.[3] It was closed down in 1964 and did not resume publication until 1970, when Faiz Ahmed Faiz started producing new issues of *Lail-o-Nihār* from Karachi. It was shut down again during General Zia-ul-Haq's martial law, though its "declarations" were at one point bought up by *Al Fatah* to circumvent bans on progressive publications targeting other magazines.

Al Fatah | The Victory

Al Fatah or The Victory was launched in the 1970s. Irshad Rao (c.1945–present) was the editor, and it circulated well into the 1990s, albeit intermittently because of multiple bans on it by sitting regimes. Ironically, despite being a magazine known for its pro-Pakistan People's Party leanings, Bhutto's PPP government was the first to crack down on its production and circulation. This only burnished its widely critical and solidly Left reputation. Throughout its history, for instance, *Al Fatah* penned critical articles and poetry on the 1971 war in East Pakistan, now Bangladesh.

Al Fatah took a strong stance on the side of multinationalism, insisting much like Bhutto's main opponents, NAP, that Pakistan was a country made up of multiple nationalities and languages and that each of these should be seen as integral to what constitutes Pakistani national identity. It was in this vein that *Al Fatah* supported

[2] With thanks to Mir Mohammad Ali Talpur who co-authored a Digital Teaching Tool on *Jabal* with Mahvish Ahmad, as part of a joint initiative between Ahmad Salim's SARRC and Revolutionary Papers (RP), a transnational collaboration investigating twentieth- and twenty-first-century anti-colonial and left journals as sites of critical knowledge production. Access the RP/SARRC Digital Teaching Tool at tools.revolutionarypapers.org/jabal-the-voice-of-balochistan/.

[3] The editors, respectively, of *Daily Pakistan Times* and *Daily Imroz* Mazhar Ali Khan and Ahmad Nadeem Qasmi resigned. Editor of *Lail-o-Nihar* Sibte Hassan was fired.

Figure 3.4 *Lail-o-Nihār* cover declaring that the days of dictatorship are coming to an end, November 1, 1970, SARRC Collection

Figure 3.5 Cover of *Al Fatah*, February 10, 1970, SARRC Collection

Bhutto's declaration of Sindh as a bilingual province, with equal stature for both Sindhi and Urdu. At a time of excessive splits within the Pakistani Left between pro-Soviet and pro-Chinese camps, *Al Fatah* was known as an anti-Soviet, pro-China magazine. In fact, the Soviet Press and Information Department often tried to print in *Al Fatah* for the purposes of influencing the Pakistani Left.

Though circumscribed by Bhutto, *Al Fatah* was banned by Zia. The military ruler declared the magazine anti-Pakistan. In order to circumvent the total closure of *Al Fatah*, Irshad Rao would find a magazine that was still legal, and buy up the "declaration" in order to continue publishing *Al Fatah* content in other magazines. To ensure that its readers were able to identify the provenance of the new content, *Al Fatah* would print a small logo somewhere on the front cover declaring that readers should consider the content in the magazine they were holding identical to that which would normally be printed in *Al Fatah*. Articles by *Al Fatah* were carried in other progressive magazines, such as *Awāz* and *Lail-o-Nihār*. This would be followed by the sentence: "*Al Fatah* will be reprinted [in its original form] as soon as our declaration is restored!" It is considered multinationalist, anti-feudal, anti-capitalist and pro-worker, with publications only dwindling after the fall of the Soviet Union in the late 1980s and early 1990s.

Awāz | Voice

Awāz was first published in the late 1970s under the editorship of feminist Urdu poet Fehmida Riaz, widely known for her progressive, feminist, anti-military, pro-democratic, and socialist political and literary writing. Initially conceived as an independent magazine, it railed against Zia's military regime. *Awāz* also offered a home to other banned magazines—especially *Al Fatah* and *Meyār*—despite having their "declarations" or permissions to publish revoked by Zia. For instance, *Awaz*, issue no. 4, published in 1978, is a reprint of the magazine *Meyār*, which was founded in 1976 by Mehmood Shaam and was known as progressive, leftist, and supportive of the PPP. This issue contains a range of articles critiquing martial law under Zia, as well as documenting and presenting lists and photographs of opponents arrested by the military regime.

Awaz propagated an anti-Zia, socialist, and Third World internationalist position, regularly publishing original progressive literary content. This included *shuhadaaye falasteen ke naam*, a poem penned and published for the first time in *Awāz* by Faiz Ahmed Faiz in an issue in 1981. The decision to take such a solid stance against Zia on the pages of *Awāz*, including his 1979 hanging of Bhutto, made Fehmida Riaz a target of the military regime's wrath. She was placed under surveillance, and at least ten criminal cases of sedition, carrying the death penalty, were registered against her. Her husband, the leftist political worker Zafar Ali Ujan, was also thrown in jail. To escape the charges, she went to India under the pretense of being invited for a *mushaira*, and secured asylum there under Indira Gandhi's government with the help of fellow Indian novelist and poet, Amrita Pritam. She spent her years there as a poet-in-residence at Jamia Millia Islamia, Delhi, with her husband eventually joining her once he was released from jail.

Figure 3.6 Cover of *Awāz* issued in coordination with *Meyār*, September 1978, SARRC Collection

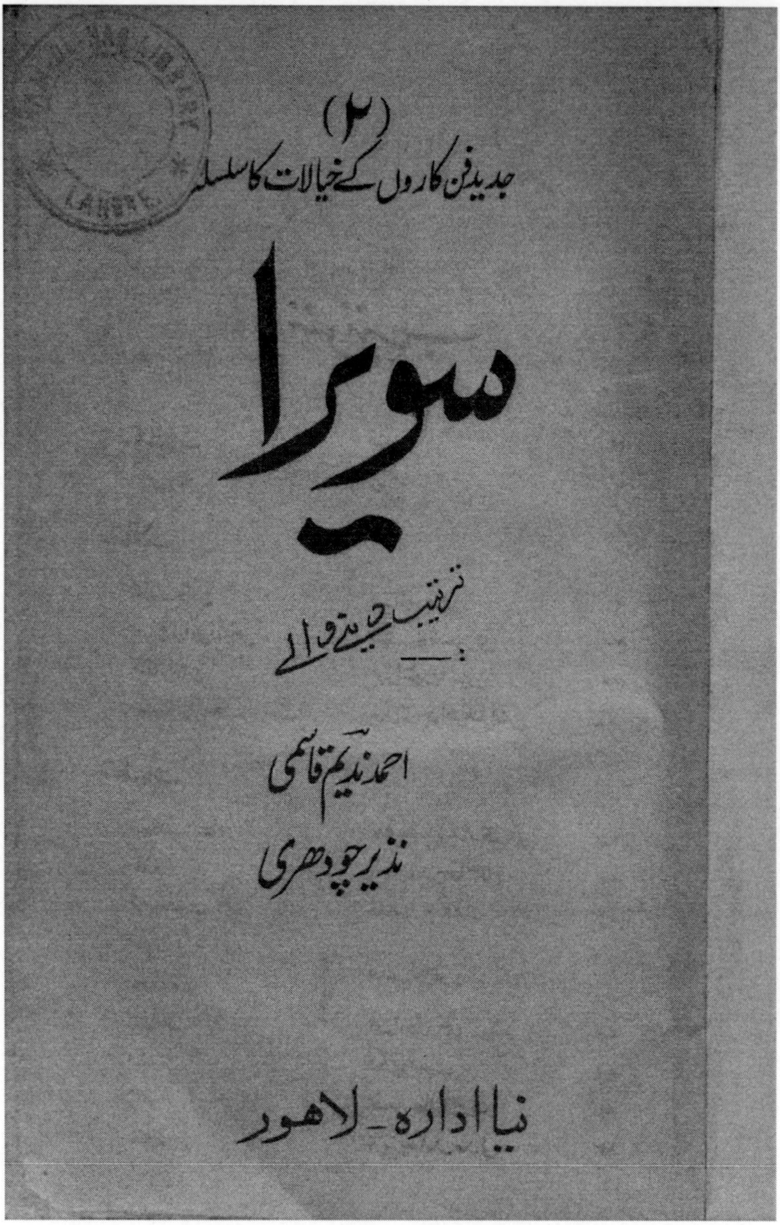

Figure 3.7 An edition of *Sawera*, Lahore, 1947, edited by Ahmed Nadeem Qasmi and Nazeer Chaudhry, SARRC Collection

Sawera Lahore | Dawn Lahore

Sawera—a monthly, and the literary organ of the Progressive Writers Association—was launched just before Partition. Its continuity into post-1947 Pakistan puts it on the list of the few publications that span both time periods with editions coming out until the late 1970s. Founded in England in the 1930s by Sajjad Zaheer, Mulk Raj Anand, and others, the Progressive Writers Movement, closely affiliated with the Communist Party of India, had a commitment to building a new literature that would aid the liberation of the masses. Along with *Adab-e-Latif* and *Naya Adab*, *Sawera* is critical to understanding the development of progressive writing in the Urdu language in South Asia. While *Sawera's* most famous editor remains Ahmed Nadeem Qasmi, in the 1940s and 1950s single editions were edited and curated by a range of progressive literary figures, including Sahir Ludhianvi, Ahmad Rahi, Zaheer Kashmiri, and Hanif Ramay.

Starting out as a magazine that would publish a wide range of authors critical of the society that stood before them, ideological lines were sharpened in a new manifesto issued in 1950, which set out distinctions between progressive writing and "non-progressive" writing. This attack led to the purge of a range of authors from the pages of *Sawera*, including Sadaat Hassan Manto and Noon Meem Rashid, for "decadent" writing influenced by "bourgeois psychology." Carrying the works of Faiz Ahmed Faiz, Krishan Chandar, Ismat Chughtai, Sajjad Zaheer, Qaifi Azmi, and Sibte Hassan among others, *Sawera* remains the tour de force that printed the bulk of socialist literature that continues to be read. Surveying its pages, one moves between poetry, short stories, political essays, and translations of progressive writers from across the world, including Pablo Neruda and Ilya Grigoryevich Ehrenburg.

Mazdoor Kissan Party Circular | Worker's Peasants Party Circular

The *Mazdoor Kissan Party Circular* was the official organ of the Mazdoor Kissan Party (MKP). In total, at least a hundred issues were produced during the party's heyday in the 1970s. Published on cyclostyled sheets, and distributed by hand, it was meant to be circulated only among party members. Despite a decline in the party's organizing and eventual splits, the *Circular* continued to run well into the 1980s and 1990s, undergoing changes in its name, from the *Circular*, to *Proletari*, and finally, *Bulletin*. Despite the publication surviving under different names, it is this period that captures the fullest development of Maoist political consciousness and organizing in Pakistan, and can be read alongside the development of the contemporaneous Naxalbari movement in India, often referenced to in the *Circular*.

The *Circular* is important because it attempted to reckon with the national question in Pakistan after the independence of Bangladesh. It was also a space to encounter the MKP's most famous general secretary, Major Ishaq Mohammad, and his writings, though it also captured developments in the MKP's Khyber Pakthunkhwa and Sindh chapters. Not only does the *Circular* tell the story of the Hashtnagar struggle, it is also an

Figure 3.8 Ho Chi Minh featured in an *MKP Circular*, 1975, SARRC Collection

important space to learn about struggles that are less spoken about, such as the strikes and factory occupations in Landhi in 1972, or the Dehat Mazdoor Tanzeem (Rural Workers Organization), which deserves attention on its own for fashioning a kind of synthesis between the Harappan civilization and Marxism. The MKP circular would often carry the price list of essential items, keeping tabs on how the market was being

Figure 3.9 Peasants facing a tank, *Dehqan*, November 28, 1971, SAARC Collection

controlled or not. The *Circular* remains an important space for discussions around the relationship between literature, culture, and revolutionary practice in Pakistan.[4]

Dehqan | Peasant

Dehqan, a weekly, named for the word 'peasant' in Persian, offers a glimpse into the world of its editor Sheikh Mohammad Rasheed, known as Baba-e-Socialism, and the socialist groupings within the Pakistan People's Party. Launched in late 1971, the magazine's tagline boldly carries one of Iqbal's more powerful couplets, "*Jis khet se dehqan ko mayasar na ho rozi, uss khet ke har gosha e gandum ko jala do*" (Burn each kernel of wheat in that field, which does not yield a peasant's livelihood), reflecting the close connection Rasheed had with the West Pakistan Kissan Committee and the demand for substantive land reform in the country, which mobilized hundreds and thousands of peasants in East and West Pakistan. Much like other Left-wing magazines of the times, *Dehqan* also stood out for its punchy cover art, such as the image of two peasants standing in front of a tank, designed by Lahore-based architect Kamil Khan Mumtaz.

Started at a time when a socialist revolution in Pakistan seemed imminent, *Dehqan* captures both the hope and contradictions of this period. The cover image featured came out on the eve of the Bangladesh war of independence with the editorial titled, "Who wants war?" boldly questioning the logic of war and blaming the Jamaat-e-Islami for playing puppet to the establishment. The magazine also covered the ban on NAP, both condemning the ban and critiquing NAP at different points. For example, a 1972 editorial questions NAP's criticism of the Hashtnagar peasant struggle. Each edition of the magazine had separate sections on farmers', students', and labor movements in the country, as well as a section on ongoing global anti-colonial and anti-capitalist struggles. The magazine also reprinted a special issue featuring an Urdu translation of Mao's 1927 Report into the Peasant Insurgency in the Hunan District, putting a commitment to peasant struggle at the very heart of the magazine.

Bibliography

Ahmad, Mahvish, and Talpur Mir Mohammad Ali. 2021. "*Jabal*: The Voice of Balochistan." Revolutionary Papers. https://tools.revolutionarypapers.org/teaching-tool/jabal-the-voice-of-balochistan/. Accessed November 16, 2022.

Asdar Ali, Kamran. 2015. *Surkh Salam: Communist Politics and Class Activism in Pakistan*. Karachi: Oxford University Press.

Kazmi, Sara. 2021. "Mazdoor Kissan Party Circular." Revolutionary Papers. https://tools.revolutionarypapers.org/teaching-tool/mazdoor-kissan-party-circular/. Accessed November 16, 2022.

Toor, Saadia. 2011. *The State of Islam: Culture and Cold War Politics in Pakistan*. London: Pluto Press.

[4] With thanks to Sara Kazmi, who authored a Digital Teaching Tool on the *Mazdoor Kissan Party Circular* as part of a joint initiative between Ahmad Salim's SARRC and Revolutionary Papers.

Part Two

Nationalism's Many Violences

4

1971: Pakistan's Past and Knowing What Not to Narrate

Nayanika Mookherjee

The day Pakistan builds a memorial in Lahore or Islamabad acknowledging how the Pakistani army killed and raped Bangladeshis during 1971—I can think of pardoning Pakistan.

—*Dr. Meghna Guhathakurta, interview with the author, November 2016*

Dr. Guhathakurta's comment above reflects her experience as a teenager in 1971, when she witnessed her father being fatally shot by the Pakistani army in front of their home in the staff quarters of Dhaka University. Her father, Professor Jyotirmoy Guhathakurta, taught English at the university and was targeted, as he was a Hindu professor. Meghna, a professor of international relations, was a member of the Bangladesh Human Rights Commission. She is also a member of Projonmo Ekattor (Generation 71), an important organization in Bangladesh composed of children (now adults) whose parents were killed as part of the Pakistani army's attempt to kill East Pakistani intellectuals, particularly those who were part of the minority Hindu community. As a result, members of Projonmo Ekattor have an iconic status in Bangladesh as survivors. This statement by a member of Projonmo Ekattor would also be deemed to be highly politicized and not necessarily an unmediated voice of "the people." Nonetheless, these individuals are also highly respected as critical voices against both the role of the Pakistani army during 1971 in East Pakistan and of Bangladeshi nationalism, including the role of the Bangladeshi army's oppression of the indigenous communities in the Chittagong Hill Tracts since the 1980s.

In 1947, with the independence of India from British colonial rule, a sovereign homeland for the Muslims of India was created in the eastern and northwestern corners of the subcontinent as West and East Pakistan. The two wings of the country were separated not only geographically but also by sharp cultural and linguistic differences. Successive Pakistani governments embarked on a strategy of cultural assimilation toward the Bengalis in East Pakistan. Resistance to this program, and more generally to West Pakistani administrative, military, linguistic, civil, and economic control for over two decades, culminated in 1971 with a nine-month-long war between the Pakistani army and the *Mukti Bahini* (East Pakistani/Bengali liberation fighters) supported by the Indian army, which officially joined the war in its last ten days. This conflict resulted in the formation of Bangladesh.

The creation of Bangladesh in 1971 coincided with the death of around fifty intellectuals (Mookherjee 2007),[1] three million civilians, and the rape of two hundred thousand women (according to official, contested figures) (Mookherjee 2015: 8, 22, 35) by the West Pakistani army and Bengali and non-Bengali East Pakistani Collaborators. In my book *The Spectral Wound: Sexual Violence, Public Memories and the Bangladesh War of 1971* (Mookherjee 2015), I argue that the Bangladesh case is distinctive, in comparison to other instances of sexual violence in twentieth- and twenty-first-century wars, in that rather than silence there was widespread public recognition of wartime rape in independent Bangladesh. This was evidenced in the globally unprecedented event of the Bangladeshi government's declaration of women who were raped in 1971 as *birangonas*, or "brave women" (ibid. 129–58). Thereafter, in independent Bangladesh the figure of the raped woman became present in photographs, advertisements, testimonials, and various literary and visual representations. This enumerative community of "3 million dead and 200,000 raped" has been further canonized in the last two decades of nationalist commemorative discourse concerning the war in Bangladesh. A notable consequence of such canonization is the absence of discussion of the rape of Bihari women in East Pakistan by the Bengali liberation fighters within this nationalist narrative.[2] The Biharis are held to have supported the Pakistani army, and so pose problems for the nationalist narrative in Bangladesh. After 1971, the Biharis were left stranded in deplorable conditions in the Geneva Camp in Dhaka and continued to occupy a liminal space in South Asian politics for several decades, with neither the Bangladeshi nor the Pakistani government accepting them as citizens (Siddiqi 2013). Only in 2008 were they granted Bangladeshi citizenship instead of their anticipated Pakistani citizenship. In the last couple of decades, many feminist scholars, filmmakers, and activists within and beyond Bangladesh have begun to examine the attacks on Biharis, complicating the nationalist narrative (Akhtar et al. 2001; Mokammel 2007).

This lively and contested memorial culture contrasts starkly with the situation in Pakistan, where discussion of the 1971 war is rare and its public memory is characterized not by silence and erasure, but by a conscious nonnarration. Discussions with various Pakistani scholars, students, and the younger generation highlight a similar gradual process: the older generation within the families have been willing to talk about the trauma of Partition; some others are today keen to elaborate on the authoritarian role of the Pakistani army in Balochistan; and increasingly there is acknowledgment of the role of the Pakistani army in the killings of East Pakistanis with important parallels drawn with Balochistan. The sexual violence of 1971, however, only tends to be acknowledged when the younger generation—having heard about it elsewhere—have interrogated

1 The loss of the intellectuals is commemorated each year on December 14 on the Martyred Intellectual Day in Bangladesh. See Nayanika Mookherjee, "The Dead and Their Double Duties."

2 I have not been able to work with any Bihari women survivors, but Saikia (2011) includes the experiences of a Bihari woman. Also see Siddiqi (2013).

their family members about it. Instead of an active forgetting, what exists in Pakistan, then, is a process of "apparent amnesia," (Forty 1999: 8) or what I refer to as a strong sense of remembering what *not* to narrate. This apparent amnesia can be understood in light of comments made by some Pakistani commentators who have suggested that "to understand Pakistan through 1947 is the wrong lens. The hurt that moves Pakistan is from a wound more recent—1971." (Hussain 2009). In thinking through the relation between family, nation, and the memorialization of sexual violence, this essay argues that 1971 is a wound that cannot be named in histories of Pakistan. What then does it mean to ask for a memorial for this war? How is it possible to commemorate a wound that cannot be named?

The memorialization of valor and loss in war by governments and other groups through statues, monuments, memorials, and other artifacts presumes that material objects stand for and embody memory, that these are "exchangeable currencies" (Forty 1999: 15). The memorial imperative is based on the externalization and communication of private pain as public and is an injunction directed at that public to remember. At the same time, memorialization also runs the risk of consigning an event to oblivion once it is tied to the memorial as an object of recall. While memorials are part of nation-building and Pakistan has built many monuments to its leaders and its army, the desire for foundation and national cohesion remains haunted by that which it *cannot* narrate—the events of 1971. For the members of Projonmo Ekattor, the call for a memorial has a different temporal and moral imperative; it is not only an attempt to contest the apparent amnesia prevalent in Pakistan but also a demand to symbolically enact and represent remorse, atonement, and apology from Pakistan for its role in 1971. This might then provide the conditions within which Meghna and others like her could consider the possibilities of "thinking of pardoning Pakistan."

In the Pakistani nationalist narrative, 1971 exists as a war in which the East Pakistanis seceded, betrayed the idea of Pakistan as the homeland for South Asian Muslims, and were supported by India, who are understood to have provided encouragement to the Bengalis to separate, and in the process used the conflict to divide Pakistan. That these views are well embedded within the Pakistani government is evidenced in the white paper it published on March 2, 1971.[3] In India, 1971 is primarily seen as an Indo-Pakistani war[4] (occurring at a conjuncture of Cold War politics). West Pakistanis are also deemed to have looked down upon East Pakistanis, and racialized and gendered discourses toward Bengalis have persisted over time. To call some West Pakistanis "Bengalis" was taken as something of an insult (Jafar 2013; Mookherjee 2015).

What implications does the consigning of 1971 to a nationalist narrative of "Bengali betrayal" and "Indian aggression" have for Pakistan's history?[5] And what propels this

[3] Pakistani Government, white paper, March 2, 1971.

[4] An internet search for *Muktijuddho* (Liberation War of 1971) yielded links to 45 sites, "Bangladesh Liberation War" yielded 1,428 sites, and "1971 Indo-Pakistan War" yielded 3,323 sites

[5] From the Partition scholarship, sexual violence across communities (often bureaucratically referred to as "abduction" or "recovery") has predominantly been documented in the case of the northwestern border between India and West Pakistan. The Nehru–Liaqat Pact recommended setting up a committee to find missing girls on the eastern border (Dr. Meghna Guhathakurta, pers. comm.).

insistence on not narrating the rapes carried out by West Pakistani armies on the population of East Pakistan? Could it be the hold the Pakistani army has on its people, as demonstrated by activist Pakistanis who have struggled against the army over the years and yet have connections to the army, even in their own immediate families? Could it be out of shame of the rapes perpetrated? Could the events of 1971 simply be too recent to narrate accurately? Is it conditioned by the still-active pain of losing East Pakistanis as one's fellow citizens, as well as the country's rich resources while at the same time, in my personal communication with Pakistani activists, referring to East Pakistan as a "burden"? Or does it emerge from an anger and indignation at Pakistan's loss of face and territory to the "dark, lazy, effeminate, half-Muslim Bengalis," (Mookherjee 2015: 163) and its defeat by its nemesis the Indian military in 1971, which was a tremendous humiliation for Pakistani leaders, their military, and their citizens? A quiet consensus around what should *not* be narrated in post-conflict situations is also evident in contexts like Bosnia and Rwanda (Burnett 2012; Zarkov 2007), spurred in these cases by the proximity of the different communities that perpetrated sexual violence. But what role, then, does Pakistan's geographical distance from Bangladesh play? Has it facilitated amnesia among West Pakistanis, many of whom were ignorant, willfully or otherwise, of what really transpired in East Pakistan during 1971 or were told that the army was quelling the rebellion successfully in East Pakistan but then suddenly surrendered, leading to an independent Bangladesh? At the same time, how are narratives and narrations affected by the fact that the filial proximate self of East Pakistan overnight became the Other for West Pakistan, and as such needed to be put at a distance emotionally and also in terms of memory- and state-making? What implications does this elusive presence of 1971 have for the imagination or pursuit of possible futures? How do we understand these questions in light of a destabilizing Pakistan, whose army remains central to politics and society, and with regard to an economically buoyant and apparently stable Bangladesh, which, for the last two decades, has invested in a nationalist historiography of 1971 but where a critical narrative is also emerging?

The following discussion takes as its point of departure the narrativization of the sexual violence of 1971, in my book *Spectral Wounds*. In the first section, I explore the different ideas of Pakistan at particular historical moments in Bangladesh and Pakistan, and responses the book has generated. In the second section, I relate the wound of 1971 in both Pakistan and Bangladesh to the ambiguous positioning of 1947 in respective national narratives. These discussions give us insight into what the wound of 1971 means for attempts to narrate history in Pakistan; it also opens up the question of apology and forgiveness, tying the shadowy past of East Pakistan to ongoing struggles in Balochistan. In the final section, the debates concerning apology allow us to reflect on the possibilities of memorializing 1971 in Pakistan.[6]

This essay draws on long-term ethnographic research on the public memories and nationalist narratives of sexual violence during the Bangladesh war of 1971 along with discussions with various Pakistani scholars and students, engagement with historical

[6] Pakistan is not the only state that is selective in its history writing. India and Bangladesh have also skewed historical narratives and continue to do so today.

sources, government documents, textbooks, blog posts, press articles, and other secondary materials. By deploying a broad lens across these sources, I aim to illuminate the high stakes that scholarship and public discourse in this area must negotiate and offer some reflections on the intersection of history, family, nation, (non)narration, and apology. At the same time, I remain cognizant of the shifting contexts and readings of these historical instances so as not to reproduce the coloniality of the present in which negative ideas of Pakistan are perceived in today's Islamophobic world. Nonetheless, the injustice perpetrated in East Pakistan by the Pakistani state cannot be unwritten or negated.

Spectral Wound: Narrativizing Sexual Violence

The book focused, by means of ethnography, on the post-conflict public memory of the history of rape during the war of 1971 in independent Bangladesh. Addressing how the experiences of 1971 manifests today among women themselves and their families, the book triangulates the narratives with various representations (state, visual, and literary) as well as contemporary human rights testimonies. It ethnographically analyzes the social life of various kinds of testimonies, examining how the stories and experiences of raped women of the 1971 war became part of a broader set of national discourses and debates. It explores how visual and literary representations of the raped woman create a public culture of "knowing" and remembering her which in turn informs the processes of testifying and human rights. The book argued that identifying raped women *only* through their suffering creates a homogenous understanding of gendered victimhood and suggests that wartime rape is experienced in the same way by all victims. Against this *The Spectral Wound* sought to highlight the varied experiences of raped women during 1971 through a political and historical analysis of wartime rape.

As such, the book aimed to counter the assumption of silence relating to wartime rape and locates the post-conflict narratives within wider political, literary, and visual contexts. In doing this research as a Bengali Indian, I have always been very conscious of how this project could reinforce enmity between India and Pakistan based on the role of each of these countries during the war of 1971. Instead, *Spectral Wound* decenters these South Asian stereotypes in terms of the roles ascribed to each of these countries in relation to the Bangladesh war of 1971: that of India as "savior" only, Pakistan as "perpetrator" only, and Bangladesh as "victim" only.[7] Today, in the context of India's subcontinental "Big Brother" politics, India is reviled in Bangladesh while its role during 1971 is represented in a mostly positive light due to a literary and linguistic propinquity among the literary intelligentsia in West Bengal and Bangladesh. Nonetheless, conceptions about lack and excess on both sides also exist. Pakistan is also variously considered in Bangladesh: with a lens of hatred due to 1971, as well as affinity due to religious proximity, or indifference.

[7] See Mookherjee (2012) for an elaboration of this point.

Bangladeshi history books of the late 1970s and 1980s, effectively deterritorialized the Pakistan army by only describing them in general terms such as "invader," "enemy," or "friendly." According to Bangladeshi Left-liberal activists, this led to the institutionalization of a *bikrito* (distorted) history, as these faceless references to the army led many among the younger generation to refer to the Indian army as invaders and the Pakistani army as friendly. In contrast, for Left-liberal activists, the Indian army is deemed friendly and the Pakistani army the invader. While the role of the Indian army during the 1971 war could be critiqued in terms of transgressing the sovereignty of Pakistan, the reference to the Pakistani army as friendly in Bangladeshi history textbooks of the 1980s flies in the face of the innumerable instances of killings and rapes carried out by the West Pakistani army and their East Pakistani collaborators. There is no doubt that the Pakistani army did kill and rape huge numbers of East Pakistanis, although as indicated these numbers continue to be contested. The contestation of the numbers however cannot negate the atrocities carried out by the Pakistani army. The Hamdoodur Rahman Commission of Enquiry, appointed in 1971 by the president of Pakistan to inquire into the circumstances of Pakistan's surrender, includes witness statements like "the troops used to say that when the commander [Lt. Gen. Niazi] was himself a raper, how they could be stopped?"[8] In Bangladesh this deterritorialization is predominantly read as a pro-Islamic (often conflated with pro-Pakistani) move by the military governments of General Ziaur Rahman (1975–81) and General Ershad (1982–90). The lack of mention of the instances of rape carried out by the Pakistani army during the war of 1971 in the Bangladeshi history books of the late 1970s and 1980s is above all deemed an attempt to focus on the role of the Bangladeshi military in securing the independence of Bangladesh and to downplay the role of the civilian population in 1971.

The difficulties in narrating the rapes of 1971 became evident in another register, this time in response to the book. When teaching about 1971 and presenting at conferences and seminars, I have frequently had Pakistani students approach me to express their enthusiasm for the book and get it signed for a family member who fought in the war of 1971 and who is also critical of it. Further, I have taught numerous students whose parents were members of the Parliament in Pakistan. They have emphatically added that they were not told anything about the rapes carried out by the Pakistani army either in their school textbooks or by their family members. This links to Ayesha Jalal's formulation on how "the history of Pakistan has been conjured and disseminated by the state-controlled educational system" (Jalal 1995: 74) and that "Pakistan's history textbooks (are) among the best available sources for assessing the nexus between power and bigotry in creative imaginings of a national past." (ibid. 78). Jalal, though referring to Pakistani historiography, is referencing events before 1971 and hence does not address how the Bangladesh War of 1971 is included and treated in Pakistani textbooks. In Pakistan, 1971 is predominantly evoked to analyze military strategy—or is seen as "a civil war of brothers killing brothers; as a story of betrayal within a family saga," (Saikia 2011: 64). In textbooks, 1971 features primarily as an India–Pakistan war, suggesting

[8] Pakistan Government, *Hamdoodur Rahman Commission of Enquiry, 1971*, August 2000.

that the East Pakistanis were headed by Hindu teachers and that Sheikh Mujib and *Mukti Bahini* (liberation fighters) spearheaded the "betrayal": "poisonous propaganda" was produced, in these accounts, by the conflated forces of "separatist elements and pro-Hindu teachers," (ibid. 27). Importantly, younger-generation Pakistani authors such as Anam Zakaria and others have also been exploring the process of history writing in Pakistani textbooks with regard to 1971. The class 9 and class 10 Pakistan studies textbook of the Federal Textbook Board of Islamabad described the Indian-backed agitators as "unruly, uncontrollable and violent" (Zakaria 2010). Bengalis are presented as the instigators of all bloodshed. An excerpt reads:

> Raging mobs took to streets ... banks were looted and the administration came to a halt. Public servants and non-Bengali citizens were maltreated and murdered. Pakistan flag and Quaid's portraits were set on fire ... reign of terror, loot and arson was let loose. Awami League workers started killing those who did not agree with their Six Points Programme. Members of Urdu-speaking non-Bengali communities were ruthlessly slaughtered. West Pakistani businessmen operating in East wing were forced to surrender their belongings or killed in cold blood, their houses set on fire. Pro-Pakistan political leaders were maltreated, humiliated and many of them even murdered. Armed forces were insulted; authority of the state was openly defied and violated. Awami League virtually had established a parallel government and declared independence of East Pakistan. (ibid.)

The textbooks suggest that the Pakistani army was further defamed by being blamed for the killings of East Pakistanis, which they say were actually carried out by Awami League militants. As mentioned earlier, increasing attention is being given in Bangladesh to the killings and rapes carried out by the liberation fighters on the Bihari communities in Bangladesh, who were deemed to be collaborating with the Pakistani army. But the scale of this comparison with the enumerative community of the 200,000 women raped by the Pakistani army and local collaborators is dissimilar. Pakistani authors see this rewriting of the history of 1971 as part of the Pakistani state policy to "eradicate, deny and distort its history." (ibid.)[9] Recent O-Level history textbooks in Pakistan mention the indiscriminate killings in 1971, but not the rapes. The aforementioned Hamdoodur Rahman Commission of Enquiry, which did address the issue of rape in 1971, has only been a public document available to all Pakistani citizens since 2000. After my presentations in conferences and seminars, other scholars have told me that they have contacted their families to ask them if the rapes happened, which was confirmed by their parents and family members. Scholars who have had conversations with their parents after listening to presentations on this issue shared their astonishment as to what their Left-liberal parents had remembered not to narrate. They compared this condition to the manner in which stories of the atrocities carried out by the Pakistani army in Balochistan in 1973 are regularly transmitted in Pakistani

[9] A similar process of changing the history of 1971 exists in Bangladesh based on interparty politics. See Nayanika Mookherjee, *Spectral Wound: Sexual Violence, Public Memories and the Bangladesh War of 1971* (Durham, NC: Duke University Press, 2015), ch. 2.

activist families.[10] The accounts of rapes in Bangladesh are, in contrast, consigned to a zone of apparent amnesia and nonnarratability.

The reference to Balochistan is important to think through when discussing the Bangladesh war of 1971. Since Balochistan became part of Pakistan (in 1948), the Pakistani state has brutally suppressed four Balochi insurgencies/uprisings—in 1948, 1958–9, 1962–3, and 1973–7 (Hussain 2013; Jafar 2013; Siddiqi and Hanif 2012). The separatist/independence movements in Balochistan and Bangladesh have intrinsic parallels, as they were both occurring around the same timeframe. First, both the regions were rich in resources and yet were economically marginalized by the Pakistani state. Second, like the Six Point program of the late Sheikh Mujibur Rahman of Bangladesh, most Balochis agitated for regional autonomy and not independence or secession. But with the introduction of a new Pakistani constitution in 1956, provincial autonomy was restricted, and the "One Unit" concept of political organization was enacted. The first revolt in the 1970s in Balochistan was ruthlessly put down by the Pakistani army led by General Tikka Khan, who earned the nickname "Butcher of Balochistan" and was also called "Butcher of Bengal" because of his brutal attacks in East Pakistan. In 1971, at the height of the Bangladesh war, processions were taken out in Quetta in favor of independence for Balochistan (Jafar 2013). Third, like the practice of abduction and killings of minority communities and intellectuals by the Pakistani state in East Pakistan in 1971, target killings, abducted and missing persons, sectarian trouble, and dumping of corpses carried out by Pakistani state authorities became common in Balochistan during the 1973 movements. The periods of 1948, 1958, 1962–9, and 1974–7, as well as the current post-2000s eras, have seen varying degrees of violence in Balochistan. The general crackdown on nationalist activity throughout the past many decades has been a cause of deepening animosity toward Pakistan among the Balochis. Pakistani commentators have made comparisons between the two regions, warning against the possibility of Balochistan becoming another Bangladesh, seceding from Pakistan and disrupting Pakistan's territorial integrity.

There are various reasons why there might be a reticence to talk about 1971. First, even though East Pakistan is deemed to be a "load" today, there is an overall melancholy among Pakistani activists as to what might have been if East Pakistan had remained with Pakistan. The example cited is of Bangladesh's enviable position as a source of production in agriculture, industry, and export goods, and activists lament the lack of similar development in Pakistan. Today, ironically, Bangladeshi personnel experienced in the garment industry are brought over to supervise and oversee production on the work floors of garment factories in Pakistan. Second, Pakistani scholars point out that the rapes in 1971 are not discussed, as they would end up as ammunition for a critique of Zulfikar Ali Bhutto, whose lack of compromise in negotiations with East Pakistani leader Sheikh Mujibur Rehman (after the latter's victory in the 1970 elections) contributed to the outbreak of the Bangladesh war (personal communication). Bhutto became Pakistan's president in the aftermath of the war after Bangladesh was formed and was popular among the Pakistani Left-liberal communities for leading a social

[10] Even though it is discussed in families and activist circles, the issue of Balochistan is much more difficult to raise publicly as censorship about it continues to be exercised.

democratic government, being less religious (though like the secular Sheikh Mujib, he drew heavily on Islamic populism) than Zia-ul-Huq (1977–88), who became the Pakistani head of state after deposing Bhutto. Third, those in the Pakistani army who were prisoners of war after 1971 refuse to talk about the conflict and are more willing to speak about earlier conflicts such as Partition. What is significant to note here is what constitutes "knowledge" within intergenerational transmission of memories of conflict. In Pakistan, Partition violence is the predominant point of renarration by the grandparents' generation; the "unfair" conflict in Balochistan is what one's parent's generation would be willing to discuss, and 1971 did not figure as knowledge that needed to be transmitted. In liberal circles, the example of Balochistan is cited as a way of criticizing the Pakistani army. The significance of bringing East Pakistan and Balochistan into conversation when discussing Pakistan's past is best brought out in a comment by Pervez Hoodbhoy (a noted academic and Professor of physics at the Quaid-e-Azam University in Islamabad): "Because the lessons of East Pakistan have been lost, most Pakistanis cannot understand why Balochistan is such an angry province today."[11]

Yet concerns about maintaining the territorial integrity of Pakistan and preventing Balochistan from seceding also makes one less critical of the army. In those instances, the example of 1971 and its killings (not the rapes) become a note of caution of what could happen with Balochistan. Obviously there have been a quite few dissenters who have criticized the Pakistani army's role in the 1971 war—among them Tariq Rahman, Colonel Nadir Ali, Ahmed Salim, and others who either fought in the war or went to jail for protesting it—who have never been silenced.[12] But there is no public memory of 1971 in Pakistan. Instead, 1971 is remembered as an illustration of how India "crushed" Pakistan. Today, it is the younger generation in Pakistan who have started to delve into the atrocities and rapes perpetrated in East Pakistan in 1971 by the Pakistani army in television talk shows, novels, blogs, press columns, and articles.[13]

Meghna Guhathakurta's demand for a memorial is constrained by the nonnarratability of this history of rape of 1971 based on different readings, contexts, and configurations of the idea and past of Pakistan. The forms through which intergenerational memory is transmitted and knowledge about violent conflicts is constructed makes it difficult to translate these ambiguities into a memorial form. Hence Pakistani activists compare the state's role in 1971 and Balochistan as a way of critiquing the army. However, while Pakistani state atrocities in Balochistan are easily narrated in families, the many instances of wartime sexual violence during 1971 remain undiscussed. The year 1971 also becomes an important illustration of

[11] M. Hussain and Imtiaz, "School Books in Bangladesh and Pakistan." www.sacw.net/article1767.html (accessed December 2018).

[12] Various civil society actors, such as the Women's Action Forum, as well as poets and writers, have expressed an apology for the Pakistani army's actions.

[13] In late 2021, in the fiftieth anniversary year of 1971, these events have finally been broached in broadcast media, in TV serials, in a popular film *Khel Khel Mein* directed by Nabeel Qureshi, and in a documentary by Javed Jabbar entitled, "Separation of East Pakistan: The Untold Story." The fictional film suggests India was at fault by stoking a disagreement between two "brothers," whereas the documentary, which purports to be a serious read of history, minimizes the role of the military.

secession, which if followed in Balochistan would affect the territorial integrity of the already beleaguered Pakistani state. So reticence about criticizing the Pakistani army and the absence of a memorial for 1971 are caught up in the quagmire of these diverse dilemmas, which are also linked to how 1947 is a problematic origin year for both Pakistan and Bangladesh.

Pasts Disavowed: 1947 and 1971

The Bangladeshi scholar Anisuzzaman argues that 1971 is not a negation of 1947, but in the interests of Bengali nationalism 1971 needs to be disconnected from the birthmarks of 1947 (Anisuzzaman 1995). I have noted the silence relating to Partition and 1947 in Dhaka on the occasion of the fiftieth anniversary of independence of India and Pakistan among the Bangladeshi Left-liberal community (Mookherjee 2015). The silence of Bangladeshi state and civil society on 1947/Partition juxtaposed with their extensive memorialization of 1971 is a phenomenon worth noting. In fact, to raise the specter of Partition today is to betray the cause of secularism or to acknowledge the power of communalism, as a large part of the Bengali Muslim middle-classes and rich peasants swung toward Partition in the 1940s leading to the creation of Pakistan (Samaddar 2013). Both West and East Pakistan had a "radical and unprecedented beginning" based not on blood and soil but on the universalizing promise of Islam (Devji 2013). In they were not forgetting or burying the past but, in what Devji refers to as "an anti-historical thinking," were ensuring a break with the past in order to focus on forging new futures. In East Pakistan, a large part of the same classes swung dramatically away from their Islamic identity shortly after (Khan 2000), which led eventually to the formation of Bangladesh in 1971.

It is worth noting here the fluctuating allegiances of Bengali Muslims to the Pakistani movement, which has been referred to as a "double burden" for Bengali Muslims who are required to prove their genuine commitment to both components of a hyphenated identity (Siddiqi 2012). The example of Abul Mansur Ahmed, who supported the Pakistan movement intermittently but was then jailed in Pakistan for supporting Bengali language rights, is an illustration of the intellectual *and* literary foundations of Bengali Muslim identity that did not fit into the dominant identity framework of either India or Pakistan.[14] This fluidity was enabled in part by the fact that the idea of Pakistan was linked in specific contexts to protests against economic suffering and exploitation, effectively tying together class and religious identities. This fluidity was arguably lost in the wake of 1947, the establishment of the state of Pakistan curtailing certain possibilities, and thus the sharpening of a distinct Bengali Muslim literary identity and cultural milieu after Partition. Such fluctuating and complex allegiances can render 1947 unspeakable in Bangladesh.

On the other hand, the formation of Bangladesh was deemed by West Pakistanis to be a successful "dismemberment" by India (Naqvi 2014), by which it seared apart

[14] For the distinctive cultural politics of Bengali Pakistanism, see Sartori, "Abul Mansur Ahmed"; Bose, *Recasting the Region*.

the vital limbs of Pakistan. This understanding is noted in various academic, military, and press publications, and it has come to be the most dominant Pakistani perception. Dismemberment is the action of cutting off a person's or animal's limbs. It also refers to the action of partitioning or dividing up a territory or organization. As mentioned before, some Pakistani commentators have suggested that "to understand Pakistan through 1947 is the wrong lens. The hurt that moves Pakistan is from a wound more recent—1971" (Hussain 2009). The idea of dismembering Pakistan's limbs and hence its weakening by India through the creation of Bangladesh in 1971 belies arguments about the uncertainty around territorial imaginaries in early Pakistani political thought (Devji 2013). In fact, Jalal has proposed that the confinement of geographical space and being besieged from within and outside led to a state-inflected "creativity" (distortions) into the enterprise of collective remembrance (Jalal 1995: 76). The process of nationalizing Pakistan's past in textbooks through the introduction of Pakistani studies has similarly been vexed by the twin issues of historic origins and national sacrifice (ibid. 76–8). For Bangladeshi historians, the contested nature of origins is also inherent in the term *dismemberment*, and their views have parallels with Hussain's earlier argument that Pakistan needs to be understood through 1971 rather than 1947. The response of Bangladeshi historian Afsan Choudhury to the term *dismemberment* is that

> the error lies in the understanding of 1947, making it sacred and fundamental. 1947 is about present India-Pakistan, not us. The Partition of 1947 was not the great tragedy for us. Our history is the tragedy of One Pakistan in 1947. That's when Bangladesh was actively born. After the failure of the united Bengal Movement, activists gathered in Calcutta and decided to set up a separate state. We were never Pakistanis, we were in the waiting room to be Bangladesh. (Choudhury, pers. comm. July 2017)

The uncertain place 1947 and Partition occupies for Pakistan also needs to be elaborated. Historians have noted that

> the creation of Pakistan marked a partition not simply of the subcontinent but of the Indian Muslim community itself has made the fitting of the creation of Pakistan into any simple narrative of Muslim community extremely problematic. The emergence of Bangladesh in 1971 made this even more difficult. While the creation of a Muslim state in 1947 is generally celebrated in Pakistani historiography, the actual partition of the subcontinent often has about it an air of betrayal. (Gilmartin 1998: 1068–9)

Emerging as a moral community in territorial terms, the territorial disjointed reality of Partition had, however, destroyed the essential cultural meaning of that sense of place as a Muslim homeland and highlighted the ambiguities prevalent in the process of nation-making for Pakistan.

While generating great support in East Pakistan for the formation of Pakistan in 1947, the process of sharpening the distinct Bengali Muslim literary identity and cultural milieu in East Pakistan started soon after Partition. As a result, Bangladeshi historians would refute the language of dismemberment to counter the argument that East Pakistan was a "limb" of West Pakistan. The year 1971 is when everything started for East Pakistan, at least to many Bangladeshis. Compared to the Partition of 1947, which is owned as a huge victory in Pakistan, 1971 is viewed as a great loss (Zakaria 2017). Nonetheless, some have argued that instead of 1947, 1971 is one of the originary wounds for Pakistan. In short, for very contrasting reasons, 1971 could be deemed a focal point for the existential entity of both Bangladesh and Pakistan, and the problems of memorializing it in Pakistan become part of these contested narratives about 1947.

"History Does Not Forgive": The Question of Apology

Ernest Renan, in attempting to identify the nation as a form of morality, argues that "what one really understands despite differences is having suffered together—indeed common suffering is greater than happiness" (Renan 1896: 81). Yet in Pakistan, through these intertwined and varied narrations of family and nation, one gives oneself histories and identities through a non-storytelling that is beyond suffering.[15] This non-storytelling about 1971 is distinct from Renan's ideas of forgetting, which he calls a historical error that is essential for the making of the nation. For Renan, forgetting past acts of violence was essential for the future of the nation. The way in which Balochistan can be narrated to the younger generation and the rapes in Bangladesh can be remembered to not be narrated highlights the varied ways in which the 1971 war and its consequences are palpable in contemporary Pakistan. As dissident Colonel Nadir Ali noted in his article on 1971, "In the Army, you wear no separate uniform. We all share the guilt. We may not have killed. But we connived and were part of the same force. History does not forgive!"[16]

In 2002, President Pervez Musharraf of Pakistan expressed regret for the events of 1971 during an official visit to Bangladesh; it was the first time a Pakistani military ruler had done so. When visiting the national war memorial (where all foreign dignitaries are taken in Bangladesh and which features on the Bangladeshi currency) at Savar, near Dhaka, he left a handwritten note in the visitors' book: "Your brothers and sisters in Pakistan share the pain of the events in 1971. The excesses committed during the unfortunate period are regretted. Let us bury the past in the spirit of magnanimity. Let not the light of the future be dimmed" (quoted in McCarthy 2002).

His expression of "regret" and not apology was met with widespread criticism by the then opposition party Awami League, though it was welcomed by the BNP government. Amid heavy security, Bangladeshi students and activists clashed with police in Dhaka and had planned a full day of nationwide strikes to demonstrate

15 The Pakistani poet Iqbal also critiques Renan's idea of the moral consciousness essential for the formation of the nation. He says Indian society is inherently anti-national, as various castes and religious groups are unable to exert their individuality from their collective to contribute to the bigger idea of the nation. See Devji, *Muslim Zion*, 118.

16 Ali, "A Khaki Dissident on 1971." https://www.genocidebangladesh.org/a-khaki-dissident-on-1971/ (accessed April 2022).

against the visit of the general, who was "not welcome." The activists also considered his inadequate expression of regret as a manipulative way of ensuring successful trade links with Bangladesh. As well as trampling democracy in Pakistan, they saw this empty gesture as a means of legitimizing and securing his dictatorial rule there, which also sought to humanize him as a military general. The ambiguity in his note centers on the terms *excesses* and *magnanimity*. It is not clear from this statement to whom he ascribes these excesses. Also, by not burying the past, Bangladeshis are blamed for lacking magnanimity and holding a deep "grudge" toward Pakistanis. As a result, in 2012, when the Bangladeshi foreign secretary demanded an apology, the then Pakistani government said it had "regretted in different forms and ... it was time to move on."[48] That Pakistani governments have not even engaged with what happened in East Pakistan—forget moving on—is well formulated in a book on apology by Pakistani writers, edited by Ahmad Salim. In this book Shehzad Amjad powerfully notes: "The question of the fall of Dhaka continues to trouble the deepest recesses of our collective consciousness, fueling anxieties about our future, obstructing our emergence into a tolerant and self-respecting society. The struggle for 'Pakistan' is not yet over" (Amjad 2012).

Conclusion

If historicity is the provocative entry point into the politics and public life of Pakistan, what does the lack of historicity and public life related to 1971 in Pakistan tell us about the configurations of its past? This essay has explored the unsettled potential of 1971, the implications it has for the past of Pakistan, and its processes of history writing through the lens of the demand for a memorial on 1971 with which I started this essay. Projonmo Ekattor's call for a memorial in Pakistan locates the analogous relationship between material objects and human memory squarely at the center of this demand. It is assumed that the durability of such objects enables the prolongation and preservation of a memory beyond its existence. At the same time, it is apparent that as soon as we have memory fixed to an object, it becomes slowly consigned to oblivion. In short, memorialization can enable forgetfulness (Forty 1999; Mookherjee 2007), even if we wish for apologies and forgiveness.

To this day, the war of 1971 is rarely discussed in public in Pakistan and is still regarded as a tragic loss that tarnished the reputation of the nation's military. Further, there is an explicit nonnarration of the history of rape of 1971. That there is an intergenerational and interfamilial apparent amnesia on 1971 in Pakistan is evident in textbooks, architecture, and built structures. I have examined how global geopolitics, intergenerational selective memory, the troubled foundations of 1947 for both Pakistan and Bangladesh, the parallels between Balochistan and East Pakistan, and the possibility of weakening the territorial integrity make the history of rape of 1971 nonnarratable and hence the memorialization of it unfeasible.

Shehzad Amjad's aforementioned quote about apology and the struggle for Pakistan's future, however, seems to hinge on the wound of 1971. Hence Projonmo Ekattor's call for a memorial has a different temporal imperative. The call also demands that the memorial be a symbol of remorse, atonement, and apology from Pakistan for its role in 1971. This might trigger memories and questions of 1971 in Pakistan as well as run the risk of sanitizing and freezing this memory. For *Projonmo Ekattor*, however, this memorial is the condition on which they position their forgiveness toward Pakistan for the loss—personal and national—they endured as a result of the violence perpetrated by West Pakistan in East Pakistan in 1971. While very much aware of the "sentimental politics" (Berlant 1999) that can be implicit in the politics of offering an apology (Mookherjee et al. 2009), members of Projonmo Ekattor, as children of all the martyred intellectuals, are also setting out the conditions in which the offering of apology and possible acceptance through forgiveness can occur. Hence here the call for a memorial is a challenging and subversive call for apology and justice in the first instance and a demand for the memorial to be built as a condition for them to grant forgiveness. However, the expression of making amends for this elusive past is mired in its dilemmas. Nonetheless, it is this will to memorialize that can address the shadowy pasts and histories of Pakistan in the first instance.

Acknowledgments

Discussions with various Pakistani colleagues at the "Infrastructures of Gendered Violence" workshop held at Cambridge University on June 22–3, 2017, enriched this essay immensely. A draft of this essay was also presented in the Bangladesh Studies Network Meeting in Edinburgh on June 8, 2018, and I am thankful for the comments received. Warmest thanks also to Anam Zakaria and Chris Moffat. Thanks to Kamran Asdar Ali and Asad Ali for including my article in this volume and to Duke University Press for their permission to republish the original article: "71: Pakistan's past and knowing what not to narrate" (Mookherjee 2020), in the Special Issue: "The Past for Pakistan: History and the Republic." *Comparative Studies of South Asia, Africa and the Middle East* 39 (1) (2020): 280–305. Duke University Press. https://doi.org/10.1177/0069966720917923.

Bibliography

Ahmed, Syed Jaffar. 2017. "Pakistan Blundered by Making Urdu National Language, Not Mentally Accepting Hindus as Pakistanis." *Wire*, April 5. thewire.in/121307/pakistan-jamshed-marker-interview/. Accessed January 22, 2018.

Akhtar, Shaheen, Suraiya Begum, Hameeda Hossein, Sultana Kamal, and Meghna Guhathakurta (eds.), 2001. *Narir Ekattor O Juddhoporoborti Koththo Kahini* (*Oral History Accounts of Women's Experiences during 1971 and after the War*). Dhaka: Ain-O-Shalish-Kendro (ASK).

Ali, Nadir. 2011. "A Khaki Dissident on 1971." *Viewpoint Online*. https://www.genocidebangladesh.org/a-khaki-dissident-on-1971/. Accessed April 2, 2022.

Amjad, Shehzad. 2012. "We Owe an Apology," in Ahmad Salim (ed.), *We Owe an Apology to Bangladesh*. Dhaka: Shahitya Prakash, 13–17.

Anisuzzaman. 1995. *Identity, Religion, and Recent History*. Calcutta: Naya Udyog for Maulana Abul Kalam Azad Institute of Asian Studies.

Berlant, Lauren. 1999. "The Subject of True Feeling: Pain, Privacy, and Politics," in Austin Sarat and Thomas R. Kearns (eds.), *Cultural Pluralism, Identity Politics and the Law*. Ann Arbor: University of Michigan Press, 49–83.

Bose, Neilesh. 2014. *Recasting the Region: Language, Culture, and Islam in Colonial Bengal*. Delhi: Oxford University Press.

Burnett, Jennie. 2012. *Genocide Lives in Us: Women, Memory and Silence in Rwanda*. Madison: University of Wisconsin Press.

Dawn. 2012. "The Apology Issue." November 10. www.dawn.com/news/763045. Accessed January 22, 2018.

Devji, Faisal. 2013. *Muslim Zion: Pakistan as Political Idea*. London: Hurst.

Forty, Adrian. 1999. "Introduction," in A. Forty and S. Kuchler (eds.), *The Art of Forgetting*. Oxford: Berg, 1–18.

Gilmartin, David. 1998. "Pakistan and South Asian History: In Search of a Narrative." *Journal of Asian Studies* 57 (4): 1068–95.

Government of Pakistan. 1971. White paper, March 2.

Government of Pakistan. 2000. Hamdoodur Rahman Commission of Enquiry, 1971, August.

Hussain, Khurram. 2009. "To Understand Pakistan, 1947 Is the Wrong Lens." *Outlook India*, November 9. www.outlookindia.com/magazine/story/to-understand-pakistan-1947-is-the-wrong-lens/262535. Accessed January 22, 2018.

Hussain, Misha, and Huma Imtiaz. 2010. "What Do School Books in Bangladesh and Pakistan Say about 1971 War?" *South Asia Citizens Web*, December 18. www.sacw.net/article1767.html. Accessed December 2018.

Hussain, Zahid. 2013. "The Battle for Balochistan." *Dawn*, April 25. www.dawn.com/news/794058/the-battle-for-balochistan. Accessed January 22, 2018.

Jafar, Ghani. 2013. "Of Bangladesh and Balochistan." *Pakistan Today*, October 15. www.pakistantoday.com.pk/2013/10/15/of-bangladesh-and-balochistan. Accessed January 22, 2018.

Jalal, Ayesha. 1995. "Conjuring Pakistan: History as Official Imagining." *International Journal of Middle East Studies* 27 (1): 73–89.

Khan, Mushtaq. 2000. "Class, Clientelism, and Communal Politics in Contemporary Bangladesh," in K. N. Panikkar, Terence J. Byres, and Utsa Patnaik (eds.), *The Making of History: Essays Presented to Irfan Habib*. New Delhi: Tulika, 572–606.

McCarthy, Rory. 2002. "Musharraf Faces Storm on Mission to Bangladesh." *Guardian*, July 30. www.theguardian.com/world/2002/jul/30/pakistan.bangladesh. Accessed January 22, 2018.

Mokammel, Tanvir, dir. 2007. *Swapnabhumi* (*The Promised Land*). Dhaka: Kino-Eye Films and Shafiur Rahman.

Mookherjee, Nayanika. 2007. "The Dead and Their Double Duties: Mourning, Melancholia, and the Martyred Intellectual Memorials in Bangladesh." *Space and Culture* 10 (2): 271–91.

Mookherjee, Nayanika (ed.). 2009. "The Ethics of Apology: A Set of Commentaries," contributions by Nayanika Mookherjee, Nigel Rapport, Lisette Josephides, Gillian Cowlishaw, Ghassan Hage, and Lindi Todds, *Critique of Anthropology* 29 (3): 345–66. https://doi.org/10.1177/0308275X09336703. Accessed January 22, 2018.

Mookherjee, Nayanika. 2012. "The Absent Piece of Skin: Sexual Violence in the Bangladesh War and Its Gendered and Racialised Inscriptions," *Modern Asian Studies* 46 (6): 1572–601.

Mookherjee, Nayanika. 2015. *The Spectral Wound: Sexual Violence, Public Memories and the Bangladesh War of 1971*. Durham, NC: Duke University Press.

Naqvi, Lubna Ejaz. 2014. "A True Perspective: Dismemberment of Pakistan 1971." *Dispatch News Desk*, December 14. dnd.com.pk/true-perspective-dismemberment-pakistan-1971/84333. Accessed January 22, 2018.

PTI, Islamabad. 2010. "Pak Textbooks Still See '71 War as Conspiracy." *Daily Star*, December 17. www.thedailystar.net/news-detail-166327. Accessed January 22, 2018.

Renan, Ernest. 1896. "What Is a Nation?," in W. G. Hutchinson (trans.), *The Poetry of the Celtic Races and Other Studies*. London: Walter Scott Limited, 163–76.

Saikia, Yasmin. 2011. *Women, War, and the Making of Bangladesh: Remembering 1971*. Durham, NC: Duke University Press.

Samaddar, Ranabīra. 1995. *Many Histories and Few Silences: The Nationalist History of Nationalism in Bangladesh*. Calcutta: Azad Institute of Asian Studies.

Sartori, Andrew. 2007. "Abul Mansur Ahmad and the Cultural Politics of Bengali Pakistanism," in Dipesh Chakrabarty, Rochona Majumdar, and Andrew Sartori (eds.), *From the Colonial to the Postcolonial: India and Pakistan in Transition*. Oxford: Oxford University Press, 19–36.

Siddiqi, Dina Mahnaz. 2013. "Left Behind by the Nation: 'Stranded Pakistanis' in Bangladesh." *Sites: A Journal of Social Anthropology and Cultural Studies* 10 (2): 150–83.

Siddiqi, Farhan Hanif. 2012. *The Politics of Ethnicity in Pakistan: The Baloch, Sindhi and Mohajir Ethnic Movements*. London: Routledge.

Zakaria, Anam. 2017. "By Marking Genocide Day, Bangladesh Seeks to Remember What Pakistan Wants to Forget." *Scroll.in*, March 25. scroll.in/article/832420/by-marking-genocide-day-bangladesh-seeks-to-remember-what-pakistan-wants-to-forget. Accessed January 22, 2018.

Zarkov, Dubravka. 2007. *The Body of War: Media, Ethnicity, and Gender in the Break-Up of Yugoslavia*. Durham, NC: Duke University Press.

5

Left Behind by the Nation: "Urdu Speakers" in Bangladesh

Dina Mahnaz Siddiqi

Introduction

What does it mean for a nation to have "left behind" its citizens? How did legal citizens come to see themselves as "stranded" after East Pakistan became independent Bangladesh in 1971? What accounts for the awkward place of so-called stranded Pakistanis (or Urdu-speaking minority, as the new generation in Bangladesh prefers to be called) in national consciousness today?

Addressing these questions forces a reconsideration of standard nationalist historiography in Bangladesh, which tends to elide or erase the 1947 Partition of British India. Indeed, the presence within Bangladesh's borders of those "who never left Pakistan," gestures to a history that has been rendered unspeakable because of its incongruity with the dominant national project. In this essay, with reference to the making of "stranded Pakistanis," I argue that foundational narratives of the Bangladeshi nation cannot but disavow the moment of the 1947 Partition, for any such acknowledgment fundamentally troubles the idea of a core/preexisting Bengali secular identity. By extension, and more significantly, the recognition of the 1947 Partition necessarily involves an interrogation of (East) Bengal's participation in what has been called "the Pakistan experiment." The erasure of the 1947 Partition from official memory, then, represents an attempt to paper over the fissures and contradictions involved in the making of a secular unified Bengali nation-state.

Nationalist desire for narrative permanence and fixity of territory/identity invariably comes into tension with the historical contingencies and complexities of identity/border-making in practice (see, for instance, David Ludden 2003). Arguably, such contradictions are characteristic of all nationalist-modernist projects, which in themselves are necessarily exclusionary since the quest for national purity calls for the assimilation, suppression, or outright excision of difference.

Unpacking the cartographic anxieties and contradictions underlying the ethno-territorial project of Bengali/Bangladeshi nation-making does not simply foreground the limits of nationalist historiography. Rather, the study of the 1947 Partition remains critically important for understanding the cultural politics of citizenship, belonging, and national identity in Bangladesh today. Reading the history of 1971 without taking into account 1947 does not only produce incomplete histories; such a move obscures the historically constitutive processes through which categories of (national) Self and Other are produced and naturalized, and the dynamics that allow for the privileging of some narrative accounts and simultaneous displacement of others. Put differently, the inability of Bangladeshi nationalist historiography to come to terms with Partition/ Pakistan ensures the exclusion not just of "Biharis" but of all other non-Bengali-speaking minorities from national belonging.[1]

Partitioned Histories

The figure of the "stranded Pakistani" represents an enduring if neglected instance of the continued weight and paradoxical effects of the 1947 Partition. Commonly known as Biharis (although many came from much further away than Bihar) these non-Bengali-speaking Muslims migrated to East Bengal either in the aftermath of communal riots in Bihar in 1946 or after Partition in 1947. A heterogeneous group differentiated by class interests and regional distinctions, they were tied together primarily by their linguistic difference from the Bengali-speaking majority in East Pakistan.

It bears repeating here that Partition did not necessarily or exclusively signify loss, uprooting, and the horrors of communal violence for Muslims. Some scholars suggest that, for the peasantry of East Bengal, Pakistan promised a "Peasant Utopia" and a "Land of Eternal Eid."[2] In this view, the new nation was not so much a homeland for the subcontinent's Muslims as it was a new start—for Pakistan promised the dismantling of economic oppression as well as the end of religious and social discrimination. Though it has ceased to be a direct reference point in the discourses of Bengali/Bangladeshi nationalism, 1947 remains a significant marker in the reconstruction of the history of landownership in rural Bangladesh.[3] Partition provided an enormous opportunity for certain Muslim groups in Bengal to reconfigure socioeconomic relations in a landscape dominated until then by upper caste Hindu landowners. For the predominantly Muslim peasantry, Pakistan held the promise of the establishment of a just and egalitarian society, a "return" to a communitarian life. Urdu-speaking migrants could also stake a claim on such promises. Thus, unlike Hindu refugees to West Bengal, Muslims—Bengali speakers and non-Bengalis—saw East Pakistan as a legitimate destination, a place to which they had formal entitlement.

If the borders of Pakistan were theoretically open to all Muslims in 1947, the conditions for citizenship changed considerably by 1971. In the intervening years, the very idea of Pakistan had unraveled in East Pakistan; Bengalis of all classes found

[1] For an elaboration of this argument, see Dina M. Siddiqi, "Secular Quests, National Others: Revisiting Bangladesh's Constituent Assembly Debates." *Asian Affairs: Journal of the Royal Society for Asian Affairs* 49 (2) (2018): 238–58.

[2] See, for instance, Taj ul-Islam Hashmi, *Peasant Utopia: The Communalization of Class Politics in East Bengal, 1920–47* (Dhaka: University Press, 1994) and Ahmed Kamal, "A Land of Eternal Eid: Independence, People and Politics in East Bengal," *Dhaka University Studies* 46 (1) (1989): 58.

[3] I am indebted to David Ludden for bringing this point to my attention.

themselves culturally and economically marginalized by non-Bengalis. The latter were primarily bureaucrats, industrialists, and military personnel, often Punjabi rather than Urdu speakers. By the 1960s, calls for greater regional autonomy and more equitable resource distribution came to be squarely situated within a movement for Bengali linguistic and cultural autonomy. The corresponding production of a monolithic non-Bengali Cultural Other in the Bengali imaginary left little space for distinctions among "Urdu speakers," the most powerful of whom were ethnically Punjabi.

The open collaboration of *some* Urdu speakers with the Pakistani army in the latter's brutal suppression of and genocidal war on Bengalis in 1971 rendered *all* "Biharis" into permanent national pariahs. At the end of the war, leaders on behalf of the "community" formally opted for Pakistani citizenship, although the Pakistani state accepted only a handful of people, primarily those who had actively collaborated with the Pakistani army during the war. The remaining population was cordoned off in camps in the capital and other cities awaiting a future over which they appeared to have little control. Unable to claim United Nations refugee status due to technicalities, this ethnic and linguistic minority became effectively stateless.

Successive Pakistani governments have refused to take "back" these people, most of whom have never been to (West) Pakistan. Fifty years later, younger generations have lived their entire lives within the cramped perimeters of makeshift camps scattered across Bangladesh. The Geneva Camp in Mohammadpur, Dhaka, is iconic in this respect. Located in the heart of the capital city, the camp constitutes a no-man's land, a site that most Bangladeshis barely acknowledge, even though its borders bleed into neighboring areas. This spatial ambivalence characterizes the place of Biharis in the nation. On the one hand, Biharis constitute an invisible minority, erased from the historical, cultural, and national landscape.[4] On the other, they are subject to significant nationalist hostility; indeed, the term "Bihari" continues to be synonymous with *dalal* or wartime collaborator.

The loyalties of Urdu speakers may not have been with the Pakistani regime per se, but their identities and interests were deeply entangled in the idea of Pakistan. In an insightful and provocative review essay, Irfan Ahmad observes that "if India's Partition resulted in the birth of Muslim camps in Delhi and Hindu camps in Lahore in the mid-twentieth century, its sordid trail continues well into the twenty-first century in places such as Dhaka's Geneva Camp" (Irfan Ahmad 2012: 494). Indeed, the pre-histories of 1971 continue to haunt the Bangladeshi nation today, not least in relation to "stranded Pakistanis."

4 It is only in the last two decades or so that the subject of Bihari (non) citizenship has entered mainstream cultural discourse. Filmmaker Tanvir Mokammel produced the documentary *Promised Land* in 2007 to critical acclaim and some criticism. Short story writer Mahmud Rahman has also dealt with the topic. Earlier, in 1994, an English-language novel featured a protagonist who cites the "indiscriminate slaughter of the Biharis by Bangladeshis after 1971" for his leaving Bangladesh in disillusionment after the Liberation War. The author, Adib Khan, does not record any specific incidents of violence. See Adib Khan, *Seasonal Adjustments* (Australia: Allen and Unwin, 1995).

Partition's Ghosts and Cracks in the National Story

It may well be that the periodic emergence of Partition's ghosts constitutes a central feature of Bengali/Bangladeshi nationalism. The active forgetting of the fractious histories of Partition renders the historiography of Bangladesh slightly askew of the rest of the subcontinent, at least in relation to the recalling of Partition. In India and Pakistan, dominant historical narratives culminate in the story of "Freedom at Midnight" in 1947. This celebration is notably absent in Bangladesh. In the weeks leading up to the 50th anniversary of Indian and Pakistani Independence, BBC World and CNN International, both cable channels available to Bangladeshi audiences, devoted extensive coverage to related events. In contrast, Bangladeshi newspapers and other media exhibited a muted interest in the anniversary or ignored it altogether. That the 1947 Partition/independence appears to have become a non-event in a state that was once part of Pakistan is a feature of Bangladeshi historiography worth revisiting.

I suggest that from the perspective of the national story, 1947 does not merit remembrance, let alone celebration, for it disrupts a carefully constructed teleology of an a priori, secular Bengali nation waiting to come into formation. Partition—and its corresponding violence—unsettles the secular story of a unified preexisting Bengali identity that comes into its own in 1971. For, to formally mark the division of Bengal in 1947 is to acknowledge the histories of violence and fractures within "Bengali" as a (political) category. In this framing, Partition cannot constitute *true* independence; it denotes one more moment in the continuing history of Bengal's colonial domination, marking the transfer of power from the British to the West Pakistanis. Thus Bangladeshi historians routinely refer to the double cloak of colonialism when discussing the period between 1947 and 1971. The official timeline of the nation nods to 1905—the "first" Partition of Bengal (and Assam) province—and moves on to 1952 (the inauguration of the language movement) as foundational moments.

This "secular" version of the national story must mute the Bengali-speaking peasantry's enthusiasm for Pakistan as documented by Ahmed Kamal and others. Nor can it absorb more complicated interpretations of the so-called double cloak of colonialism. For instance, some Bangladeshis refer to 1947 as the *first* independence, meaning that Bengali Muslims had to first separate from upper caste Hindu dominance, hence the need for a break in 1947, before they could be independent (Gautam Ghosh, personal communication).

The ideological moorings of Bangladesh's nationalism are grounded in the existence of a pre-existing and *secular* Bengali identity, one that underplays or blurs religious distinctions. Against this backdrop, the specter of Partition can be construed as betraying the cause of secular nationhood. Overt engagement with Partition's violence entails the existence of sectarian identities and by extension the "disunity" of Bengali national identity, thereby destabilizing the grounds for the nation's coming into being. This may be why public recognition of 1947 in narratives of the Bengali nation has been muted at best. It may explain why, for instance, the Asiatic Society's three-volume history of Bangladesh skirts around the events and debates surrounding Partition, without actually *naming* or classifying the latter as such (Islam 1992).

The Making of Muhajirs

The Partition of Punjab and Bengal led to the displacement of anywhere from 11 to 18 million people. The actual numbers may be much higher, but exact figures from this period are notoriously difficult to compile. The number of incoming refugees between 1947 and 1951, as reported in the Indian and Pakistani census of 1951, is 7.29 and 7.22 million, respectively (Kudaisya 1995: 73). Of the 7.22 million Muslims coming into Pakistan, only 699,000 were enumerated in East Pakistan in the 1951 census, constituting only 1.7 percent of the total population of East Pakistan (Government of Pakistan 1953: ii). In contrast, the 1951 Indian census enumerates 2.55 million refugees coming in from East Bengal. Some writers conflate the terms Muhajir and non-Bengali, counting all of the nearly 700,000 individuals who entered East Bengal as "Biharis." However, the 1951 Census enumerated a total of 118,181 "Urdu-speaking" refugees in East Pakistan.[5] The vast majority of these, 97,349, were from Bihar. Of the remainder, 18,819 were from Uttar Pradesh and 2,002 from Punjab or Delhi (Kamaluddin 1985: 224).

Vicious riots in Bihar in the aftermath of Direct Action Day and the massacre of Hindus in Noakhali in 1946 were instrumental in the uprooting and relocation of Muslims from Bihar into Bengal. In almost one week of rioting, 7 out of 16 districts and 750 out of 18,696 villages in Bihar were affected (P. Ghosh 1991: 275). For the most part, the Bihar riots disrupted the lives of the rural populace, who lived in relatively small and isolated groups, making them easy targets of "roving mobs." Survivors took refuge in camps in Patna and other big towns, while rumors of more attacks persuaded many who had not been affected to seek shelter elsewhere. Migration began in earnest in November 1946. Papiya Ghosh estimates that around 60,000 Muslims moved to Bengal between the third week of November and the end of December 1946 (ibid. 282). By January the flight of people slowed down and some people even returned home. Refugees from Bihar also sought shelter in the Sindh and Punjab.

The influx of refugees continued long after Partition, increasing during moments of tension across borders: the 1950 riots in Calcutta, and anti-immigrant agitation in Assam; outbreaks of violence in Madhya Pradesh and Uttar Pradesh in 1961; scattered incidents in Assam and West Bengal in 1962 and all over eastern India during the Hazratbal episode in Kashmir (see H. Feldman 1969: 148). The 1961 Census puts the number of Urdu-speaking people in East Pakistan at 640,000, an increase of almost 500,000 from the 1951 census. According to one source, at least 800,000 Indian Muslims, mainly from West Bengal, entered East Pakistan during the 1964 riots. These figures constitute only those who were registered in camps (Kamaluddin 1985: 222). By December 1967, another 540,000 from the border states of Tripura, Assam, and West Bengal mainly, entered East Pakistan.

[5] In a 1991 essay, Papiya Ghosh states that 14.5 percent, that is, 101,500 of the East Pakistan immigrants were from UP and Bihar. She does not mention a source. P. Ghosh, "The 1946 Riot and the Exodus of Bihari Muslims to Dhaka," p. 275.

Theodore Wright has remarked that "it is clearly a matter of propinquity that the main outflow was to the east, particularly for those who could not afford the journey to West Pakistan" (cited in Ghosh 1991: 283). Given differences in language and ethnicity, this makes sense. It is worth recalling, however, that the national borders between India and Pakistan cut through much older routes of travel. Many Bihari Muslims journeyed on already familiar, if circular, corridors of migration. Refugee movements produced by Partition disrupted or overrode earlier patterns of migration. Under new and much more brutal conditions of forced mobility, for many "Urdu speakers," "Pakistan came to be visualized as the embodiment of the sacrifice of the Bihar Muslims in the riots of 1946" (314), in Papiya Ghosh's words. Despite this sense of sacrifice and right to belong to Pakistan, this population found itself awkwardly poised between the predominantly Bengali citizenry and state authorities.

Strangers in the Homeland: The Dangerous and Disloyal Muhajir

> "I am originally from Lucknow. I came to the then East Pakistan because we were guided by revolutionary emotions."
>
> Resident of Geneva Camp
>
> "Cigarettes between fingers and betel leaves in the mouth, we will fight and win Pakistan" -- who knew the chant would lead to this [predicament]?"
>
> Resident of Geneva Camp

The term "Muhajir" was part of Pakistan's political vocabulary from the outset. Its application to refugees from India marked a conscious effort to rally support among those already living in what had become Pakistan for the task of welcoming and then looking after the large numbers of people pouring in from across the border (Ansari 1995: 95).

Sarah Ansari notes:

> Refugees caught up in large scale, often involuntary migration as a result of political conflicts in the 20th century, have been forced to move to places over which they have little if any personal claim. In contrast, Muslims leaving India for Pakistan at Partition perceived themselves to be migrating to a place of refuge which "*belonged*" to them as "Pakistanis" just as much as it did to the Muslims whom they found living there. This naturally complicated the whole issue of their resettlement. They presumed themselves to be there not by kind invitation but *by right*. (Ibid.: 96, emphasis added)

Ansari goes on to suggest that for many uprooted Muslims, the support they received from fellow Muslims formed a vital part of their understanding of their predicament, influencing the way they put down new roots. Since Partition occurred during the month of Ramadan, it allowed many refugees to draw parallels between themselves and the original Muhajirs. Those people already living in Pakistan could then be seen as *ansars*, modern equivalents of the people of Medina who gave refuge to Mohammed and his followers.

The politicization of the refugees/Muhajirs proceeded along distinct registers in the two wings of Pakistan. In the West, the category was ethnicized rapidly, and came to index Urdu-speaking Pakistanis. Muhajirs in West Pakistan eventually formed their own political party, the Muhajir Quami Movement (MQM), which became an influential oppositional movement *within* the ethnic politics of Pakistan. In contrast, "Urdu speakers" in East Pakistan soon found themselves written out of the emergent political formation; indeed, the movement for regional and linguistic autonomy negated and devalued the narrative of sacrifice on which their claim to the nation hinged. A large portion of the Urdu-speaking educated upper and middle classes who had initially sought refuge in East Pakistan moved to West Pakistan, which afforded better economic and social prospects for those with social capital and connections. Non-Bengali Muslims who stayed on in East Pakistan tended to be refugees with little formal education and even less in the way of capital and connections.

Despite a robust sense of sacrifice and deeply felt right to belong in (East) Pakistan, Urdu speakers found themselves inhabiting a decidedly ambivalent national space. To most Bengalis, Biharis constituted a single community that had constructed self-contained ethnic enclaves, thereby proclaiming and reproducing a sense of superiority and cultural distance from the majority population. By this logic, the structural and linguistic constraints of everyday life that produced a certain "aloofness" among Urdu speakers could be recast as intentional racialized distancing. The Pakistani state's preferential treatment of selected non-Bengalis, mainly industrialists, reinforced this framing; the condition of privilege came to be associated with all "Biharis." Indeed, the government actively discouraged assimilation and took for granted that non-Bengalis would be allies. Resented as privileged outsiders, the majority of Urdu-speaking "non-locals" were in fact greatly disillusioned with their situation in East Pakistan. Unemployment rates were very high, with a preponderance of temporary or underemployment. Education, especially higher education, came to be a particular source of dissatisfaction, because of language problems.

When war broke out in 1971, some Urdu speakers, attached to the idea of Pakistan, actively sided with the Pakistani army (as did a number of Bengali Muslims). Regardless of actual political inclinations, all Urdu speakers found themselves identified with the Pakistani cause. Bihari as a moniker came to be inextricably linked in national memory with Pakistani army brutality. The extent to which Urdu speakers were involved as volunteer members or *razakars* in *al Badr* and *al Shams,* the notorious paramilitary groups responsible for some of the worst wartime atrocities, remains a matter of dispute. Leaders of the "stranded Pakistanis" vehemently deny any involvement; they point instead to the recruitment of Urdu speakers to the East Pakistan Civil Armed Forces (EPCAF), a separate force posted mainly in border regions, and tasked with policing national borders. Few Bengalis have ever heard of EPCAF. *Razakar*, however, is a household word denoting wartime collaboration and generalized treachery. In national collective memory, all Biharis are closely associated with Pakistani army atrocities, naturalizing the identity between Bihari/Razakar and Pakistani (therefore of dangerous and disloyal non-citizen). It is a great irony of history that in 1971 the

Pakistani army turned on their heads the allusions to Islamic history invoked in 1947. Arabic and Persian words once held to be sacred came to carry, by the end of the war, a radically profane and negative set of meanings. Permanently linked to Bihari (and Bengali) collaboration/betrayal, these terms still evoke fear and disgust rather than respect and piety.

Neither Citizens nor Refugees

> "We have no moral right to stay here as we failed to protect our dear Pakistan from breaking up ... This is why we want to go to our *opted* land."
>
> Nasim Khan, Stranded Pakistanis General Repatriation Committee (FEER 1989: 28)

An estimated 900,000 Urdu speakers remained in Bangladesh at the end of the war (Feith 1972: 22). Most affluent Biharis left newly independent Bangladesh to settle abroad, some heading for India. As in 1947, those who remained possessed minimum social or financial capital. Conditions were poor enough for residents in several makeshift camps to hold up placards to visitors that said, "Give us poison."

Early efforts by the Stranded Pakistanis General Repatriation Committee (SPGRC) to claim Pakistani citizenship and official UN refugee status did not succeed. Camp dwellers found themselves in a peculiar and anomalous space. To count as a refugee, an individual must prove he or she is a national of one country with a well-founded fear of persecution from the authorities of that country.[6] Pakistan's disavowal of their claims to citizenship rendered Biharis ineligible for recognition as refugees from that country. Meanwhile, in a conciliatory gesture in 1973, Mujib had declared, "The non-Bengalis who were citizens of Pakistan and residents in the then East Pakistan will be treated as equal citizens *if* they declare allegiance to the government of Bangladesh." This ostensibly inclusive proclamation effectively rendered those Urdu-speaking East Pakistani citizens who had in the interim applied for "repatriation" to Pakistan (through the International Committee of the Red Cross) non-citizens of Bangladesh. For the very *act* of seeking Pakistani citizenship signified betrayal, the anti-thesis of allegiance to Bangladesh. Paradoxically, declaring these people Pakistanis, as the government did, carried no legal validity, for Pakistan was not bound and still is not legally bound to accept them. After all, they were not born on what is *now* Pakistani soil. From the perspective of Urdu speakers, the nation of Pakistan (along with its citizenship-conferring state apparatus) had abandoned part of the territory and people of which it had once been an integral part, leaving the former in a liminal zone. Neither citizen, nor refugee, Urdu speakers appeared condemned to a form of civil death.

[6] The 1951 Refugee Convention of the United Nations defines a refugee as someone who "owing to a well-founded fear of being persecuted for reasons of race, religion, nationality, membership of a particular social group or political opinion, is outside the country of his nationality, and is unable to, or owing to such fear, is unwilling to avail himself of the protection of that country." http://www.unhcr.org/pages/49c3646c125.html.

The "legal fiction" of civil death has been challenged successfully in the intervening years. In 1984, the case of Muktar Ahmed, 34 DLR (1984) 29, the High Court Division of the Supreme Court, presided over by Justice Shahabuddin Ahmed and Justice Rafiqur Rahman, declared:

> The mere fact that he filed an application for going over to Pakistan cannot take away his citizenship. The Bangladesh Citizenship Order, P.O. 149/72, has enumerated different situations in which a person shall be deemed to be a citizen of Bangladesh, but it has not discriminated among its citizens no matter in which way they have become citizens of this country. So, the petitioner is on the same footing as any other citizen. His citizenship, therefore, clings to him. (Nahar 1997: 7)

While these battles were being fought, a new generation of Biharis has come up, knowing no home other than the camps in which they were born. This generation has no direct memory of Partition or, in the case of some people, of 1971. Most speak Bengali fluently and do not have attachments to places outside Bangladesh. Acutely aware of their marginalization, younger Urdu speakers have invested much energy in "becoming" Bangladeshi. The Stranded Pakistanis Youth Rehabilitation Movement was at the forefront of legal initiatives that culminated in a 2008 High Court ruling directing the government to recognize Urdu speakers as Bangladeshi nationals.[7] In response to the ruling, Sadakat Khan, president of the movement, declared, "This is a historic achievement. We had been waiting for decades, while living an inhuman life in the camps. Why we should go to Pakistan? We don't belong to Pakistan. We don't want to go to Pakistan" (Majumdar 2008)

Bangladeshi citizenship and all that it offered—including escape from civil death—was not enough for many older Urdu speakers. Speaking on behalf of the SPGRC, Shoukat Ali remarked: "We have full respect for the court but we reject its ruling. Pakistan is our home and we want to exercise our citizen rights only after going there" (ibid).

Remapping Memories

It is instructive to trace the points of intersection and disjunction between personal and official narratives of the nation. Javed Hasan (a pseudonym) was born in Bihar

[7] In 2003, the Supreme Court of Bangladesh (High Court Division) ruled on a petition submitted by ten Urdu speakers, born both before and after 1971. In a landmark decision, the court declared that all ten were Bangladeshi citizens with the right to vote and directed the government to register them as voters. The 2003 decision was limited to the original ten petitioners. Five years later, in May 2008, in response to another petition, the High Court ruled that Urdu speakers were to be considered Bangladeshi nationals, regardless of whether or not they had opted to be "repatriated" to Pakistan. See UN High Commissioner for Refugees, *Note on the Nationality Status of the Urdu Speaking Community of Bangladesh*, December 17, 2009. www.unhcr.org/refworld/docid/4b2b90c32.html See also Azad Majumdar, "Bangladesh Citizenship Rights Divides Biharis," Reuters (Dhaka). http://in.reuters.com/article/2008/05/20/idINIndia-33670220080520.

in 1944. He is a resident of a camp in Khulna, although he spends most of his time in Dhaka. He says he has no profession or employment—his profession is to protest or demonstrate (*andolon kora*).[8] He obviously has no recollection of the Partition, but has heard stories from his father and other senior males in the family, and no doubt from SPGRC leaders. His narrative is emblematic in this respect, representative of an older generation's official collective memory:

> There were riots in '46. Then, once Pakistan was born, all the British employees went to Britain; the Muslim League high command secretly rounded up all the Muslim government employees and told them Pakistan had become a Muslim country and that they *must go there to help build the country*. They printed special forms -- one for those who wanted to go temporarily and others who wanted to move permanently. This was a directive especially for government employees. My uncles who stayed behind didn't work for the government. *They didn't have to leave*. They had their land and their business. *At the time, there was nothing here [East Bengal/Dhaka]. Only swamps and canals. No establishment or administration was here [to deal with the refugees]*. Many people were shifted from one district to another. Although my father applied, because there wasn't enough space, he was made surplus.
>
> My father used to be stationmaster at Shialdah Railway Station but didn't return to his job in the Railway, he became the headmaster of Quaid-e-Azam High School in Saidpur [then part of Rangpur district in East Bengal]. My father came first, then he sent for us. At the time, very few men came with their "full family." A lot of people couldn't adjust here, they eventually left [returned to India]. (Emphasis added throughout)

Javed Hasan's sense of belonging to (East) Pakistan is not as strong as one might have expected. Hasan has grown up with nostalgia for a life left behind in India where, according to him, Urdu speakers/Biharis had social standing and clout. He returns to this topic later in his account. As he represents it, the decision to migrate to East Bengal/East Pakistan—a land of "only swamps and canals"—was more of a compulsion than a choice for his father. Coming to the east was a sacrifice that Muslims were called on to make, to help build the new nation. The theme of sacrifice is central to his construction of community and national identity.

> Many people died in the riots of Bihar. Of those who survived, many went to East or West Pakistan. Our car [railway carriage] was going towards Punjab but there was so much killing and violence—the Sikhs were stopping trains to murder the passengers. So the government turned the train around and made us return to Calcutta, then pushed us into East Pakistan. The Sikhs, you know, have done very well for themselves, I mean politically, in the Punjab. Quaid-e-Azam [Jinnah] tried at one time to avoid the division of Punjab—he urged the Sikhs to stay, promised

[8] The stylized nature of his prose probably reflects his self-positioning as a "professional agitator" for the SPGRC.

> their leaders they would have full rights but Nehru and Gandhi lured them away with talk of religion and what not. Got them all riled up. Some Muslims were killed. The record has underestimated the numbers killed in all. I would say around 60 lakhs (6 million) died. *The most deaths were in Bihar. Without the deaths, Pakistan could not have been created.*

The passage above is notable for several reasons. Here Sikhs, rather than Hindus are invoked as the Other. In a reversal of "commonsense" Partition narratives, Nehru and Gandhi are held responsible for the division of the Punjab and for instigating communal violence. Most striking, for Javed Hasan the sacrifice of Muslim blood is fundamental to the emergence of Pakistan. (Notably, Muslims in Bihar are situated at the forefront of this sacrifice.) The statement that Pakistan could not have been created without the deaths of Muslims forces a recalibration of the meaning of communal violence during Partition. What could be seen as senseless horror and loss is here transposed into meaningful sacrifice for the future. (This resonates with the idea of the "first" independence noted earlier.)

Javed Hasan goes on to reflect on post-Partition life in India for the Muslim minority. Curiously, India is here represented as a place where Muslims still hold sway, in implicit comparison to Muslim-majority Bangladesh.[9]

> I lived in Saidpur until 1974, when I moved to Khulna. There I'm a leader of the party [SPGRC], which has a wing in Khulna. I have to stay in Dhaka most of the time since all the embassies, political parties, NGOs and journalists are based here.
>
> Although we were a minority in India, by that measure, we aren't doing so badly there. Even today, in UP, CP and Bihar, Hindus never challenge the word of Muslims. All the *bichar* [informal village mediation] is done by Muslims, Hindus accept this *bichar*. India has Muslims in many high posts. It's had two Muslim Presidents. When the foreign minister came, his secretary was Muslim. Have you heard of Hamid Khan? All the most famous Indian film stars are Muslim. No one has been able to beat the voice of Nurjahan in singing. Even though Lata is around, thousands of Nurjahan's songs are popular in India. It's because of *our* heritage—places like the Deoband Madrasa, Aligarh University, the Red Fort and other big mosques and shrines, it's because Muslims were in power that they were able to accomplish so much. It's our good fortune that Muslims still have some influence in Bihar. [At this point he launches into a long story about the *rewaj*, i.e., the customary practice of hierarchy and propriety among status groups that he claims is still maintained in Bihar.]

[9] Papiya Ghosh also notes the "glowing recall of the Bihari homeland" in the SPGRC's reconstruction of Partition in the 1980s. See P. Ghosh, *Partition and the South Asian Diaspora: Extending the Subcontinent* (New Delhi: Routledge, 2007), 61. My interviews were taken several years before the 2002 pogroms in Gujarat, India. In light of the latter, and current fears of an impending genocide of Muslim Indians, it is unlikely that such nostalgia for their time in India persists, at least to the same extent.

Clearly the speaker feels a strong sense of identity with Muslims across India, not just Bihar, as evinced by his use of the pronoun we. The slippage between Biharis and Muslims, between Urdu-speaking Muslims in Bangladesh and Muslims in India, and between an imagined Muslim community and the glories of its cultural heritage in the golden age of Muslims (the Pakistani singer Nurjahan, Moghul-era Red Fort, and British-established Aligarh University) are instructive. By implication, neither Bangladesh nor Bengali-speaking Muslims falls within his definition of Muslim community.

The location of Pakistan and the meaning of East Pakistan after 1971 shift in his narrative accordingly.

> *I've never been to Pakistan, nor has my father*. I haven't been to Bihar in 50 years although we still have a share in the land. It's only since we came here that we've been divided. In Pakistan, we are called Muhajir. Here, we have been given 4 names—refugee, non-Bengali, Bihari and Stranded Pakistanis. Bhutto was only interested in taking back the Punjabis, he knew he needed Punjabi support to remain Pakistan's President.

For someone born in 1944 to claim that neither he nor his father had ever been to Pakistan says something very specific about the shifting meaning and territoriality of Pakistan. Javed Hasan's time in what was East Pakistan between 1947 and 1971 no longer counts as ever having been in Pakistan. It is as though the emergence of Bangladesh erases its past meaning as East Pakistan (a line of thinking that is consistent with Bengalis nationalist ideology, it should be noted). At the same time, when Javed Hasan speaks of Bengalis, implicitly he equates them with Hindus, echoing older colonial and Hindu nationalist tropes. So below, when he talks about "we Muslims" no longer being safe, he clearly does not include Bengali-speaking Muslims. He reconstitutes the putative opposition between Muslim and Bengali, constructing boundaries around Muslim identity that are given content elsewhere, outside the territory that is now Bangladesh.

> Once the tripartite agreement was drawn up, *we Muslims* were no longer safe. The Bengalis knew they had their homeland; there was much torture, looting and destruction. People died. We had to abandon our homes, find some place of refuge. The Red Cross camps here and there were places of protection. We fought for Pakistan, we made Pakistan, after creating Pakistan, and we wanted to stay in Pakistan.
>
> The UNHCR secretary tells us that we can't be listed as refugees because we're still on the soil we lived on before. (*apnara je matitay chhilen, she matitay achhen).* We say yes, we are still on the same soil, but our country (*desh*) has left us behind. People leave their desh but now we find that our desh has left us.

Paradoxically, for Urdu speakers to regain rights to the nation, they needed to embrace the identity of the refugee, the stigma of which the *bhadralok* sought to cast off.

> Our predicament is that we cannot be listed as refugees. The UN people tell us that a refugee is someone who has left their home. But we left behind places [uses the Bengali word *jaiga* meaning place, rather than *bari* or *desh* meaning home]. We came from Khulna, from Saidpur, from Mymensingh. It's our great sorrow that the UN runs around trying to conserve snakes, tigers and other wild animals, pours crores of dollars into fish breeding, but nothing for this human being, this Mussulman. No one counts us as human; other Muslims don't count us as Muslim, in Bihar Hindus don't think of us as Bihari, Bengalis don't think of us as Bengalis and the UN won't recognize us as refugees.
>
> Bengalis are always telling us to become Bengali but what does it take? I mean, here I am talking to you in Bangla. Tell me the *kalma* [formal declaration of faith for Muslims/here something like a magic charm] that will make me Bengali, so I will no longer be called a Pakistani, Bihari or a refugee.
>
> Pakistan says we're not Pakistani but if those of us from UP, CP and Bihar had not taken the Muslim League initiative to heart would Quaid-e-Azam have been able to come from Punjab to build up Pakistan by himself? Would A. K. Fazlul Haq have been able to create Pakistan from Bengal alone?

Here, Javed Hasan elaborates on the idiom of sacrifice that runs through his narrative. For him, it is Muslims like him, from North India rather than from Punjab or Bengal, who are the *true* nationalists (a move that displaced Hindu *bhadralok* also make, see G. Ghosh 2007). Hasan then goes on to reinscribe an older trope that pits a homogenous Bengali community to that of Muslims. In his version of the Bengali/Muslim dichotomy, the exertions and sacrifices of North Indian Muslims rescue Muslims in Bengal from the oppression of high-caste Hindu landowners.

> Would they have been able to withstand Hindu conspiracies? In Bengal, a Muslim didn't have the right to even walk past a *jomidar* [high status, large landowners who wielded enormous authority over local populations. The majority in Bengal were Hindu] house with his umbrella open [to do so was considered disrespectful]. No matter what great positions they are in now, at the time, they didn't have the power to stand in front of the Chatterjees, Bannerjees and Mukherjees [high-caste Hindu lineages]. Even after Pakistan was created, Muslims couldn't slaughter during *qurbani* openly for a while. In Khulna, I saw how they had to pay Raja Suresh Ghosh 50 Taka for each cow.
>
> So three generations have grown up crippled—lacking in proper education, assistance, even medical care. Today, there are so many initiatives being taken worldwide to improve the status of women. But no NGO, Islamic organization or UN body gives us a second look. All because we're not officially refugees.
>
> My paternal grandfather had two wives. My father was one of 6 brothers. He had three stepbrothers. These three uncles didn't leave [India]. Of the six brothers, three left for Karachi, two came to Saidpur and one stayed back in Bihar. At first, all three of my mother's brothers and one sister also stayed back. Later, one of my uncles joined us here. The other two remained in Bihar, with full family. They're

> doing quite well, actually. They're happy. What could possibly happen? There are at least 22 crore Muslims in India.
>
> We had a lot of influence in 1971. Now, people *still* torture us. No one can bring back that power. I was in Saidpur during the nine months of the war. I lived there until 1974. I never faced any harassment. Nothing happened in Saidpur town—it was a calm and safe place. *No Bengali ever died there, no military operations ever took place, no mukti bahini [Bengali guerrilla army during the 1971 war] ever walked down the street and called out to me "hey you, you shala—come here."* What happened in Saidpur is that we maintained control—you understand we were young men then. It was decided that no one would be harassed in Saidpur. There was an attack on Saidpur but it was by outsiders and Pakistanis. There were no mass killings in Saidpur after liberation, it was normal.

Here Javed Hasan resorts to the common rhetorical device of blaming unnamed outsiders for violence, thereby muting potential tensions between Bengali and Bihari communities that the telling of this story and the acknowledgment of violence open up. He also distances Biharis from any violence inflicted on Bengalis by insisting that the *Razakars* (collaborators) were Bengali, not Urdu speakers.

> The main thing that keeps us apart from the mainstream Bengali population today is the celebration around December 16th, February 21st and March 26th. During these three months, all the plays, songs, lectures and cultural functions, in all of them the role of the enemy is shown by using Urdu, and they show some Bihari *Razakars. There were no Bihari Razakars, I must make this clear, the Razakars were not Bihari—the Razakars were Bengalis from here. All these Razakars—they were your people and the Muslim League here certified them.* Biharis stayed in their own towns. Yes, the government did set up the East Pakistan Civil Army Force but they only fought in the front, that doesn't mean at the same time, they were raiding and destroying villages. They only fought the Indian army at the border, never any Bangladeshis. Using Urdu just makes the locals furious with us. The friendships we build up so carefully in nine months is destroyed in three [during Independence celebrations between December and March].
>
> All we want is to live honestly. Give me a factory; give me an agreement and proper rates and I will give you the goods on time. All I ask is for you to give me a factory.

Beyond the Quandaries of National Belonging

UNHCR's logic for Bihari ineligibility for refugee status, as mediated by Javed Hasan's experiences, foregrounds the paradoxes of national identity produced by the 1947 Partition. Much like the Hindu Bengali migrants tracked by Gautam Ghosh, Biharis did not leave the nation, but the nation seems to have left them. Of the former, Ghosh writes in "Outsiders": "One might say that, with the Partition, the Indian nationalism which they had constructed suddenly left them behind, abandoned, and they then 'followed' it to India seeking to preserve their central role within it."[10]

Pakistani nationalism too abandoned Urdu speakers in East Pakistan/Bangladesh. The difference is that "stranded Pakistanis" could not follow this nationalism or, after 1971, even claim a rightful place in the nation for which they felt they had sacrificed so much. The proper homeland—the one that could not have been created without their struggle—had vanished literally under their feet, even though they had not moved, they were still literally on the same soil. The same reasoning that denied them refugee status undid their claims to both Pakistan and Bangladesh.

The still unfolding trajectory of Biharis in Bangladesh challenges the singularity of conventional Partition narratives. It is a reminder that nation-making processes in South Asia are shot through with fractious histories of 1947 that continue to jostle for recognition within unequal fields of power. Entering the predicament of the "stranded Pakistanis" through the story of Partition allows us to pose 1947 and 1971 as two interrelated (and mutually constitutive) moments rather than as separate and contradictory events. This move also throws into sharp relief the ways in which older meanings of Partition (and of Pakistan) were disrupted, displaced, or reconstituted by the 1971 war.

The experience of Partition for Muslims in East Pakistan was not homogeneous—distinctions arose not only between those who were refugees/migrants and those who never left East Bengal but also within the category of refugee itself. Further, those who celebrated the coming of independence did not share one uncomplicated strand of feeling. The "festival of freedom," and euphoria at Partition documented by historians of East Bengal was not uniformly shared (see Hashmi 1994; Kamal 1989). Ahmad Kamal notes that the word "euphoria" both reveals and hides the contradictory expectations embedded in the idea of Pakistan (Kamal 1989: 58). Indeed, the vagueness and imprecision of what constituted Pakistan exacerbated the tensions between different communities. For most non-Bengali speakers, East Pakistan would remain an alien space in which they had to constantly renegotiate their identities, precisely because their vision of Pakistan was ultimately different from that of most Bengalis. After 1971, Pakistan was no longer theirs to claim.

Thus, Bangladesh's sovereignty created a permanent rupture in identity—a civil death—for Urdu speakers in East Pakistan. Those who had previously mediated belonging and citizenship through the idiom of sacrifice to the Muslim nation found themselves excluded by the terms through which the Pakistani nation was redefined in 1971. Urdu speakers became the new Bengali state's enemy Other at the moment that the Pakistan they knew quite literally ceased to exist under their feet. The nation left them, even though they were still on the same soil. They could not follow. This paradoxical condition was rooted in the shifting relationships between national and territorial identities generated by the 1947 Partition. Ambivalence and tensions

[10] G. Ghosh discusses the reconstitution of the relation between 1947 and 1971 by Hindu migrants to India for whom the memory and loss of Partition continue to resonate strongly. "Outsiders at Home? The South Asian Diaspora in South Asia," in Mines and Lamb (eds.), *Everyday Life in South Asia* (Bloomington: Indiana University Press, 2002), 326–36.

around Partition were not only productive of identities; on occasion they erased claims to belonging altogether. For those in danger of permanent civil death, recourse to the idiom of sacrifice no longer sufficed. Both refugee and citizen at the moment of Partition, Urdu speakers in East Pakistan, were rendered non-citizens and non-refugees in independent Bangladesh.

Willem van Schendel has for long advocated the writing of *post-nationalist* histories of Bangladesh, histories that go beyond "getting Bengali nationalism right" (van Schendel 2001: 134). Noting that contemporary political disputes in Bangladesh are fundamentally conflicts about what constitutes the *common history* and *common destiny* of the inhabitants of the country, van Schendel reminds us that the study of history is always a study in power relations and that debates over the definitions of Bengali/Muslim/Hindu obscure underlying bids for power. Van Schendel argues for a "pluralist" critique of national narratives, one that would confront the exclusionary and inegalitarian aspects of such narratives as they have developed since 1971. Such a project could help in defining "new, more pluralistic, inclusive and democratic notions of what it could mean to be Bangladeshi citizen in the twenty-first century" (ibid).

This essay is written in a similar spirit. It is a call to denationalize the writing of history in Bangladesh, that is, to move away from statist and teleological versions of history in order to address the incongruous and that which has been rendered "unspeakable" through nationalist myth-making. By unspeakable I refer not only to the subaltern's inability to speak/be heard/have a voice. The precondition for subaltern speech to be heard (and not automatically marked as being *against* the nation) lies in revisiting the processes through which categories such as Bihari and Bengali are produced and naturalized and of the silencing, erasure, and displacement of some histories and the privileging of others. Only then can we begin to reimagine more inclusive and just forms of belonging and citizenship.

Bibliography

Ahmad, I. 2012. "Modernity and Its Outcast: The Why and How of India's Partition." *South Asia: Journal of South Asian Studies* 35 (2): 477–94.

Ansari, S. 1995. "Partition, Migration and Refugees: Responses to the Arrival of Muhajirs in Sindh during 1947–48." *South Asia* 18: 95–108.

Chattopadhyaya, H. 1987. *Internal Migration in India: A Case Study of Bengal*. Calcutta: K. P. Bagchi.

Elahi, M., and S. Sultana. 1985. "Population Redistribution and Settlement Change in South Asia: A Historical Evaluation," in L. Kosinksi and M. Elahi (eds.), *Population Redistribution and Development in South Asia*. Boston: D. Reidel, 15–35.

Feith, H. 1972. "Bihari Sorrow," *Far Eastern Economic Review*, May 13, p. 22.

Feldman, H. 1969. "The Communal Problem in the Indo-Pakistant Sub-Continet: Some Current Implications." *Pacific Affairs* 42 (2): 145–63.

Feldman, S. 1999. "Feminist Interruptions: The Silence of East Bengal in the Story of Partition." *Interventions: International Journal of Postcolonial Studies* 1 (2): 167–82.

Feldman, S. 2003. "Bengali State and Nation Making: Partition and Displacement Revisited." *International Social Science Journal* 55 (177): 111–21.

Ghosh, G. 2002. "Outsiders at Home? The South Asian Diaspora in South Asia," in D. Mines and S. Lamb (eds.), *Everyday Life in South Asia*. Bloomington: Indiana University Press, 326–36.

Ghosh, G. 2007. "The (Un)Braiding of Time in the 1947 Partition of India," in A. Grafton and M. Rodriguez (eds.), *Migration in History: Human Migration in Comparative Perspective*. New York: University of Rochester Press, 53–85.

Ghosh, P. 1991. "The 1946 Riot and the Exodus of Bihari Muslims to Dhaka," in S. Ahmed (ed.), *Dhaka: Past, Present and Future*. Dhaka: Asiatic Society of Bangladesh, 305–18.

Ghosh, P. 2007. *Partition and the South Asian Diaspora: Extending the Subcontinent*. New Delhi: Routledge.

Government of Pakistan. 1953. *Census of Pakistan, 1951. Population According to Economic Status (Tables 11 and 19-C)*. Census Bulletin No. 4., Ministry of Interior, Karachi, p. ii.

Hashmi, T. 1994. *Peasant Utopia: The Communalization of Class Politics in East Bengal, 1920–47*. Dhaka: University Press.

Islam, S. (ed.). 1992. *History of Bangladesh 1704–1971, Vol. 1, Political History*. Dhaka: Asiatic Society.

Kamal, A. 1989. "A Land of Eternal Eid: Independence, People and Politics in East Bengal." *Dhaka University Studies* 46 (1): 58.

Kamaluddin, S. 1992. "Bihari Refugees to Return to Pakistan." *Far Eastern Economic Review* 155 (25): 23.

Kamaluddin, S. 1989. "Left in Limbo." *Far Eastern Economic Review* 146 (42): 23.

Kamaluddin, S. 1989. "Prisoners of Peace." *Far Eastern Economic Review* 143 (4): 28.

Kamaluddin, A. 1985. "Refugee Problems in Bangladesh," in L. Kosinksi and M. Elahi (eds.), *Population Redistribution and Development in South Asia*. Boston: D. Reidel, 221–36.

Kaushik, S. N. 1988. "Pakistan's Relations with Bangladesh," in S. R. Chakravarty and V. Narain (eds.), *Bangladesh: Volume Three, Global Politics*. New Delhi: South Asian Publishers.

Khan, A. 1995. *Seasonal Adjustments*. Australia: Allen and Unwin.

Kudaisya, G. 1995. "The Demographic Upheaval of Partition: Refugees and Agricultural Resettlement in India 1947–67." *South Asia* 18: 73–94.

Ludden, D. 2003. "Maps in the Mind and the Mobility of Asia." *Journal of Asian Studies* 62 (4): 1057–78.

Majumdar, A. 2008. "Bangladesh Citizenship Rights Divides Biharis." Reuters (Dhaka). http://in.reuters.com/article/2008/05/20/idINIndia-33670220080520.

Malkii, L. 1995. "Refugees and Exiles: From 'Refugee Studies' to the National Order of Things." *Annual Review of Anthropology* 24: 495–593.

Mokammel, T. 2007. *The Promised Land*. Dhaka: Kino-Eye Films.

Nahar, S. 1997. "Biharis in Bangladesh: The Search for a Home." *Weekly Holiday*, June 13.

Rahman, M., and W. van Schendel. 2003. "'I Am *Not* a Refugee': Rethinking Partition Migration." *Modern Asian Studies* 37 (3): 551–84.

Siddiqi, Dina M. 2018. "Secular Quests, National Others: Revisiting Bangladesh's Constituent Assembly Debates." *Asian Affairs: Journal of the Royal Society for Asian Affairs* 49 (2): 238–58.

UN High Commissioner for Refugees. 2009. *Note on the Nationality Status of the Urdu Speaking Community of Bangladesh*. December 17. https://www.refworld.org/pdfid/4b2b90c32.pdf. Accessed November 17, 2022.

Van Schendel, W. 2001. "Who Speaks for the Nation? Nationalist Rhetoric and the Challenge of Cultural Pluralism in Bangladesh," in W. van Schendel and E. Zurker (eds.), *Identity Politics in Central Asia and the Muslim World*. London: I.B. Tauris, 107–28.

Zamindar, V. 2007. *The Long Partition and the Making of Modern South Asia: Refugees, Boundaries and Histories*. New York: Cambridge University Press.

Acknowledgments

An earlier version of this article, Left Behind by the Nation: 'stranded Pakistanis' in Bangladesh by author was published in *Sites: A Journal of Social Anthropology and Cultural Studies*, 10 (2) (2013). It is being republished with permission from the Journal.

6

Invisible Borderlines

Naila Mahmood

Ami mayyamanush. Bangali mayyamanush. Aar ami gorib manush. Aapnarey kouner moto amar kono kichha nai.
(I am a woman. A Bengali woman. And I am poor. I have no stories to tell you.)
—*Fazeelat, 2014*

I met Fazeelat in 2001, while she worked as a domestic help in an apartment in Karachi. She had a quiet, forlorn demeanor and spoke in faltering Urdu, heavy with Bengali accent. Fazeelat was one of the thousands of impoverished Bengalis who had migrated to Pakistan from Bangladesh, in the aftermath of the 1971 Bangladesh war of independence—one of the most gruesome and violent conflicts in the history of contemporary South Asia.

Before 1971, present-day Pakistan and Bangladesh were part of a common federal entity separated by approximately 1,500 miles of Indian territory. Economically and culturally subjugated by West Pakistan, the Bengali-speaking province of East Pakistan, with a larger population, was systematically denied its fair share in the national economy and in governance. In December 1970, national elections were held in Pakistan. These were the first elections to be convened in the country on the basis of adult franchise. In these elections, the Awami League, a political party primarily representing the Bengali population, led by Sheikh Mujibur Rahman, won the majority of parliamentary seats. Hence, it was the Awami League's constitutional right to form the national government in Pakistan. Instead, between January and March 1971, the ruling West Pakistan–based military junta twice postponed the dates for convening the legislature (the National Assembly), refusing to commit to a peaceful transfer of power. In March 1971, the military government initiated an armed offensive, "Operation Searchlight"—a brutal and murderous crackdown on its own citizens of the Eastern Wing. This premeditated violence morphed into a gruesome, nine-month-long civil war. By popular estimate, about three million lives were lost in this conflict, while millions fled the violence and carnage and became refugees in the bordering state of India. Bengali resistance and a full-scale war with

India on the Eastern and Western fronts of united Pakistan resulted in the eventual independence of East Pakistan and the creation of a new nation-state of Bangladesh in December 1971.

Before independence, East Pakistan/Bangladesh was an economically neglected region of Pakistan. For many years before and after independence, it was racked by successive onslaughts of natural disasters such as floods, cyclones, and droughts and by a gruesome famine in 1974. These events intensified the effects of the colossal economic damage caused by the war, severely affecting industrial workers, small peasants, agricultural laborers, and rural communities. Political and economic instability also escalated in Bangladesh with the assassination of President Sheikh Mujibur Rahman in 1975, triggering a chain of army coups, assassinations, and violence.

The dire situation in Bangladesh in the aftermath of the war led many poor Bangladeshis like Fazeelat, to illegally migrate to both India and Pakistan. Most Bangladeshi migrants who went to India settled in the same geographic region, in states along the Indo-Bangladesh border, particularly in West Bengal and Assam, connected by similar geographical, cultural, and linguistic linkages. Thousands, however, trekked across India, destined for the port city of Karachi, endangering their lives to enter a country which had committed massive war crimes in Bangladesh. For most Bengalis, the decision to migrate to Pakistan was driven by greater economic security and by the support offered by migrant social networks formed around kinship and common community origins. Subsequent chain migrations and movements across borders into Pakistan were also motivated in large part by economic imperatives and social affinities. From the viewpoints of these migrants, the idea of nation, borders, and national territories became subservient to survival. Their experiences, memories, points of view, and varied lives offer an alternative dimension, a diverse way of relating to the past and challenges the dominant idea of nationhood in nationalist histories, and needs to be told.

Most migrants crossing national borders suffered hardship, abuse, physical harassment, and even loss of life to arrive at the port city of Karachi. Fazeelat, like many other Bengali migrants, was brought to Pakistan by extortionate traffickers called *dalals*. Many women recount the border crossings with pain that has not diminished with time—emotional scars of physical assault by migrant smugglers or border guards, deaths, and disappearances—unreported, uninvestigated silent stories that became an inescapable part of the collective migrant journey.

Once inside the supposed sanctuary of the Pakistani borders, mostly in the city of Karachi, the Bengali population took up menial jobs as domestic servants, factory workers in the fishing industry, day laborers, and workers in informal industries. After living and working in Pakistan, in some cases for more than thirty years, they remained unrecognized and undocumented, despite being part of the domestic labor force. The state still ignores and criminalizes the existence of a generation of Bengalis that were born and raised in Pakistan, but are not recognized as citizens.

Pakistan's National Aliens' Registration Authority (NARA), which was formed in 2001, explicitly targeted ethnic Bengalis as "illegal aliens," regardless of their individual histories of migration. Today, an estimated three million Bengalis remain stateless and trapped in Pakistan, structurally excluded from stable jobs, education, land ownership, and free movement.

Bangladeshi immigrants also became victims of preexisting anti-Bengali prejudices in Pakistan. Their class, language, and mannerisms made them easy targets of discrimination and ridicule. Bengali women faced unique and difficult challenges—besides the ethnic and class prejudices suffered by Bengali migrants, they also had to endure and navigate patriarchy and gender discrimination. In present-day Pakistan, these stateless women have no social standing, political power or cultural agency, and limited economic means as they negotiate their past, present, and future within a hostile society. In Fazeelat's words, she is inaudible and invisible because she is a woman, is poor, and a Bengali.

Fazeelat had lived in a village near Munshiganj Sadar, about four hours south of Dhaka. When her husband, a peasant who worked on a small farm, died in 1978, she struggled to support her young family. Her older brother had migrated to Pakistan, and sent back money and photographs of what seemed like fancy places in Karachi. Fazeelat's family encouraged her to go to Pakistan, where wages were higher, promising that they would look after her children.

Fazeelat connected me to some immigrant Bengali communities that live in clusters of informal settlements in different parts of Karachi. I visited their homes and spent several months listening to the stories of Bengali women, as they unburdened their memories of war, border crossings, the staggering hardships of their immigrant lives, their longing for their families left behind and their many unanswered questions.

To document these untold stories of marginalized lives, I drew from their first-hand testimonies and observations of their lives. I photographed letters, photos, and little mementos from their past that were redolent with the intensity of displacement and separation. These interviews developed into a small documentary project, with photo-narratives that expanded on traditional storytelling. Here, I attempt to zoom in on one personal story, Fazeelat's, across time and geography—a story scored with tragic notes of exile and homelessness, as she struggles to be reunited with her children.

These stories of individual women take the form of nano-histories that reveal the broader structures of injustice that have dominated gender and labor politics and national policies toward minorities and marginalized populations in Pakistan. For me, these tragic stories highlight the emotional dimensions of armed conflicts and foster a better understanding of the sociopolitical milieu in which the 1971 war was waged, contesting, at the same time, the national narrative that dominates the historiographical landscape of Pakistan.

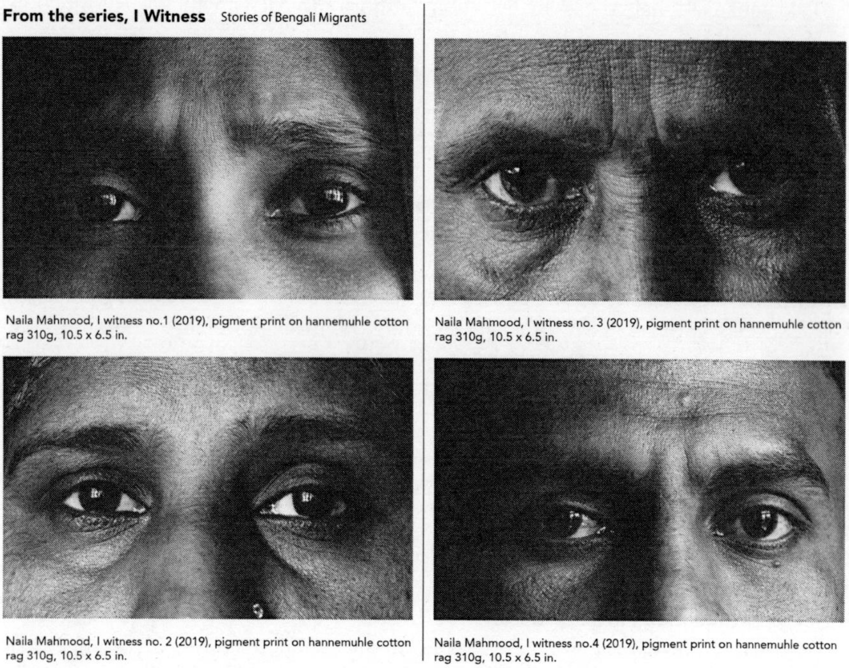

Figure 6.1 Photos from the series *I Witness* by Naila Mahmood

When I encounter
The land of unfulfilled desires and hopeless expectations
I cannot bear to look that way
I tell myself I must flee
Escape where hopes and desires are joyous luxuries
Not the detritus of broken lives[1]

River Currents

"Be strong. Take care of each other. I will be back soon. I will bring you bangles and toys," Fazeelat had told her children.

Leaving her five children behind in her village in Bangladesh, under her brother-in-law and his wife's care, Fazeelat joined a group of would-be migrants. They were led by an agent, the *dalal*, on a perilous journey to Pakistan, across lands sundered by politics and war. They spent days trekking in scorching heat. To evade the authorities, they often moved through the welcome coolness of the night. The *dalal* led them to abandoned huts, mosques, shelters, swamps of *sundra* mangroves, and mosquito-infested *gewa* marshes.

1 Anjum Altaf, *Transgressions: Poems Inspired by Faiz Ahmed Faiz* (New Delhi: Aakar Books, 2019), 42.

Was it three months or seven? She lost sense of time as the days and nights blurred across the neat divisions of any calendrical order. There were too those rare days when she did not feel hunger. The group had swollen to nineteen, joined by a young couple with a small boy, and two teenage sisters from Gopalpur in search of their father. They crossed Western Bengal, Bihar, Utter Pradesh, Haryana; exhausted by the unpredictability of each day. The small boy's insistent wails of *Aami baari jete chaaee, Aami baari jete chaaee* (I want to go home, I want to go home); began to fade.

Eventually, after she had lost all trail of time, there was the river—the final crossing—and freedom. Or danger of a different kind. Waist-deep waters, the ends of their sari *palloos* tied together, the gray-watered eddies; terrified, starved children clutching to their mothers, the night under the bridge, flash lights, boots, the detention center.

They were huddled in the corner of the room, crouched on the floor.

"Do you have any Indian cassettes?" The uniform looked down on them.

The *dalal* got up, steadied his feet, and whispered some words to him. The uniform left.

The early morning lulled Fazeelat to sleep. She awakened to an unyielding silence, as the cold seeped through the cement floor. The two girls from Gopalpur were gone. The price of freedom—the "Indian cassettes" so desired at the border.

The group was released an hour later. Fazeelat had survived one arduous journey, a liberation of sorts, but another long, forbidding journey had just begun.

Three weeks later, in Ganda Singh Wala village, near the border city of Kasur, two unconscious girls were found in a small graveyard and taken to the district hospital in Kasur. They only spoke Bangla.[2]

Invisible Borderlines

The borders she crossed to get to Karachi were perhaps more permeable than those that awaited her arrival.

When people looked at her, they could only see an enemy, a defeat, a history that had to be forgotten. The roundness of her vowels and the weight of her consonants, the way her mouth shaped *Urdu* words stirred anxieties and resentment of a lost war.

They could hear it when she was quiet and still. They could see it through the blackness of the veil covering her face.

The slurs, that were cultivated and crafted. *Kaali Bengaalan*—the black Bengali—the color of her cast iron skillet, the *tawa*, broken in by years of use.

These borders were resolute.

[2] Interviews with migrant women pointed to widespread use of abusive language, implicit derogatory terms and sexual abuse by border guards. Arif Hasan writes "The other serious issue that has surfaced is that Bengali and Burmese women are trafficked to Karachi for purposes of prostitution. It is estimated that 200,000 Bangladeshi women have been trafficked to Pakistan in the last 10 years, and many of them have been sold to the slave trade for US$ 1,500–2,500 each. At present, there are more than 2,000 Bangladeshi and Burmese illegal migrant women in prison and in shelters in Karachi," p. 38. https://journals.sagepub.com/doi/pdf/10.1177/0956247809356180.

She had to remove the symbols of her past, relieve herself from the burden of identity. She unwrapped her midriff-bearing, arm-showing *sari* and put on a more demure *shalwar kameez.* Her body had to realign, make adjustments. There was comfort here, she could now dissolve in the hypnotic movements of the crowds, in the amorphous fogs of human shapes, temporarily escaping the constraints of her ethnicity.

Could she ever call this place home? She asked herself this often.

"This is not my home. Not my home," she would always reply. "My home is in the past. And the past is gone."

A fugitive of time and geography. Not even a number in the census. Undocumented. Stateless.

"Ami amar šantander-o khaoyate parini. Amar kono upay ni, amar kono upay chilo na"

(I could not even feed my children if I stayed back. I had no recourse, no way out.)

With limited employment options, she worked as a domestic help in private homes, looking after children—cleaning, sweeping, cooking. She lived with her employers and would visit her brother twice a month. Isolated from other Bengali migrants and vulnerable to the scrutiny and sexual overtures of her employers and other domestic help, she toiled away with a singular mission—to marry her teenage daughters. She borrowed money for their dowries, sliding ever deeper into poverty and debt.

Jai Namaz (the Prayer Mat)

Fazeelat had packed a small bag of boiled rice, dried coconut, a sari, three photographs, and a prayer mat for her journey to Pakistan. The prayer mat was a muddied white cloth of duck egg color. Her friends, Noor Jehan and Shahida, had toiled every day for weeks with the *kantha tanka*, till the last vestiges of light would slow their adept rhythms of colors and threads, as they crafted a parting gift for Fazeelat. They embroidered borders of undulating lines and concentric circles, of boats and stars and trees on the *jai namaz*, unaware of how these symbols would mark Fazeelat's journey into a new life.

The prayer mat was Fazeelat's portable sanctuary. Entangled in its threads were childhood bonds bearing memories of fraternity, love, separation, perseverance, and fortitude. She would spread it open five times a day and stare at the lines of running stitches, as she raised her index finger in *shahadat*, giving evidence of the invisible oneness of God. The lines conjured up images of the trickling tributaries of *Brahmaputra*, small rice fields, and little ravines that had taken them to Hindustan. The lapping of water against the hull, the last damp smokey whiffs of bamboo, and the slowly enveloping darkness for which they had waited all day. She would watch her boat move slowly along these sewn paths of curving, overgrown rivulets on her mat.

During the edgeless hours of early morning, she would lay awake on her prayer mat, the *jai namaz*. As the *Fajr Azaan*, the call to prayers, drifted across the predawn sky, she would go back to her village once again—to her children, to the courtyard, to a place of solace where nothing painful could touch her—not even the haunting evocations of a murderous war.

Intersecting Worlds

The fierce sadness of 1,500 miles of separation, over twenty-six years of exile.

Aami baari jete chaaee.

(I want to go home.)

Fazeelat would murmur this mantra in her sleep even as her breathing, increasingly labored, measured out the shortening of time. There was less of it, maybe very little. She would raise her leathery hands, swollen with inky veins, and pray for a reunion with her children—for her home.

"Amar Chaowalder na deykha ami kyamoney ei duniya chhayra jamu? Amar aar kono upay nai, mushkil aashaner aar kono raasta nai. aamar bachon lagboi. aami bachtey chai."

(How can I die without seeing my children? There is no recourse, there is no way out. I have to stay alive. I have to stay alive.)

Then she found Ismail, the carpenter. He was returning to Jessore with his sons with one-way travel permits, being issued by the Bangladeshi embassy.

"It's the *galla katta* scheme, the slit throat, its one way, no way back." As he spoke the words, a distinct feeling unlocked inside of her—the possibility of return.

As the airplane lifted her above the clouds, she finally felt weightless, unburdened by years of pain, floating above the borderlines that separated the past from present, here from there, us from them.

She closed her eyes and felt the damp caress of the *shital pati* mat against her body, the taste of the monsoon rains, the sweet, woody smell of warm *kancha kola* plantain on a cart, the mud-colored dog barking under the mango tree, the gentle lapping of cool water against her shins in the marshes, the velvety spread of water lilies softly brushing her skin as she picked *shapla* flowers, the soothing lull of a distant flute. She was home.

"All Pakistanis form a separate line," boomed a uniform in a sharp, thunderous voice, breaking her daydreaming spell. "Are you carrying any money? Dollars?" said the steely eyes. "Hey you! Leave your bag here."

Pakistani? Money? No. No. There is a mistake. This is my home. Look at my face. I am Fazeelat. Hear my words. This is my home.

The city roads were tangled by wriggling swarms of cycle rickshaws driven by reedy men with sun-burnt skins. The city had grown and Fazeelat could no longer recognize the slender, intriguing town of her youth. Fazeelat's daughter lived in a dilapidated building with a frayed curtain for the front door, a steep staircase with no railings, wedged in narrow lanes of a community of textile workers. She looked around for glimpses of familiarity but found none—Noor Jehan, the village, the wind-swept courtyard, the terra cotta water jars, *shapla* ponds of water lilies, her youth, her past, her sense of belonging. What hung indelibly was the phantom of dreams and regrets. And Shahida, who radiated with the exuberance of belonging and continuity. It was Fazeelat's fate after all—the fate of an immigrant, an exile, to chase time, memory, history, a sense of home.

She would lay in her bed, under the staircase, and listen to the strange inflections of her grandchildren's Bengali, as the rain pounded on the corrugated sheets of tin roof. *Aami baari jete chaaee.* She would whisper. I want to go home. A faint sigh from the abyss of her ever present distress, from the irreconcilable space between her past and present, from the decrepitude of her two intersecting worlds.

Her small voice, fatigued by the burden of unanswered questions, would move across warm breezes, in search of a home, across the currents of river *Padma*, the Ganges, where the debris of all dead dreams subsist.

Fazeelat died ten months after returning to Bangladesh. According to her wishes, she was buried in a graveyard in Munshiganj Sadar, where she was born.

Part Three

Alternate Registers, Other Histories

7

Un-archiving Baloch History

Adeem Suhail

The year 2021 dawned on Kechh shrouded in the veil of mourning. Baloch rights activist Karima Baloch had died in exile under mysterious circumstances. As her earthly remains returned to Balochistan, to be interred in her village, the funeral procession was hijacked by security officials. Her body was held hostage, her town placed under curfew, telecommunication services suspended, and mourners forcibly dispersed.

In death, she continued to animate the struggle to which she had devoted her life. Karima had done so under immense pressures and personal costs. First as a student activist, then as a political dissident, she traveled to the remotest parts of Balochistan becoming as much an advocate for Baloch rights as for the crucial role that women had to play in the struggle. She was forced into exile for all that she was and threatened to become and may yet have paid the ultimate price for her courage. In so doing, she became, perhaps, the first woman leader and political activist to have paid the blood toll that all Baloch must to enter the historical Archive in Pakistan.[1]

The Archive's Blood Toll

In the geography claimed by Pakistan, the Baloch peoples are marked by the historical archive for a blood toll as the condition of inclusion. The toll does not guarantee the terms of inclusion. Archive here does not merely allude to a material collection of documents, histories, and other representational forms, although it encompasses those objects. Rather, here "archive" denotes a site of selection and classification, of framing and authorizing the limits of what aspects of a people's life can become history (Pandey 2012: 37). Political power is predicated on differential access to this site (Galison 2004). The blood toll is the price exacted for contesting and being subjected to the epistemic violence of nationalist historiography.

Baloch inclusion into the narratives of the nation-state sequence in Pakistan began with the annexation of the Makran Coast and the Kalat Khanate in 1948 and the subsequent masking of the original violence in "statist" narratives (Baloch 1987; Kutty

[1] This is not to undermine the numerous cases of abduction, abuse, assault, and various forms of sexual violence against women in Balochistan. These practices are pervasive, true as day for all military occupations, condemnable in each instance.

2009).[2] Subsequent histories have contended with this originary violence that carries with it a constant reminder of the synthetic nature of Pakistan as the afterlife of the empire (Chatterjee 1993; Kolsky 2005). Much as in the colonial era, the landscapes the Baloch inhabit are frontiers over which those who claim to speak on behalf of the state carve *etatization* in blood (Badal Khan 2017; Bangash 2015; Rahman 1996). This has resulted in a decade-long struggle for dignity, rights, self-determination that is reflected in the discursive space of the archive. Culturally diverse and peripatetic, the Baloch are thus normalized into legibility (Swidler 2014).

Baloch history obtains through cathexis: acquiring shape and substance through libidinal investments in the narrative acts of violence. The archived narrative is thus inclined toward accounts of violent struggle, strife, death, and sacrifice. Where the archive assembles under the sign of the state, this inclination is palpably malign. However, even where that assemblage is challenged, the discursive terrain of contestation recapitulates the dominant mode or *genre* authorized by the archive.

"Struggle" is the genre the archive authorizes for the Baloch in Pakistan. In this genre the Baloch features as a stock character: as a recalcitrant subject of the state, a putative victim of anachronistic and violent modes of social organization. Punching discursive holes in this blood-soaked fiction is an important tradition of dissident Baloch historiography speaking back to statist narratives (Ahmad 1977; Baloch 1985; Mazari 1999). The generic figures populating the counter-archive is a valiant hero resisting violent subjection and extraction, the suffering body (*-politic*) becoming the object on which the fictions that sustain the postcolonial nation-state are carved out as history. Evidently, insofar as this counter-archive assembles itself in response to statist fictions, it accepts the basic tenets of the terrain over which the contest over the archive is waged. Broadly, in this terrain the subject of Baloch history becomes *gendered* (male), *spatialized* (in the hinterlands of agrarian and urban landscapes that constitute the spaces of the nation), and *temporalized* (the time of the Baloch is the time of insurgency/struggle) (Baloch 1982).

This article primarily draws on the concept of "unarchiving" as a methodological exercise as suggested by Gyanendra Pandey (2012). Traditional historians, as Pandey maintains, argue that there can be no history outside of the discursive terrain of the archive. In *Unarchived Histories* (2014) and *A History of Prejudice* (2013) Pandey goes on to develop and populate a framework for unarchived histories, where lives and "practices, which are not events, not datable or even nameable" (2012: 37) can be posited against the authority of the archive.[3] Unarchiving thus involves juxtaposing

[2] Contrary to popular (mis)representations in Pakistan as territorial tribal society, the Baloch can be considered a diverse and peripatetic people who have maintained kinship networks that span centuries and oceans. Peoples who claim Baloch kinship inhabit the Indian Ocean littoral, speaking many languages, nominating diverse ethno-racial identities of belonging and practicing an entire gamut of social functions across diverse locations. The rule of colonial difference in British India canalized this diverse, multilingual, and transoceanic cosmopolitan polity into an ethnic formation at the frontiers of empire. To truncate a long and complicated history, we may assume that all political settlements in postcolonial Pakistan inherit the British production of Baloch ethnicity as a tribal, frontier polity.

[3]

> For the disciplinary historian, the archive may fairly be described as a site of selection and classification, of framing and authorizing—and hence making intelligible. In Foucauldian

the putatively senseless, the unremarkable, and the *trifling* as a modality of historicity beyond the common sense of the archive. The archive normalizes objects that can be selected, classified, and categorized. Unarchived histories pose a "menace" to the archive's pretensions as history's "commencement" (origin) and "commandment" (authority), the exclusive and unquestionable ground for historical knowledge (Derrida 1996).

As unarchived histories, I present here biographical fragments of the lives of two women: Azra Bibi and Babli Baloch. They appear here as fragments, not as a positive countervailing "evidence" that weighs in, one way or another, on the archive's common sensical mode of appropriating the Baloch. These fragments index a different subject position, that nevertheless emerges from the lived experience and understanding of Baloch life in Pakistan. As such, they implicate rather than deconstruct the would-be archivist's libidinal investments in the expansion, rectification, validation, and sanctification of the archive (Pandey 1992: 47).

Azra and Babli stage a potent refusal to conform to the common sense of how, wherefrom, and what as, the Baloch enter Pakistani history where normally, they would not appear at all, or be deemed insignificant and unsignifying to the authorized genre of archiving Baloch history. In substituting these fragments to pose as a "people's history" (this volume), this essay destabilizes the grounds on which state-making violence and the vicissitudes of resistance exact the blood toll. Their *being* indexes an expository bar on the perpetuation of the archive's deathly fetishism. This essay asks: What does it mean to foreground the unremarkable but vibrant life of two woman as the principal locus of Baloch lifeworlds through and across the Pakistani postcolony? What is the worth of the mundane when the archive stages existential contests? Is the contrapuntal movement of humbler lives dissonant with the symphonic dialectic of domination and resistance?

The Trifling Lives of Azra Bibi and Babli Baloch

The location from which we populate Baloch lifeworlds in this essay is the historic neighborhood of Lyari, Karachi. Community elders claim that where now runs the Mauripur highway along the southern edge of Lyari, there once stood a sign that read "Welcome to Balochistan." It disappeared sometime in the 1950s. Contemporary Karachi holds the largest urban population of Baloch residents in the world. Indeed, the Baloch of Kechh Makran claim belonging to lands along the isthmus of River Lyari centuries before the British decided to turn Karachi into a city in the late nineteenth century.

terms, the archive authorises what may be said, laying down the rules of the "sayable," negating (making inaudible and illegible) much that comes to be classified as "non-sense," gibberish, madness, and is dispatched therefore to a domain outside agential, rational history. In this process of selecting, framing, authorising, as even the most hard-boiled of traditional historians will acknowledge, every archive necessarily excludes a great deal that is not of direct interest to its custodians (Pandey 2012: 37–8).

Elsewhere, I have chronicled how significant the Baloch working class was to Karachi's birth as a city (Damohi 2013; Suhail and Lutfi 2016). The city has, from inception, functioned as the intellectual and political hub of Baloch nationalism in all its diverse expressions. Much of this history, and Karachi's history, as a cosmopolitan Indian Ocean entrepot was erased in the cataclysmic transformations wrought by Partition in 1947. This essay builds on that work without retreading that ground. Karachi's Baloch have been subsumed into discourses that continue to describe the city in terms of ethnic strife. Challenging such erasure, Baloch urbanisms have left traces on various parts of the city since its first rudimentary ramparts went up in 1728 (Suhail 2019).

In the biographies of Azra and Babli I recover the trace of the ways in which being in and of the city, both forged and expanded the possibility matrices for being Baloch in the world. Azra expands it geographically: across deserts and seas to kin in Iran and the Arab Gulf States. Babli expands our conceptions in other ways, insisting on the visibility and agency of Baloch and Afro-Baloch women in processes that sustain and reproduce Karachi. Her active participation in the electoral and patronage politics, as a single mother, confounds normative accounts of who brokers these operations (Mohmand 2019). Both women find complicated emancipatory horizons in the often-dubious spaces of the market and the kin-group. Aditi Saraf has recently explored how commerce and markets can become sites of solidarity and resistance in the context of Indian-Occupied Kashmir (Saraf 2020). Similar dynamics have been explored in other situations in Occupied Palestine (Tamari 2011). Azra, in the founding of Lyari's iconic JhatPat Market, and Babli, in forging an entrepreneurial self that aims to lift her whole neighborhood give us the blueprints for an unarchived history of the Baloch.

Azra's Oceans

I met Azra Bibi, when collecting oral histories in Karachi's historic old city neighborhood of Lyari. Very early into our conversation, Azra had already laid claim to Lyari and the larger cosmopolitan Baloch world it was connected to for herself. At the time, my investigations were motivated by an interest in the longue durée of political mediation in Lyari. I was one in a gaggle of scholars who at the time came to study the Lyari Gang War. The weight of her claims gave pause to those preoccupations, disarming all my impulses at gatekeeping away her claims on the city, her people, their world, and history.

The twenty-first century dawned on the hitherto peaceful, diverse, and cosmopolitan old city neighborhood of Lyari in red hues of blood as putatively murderous gangs fought the "forces of order" as much as they fought each other. Lyari was, until recently, a bastion of Karachi's old city charm and bonhomie in a city often rife with violence identified with ethnic and sectarian difference. The so-called gang war launched a thousand probes, including mine, from journalists, scholars, NGOs, the military, the police, politicians, and TV pundits into and onto Lyari, with a clear interest in violent marginality. Dubbed as an "exceptionally violent" gangland, Lyari was discursively transformed into a place where young Baloch men played out tired fantasies of urban youth living fast and dying young violent deaths putatively exemplifying the city's "ordered disorder" (Gayer 2014).

Fear was deployed in narratives about Lyari to several, often competing ends. It catered to widely differing publics and interests. Each instance indexed a fascination with young Baloch men who wield violence. The fetishization of Baloch vectors of public violence has become a regular foil for legitimating state violence in Pakistan. The Baloch body becomes a "disorder" that beckons state-ordering mechanisms. Enabling this highly constructed discursive stability that hinges on the question of violence are not just state security apparatuses but also "progressive" academics and activists, "local" politicians and community leaders, and crime-beat journalists out for scoop, together conspiring to collocate violence and masculinity under the sign of the Baloch. Good faith or suspect, all are driven by a motivating drive: we do not know enough and need to learn more about the Baloch-as-object. The object *dazzles* us. It beckons, as if there, to be studied, identified, differentiated, recorded, and recoded. In each instance, the will to knowledge begins in uncertainty and calls for compulsive repetition: probing, penetration, messiness, seeking to be quite indelicately intimate with the suspended subject/object. Some do it with bullets, others with the pen. Some purple blotches on dead Baloch bodies look eerily like so much spilled ink.

Azra Bibi, in her reconstructions of Lyari and the Baloch world through biography, was determined to thwart such partial objectification. This essay places Azra Bibi in particular, and Baloch women in general, at the center of the process of worlding the history of a place and people overdetermined by the contest over how they may become archivable objects. My meetings with Azra were mediated through the intercession of my friend and her niece, the journalist Hina Rind. Azra introduced herself as a comfortable business owner, investor, and as a repository of the regularly overlooked cosmopolitan potency of Baloch lifeworlds. She made it clear that she would paint Lyari in her own peculiar palette. Defying archival expectation, she frames her story as her triumph. The triumph of her body and subjectivity, her womanhood, her Balochness: a never occupied free country (Steedman 1987).

Azra was born in Karachi's old city neighborhood of Lyari in the prominent Rind family sometime in the early 1930s. The Lyari Azra was born into was a world apart from the "violent gangland" and "urban slum" it passes as in dominant discourse today. The slow-moving sludge of refuse and excreta that the Lyari River has now become, was then a seasonal river. Her Karachi was an Indian National Congress bastion in a Sindh dominated by the All-India Muslim League.

Her father was an interesting man, who is not altogether anomalous in a cosmopolitan Indian Ocean entrepot, where the confluence of languages, cultures, ideas, things, and the people that carry them, were primed to birth a new thing. The man had migrated to Karachi from the Kechh region of upper Makran, where he had left behind the village, family, and many acres of palm orchards along the Dasht River to explore more interesting horizons in the colonial city. In the 1920s, he had moved to Karachi to "educate himself" but ended up, by the time of Azra's arrival, becoming a "Jobber" in Lyari.

The Jobber was a prominent feature in the working-class Lyari of the booming 1940s. The Jobber was a community elder in Lyari with a strong position among his kin group in the city's immediate hinterlands in Balochistan, Kutch, and Sindh. He was usually a relatively affluent tribal patriarch with a sizable residence or stake in unallocated "wastelands" in and around Lyari who would arrange for the selection and accommodation of cheap labor brought in from the hinterlands involved in port operations and industry in Karachi. The Jobber thus was an important intermediary between the Sindhi Hindu or Parsi (Gujarati) capital that had an interest in the growth of the city, the British administrators who in many respects shared this interest and resided in Karachi, and the largely Baloch Muslim or Kachhi Dalit labor that resided primarily in Lyari. The Jobber was an important position that commanded the respect of both the laboring masses and from those interests that would appropriate that labor.

Azra, his youngest daughter, was important to this important man. Azra recalls with misty eyes how she would shadow her father as he ran *baithaks*: gatherings where folk community members in old Chakiwara would come to him for advice, dispute resolution, work, or other forms of assistance. At these *baithaks*, Azra and her brother both received an education in the world and how to lead an ethical life within it. Despite her father's insistence on schooling and her recalcitrance with it, Azra believes their true education was in these daily gatherings. Azra's brother would go on to be one of the most prominent and well-respected leftist community leaders in Lyari. Azra would become a shrewd businesswoman.

Unlike her studious brother, Azra's interests spanned the breadth of the Baloch world. As a curious young girl growing up in a city changing rapidly after Partition—losing nearly the entirety of its Sindhi Hindu majority, and yet managing a 400 percent increase in population as migrants arrived—Azra's memories are pegged to the Lyari River and her world that stretched into the Arabian Gulf. She would be eager to receive relatives that kept arriving and leaving, from and to Kechh, Iranian Makran, and to Oman across the Arabian sea. The lives of this peripatetic kin fixated her city-dwelling fascination, and she would yearn for the annual trips her family would take back to their kin's orchards along the Makran. Repeatedly, she would remind me how clean and clear the river waters were in her time when she swam it, that a fascinating "jungle" lay beyond it, one they were forbidden to explore, but did nonetheless, the thrill of excitement as aunts and uncles and cousins and neighbors would travel as if in a merry caravan back to the old country that now lay across three national boundaries and international waters.

By the late 1950s as political turbulence rocked the Pakistani state, and its military junta precipitated its first antidemocratic putsch her teen-aged brother, best friend and confidant, was drawn further into the political intrigues that ensured that the inequity between the city's working poor—both old Baloch kin and new Muhajir migrants—and the city's industrialist elites would grow at an alarming rate. Her brother became a leftist youth activist, a voice for Baloch rights, and within the community in Lyari, a budding successor to her father's leadership position. From their father, who had come to play the role of an influential (and relatively affluent) patriarch in the kin network, the siblings inherited a sense of responsibility to their people. Within this milieu, being a "Baloch nationalist" and a "socialist" were considered synonymous.

The memorable exploits of Lyari's great socialist leaders continue to animate progressive political dissidence in the city and is memorialized in an important and growing counter-statist archive of progressive politics in Pakistan (Ali 2015; Baloch 2013). Her brother joined this legendary cohort of leftist, communist, and Baloch nationalist political activists in Karachi. The group met in the Rind family house courtyard and was dubbed the Leningrad Circle (Baloch 2017). The Leningrad Circle comprised some of the most important men who came to define the spirit of horizontal solidarity and resistance that became a hallmark of political consciousness in Lyari.[4]

Azra also laid claim to the axiom that animated this politics, repeated to me by many other figures (mostly men) I interviewed, which was a variation on "what all we claim as ours is the charity of the dispossessed amongst us." However, she articulated this cosmopolitical inheritance in different, perhaps far more expansive if largely invisibilized spheres. For example, her passing mention of the famed Leningrad Circle is a view from *inside the house*, where the invisible labor of women, perhaps signaled in the tea and snacks served to attendees, enabled the Circle to meet regularly (Elyachar 2010; Pernau et al. 2015)). However, Azra does not dwell on the matter long. It is, as she describes in a different context, a parallel path that her brother took in executing his social responsibilities to his kin, neighbors, and comrades. Azra's path led to cultivating herself as a business owner, an investor, but also as someone who had made these investments in the Baloch world. Hers was an internationalism, a Baloch nationalism, and solidarities of a different order.

Azra, in her own words, had inherited from her father a fascination for "her people's country," the Makrani coast that undulated into Kechh beyond which the Pak–Iran border was sketched and regularly ignored by her folk, connecting her to kin in Sarbaz in Sistan-Balochistan, Iran. Her interests were in querying uncles and cousins, who would make regular trips to and from neighboring Oman, and later, Dubai, as workers and small-business owners. Her ambitions spanned the breadth of this transnational, transoceanic world and saw Karachi as the launchpad for her cosmopolitics rather than its sole object.

The story she tells therefore of being Baloch is one that denies geographic situation, and a tarrying with the temporality of "the Baloch struggle." Illustrative is the way in which she describes transcending the perceived Baloch domestic sphere of the statist archive. Azra and her niece Hina both avidly relate the ways in which "Lyari traditionally celebrates" weddings. She loved the weddings because they allowed her access to what she had learned was her only "*sarmaya*": her kin. Kinship for Azra was more a theme with which she could play rather than a structure that caged her.

Her playful resignification of Baloch kinship networks is hidden within her answers to my questions of why she loved the weddings while at the same time proclaiming, at once matter-of-factly and with pride, how she had convinced her father that she was

[4] Storied names such as Narayan Das Bisla, Faiz Ahmed Faiz, Usman Baloch, Nazir Ahmad, Zulfikar Ali Bhutto, Tufail Abbas, Mairaj Mohammad, Rahim Baksh Azad, Mairaj Muhammad, Ghaus Baksh Bizenjo, Akbar Barakzai, Osman Baloch, Lala Lal Baksh Rind, and Saba Dashtiari were at one time or another a part of the Circle.

neither interested in marriage nor ever would be. Nevertheless, she would point to having developed an affinity for events where the extended kin group had an excuse to assemble in their homes in Lyari, Gulshan, and Malir. She speaks of these events as almost mundane but felicitous forms of communion with being Baloch in all the ways one could be (cf. Berlant 2016; Harney and Moten 2013).

The Rinds, she would proudly claim, are a large clan that span oceans and countries, producing all sorts of daughters and sons. For instance, she recalls how one of her favorite parts of the wedding ceremony were the "dancers" that were brought in from Napier Road. "You have no idea the kinds of fun we could have in the *zenana* precisely when the male gaze was not around," she teases. In her youth, the wedding ceremony in Lyari would involve a tented-off side street with one side reserved for the men and the other for women, both participating in mirrored celebrations and rituals. It is from this sense of "mirroring" that she realized that kinship is not simply family relations but allows for other forms of arrangements and engagements. This realization is what enabled her to organize her life around two poles: the physical space of the market, and the space of the transnational Baloch kinship network to which, being in the city she was both tethered but also at a distance.

By the 1970s, Azra's kin group had strong footholds in services and labor sectors of the booming petro-economies of Arab Gulf states. The function of the Jobber that her father had performed in Karachi was being performed by cousins and uncles all along the Western Indian Ocean entrepots. Despite the hardening of national boundaries in this region, especially given the Baloch insurgencies in Pakistan and Iran, her kin continue to traverse along their centuries-old networks even as they were constantly being extended along new nodes.

One of the ways the kin networks reenergized themselves was through periodic movement: migrations, visits, and "caravans" traveling back and forth both by sea and land and "temporary settlements" that may range from a few months to generations. While much of the recent burgeoning literature in Indian Ocean studies accounts for how men move along these axes, the absence of women in these movements as anything other than cargo (slaves, indentured, "family," or pilgrims) is complicated by accounts such as Azra's that evince a vibrant movement across borders of women engaged in small-scale production and exchange through kin networks (cf. Lowe 2015).

Azra organized and scaled up this already vibrant if invisible economy of exchange. Choosing to remain unwedded, Azra recalls being a perennial co-babysitter, helper, busybody, confidant, and friend to women within her neighborhood in Gul Mohammad Lane. Many of her friends and kin were also involved in producing homemade products such as clothing, beddings, knitwear, and other items that they would take to trips into Kechh and further in Iran in what Azra describes as caravans of kinwomen. From Iran, whenever they were done visiting their family, they would bring back other small household items (towels, tea, rubber slippers, etc.) that they would be able to sell in the neighborhood. Azra decided to organize and rationalize the production and exchange along this network. According to Azra, she was one of the pioneering traders (if not *the* pioneer) who constituted what later came to be known as Lyari's famous JhatPat market.

Lyari, insofar as it is *the* oldest part of the city, is home to storied markets. JhatPat, over the years, had become a unique feature of neighborhood life in Lyari. Here, Pakistan's endemic patriarchal masculinity's monopolization of public spaces is revitalized by the activities of women vendors, customers, spectators, selling groceries, towels, clothes, folk crafts, toys, and knick-knacks. The atmosphere is not only punctuated by the usual smog, sounds of traffic, and muck on shoe but also by women's laughter, banter, loud and aggressive anger in an aural and sensorial shock, because it cannot be obtained anywhere outside domestic spaces.

My friend, Ramazan Baloch, Lyari's respected historian-in-residence once remarked on the ingenuity and "business acumen" of the women who ran JhatPat. "Some women" created their own cheap supply sources for everyday items and built this institution that now "belongs to Lyari." The men worked the port, the fisheries, manual labor: their spaces were elsewhere in Lea Market and Khajoor Gali and Joria Bazaar; only women sold goods at JhatPat. The cacophony of Kachhi, Balochi, Sindhi, Urdu, Pashto, and Memoni (Gujarati) reminds one that this is what the "Old City" of a cosmopolitan Indian Ocean port city should sound like.

The history of economic activity in both modes of history writing done by and for the Baloch is dominated by men. As such only specific forms of mobility and exchange are legible to an archive that builds on colonial and thus, at best, partial forms of representing practices and structures in subject societies (Spivak 1985). Anthropologists have long chronicled the crucial role women play in economic life across the world; empirically contradicting presumptions that (European) forms of individualism alone afford women freedom of mobility and choice of practice (Freeman 2001; Mintz 1971). Scholars have ethnographically detailed women's involvement in transnational markets and entrepreneurial activities sustaining and inhering within forms of specific modes of sociality (Elyachar 2010; Seligman 1989). Lyari's Old City bonhomie is sustained through the *hypervisibility* of spaces such as JhatPat that memorialize what once Karachi was and has the potential to be again. Here I gesture toward JhatPat, which deserves its own in-depth treatment elsewhere. For, with JhatPat, Azra is making a claim on behalf of a very specific genealogy of practice, what Engseng Ho has identified as "genealogy as method, genealogy as gift" (Ho 2006). Here, however, the genealogy of practice is transmitted through kinwomen. It is a genealogy of practice given from mother and aunt to daughter, from neighbor to neighbor, knitting the fabric of community in a working-class public space in Karachi that is wholly feminine.

Baloch women weaving and wandering in and out of Karachi were not waiting for a niche of agency, they had been carving out their own circuits for generations. The spaces they produce are not forged in contradistinction from oppressive and calcified kinship structures, the masculinist space of the market, nor culturally informed curtailment on women's mobility. To the contrary, Azra and *her* comrades built their space *through* these structures, by subverting them. Indeed, when the gangs of Lyari would ascend into dominance three decades after Azra has already claimed the Baloch world for herself and her sisters, they would learn from the women their traditional routes, their business strategies, their modes of redirecting kin and cooperation across transnational networks albeit toward their own nefarious ends. The route to influence within the community was through investment in its structures and traditions.

Indeed, by the 1990s, Azra Bibi had diversified her own portfolio by investing her money in the string of nephews and great-nephews who were moving to Dubai and other Gulf states to set up their own small business. These included car repair shops, restaurants, and increasingly more lucrative service sector enterprises. Azra Bibi also continued to invest in young women within Lyari by turning her ancestral home (after her brother's death) into a makeshift factory of sorts. She began to function as a private contractor to the garment industry in the city, employing young women from her neighborhood to come work for her. For many young women in her neighborhood, Azra's enterprises were their first doorways into the public workforce. Indeed, Babli, who we will discuss next, had also passed (though not lingered) through the pathways Azra had cultivated.

As scholars of colonial and postcolonial South Asia have shown us, women's bodies become a frontier over which the nation-state seeks to write itself (Sinha 2000). In this, therefore, all overt projects of etatization, as Carole Pateman and Wendy Brown would argue, recapitulate the "man in the state" (Brown 1992; Pateman 1988). Perhaps in this way, the values that visited on her ancestors both the ability to command their people's labor-power and execute their ethical responsibilities toward neighbor, worker, and kin were reworked into the space of the market by Azra Bibi. Her brother and she both had inherited these values from their father. Her brother became a celebrated local community leader, a committed leftist, for a while a member of both the quasi-Maoist NAP and later the NDP. He eventually went to prison in the Movement for the Restoration of Democracy (MRD) during the Zia dictatorship. She too fought for her people in her own way. In owning and rearticulating the channels of Baloch kinning, kenning, and mobility, she mounted a "trifling" mode of nurturing Baloch futures in a mode more in line with her ancestors, men, *and* women of the Makran, than perhaps the resistance organized by her celebrated brother.

Babli's City

The Baloch were not just present at the birth of the city, they were the hands that built it. In the late nineteenth century, the British colonial government accelerated the development of Karachi into a port city importing as much cheap labor from the hinterlands as could be mustered for the massive public works projects. It is at this time that thousands of ex-slaves flocked into British Karachi from the Omani controlled parts of Makran coast. While slavery had been abolished in the British Empire at the time, it persisted in Britain's vassal state of Oman: the uneven legal–political geography ensuring cheap emancipated labor at the frontiers of the empire. In Karachi, though retaining certain distinctive features of language, religion, and culture from East Africa, the Afro-Makrani ex-slaves and their descendants of African origins took on the Baloch identity, and "Baloch" became a common surname among these groups (Suhail and Lutfi 2016).

A few decades on, in the 1930s, a progressive movement aimed at democratizing and modernizing the state of Kalat (what is now the Pakistani province of Balochistan) was being led by a vibrant young group of statesmen including Mir Ghaus Baksh Bizenjo and Mir Gul Khan Nasir. This group of young reformers, poets, socialists, and nationalists were centered in and around Karachi and became the forefathers of the Baloch nationalist movement. By then Karachi was home to presses, schools, publication houses and a hub of Baloch intelligentsia. As the anthropologist Hafeez Jamali once remarked, supporters of the nationalist movement began shedding clan names for the surname Baloch. Thus, by the 1940s, the Baloch in Karachi converged into a highly inclusivistic kinning and group-formation comprising a wide spectrum of religio-sectarian and ethno-racial difference in favor of large geographical networks of kinship and cooperation (Barth 1981, Jamali 2014, Scholz 1996, Titus 1996).

The Afro-Baloch, nevertheless, rarely feature in the archive on Baloch history especially as constitutive subjects within the group. Insofar as the geography and temporality of Baloch history has been limited by colonial and statist narratives to "feudal hinterlands," this highly diverse, cosmopolitan, and urban population is obscured in the contested terrain of the archive, often featuring but as "curiosities" in the margins of "larger" histories (Lutfi 2018). The trivialization of Afro-Baloch lives belies the role their group continues to play in charting out Baloch futures in the city. A "trifling" instance of this was the ways in which Babli Baloch, a young, widowed Afro-Baloch woman came to play a key, if silenced, role as a Pakistan People's Party community organizer, an activist for public health measures in the community.

The Afro-Baloch of Karachi in their vast majority are embedded within Karachi's old city central township of Lyari. Lyari is one of the most densely populated sectors in the city of Karachi. It is the smallest township out of the nineteen that constitute the city, accounting for nearly 9 percent of the city's population. Nevertheless, in terms of the basic healthcare infrastructure, and especially women's health and maternity homes, it remains criminally underserved. The dearth of resources allocated to Lyari may partially be attributed to the fact of its cosmopolitan, and diverse character, as its multiethnic harmony did not render it an easy fit into the "ethno-nationalist" turn in the city's politics. To date, across main Chakiwara Street, you could pass laborer and shopkeepers speaking Balochi, Sindhi, Gujarati, Bengali, Pashto, and Urdu. With the advent of the brutal Lyari Gang War (2002–16) that resulted from the breakdown of relations between multiple political and economic interests in the Old City area of Karachi, the orphaning of this constituency in the city was exacerbated. Babli's generation, coming of age in this milieu had to make their own breaks amid the intensities of urban violence and elite neglect.

* * *

Babli and I smoked cigarettes on a wooden bench that lay in the compound of Lyari Medical Facility (LMF) where she worked. The bench was usually occupied by grizzled men who self-identified as local community elders. They sat under the shade of the giant *peepal*, reading the lurid rag *Jaanbaaz*, dribbling red streaks of *gutka* over the bloody pictures of young Baloch men lost to the Lyari Gang War.

Jaanbaaz was exactly the kind of fetish object players in the contest over the Archive thirst for (Gayer and Kirmani 2020). At the height of the gang war (2010–14), it became the most widely read publication in the locality. It thrived on publishing gratuitous photographs of the war's brutalized victims and sketched sensationalized stories of its combatants. The accounts of cold-blooded murder it chronicled were often highly embellished—and sometimes clearly fabricated (Rahman et al. 2017). *Jaanbaaz* curated the tableaus of intense violence ostensibly orchestrated by the gangs for the curious gaze of those for whom Lyari served up the blood toll that allowed the "Baloch gangs" to become archivable in narratives on Karachi. *Jaanbaaz* commodified fear and insecurity in Lyari for mass consumption. The hunger for death in Baloch Lyari was sublimated in the newspaper archive, indexing the libidinal investments of a diverse ensemble of "professionals" compiling the archive.

Babli too enjoyed what *Jaanbaaz* and the archivists were selling. In fact, it was precisely this pall of death and foreboding that ensured the *absence* of the city's elite from Lyari's geographical domains and allowed low-level party workers and political brokers, such as her, to play an outsized role in the future of their people. Babli was an ardent party worker for the Pakistan People's Party. Her adherence to the memory of the slain Benazir Bhutto was devotional. During our smoke breaks, Babli would invariably be lured into animated defense of the party to the annoyance of the community leaders who consumed, with ample condescension, the arguments of someone they dismissed as a loud-mouth Afro-Baloch woman.

Never mind that most of the "respectable" community elders each had their own history with the party. Many of them had joined the party during the 1970s when labor unionists and community leaders in Lyari had held two seconds of sway in Zulfikar Bhutto's pro-labor populist government. The Baloch of Lyari, insofar as they were also aligned with working-class politics, had long supported the party as well. Since the 1990s, however, this leadership, having borne a decade of persecution from General Zia's violent dictatorship, had seen those early promises devolve into a vastly underdeveloped Baloch Karachi. The emergence of a clientelist politics where patronage to a select few without effective resource delivery had transformed a would-be cohort of urbane, educated, and politically savvy Baloch leaders into party stooges. In time the party had sidelined this older cohort of would-be leftists for young and restless gangsters.

Babli was a different kind of broker than the now disgruntled old men had once been. She was savvy to the fact that the livelihood of all who worked at the facility, including the elders, was tied to the party. And unlike them, the party still valued the energy and dedication Babli delivered for them. Consequently, she was one of the few salaried workers at the facility at a time when the public health employees were largely contract labor with few protections. Most of the facility's staff had acquired their position through intercession of the gangs or their patrons in the party. Babli was one of the few who had managed to short-circuit the hierarchies of patronage that went through the gangs or other community leaders. Her appointment was won after years of "youth activism" on the party's behalf in the Afro-Baloch quarters of central Lyari. Through the vicissitudes of being an ardent supporter through the 1990s, she had stood loyal and vocal to mobilize voters in the Afro-Baloch communities in Singo Lane, New Kumharwara, and Miran Shah.

For this she had been rewarded with salaried employment and secured rare residential quarters attached to the LMF. In her modest home, she had raised two daughters by herself. By 2016, when I began working at the LMF, her daughter had secured admission as a medical student at the Shaheed Benazir Bhutto Medical College

Lyari, established in 2012 by the PPP government as a part of the Lyari Development Package. Her steady employment at the LMF enabled her to raise her daughter despite her husband's early demise. In return, Babli has been a diligent party worker even during Musharraf's decade-long antidemocratic rule when much of the political party's local structure was dismantled by the military regime. Part of her labors also involved leveraging her labor for the patrons in the party to advocate for women in her neighborhood to get contract labor jobs in provincial government departments. For instance, much of the custodial and nursing staff during my fieldwork at the LMF owed in some way or another their jobs to her advocacy.

Over many conversations it became apparent that for Babli, her role at the LMF was not simply one of tactical survival mechanisms emblematic of small-scale brokers. It was rather important to her that what was apparent as general disinvestment on the parts of the ruling elite in the city in serving the immediate needs of Lyari's marginalized population be redressed through her intercession. This was especially true for the neighborhood's healthcare infrastructure.

Thus, when during the so-called gang war, the facility was left abandoned and rendered defunct by the higher administrators, none of whom was from Lyari, Babli, along with a few young local rising community leaders, decided to address the matter. The party at this time was unable or unwilling to help even though they occupied the provincial government. The city government, on the other hand, was dominated by the rival Muttahida Qaumi Movement (MQM) who had no interest in their rival's voting township. In this time, Babli became a leading figure in a small working group of brokers, and community organizers aimed at rehabilitating the facility.

Babli first brought the matter to comrade Habib, who was a fellow Zikri Afro-Baloch community leader in her neighborhood, and commanded respect as an energetic Afro-Baloch ex-boxer who would later go on to become the deputy commissioner of the Southern district. In recruiting Habib to the cause, Babli and her group of workers were accessing both the higher echelons of the party as well as the "deniable" but crucial support of the leading gang in the area. Indeed, local gang underboss Zafar Baloch, a key lieutenant in the Uzair Baloch gang, was soon brought to take a personal interest in the rehabilitation processes. However, rather than simply becoming turf for the People's Aman Committee (PAC) gang, Babli and Habib insisted that the facility, and in effect *all* medical facilities, be declared neutral spaces within the gang war. When Zafar decided to ignore this plea early on, the group approached another local celebrity: the brother of Rahman Dakait, the founder and ex-boss of the PAC gang. What ensued around the problem of rehabilitating the facility was a series of brokerage maneuvers that saw Rahman's brother being set up for a political career on the party's ticket with votes assured by brokers like Babli and Habib. The *cause celebre* for launching his political life would be the delivery of the facility as a fully functional maternity home. Coincidentally, Zafar Baloch was killed in a bomb blast, which made the path clearer for the group.

Elsewhere, I have chronicled in detail the intricacies involved in the rehabilitation of the facility to full functionality, which Babli and her friends were able to achieve in 2018 (Suhail 2019). Along the way, what "local" actors such as Babli, a few sweepers, and nurses began became a coalition of actors across different scales of power. They enveloped and brought into coherence of purpose the southern district bureaucracy, the local police force, the gangs, party representatives from the provincial and national level, state-employed medical doctors, and various NGOs. The facility began functioning again in 2017, inaugurated by a free medical camp where Babli's constituency from the neighborhood, mostly women and children, flocked to the facility in the hundreds to be seen to for a variety of chronic and emergent ailments by doctors reassigned to the facility as well as young medical residents from the Lyari Medical College, one of whom was proud Babli's daughter herself.

In the duration, the party has lost nearly all its support in the country, their rival MQM has been dispersed also. The gangs have been dismantled through a bloody military operation, and many of the influential men and community leaders who used to sit and disdainfully read *Jaanbaaz* have receded into further irrelevance. In the neighborhood, Babli continues to be an active organizer, especially among the women in the Afro-Baloch Zikri community. And she continues to serve as the head *ayah* at the facility, actively watching after her community's health needs. Where more visible, and putatively consequential actors have left the stage, Babli continues to perform invisible but essential mediations that make life possible in her community.

The Living Multitude

In the introduction to this volume, Kamran Asdar Ali and Asad Ali emphasize the difference between "existing peoples in their concrete actuality and plurality," and an abstract collectivity that may be referenced as the "nation," or "the people" to mobilize in defense of a specific arrangement of power. One might reference this arrangement by its folk shorthand, "the state." In one manner of reading, the state achieves etatization through multi-scalar projects of subjection, culling and conforming the actuality and diversity of life into its categorical, abstract form (Nugent and Suhail 2018). History writing, "far from being a neutral enterprise" curates as well as contests this process of *etatization*.

Synthetic postcolonial state-formations such as Pakistan have struggled to achieve etatization, often resorting to violent forms of subjection on extant polities within the territories they claim. Epistemic violence accompanies such subjection and dissident scholars from subjected polities have long mounted a struggle against the fabulations that obtain. The critical and fraught nature of the contest, however, tends to overlook "hidden transcripts," mundane practices and improvisational capacities people tend to employ in the everyday (Scott 1990).

If history is to be a "structure whose site is not homogenous, empty time" but animated by the here and now, we may best consider the heterotopic temporalities the subjects of such a history tend to occupy (Benjamin 2020). As such we may find that the socio-temporal locations in which these lives unfold is out of step with the homogenizing terrain of the commonsensical archive or the discursive modes it commands. Maura Finkelstein's *The Archive of Loss* (2019) exemplifies this impulse toward the "unarchived." In reconstructing the lives of the working classes in another Indian Ocean port city, Mumbai, the study juxtaposes the depletion and capacitation embodied in the aching, broken bodies of workers; the enduring *khastagi* of worker's *chawl* homes that acquire affective reinforcements revealing the fragility of modernity's edifices: memory, sensoria, and rumor that reinvent notions of community. In belying normative accounts of these subjects' lives, these elements reintroduce what Derrida has called the *mal d'archive* as a methodological tool rendering partial, prejudicial, and afflicted all that can permissibly be aggregated to an archive.

The archive of the Baloch struggle, as a normalized terrain of contest, is similarly buttressed by "unvisible" elements: human, affective, and physical, with all their vitality melting into the background as history in the generic mode plays out (Finkelstein 2019: 25). They would become "visible" only in moments of breakdown (Star 1999). The mundane labors of Baloch women—Karima, Azra, and Babli—uphold lifeworlds. They hold together projects across scales that rely on them: be they in the realms of public health infrastructure, political brokerage, transnational trade and entrepreneurship, the maintenance of kinship ties, or where famous revolutionary brothers and comrades can find material and emotional support as they go forth and participate in *historic* struggles.

Mubbashir Rizvi (2019) has recently chronicled ambivalent outcomes for subaltern struggles where they are co-opted into putatively "larger" movements. An important insight Rizvi offers is how lives may be burdened and broken by the desires of putative allies removed from the immediacy of consequence. In an analogous vein, Saidiya Hartman has powerfully challenged scholars to consider an ethical reckoning with "scenes of subjection" (Hartman 1997, 2019). Just living while belonging to embattled communities comes with immense pressures to signify emancipatory horizons. The mode of signification is overdetermined by the *genre* of archivable truths and histories. The genre authorized for Baloch peoples of Pakistan is that of the struggle where lives and deaths become historicized through the exaction of a blood toll.

This essay posits two lives in fragments that challenge the givenness of the constitutively bloody terrain that is the archive. Azra Bibi and Babli Baloch do not feature here as "evidence" countervailing the vicissitudes of being Baloch in Pakistan. Instead, they index a living multitude that has long passed as un-historical, trifling, and unsignifying. Azra and Babli, by fact of existence, and in representing a multitude, pose a potent refusal to the common sense of how, wherefrom, and what as the Baloch become subjects of history in Pakistan.[5]

Bibliography

Ahmad, Syed M. Faruq. 1977. *Tarikh Pakistan-wa-Baluchistan*. Karachi: Self-published.

[5] I am grateful to the participants at the *Yale Interasias Workshop* 2020, and especially Beth Derderien, Neelam Khoja, Kalyanakrishnan Sivaramakrishnan, and Jatin Dua, for reading and commenting on a terribly unready draft of this essay. The brilliance of Hafeez Jamali and Kamran Asdar Ali have been crucial to this study. Ameem Lutfi is my eternal shadow interlocutor. Zia ur Rahman and Ramzan Baloch have taught me so much. I am but an imperfect vessel that channels all the wisdom my friends share.

Ali, Kamran Asdar. 2015. *Communism in Pakistan: Politics and Class Activism 1947–1972*. London: I.B. Tauris.

Badal Khan, Sabir. 2017. "Balochistan," in Alison Arnold (ed.), *South Asia: The Indian Subcontinent*. London: Routledge, 773–84.

Baloch, Inayatullah. 1982. "Baloch Qaumi Tahrik Men 'Kalat State National Party' Ka Kirdar." *Monthly Azad Baluchistan*, December.

Baloch, Inayatullah. 1987. *The Problem of "Greater Balochistan": A Study of Baluch Nationalism*, vol. 116. Berlin: Steiner Verlag Wiesbaden.

Baloch, Liaquat. 2015. *Memoirs*. Karachi: Self-Published.

Baloch, Mir Khuda Bakhsh Bijarani Marri. 1985. *Searchlight on Baloches and Balochistan*. Quetta: Nisa Traders.

Baloch, Ramzan. 2013. *Lyari Ki Adhuri Kahani*. Karachi: Self-Published.

Baloch, Ramzan. 2017. *Lyari Ki Ankahi Kahani*. Karachi: Self-Published.

Bangash, Yaqoob Khan. 2015. "Constructing the State: Constitutional Integration of the Princely States of Pakistan," in Roger D. Long, Gurharpal Singh, Yunas Samad, and Ian Talbot (eds.), *State and Nation-Building in Pakistan*. London: Routledge, 94–118.

Barth, Frederik. 1981, "Ethnic Processes on the Pathan–Baluch Boundary," in *Features of Person and Society in Swat: Selected Essays of Fredrik Barth*, vol. 2. London: Routledge & Kegan Paul, 93–102.

Benjamin, Walter. [1940] 2020. "Theses on the Philosophy of History," in Stephen Eric Bronner and Douglas MacKay Kellner (eds.), *Critical Theory and Society: A Reader*. London: Routledge, 255–63.

Berlant, Lauren. 2016. "The Commons: Infrastructures for Troubling Times." E*nvironment and Planning D: Society and Space* 34 (3): 393–419.

Brown, Wendy. 1992. "Finding the Man in the State." *Feminist Studies* 18 (1) (Spring): 7–34.

Chatterjee, Partha. 1993. *The Nation and Its Fragments: Colonial and Postcolonial Histories*. Princeton, NJ: Princeton University Press.

Damohi, Usman. 2013. *Karachi: In the Mirror of History*. Karachi: Raheel Pub.

Derrida, Jacques. 1996. *Archive Fever: A Freudian Impression*. Chicago: University of Chicago Press.

Elyachar, Julia. 2010. "Phatic Labor, Infrastructure, and the Question of Empowerment in Cairo." *American Ethnologist* 37 (3): 452–64.

Finkelstein, Maura. 2019. *The Archive of Loss: Lively Ruination in Mill Land Mumbai*. Durham, NC: Duke University Press.

Freeman, Carla. 2001. "Is Local: Global as Feminine: Masculine? Rethinking the Gender of Globalization." *Signs: Journal of Women in Culture and Society* 26 (4): 1007–37.

Galison, Peter. 2004. "Removing Knowledge." *Critical Inquiry* 31 (1): 229–43.

Gayer, Laurent. 2014. *Karachi: Ordered Disorder and the Struggle for the City*. London: Oxford University Press.

Gayer, Laurent, and Nida Kirmani. 2020. "'What You See Is What You Get': Local Journalism and the Search for Truth in Lyari, Karachi." *Modern Asian Studies* 54 (5): 1483–525.

Gayer, Laurent, Nida Kirmani, and Zia Ur Rehman. 2017. "Bodies of Evidence," *Friday Times*, February 10.

Ginzburg, Carlo. 2013. *The Cheese and the Worms: The Cosmos of a Sixteenth-Century Miller*. Baltimore, MD: Johns Hopkins University Press.

Guha, Ranajit. 1997. *Dominance without Hegemony: History and Power in Colonial India*. Cambridge, MA: Harvard University Press.

Harney, Stefano, and Fred Moten. 2013. *The Undercommons: Fugitive Planning and Black Study*. New York: Minor Compositions
Hartman, Saidiya V. 1997. *Scenes of Subjection: Terror, Slavery, and Self-Making in Nineteenth-Century America*. Oxford: Oxford University Press on Demand.
Hartman, Saidiya V. 2019. *Wayward Lives, Beautiful Experiments: Intimate Histories of Riotous Black Girls, Troublesome Women, and Queer Radicals*. New York: W.W. Norton.
Ho, Engseng. 2006. *The Graves of Tarim*. Berkeley: University of California Press.
Jamali, Hafeez Ahmed. 2014. "A Harbor in the Tempest: Megaprojects, Identity, and the Politics of Place in Gwadar, Pakistan." PhD dissertation, University of Texas at Austin.
Kolsky, Elizabeth. 2005. "Codification and the Rule of Colonial Difference: Criminal Procedure in British India." *Law and History Review* 23 (3): 631–83.
Kutty, B. M. (ed.). 2009. *In Search of Solutions: An Autobiography of Mir Ghaus Bakhsh Bizenjo*. Karachi: Pakistan Study Centre University of Karachi.
Lowe, Lisa. 2015. *The Intimacies of Four Continents*. Durham, NC: Duke University Press.
Lutfi, Ameem. "Conquest without Rule: Baloch Portfolio Mercenaries in the Indian Ocean." PhD dissertation. Duke University, North Carolina.
Malik, Allah-Bakhsh. 1957. *Baluch Qaum Ki Tarikh ke Chand Pareshaan Patter Auraq* (Few Pages of the Troublesome History of Baloch Nation). Quetta: Islamiyah Press. (Urdu)
Mazari, Sherbaz Khan. 1999. *A Journey to Disillusionment*. Karachi: Oxford University Press, 1999.
Mintz, Sidney W. 1971. "Men Women and Trade." *Comparative Studies in Society and History* 13 (3): 247–69.
Mohmand, S. K. 2019. *Crafty Oligarchs, Savvy Voters: Democracy under Inequality in Rural Pakistan*. Cambridge: Cambridge University Press.
Nugent, David, and Adeem Suhail. 2018. "State Formation," in *The International Encyclopedia of Anthropology*. Hoboken, NJ: Wiley Blackwell, 1–9.
Pandey, Gyanendra. 1992. "In Defense of the Fragment: Writing about Hindu-Muslim Riots in India Today." *Representations* 37: 27–55.
Pandey, Gyanendra. 2012. *A History of Prejudice: Race, Caste and Difference in India and the United States*. Cambridge: Cambridge University Press.
Pandey, Gyanendra. 2012. "Unarchived Histories: The 'Mad' and the 'Trifling.'" *Economic and Political Weekly*, 37–41.
Pandey, Gyanendra. 2014. *Unarchived Histories: The "Mad" and the "Trifling" in the Colonial and Postcolonial World*. New York: Routledge.
Pateman, Carole. 1988. *The Sexual Contract*. Stanford, CA: Stanford University Press.
Pernau, Margrit, ed. 2015. *Civilizing Emotions: Concepts in Nineteenth Century Asia and Europe*. Oxford: Oxford University Press.
Rahman, Tariq. 1996. "The Balochi/Brahvi Language Movements in Pakistan." *Journal of South Asian and Middle Eastern Studies* 19 (3): 71–93.
Rizvi, Mubbashir. 2019. *The Ethics of Staying*. Stanford, CA: Stanford University Press.
Saraf, Aditi. 2020. "Trust amid 'Trust Deficit' War, Credit, and Improvidence in Kashmir." *American Ethnologist* 47 (4): 387–401.
Scholz, Fred. 1996. "Tribal Structures and Religious Tolerance: Hindus in Pakistani Baluchistan," in P. Titus (ed.), *Marginality and Modernity: Ethnicity and Change in Post-Colonial Balochistan*. Karachi: Oxford University Press.
Scott, James C. *Hidden Transcripts: Domination and the Arts of Resistance*. Yale University Press, 1990.

Seligman, Linda. 1990. "To Be In Between: The Cholas as Market Women." *Comparative Studies in Society and History* 31 (4): 694–721.

Sinha, Mrinalini. 2000. "Mapping the Imperial Social Formation: A Modest Proposal for Feminist History." *Signs: Journal of Women in Culture and Society* 25 (4): 1077–82.

Spivak, Gayatri Chakravorty. 1985. "The Rani of Sirmur: An Essay in Reading the Archives." *History and Theory* 24 (3): 247–72.

Star, Susan Leigh. 1999. "The Ethnography of Infrastructure." *American Behavioral Scientist* 43 (3): 377–91.

Steedman, Carolyn. 1987. *Landscape for a Good Woman: A Story of Two Lives*. New Brunswick, NJ: Rutgers University Press.

Suhail, Adeem. 2019. "This Is Not a Gang! Political Violence and State Formation in Contemporary Urban Pakistan." PhD dissertation. Emory University.

Suhail, Adeem, and Ameem Lutfi. 2016. "Our City, Your Crisis: The Baloch of Karachi and the Partition of British India." *South Asia: Journal of South Asian Studies* 39 (4): 891–907.

Swidler, Nina. 2014. *Remotely Colonial: History and Politics in Balochistan*. Oxford: Oxford University Press.

Tamari, Salim. 2011. "City of Riffraff: Crowds, Public Space, and New Urban Sensibilities in Wartime Jerusalem, 1917–1921," in Kamran Asdar Ali and Martina Rieker (eds.), *Comparing Cities: The Middle East and South Asia*. Oxford: Oxford University Press, 23–48.

Titus, Paul. 1996. "Routes to Ethnicity: Roads, Buses, and Differential Ethnic Relations in Pakistani Balochistan," in Paul Titus (ed.), *Marginality and Modernity: Ethnicity and Change in Post-Colonial Balochistan*. Karachi: Oxford University Press, 273–97.

Trouillot, Michel-Rolph. 1995. *Silencing the Past: Power and the Production of History*. Boston, MA: Beacon Press.

8

Queer in the Way of History

Omar Kasmani

"Is it dream, or rather delusion?"[1] Titled after the Urdu word for delusion, allure, even temptation, *Behkawa* is a twenty-six episode television serial that aired on Pakistan's Geo television network in 2012.[2] Relying on multiple storylines, it captures a range of unstraight amorous relations, many of which are eventually entangled through character arcs and journeys. Of the various tracks, however, only one deals with same-sex desire: this rare portrayal involves a well-heeled, butch-presenting media executive who pursues and lures a college-going girl from a working-class neighborhood. In parallel tracks, a divorced mother of three takes comfort in a religiously proscribed sexual liaison with her ex-husband; a death-fearing, burqa-wearing woman unapologetically pursues an extra-marital affair; a troubling and hard-to-decipher bond of love unfolds between half-siblings. Whether allusively rendered or merely suggested, the radicality of these various scenarios cannot be lost on the Pakistani viewer given the country's conservative social norms around sex and sexuality. The limits of narration are however paramount when it comes to lesbian desire. In contrast to the incest-approaching intimacy between siblings, which is abundantly articulated through dialogue, same-sex desire in *Behkawa* is never verbally expressed. Relegated to screenplay—part visual, part affective—it slides between suggesting and not really capturing. Not requited even, the butch woman's amorous pursuit of the young girl turns out to be a one-sided act of deception. In fact, one could argue that so long as same-sex desire can be dismissed as visual trickery or affective delusion, it evades a realness—only confirmed by the soundtrack's questioning refrain, *khwab hai ya phir, behkawa hai*?

This essay speculates on modes of being affectively queer in Pakistan, especially when these count as thin, allusive, or evading. It summons stories, to borrow Julietta Singh's terms, that comprise us but at the same time leave us wanting to access a fuller narrative frame. She has suitably named it "the ghost archive," that is, "everything we need to know but cannot know as we keep circling and sniffing around the edges. Everything that keeps affecting us and affecting others through us. Everything that remains right there, but just out of reach" (2018: 96). To square

[1] Refrain from the soundtrack of the television serial, *Behkawa*. Lyrics by Fasih Bari Khan.

[2] Penned by the acclaimed author, Fasih Bari Khan and directed by Mazhar Moin, the television serial was produced by Media City.

the circle, so to speak of queer and Pakistan then, it is not so much the ghostliness or for that matter the impossibility of capture that drives my interest. I am rather taken by what it means to pursue the historical in the full knowledge that it might refuse our reach and desires for certain histories. In *No Archive Will Restore You*, Singh makes the provocative contention that the archive works foremost as an "enabling fiction," a thing we make up well before we do or understand it (2018: 23). To conjure an archive thus, that is to say, to call to mind remote or removed objects and speculate on their affective relations as I here attempt is "to think of queer futures in locations where they ostensibly have no collective pull" (Arondekar 2020: 209). It would follow that in the face of "opaque hope" or "pure tease"—affects that Singh ascribes to archival work—it might well be worth exploring if acts of circling and sniffing around the edges that otherwise afflict the narration of desire in *Behkawa* can also serve as desirous modes for gathering, interpreting, feeling less-given historical textures (2018: 22). Conjuring, speculating, fabulating—these are cruisy forms of historical knowing, whose overtures seek a be/coming closer while taking us "beyond capture or a holding to a loosely situated though targeted pursuit" (Kasmani 2021). Pursuing archives that are partially rendered or momentarily available, whether hard to pin down or difficult to grapple with or which refuse the certitude of historical methods or anthropological knowing means that we tarry with shadows, that we allow ourselves the tease of ambivalence, that we do not give in to seductions of settled history and its coherent tellings, and also, that we remain open to doubt and disappointment. With these insights, this essay brings two scenes and settings, otherwise disparate, to bear upon each other. Through a common focus on lyrical verse and affect, it articulates across distinct universes, the tenuous narrative possibilities of unstraight lives and loves in Pakistan.

The first section, "Desiring in Verse" discusses the fraught and complex ways in which same-sex desire finds expressivity through the poetic. Centering the poems of the gay Pakistani-American literary figure Iftikhar Nasim (1946–2011), I explore how desiring by way of verse involves an affective terrain of in-betweenness. Trafficking across home and diaspora, religious and queer, Urdu and English, the poems in question tackle not only constraints of writing sex, intimacy, and the body but also negotiate multi-coded and eclectic grammars of desire. The subsequent section, "Mourning for Futures" ruminates on the queer entanglements of memory and temporality through the question of sonic-lyrical affect in a pilgrimage town in Pakistan.[3] I observe how Shi'i-religious lyric not only memorializes a historical tragedy, but such longing for pasts also reverberates against straight and sedimenting conditions of the present in Pakistan (Kasmani 2017). I contend that in taking unruly sonic forms, these verses ensure that certain histories can defiantly endure despite counter governance of the Pakistani state. It is this question of lyrical affect and the temporal relations that stir up by way of verse that ties these contexts despite their obvious differences. Whether we think "queerness as an outcome of strange

[3] Parts of this section have previously appeared on the blog *History of Emotions—Insights into Research*, see Kasmani (2017).

temporalities" (Halbertsam 2005: 1), or understand modes of desiring as wound up with historical disaffection (Muñoz 2009), its affect across registers, religious and sexual, is about other ways of being and belonging in time. In their side-by-side occurrence in the chapter, the scenes afford an expanded sense of people's histories outside public capture, view, or sanction. To the extent that these articulate a being affectively at odds with straight, dominant, or official ideations of Pakistan, they remain—to take license with Agha Shahid Ali's poetic verse (1997: 21)—stories in the way of history.

Unstraight in this rumination, be it to mark the orientation of lives or the character of loves, refers to oblique, radical, or less-normative conditions and prospects of the Pakistani social, or simply to those affects that betray the straight—straight being the right, dominant, or beaten path, whether understood in social, historical, or religious terms. It bears equal mentioning that I use queer as a capacious hermeneutic for understanding alterity in ways that allow a gathering of objects that include but do not necessarily cluster around questions of sexuality or identity politics. For that precise reason, queer in this deliberation does not warrant an exclusive referencing of LGBTQIA+ identities. The task of conjuring up broader histories of queer or imagining it from less-likely, possibly alternate universes—Pakistan or a religious shrine, for instance—demands methodological inventiveness.[4] It also means that we remain cognizant of the cultural and epistemological histories that terms such as queer bring to our fields as well as of the need to keep queer politically exigent. For queer to "remain that which is, in the present, never fully owned, but always and only redeployed, twisted, queered from prior usage" (Butler 1993: 19), means that queer is only as good as the work we make it do in a given historical location. Thinking queer with unstraight then, is not a drawing of boundaries between what is properly queer or not, sexual or otherwise. Rather, I employ the two terms loosely and interchangeably for conceptual volume. It means, on the one hand, staying open to "what coagulation of historical affects gives body to *queer* and to attend to what becomes of these affective histories when *queer* travels to novel historical, geopolitical, conceptual, and demographic locations." (Amin 2017: 183). On the other hand, it pushes the terms under which nonnormative social formations in locations such as Pakistan, relegated elsewhere to queer theory, can enter the purview of scholarship. Whether we describe these archives as unstraight or understand them as queer, these are instantiations of willful affect, which expand historical conditions of the present. Desiring by way of verse or sonically summoning futures aslant to official histories, being affectively queer in Pakistan, as I here propose, is about public modes and means of prevailing in and against the tyranny of straightness.

[4] To read religious life-worlds through the figure of queer signals, in my broader practice, a move from habituated lines of thinking a relationship of irreconcilable antagonism. Such conceptual affinity, however, is not in service of queering Islam or Islamizing queer, but is rather informed by the position that queer lurks ordinarily in religious life-worlds. For more on analytical categories, queer, and religion, see *Coda* in Kasmani (2022) and Castelli (2017).

Desiring in Verse

Born Iftikhar Nasim in Faisalabad, Pakistan, Ifti as he was fondly known, immigrated to the United States in 1969. He spent much of his adult life in Chicago until his death in 2011. His literary work includes verses composed in both the Urdu and English languages. In a filmed interview for a BBC documentary (2007), Ifti proudly introduces *Narman*, his collection of poems, as "the first gay book [that] ever came out in Urdu" (54:23–7). Akshaya K. Rath and Rasheda Parveen note that when published in 1994, the book "caused havoc in Pakistan, was subsequently banned and was thereafter circulated underground" (2015: 75). In the same film, Ifti complains of the homophobia and deliberate censure that he and his work have faced at the hands of the Urdu literary community. It might explain why despite having published two collections of poems, Ifti cuts a lonely figure in Pakistani literary history, also lesser known to readers in Pakistan. "My friends have left me on the road to puberty / They have ventured ahead / I wait alone for the person / Who belongs to my tribe / Who will bear the call of my body / Walk the secret path of my soul" (1994: 3–4).[5] That his work deserved a more prominent place in histories and criticism of Urdu literature was a fact not lost on Ifti himself. In an oral history interview with Kareem Khubchandani (2020), originally recorded in 2009, Ifti can be heard crediting himself with initiating the *Narmani* movement in contemporary Urdu poetry. Influenced by his style, younger poets, he claims,

> started writing about the true feeling whether it was toward the same sex or toward the woman. Before that our object of love was androgynous, you know. You cannot call him male or female. Now they started it calling whatever, if she is a woman, they will call her woman and if it is man, you did call him a man. *Narmani* poetry means true poetry, to them. (56:50–57:26).

Ifti's influence is however not limited to the literary sphere, a fact made plain in the many obituaries that followed his untimely death. Regarded as a Pakistani-American gay icon, he is remembered as a pioneer among the South Asian community in Chicago. One of the founding members of Sangat, an early South Asian LGBT organization in the United States, he was inducted into the Chicago Gay and Lesbian Hall of Fame in 1996. One obituary describes him as "a true trailblazer," someone who dedicated his life to art and advocacy.[6] But Ifti straddled multiple worlds at once. In her portrait, "*Who Is Afraid of Ifti Nasim*," Alizeh Kohari (2020) paints a larger-than-life picture of the poet, a socialite extraordinaire. "He wore a black bowler hat around town, fancy embroidered jeans, and gorgeous fur coats. He wasn't particularly rich, but as a person who knew him noted, he performed his class: it was important to him, as a self-made immigrant from Pakistan, to embody glamor, to solicit aspiration. "I would rather be looked over," he quipped, "than overlooked." He hosted a well-known radio show,

[5] Excerpt from the Urdu poem "A Gay Person" (title in English).
[6] See Amita Swadhin (2011).

wrote a weekly column for a Pakistani-American newspaper, and served as president of the South Asian Performing Arts Council of America. He also worked as a full-time car salesman. Some of these worlds, disparate as they may seem to us, meet in his poem, "A Car Salesman Blues": "My show room is my stage and / I have a stage fright. I am smiling now but my ulcer is flaring up / One more rejection and I shall fall down / Like a mud wall in the rain" (2002: 61).

As multiply-coded compositions, Ifti's poems are sutured through more-than-singular grammars. These are neither afflicted by impasse when it comes to categories, queer and religious, nor suspended between geographies, home and diaspora. In fact, notwithstanding the obvious fact that Ifti was at home with a specific scene of desi gay Chicago, his poems capture an acute and intimate understanding of the norms and forms of sexuality in Pakistani society. In an English-language poem entitled, "How to 'Kill' Your Brother with Kindness," Ifti lays bare the weave of heteropatriarchy typical of Pakistani family structures. The imperative in the poem is to topple hierarchies of male relations while navigating the overt homophobia inherent to such kin-making. The poem, full of instructions, doubles as a survival guide for a yet-to-come-out homosexual in Pakistan who must operate rather tactfully within constraints of the family. It instructs how such a person should interact with his sisters' girlfriends or why it might be beneficial for him to maintain the favor of domestic servants; it lists what not to wear or why not to give in to one's straight, older brother's superior status; it hints at the value of appearing religious or the benefits of having an upper hand on one's father by making sure that he knows that you know his secrets. The long guide of a poem culminates in the hope of outliving one's homophobic brother.

> Take your boyfriend's sister to your brother's wedding (do not exclude him)
> Dance with her all night. Dress up to the "T." Upstage your brother
> And when you are settled down call your brother and tell him on the phone
> (never in person)
> "By the way all rumors about me being gay are true."
> Hear him say, "I know it." Then tell him about his macho, homophobe, married
> childhood friend
> "I slept with him." Hear a deep silence on the other end
> "And by the way I was the top."
> If nothing else that would kill him. (2002: 52)

When it comes to writing sex, Ifti is both candid and explicit in his celebration of corporeal pleasures. A sense of sexual abandon pervades the short poem, "Nineteen Seventy's": "Sixteen men on a / face down man / Yo ho ho ho / And a bottle of 'Rush' " (2002: 33). In *Ode to a Dick*, he writes, "Genitals have a mind of their own / They like what they like" (2002: 115). Such in-your-face writing of sexual pleasure—pun intended—deviates from the veiled metaphors of love and union we often associate with Persianized registers of Urdu poetry. If it exemplifies what Rath and Parveen mean when they note that he writes "public poetry through the body" (2015: 78), it is also simply what Ifti means by "true feeling" of the *Narmani* tradition. Readers are met with surprise if not also distaste. "Good but explicitly homosexual," is how for instance Khushwant Singh described Ifti's poems, adding rather bigotedly that he would refrain from quoting them.[7] What also strikes the reader is how scenes of sexual intimacy sometimes carry within themselves traces of a violent past. The opening line of *Gerontophilia*, "One look at you and I open all my orifices" (2002: 75), though dedicated to two lovers of the poet bears an uncanny resonance with poems such as "Nocturnal," "Uncle," and "For a Dead Pedophile." In the latter, Ifti recollects scenes of sexual abuse from his early and adolescent years in Pakistan. These often lend an affective depth to poems that touch on discrimination, outsider-ness, even insults that Ifti experiences as an immigrant body in his early years in Chicago. There is also an overarching experience of rejection that the poet negotiates with his cultural and religious sense of belonging. In "Barish-e-sang," Ifti finds himself at the receiving end. The Urdu poem portrays a landscape of insult, which is both complex and far-reaching.

> The first stone came from he who slept in my bed last night, next to me
> The second stone came from he, who was like me, but was afraid of people
> The third stone was his, who I had refused to sleep with
> A fourth stone came also from a mosque, whose imam's fourth wife was younger than his youngest daughter
> One stone came from the church, whose pastor had no sexuality
> A passer-by had thrown one too for that was his habit
> The priest of a temple also hurled one, who accepted offerings from either side
> After that, I had lost consciousness.
> After that, no stone had anyone's name written on it. (1994: 22–3; author's translation)

A recurrent feature in the poems is the use of Islamic-religious tropes and metaphors. Akshaya Rath and Rasheda Parveen (2015) have argued that it is through an embracing of Sufism that Ifti is able to retain conformity with Islam. At the same time, they note, his compositions recreate a poetic culture that accommodates homosexuality. In fact, "presented as a mystic quest," they point to "a radical celebration of same-sex love which he voices with a higher degree of boldness as a gateway into the divine" (2015: 84). This perhaps is also evident in the poem, "Sufi," in which Ifti relies on sartorial inversions of gender, a rather hackneyed trope when it comes to Islamic mystical figures in South Asia. This said, for a larger-than-life, flamboyant Chicago socialite given to the love of silk, furs, jewelry and elaborate costumes, such drag is not mere literary device.

> I wear sometimes flashy
> Red garb, red lipstick,
> Adorn my hair with *sandoor*
> And *jhoomer*, my ears, nose

[7] See "World's Changing Morals" in Nasim (2002: 20).

And neck with gold ornaments
My palms and feet are painted with *henna*
I cover myself with a red *dupatta*
Head to toe, waiting for *Him* to come
And unveil me. (2002: 59, emphasis in original)

Ifti no doubt plays with Islamic-religious metaphors and renders them with queer equivalences. It would be amiss to not appreciate that he also questions the tradition. "How come thousands of prophets came down / But not one of them was gay—how odd—how unnatural," he writes (2002: 111). Striking also is the tension some of his verses perform between the poetic and the prophetic. In such instances, Ifti does not merely employ but inhabits the Sufi register. Through his verses, he claims privileged knowledge as mystics would. In the poem *Narman*—also the title of his collection of Urdu poems—he attributes to himself the experience of revelation (*kashf*) to announce an affective knowing and a radical corporeal un/becoming.

I have given birth to myself
I have endured many a pain
Of being man and woman
I have enjoyed by myself, pleasures
All of creator and creation
It is my *kashf*
a woman completes another woman
man is the other half of man
I know
how different I am from the rest of you
if you were to cut me half even
I am a creator, complete
I am past the quarrel of masculine and feminine
I am of this time
I am *narman* (1994: 7–8, author's translation)

In declaring the self as neither man nor woman (*narman*), Ifti frees himself of binaries and dualisms and through yet another Sufi metaphysic, *fana* (annihilation), announces a becoming divine: a creator, complete. It is perhaps also this paramount declaration that helps his readers dismantle the dualisms his poems perform and overcome: past and present, pain and pleasure, Sufi and gay, home and diaspora.

Mourning for Futures

As a place sacred to Hindus and Muslims, Sunni as well as the Shi'a, Sehwan draws millions of devotees from across Pakistan. The ancient pilgrimage town on the River Indus attracts in particular the country's Shi'a—mourners, devotees, pilgrims. More so because its patron saint, Lal Shahbaz Qalandar, though popularly regarded a Sufi is a direct descendant of Ali through the Isma'ili line.[8] He is by such virtue related to the *ahl-e bayt* or the family of the Prophet. Though immensely popular across Pakistan, both Sehwan and its antinomian saint do not sit straight with dominant imaginations of Islam in the nation-state. Enduring Shivaite histories, a profoundly Shi'i ascendance since the 1990s, ongoing local struggles over the town's material and spiritual heritage, not least of all a suicide attack at Sehwan's shrine in 2017 are all signs of just how deeply contested or plurally sacred the place is.[9] As I illustrate in my greater research, Sehwan is Pakistan at its complex best, where Shi'i figures, events, and temporalities are not exceptions or minor figurations but the very warp and weft of the place's ordinary mobilizations (Kasmani 2022: 26). Correspondingly, in this section, I discuss Shi'i devotional texts performed by pilgrims facing saints' tombs at two interconnected shrines in Sehwan. The three texts in question belong to distinct poetic genres such as *nauha*, *manqabat*, and *qasidah*, though what ties them is their shared citation of Shi'i holy figures and especially the tragedies around the Battle of Karbala in 680 CE.[10] I suggest that these mournful offerings bear queer import insofar as these articulate a being affectively at odds with the historical in Pakistan. In other words, these resonate and resound a historical-emotional consciousness that enables believers to critique, interrupt, and refuse a for-granted continuity of the present.

Recorded on different occasions in 2013, two of the three offerings are from the shrine of Bodlo.[11] Though much smaller in scale as compared to the shrine of Lal, it is the second most prominent site of devotion in Sehwan. The first offering is a pilgrim's lyrical tribute to Imam Hussain, the grandson of the Prophet Muhammad. The Punjabi song *Allah wangun sunda Hussain aye* (like Allah listens, listens Hussain) recounts his miraculous attributes and projects him as a figure of petition, one who is attentive and ever-listening. Listening at the same time are other pilgrims gathered at the shrine in the evening hours. To the childless, Hussain grants children, the man sings, and to the needy, Hussain is a patron, their savior. In the verses that follow, Hussain is as much admired for his willingness to battle against odds as he is remembered as a martyr. While the pilgrim sings, puncturing the song, every now and then, is the echo of a fakir in the background who concurrently calls out to Hussain as well as Ali, his father. The ambient buzz of the tomb hall adds sonic depth to the song.

The other recording from the same shrine features the voice of a woman pilgrim. Her late afternoon offering is dedicated to Abbas, the other hero of Karbala and Hussain's half-brother. The Urdu song of praise, *jhukte hain yahan shah bhi* (here surrender the

8 Lal is a hard-to-pin-down historical figure. He bears at least two more competing genealogies in Suhrawardi and Qadiri Sufi traditions, all of which are conversant with the period of his arrival in the region in the late thirteenth century.

9 For a complex and considered relationship between Sufi and Shivaite material heritage in Sehwan, see Boivin (2011).

10 For the purposes of this discussion, I refer to them simply as songs and their recitations as singing. Their Shi'i content is representative of the larger sample I have recorded between 2009 and 2018 and speaks of Sehwan's continuing Shi'i ascendance. I acknowledge that neat separations of what is Shi'i and Sunni in places like Sehwan are hard to maintain.

11 Bodlo is the penultimate disciple of Lal and thus the two sites are materially and discursively conversant with each other. This involves, among other things flows of ritual, relics, offerings, as well as pilgrims.

kings) is equally a tribute to the sacrality of Sehwan. In lyrical terms, it portrays the exemplary valor and devotion of Abbas. He is the figure who as the flag-bearer of Hussain's army at Karbala defends the family of the Prophet until his last breath.

> Your father (Ali) is god's lion, and you, the lion of Karbala!
> Known to remove hardships of whosoever is at your door
> The sky lowers itself just to kiss your *'alam*
> No place in the world equals your door, Abbas!

No place is like the place of Abbas, the woman sings. Abbas, as one might quickly observe in Sehwan, is the most ubiquitously enshrined figure in town. Countless commemorative standards in black (*ʿalam*) are erected on rooftops in Sehwan. In the refrain, *here surrender the kings*, the here of the verse is rendered continuous with the here of the pilgrim. In a stunning confluence of the lyrical and the local, the pilgrim conjures the shrine in Sehwan as the doorstep of Abbas, where all hardships are removed. She closes the offering with chanting aloud the call to Ali.

A third performance from 2011 features a group of pilgrims at the shrine of Lal, Sehwan's primary site of devotion. With the refrain *menu vir di lash te aawan de* (let me approach my brother's corpse), the Seraiki song is a mournful text in the voice of Zainab, the sister of Hussain, who witnesses and survives the tragedy of Karbala. As the lead performer delivers the opening lines, he sets the scene of a dawning catastrophe. Others in the all-male group, can be heard wailing and sobbing before they begin to sing the lament in unison. In this latter part of the text, a bruised Zainab addresses her tormentors to turn their gazes away so that she may come to her brother's corpse, cover his wounds with her *chador*, and recite Koranic verses to him on his final journey. In male voices, Zainab's gendered suffering cuts through the ambient noise of the large tomb-hall, stirring emotions of many in shrine durbar.

A point to take home is possibly a known one: singing to saints, or chanting and crying in sacred presence confirms the common perception that buried Islamic saints are listening bodies. Or, historical-religious figures, otherwise distant, are actively and sensationally in dialogue with the world of the living. More critical, however, is the attendant notion that because Shi'i holy figures are regarded as aurally immediate and intimately sense-able in a place like Sehwan, individual emotive performances exceed their singular salience and so doing reference a collectively lived situation. By this I mean that such individual and impromptu offerings, in their accumulative iterations, accrue greater historical and political charge to the extent that singing and by extension sonic affect for those who listen can open up unordinary pathways to feel, mobilize, or make current Shi'i temporal figurations in an otherwise Sunni public sphere.[12] Singing to, or longing for, Shi'i holy figures under the watchful gaze of the state, one that upholds Sunni majoritarianism, enables a critical intimacy with differently sacred geographies and temporalities. It also points to how such remembering allows believers to enfold unstraight inheritances into the contemporary, especially other or multiple religious

[12] In a study of audiocassette sermons in Cairo, Hirschkind examines the sensibilities and affects of an ethical soundscape tied to the cultivation of a pious life and moral self-fashioning.

histories of Sehwan, which are affectively at odds with Islam or its dominant narrations in Pakistan.[13]

To further sharpen its political implications, it is important to note that these sonicities survive despite governing tactics of the Pakistani state. Religious shrines and saints' places across Pakistan are public institutions after all. The project of nationalizing shrines was initiated in the early 1960s and has since involved confiscating such sites from hereditary custodians and turning these into revenue-generating sites of the state (Malik 1990). In fact, what the modern governance of shrines aims to achieve is a straightening of such shrines' radical, more-than-Islamic and often irreconcilable pasts. One of the ways in which the Department of Auqaf—a subsidiary of the ministry of religious affairs that administers shrines across Pakistan—deals with such unstraight histories is through direct material taming and architectural interventions at shrines. In the case of Sehwan, a systematic removal of Hindu relics from the shrine in the name of renovations over the years is a clear example of the Pakistani state's interest in disciplining the historic narration of the saint as well as defining his heritage in the present (Kasmani 2019). The state's anxieties around religiously complex life-worlds like Sehwan as well as the diverse inheritances these bear forth in the present are discernible in the ways in which shrines are micro-managed in Pakistan (see Ibad 2019; Strothmann 2016). Year after year, the department's constant policing of the shrine environs in Sehwan has included, among other things, painting over risqué, unsettling Shi'i texts on public walls, and replacing these with more shariah-neutral texts like sayings (*hadith*) of the Prophet Muhammad. This is particularly true of radical slogans like "*ya-Ali rabb*," literally "O Ali, god." Remarkably, however, despite its repeated painting over by the shrine administration, the chant, like Shi'i oral texts and offerings in question, thrive in sonic forms across Sehwan's many shrines.[14] My idea that sonic affects are somewhat stubborn draws criticality from Lauren Berlant's statement that "sounds … can change, potentially, how we can understand what being historical means" (2011: 36). The willfulness of sound as queer historical force—in this case the stickiness of Ali-centered texts, Shi'i chants and songs—records what audaciously endures and materially withstands in face of concrete counter measures of the Pakistani state. Bearing witness out loud to Ali as the rightful heir of the Prophet Muhammad, invoking Shi'i holy women such as Zainab in public spheres and a routine summoning of messianic figures or the imam-in-occultation at these shrines by believers upsets neat divisions of the now and the not yet.[15] In other words, such historical remembrance in sacred presence is more than a past-oriented recalling of Shi'i tragedies. Their sounding at state-run shrines, first and foremost, disturbs orders of the present in so long as it produces a critique of the contemporary. It is as much a reminder that public memory can be incongruent to official history. Surpassing

13 On the political geography and possibility of sound, Salomi Voegelin points to a knowledge of the world that lies in sound's invisible contingency even if it can't always be rendered visible (2019: 75).

14 The recordings also reveal that for such offerings to thrive, they have got to be stubborn, insisting on their own possibility amid a multiplicitous sonic-scape.

15 This is not to suggest that all Ali-centered texts always constitute as Shi'i especially because devotion to the figure of Ali is shared across Muslim communities and, in the case of Sehwan, involves also Hindu followers of the saint.

the moment in which these are performed or recorded, mourning in Sehwan, if read in Muñoz's terms (2009), serves also as a mode of desiring. It is to say that sonic-lyrical affects signal not merely backward to Shi'i pasts, in terms of a singular event, the tragedy of Karbala, but more radically to plural conditions and possibilities of a history's unstraight presence in the future. It is precisely this character that lends such religious remembering its queer historical and affective force.

Concluding Thoughts

Is religious sound rightfully queer? Are gay verses of a diasporic poet properly Pakistani? What does it mean to mourn for futures amid a fracturing relation to the historical? How is it to desire in unfinished tongues? In her visceral essay, "Of Dark Rooms and Foreign Languages," Momina Masood makes the powerful contention that "to be a Pakistani today is to know half-languages, to always not find the word, to not understand because it had never been spoken" (2019: 176). The disaffection with language we find in Masood's writing is given through the queer experience of the female body, which, though arising from the intimate, is more properly a critique of the nation-state. It compels us to confront a historical condition, that is, how grammars of desiring, broadly speaking, are circumscribed within, or must be articulated in spite of the foreclosures of expression that remain critical in geographies invented through colonization.[16] In a more recent essay, she notes, "I have no language I can want in," before arriving at the sincere admission, "I'm never certain if what I desire is flesh or its language" (Masood 2020). Her struggles aside, Masood's ruminations on sex and the body involve complex and capacious locations of desire: menstruating girls in schools, the black georgette of *abayas* between bodies in contact, female intimacy at shrines, women lovers in acts of ritual mourning and recitation all evoke a sense of queerness that is not easily expelled from the religious or devoid of the sacred. Be it through a desire for language or a language for desiring, such queerness is wound up with yearnings for historical-affective ground. Desire, then, as is also evident in the two scenes of this chapter, is a search for shared inheritances and long-temporal textures through which a certain mode of being queer, our queerness let's say, can find affective volume in the present. Precisely because here queer history is not a history of gay rights and so on, our affective meanderings from the ambivalence of *Behkawa* to half-languages of postcolony, between sexual desire and religious longing, help us question whether half-ness is always a measure of a thing's wanting, inadequate or approximating character; or, can we take it to understand how conditions of fractured-ness or in-between-ness afford expansive albeit fraught vocabularies?

This essay has pursued an enabling fiction across parallel planes though not in service of restoring a historical subject; neither are the scopes of this text expansive or ambitious enough to repair an entire history. Its labors, however, confirm that certain affective formations, as Kamran Ali (2020: 19) observes in the case of Pakistani

[16] For more on Masood's critique of Pakistan, see "Of Dark Rooms and Foreign Languages" (2019).

women's sexual politics and histories, are only available to us in small fragments. Going forward, we might better understand these as gatherings of unstraight figurations that either evade a fuller knowing when occurring singularly, or which do not historically hang together as one archive. It bears repeating that the intent of this essay has not been so much to dwell on the evasiveness of archives or the impossibility of capture as it has been to embrace the inventiveness that the task of conjuring histories of queer demands of us in encumbered locations such as Pakistan. The contribution here, it follows, is not that queer archives are captured or made visible, rather to question the straight and habituated ways of historical inquiry. In presenting two scenes alongside one another, I have in fact resisted the scholarly urge for comparison or to trace differences or similarities across settings. Ifti Nasim's poetry and the verses sung by devotees at the shrine in Sehwan are no doubt mobilizations of distinct universes. Beside-ness here is in the service of planar not egalitarian relations (Sedgwick 2003: 8), if not also a condition for partial or unstraight connections. Such acts of conjuring, or let's say desiring relations, between and across distinct settings help us appreciate, albeit in ambivalent modes, how forms of in-between-ness signal a disaffection with straight time or trouble its habitual ordering. To the extent that their expressions delineate pathways from conditions of what is to ideas and imaginings of what ought to be, these verses, no matter gay or religious, are queer visions.[17] In their lyrical-affective imaginings of otherwise worlds, they pose a challenge to linear history as much as they refuse to extend shapes of the present.

Being affectively queer is to desire in the way of history: whether driven by religious or sexual longings, no matter how meagre or minoritized each of their iterations, in such appraisal shimmers the hope that we might refuse the occlusion of queerness and by extension of queers in the narration of national and public histories of Pakistan. Such rumination is equally driven by a seduction common to my greater research, that is, to pursue the ways in which queer in the study of Pakistan can be that expansive yet critical instantiation of wilful affect that helps overcome the place's many obstinacies.[18] Put another way, queer hermeneutics serve to unsettle the nation state's dominant or sedimenting constitutions, whether these be conceptual, temporal, or geographical formations. More than anything, queer mobilizations of this essay, no matter wispy, tentative, or unfinished, are affective forces in their own right. These do not repair histories, but rather insist against the tyranny of Pakistan's further straight narration.

Bibliography

Ali, A. 1997. "Farewell," in *The Country without a Post Office*. New York: W. W Norton, 21–3.

[17] On the shared liberative potentials of religion and queer studies, Nikki Young (2017) points to their constant dismantling of temporal boundaries that divide the present (what is) from the future (what might or ought to be).

[18] For more, see introduction in *Queer Companions* (Kasmani 2022).

Ali, K. 2020. "On Female Friendships and Anger," in V. Zamindar and A. Ali (eds.), *Love War and Other Longings: Essays on Cinema in Pakistan*. Karachi: Oxford University Press, 114–30.

Amin, K. 2017. *Disturbing Attachments: Genet, Modern Pederasty, and Queer History*, Durham, NC: Duke University Press.

Arondekar, A. 2020. "The Sex of History, or Object/Matters." *History Workshop Journal* 89 (Spring): 207–13. DOI: 10.1093/hwj/dbz053.

Behkawa. 2002. [TV Serial] Dir. Mazhar Moin. Pakistan: Geo Television Network.

Berlant, L. 2011. *Cruel Optimism*. Durham, NC: Duke University Press.

Boivin, M. 2011. *Artefacts of Devotion: A Sufi Repertoire of the Qalandariyya in Sehwan Sharif, Sindh, Pakistan*. Karachi: Oxford University Press.

Butler, J. 1993. "Critically Queer." *GLQ: A Journal of Lesbian and Gay Studies* 1 (1): 17–32.

Castelli, E. 2017. "Introduction: At the Intersection of Queer Studies and Religion." *Scholar and Feminist Online* 14 (2): n.p.

Halberstam, J. 2005. *In a Queer Time and Place: Transgender Bodies, Subcultural Lives*. New York: New York University Press.

Hirschkind, C. 2006. *The Ethical Soundscape: Cassette Sermons and Islamic Counter Publics*. New York: Columbia University Press.

Ibad, U. 2019. *Sufi Shrines and the Pakistani State: The End of Religious Pluralism*. London: I.B. Tauris. E-book.

Kasmani, O. 2017. "Audible Specters: The Sticky Shia Sonics of Sehwan." *History of Emotions—Insights into Research*, October 2017. DOI: 10.14280/08241.54.

Kasmani, O. 2019. "Pilgrimages of the Dream: On Wings of State in Sehwan Sharif, Pakistan," in B. Rahimi and P. Eshagi (eds.), *Muslim Pilgrimage in the Modern World*. Chapel Hill: University of North Carolina Press, 134–48.

Kasmani, O. 2021. "Thin, Cruisy, Queer: Writing through Affect," in E. Tauber and D. L. Zinn (eds.), *Gender and Genre in Ethnographic Writing*. London: Palgrave Macmillan, 163–88.

Kasmani, O. 2022. *Queer Companions: Religion, Public Intimacy and Saintly Affects in Pakistan*. Durham, NC: Duke University Press.

Khubchandani, K. 2020. "Oral History Interview with Ifti Nasim," *South Asian American Digital Archive (SAADA)*, March 9. https://www.saada.org/item/20200309-6038. Accessed May 7, 2021.

Kohari, A. 2020. "Who's Afraid of Ifti Nasim? The Swashbuckling Life and Legacy of a Pakistani-American Gay Icon." *The Juggernaut*, June 29. https://www.thejuggernaut.com/ifti-nasim. Accessed May 1, 2021.

Malik, J. 1990. "Waqf in Pakistan: Change in Traditional Institutions." *Die Welt des Islams* 30 (1/4): 63–97.

Masood, M. 2020. "Zohra; or How I Learnt to Love and Write the Body." *Kohl: A Journal for Body and Gender Research* 6 (3), December 16. https://kohljournal.press/zohra. Accessed May 7, 2021.

Masood, M. 2019. "Of Dark Rooms and Foreign Languages," in F. Asghar and S. Elhillo (eds.), *Halal If You Hear Me*. Chicago: Haymarket Books, 176–9.

Muñoz, J. E. 2009. *Cruising Utopia: The Then and There of Queer Futurity*. New York: New York University Press.

Nar Narman. 2007. [Film] Dir. Mazhar Zaidi. London: BBC Urdu.

Nasim, I. 2002. *Myrmecophile: Selected Poems, 1980–2000*. N.p.: Xlibris.

Nasim, I. 1994. *Narman* (E-book). https://www.paknovels.com/2017/04/nirman-by-iftikhar-naseem.html. Accessed May 1, 2021.

Rath, A., and Rasheda Parveen. 2015. "The Mating Dance: Love and Exile in Ifti Nasim and Agha Shahid Ali." *Studies in Humanities and Social Sciences* 22 (2): 74–91.

Sedgwick, E. K. 2003. *Touching Feeling: Affect, Pedagogy, Performativity.* Durham, NC: Duke University Press.

Singh, J. 2018. *No Archive Will Restore You*. Montréal, Quebec: 3Ecologies Books.

Strothmann, L. 2016. *Managing Piety: The Shrine of Data Ganj Bakhsh*. Karachi: Oxford University Press.

Swadhin, A. 2011. "Ifti Nasim: Celebrating the Life and Legacy of an Avant-Garde Gay Pakistani American Muslim Activist." *Glaad*, July 29. https://www.glaad.org/2011/07/29/ifti-nasim-celebrating-the-life-and-legacy-of-an-avant-garde-gay-pakistani-american-muslim-activist. Accessed May 7, 2021.

Voegelin, S. 2019. *The Political Possibility of Sound: Fragments of Listening.* New York: Bloomsbury.

Young, N. 2017. "Queer Studies and Religion: Methodologies of Freedom." *Scholar & Feminist Online* 14 (2). Barnard Center for Research on Women. https://sfonline.barnard.edu/queer-studies-and-religion-methodologies-of-freedom/

9

Gatherings of Contemplation: Performing Other Histories in Pakistan's Sufi Shrines

Amen Jaffer

In the Islamic Sufi tradition, shrines commemorate the memory of departed saints and offer a physical portal to access their blessings. They are revered as sacred sites animated by saintly spiritual presence and are usually constructed around the tombs where saints' bodies lie buried.[1] In contemporary Pakistan, these shrines vary considerably in terms of size, scale, and significance ranging from a small, marked-off corner in a private residence, known only to a few, to grand complexes that draw millions of visitors and pilgrims and attract the patronage of governments and elites (Philippon 2014). While frequented by a diverse range of social groups, the vast majority of visitors to shrines belong to the lower rungs of the economic ladder and a significant number hail from socially marginalized castes and gender communities.

Over the past nine years, while studying this institution from the vantage point of these "ordinary" visitors in urban Pakistan, I have been repeatedly struck by the seemingly incongruent ways in which the past surfaces in the stories and conversations that I witness in these spaces. There are two common ways in which this happens. One is during the recounting of miracles of saints that seem to exist in multiple temporal registers. A story may begin with the birth of a saint in the thirteenth century, dwell on a miracle of the same saint in the colonial period, and then end up with the saint's presence in the present moment. Second, the everyday sociality forged in gatherings of visitors and devotees in these shrines appears to repeatedly bypass the present. Comprising individuals and groups from diverse socioeconomic backgrounds, these social exchanges are a site for cultivating a contemplative sensibility that tends to be removed from the here and now as participants frequently step out of their immediate temporality to communicate, reflect on, and interpret various memories and experiences from their past.

There is now an established tradition in South Asian scholarship of examining Sufi hagiographical texts, *Tadkhiras* and *Malfuzat*,[2] for their historiographical value.

[1] This is not a general rule, however, and on occasions shrines are built around sites where a saint was physically present for some time or around their objects of personal use. But even such shrines have a grave-like mound in their center that serves as a symbolic stand-in for a grave.

[2] *Tadkhiras* are memorials or compendia of biographical notes of Sufi saints that are usually compiled after their death, while *Malfuzat* are contemporary records of the religious teachings and memoirs of Sufi masters that are compiled by their disciples (Steinfels 2004: 57).

Scholars have also turned to works of Sufi poetry and fiction for understanding the historical imaginations of their authors, performers, and audiences.[3] However, the sensibilities of "ordinary" devotees in Pakistan, who lack training in any Sufi or literary tradition but have deep relations with Sufi saints and their shrines, cannot be gleaned from these sources. To excavate their alternative historical disposition, I suggest that we instead turn to the social gatherings that regularly take place in Sufi shrines across Pakistan. I am particularly interested in wayside shrines in Lahore that are generally missing from the historiography of the city. Lacking any significant state patronage or association with influential figures, such shrines are usually located in neighborhoods and graveyards across the city and may only be known to locals who frequent them in their everyday life. Their relative anonymity allows these shrines to escape significant scrutiny and emerge as an enclave for devotees, many of whom may themselves have a marginal status in their communities. Importantly, they offer space for these devotees to express and give meaning to their memories and experiences and in the process collectively construct alternative accounts of their neighborhoods and communities.

I am not suggesting that such discourses are disconnected from dominant frameworks of history and politics; rather they are forged from continuous confrontations between hegemonic histories, nationalist among others, and attempts to give meaning to everyday experiences of subaltern lives in the city. Such an approach responds to the call for pluralizing peoples' history issued by Asad Ali and Kamran Asdar Ali in the introduction to this volume. They argue that such histories do not just challenge nationalist historiography by telling different stories of the "people" but can also highlight "their differing temporalities, that is their experience of time, of the relations between past, present and future which is crucial to their historical consciousness." This essay demonstrates an alternative to the linear, empty, and homogeneous time that undergirds modern history and the nation by highlighting the historical disposition and sensibilities that are cultivated in the various social exchanges that happen in Sufi shrines. These include conversations; debates; collective preparation and consumption of food, drink, and drugs; tending to plants and pigeons; and performing prayers and Sufi rituals—but their primary site is storytelling. As I demonstrate, the contemplative sensibility and imagination of storytelling as a mode of engaging with the past does not obey the rules of modern temporality and hence often, though not always, ends up traversing the assumptions and conclusions of dominant histories.

At the same time, social exchanges in Sufi shrines are themselves wrought with contentions. While they offer mutual care and reciprocity, participants of these gatherings also treat them as a site for establishing and enhancing their social status and seeking upward mobility in the hierarchical communities associated with Sufi shrines. They are constantly jostling for position and projecting their own voice and perspective in these encounters. Thus, the historical narratives that are produced and reproduced in these settings not only face serious scrutiny and even rejection but also find support and wide circulation. It is within this complex social exchange that alternative historical sensibilities are forged and put to work in shaping a fragile and continuously shifting

[3] See Mir (2010) for an analysis of the Punjabi historical imagination through *qissa* literature.

"archive of the everyday" (Snehi 2019: 202).[4] In the rest of this essay, I focus on the assembling of this "archive" through giving meaning to memories by posing three key questions to this process: What are the distinctive practices in these shrines that create a different experience of time? How do individuals and groups that have otherwise limited agency in authoring the past collectively imagine, interpret, and re-signify history? How does participating in social gatherings and exchanging stories in shrines enable the cultivation of an alternative historical imagination and disposition? I approach these questions by combining an examination of the discourses weaved by storytelling with an analysis of the social form in which these stories are exchanged.

In recent years, there has been a welcome trend of micro-level studies in scholarship on Sufi shrines in South Asia that situate their analysis in everyday life and focus on the experiences of devotees and visitors. This emphasis has revealed important insights into a variety of social processes that unfold in this institution including assertion of national and religious identity (Rozehnal 2007; Umashankar 2012), cross-religious use of space (Bellamy 2012), localization of Islam (Mohammad 2013), functioning and reproduction of multireligious communities (Bigelow 2010), formation of postcolonial subjectivity (Ewing 1997), forging of transnational and global linkages (Werbner 2003), creation of women's space (Flueckiger 2006; Pemberton 2010; Pfleiderer 2006), and the practice of a precolonial cosmology and ethics (Taneja 2018). These studies reveal Sufi shrines as dynamic, transformative spaces that perform a variety of social, cultural, and political functions, which are interwoven with the cultivation and practice of Islam. Nonetheless, even though many of these studies pay careful attention to everyday life, they have generally ignored social activities as a site for the cultivation of sensibilities and circulation of discourse. I approach such social activities, primary among them storytelling, by first examining the social context of the Sufi shrines in which these activities are taking place. To do so, let me introduce the urban ecology of Khawaja Bihari, a Sufi shrine first established in the Moghul era, which will serve as the primary case study for this essay.

Locating the Temporality of Khawaja Bihari

Back in 2013, I visited Ghazal in her one-room residence in Mian Mir Colony, Lahore, to interview her about her connection with Sufi saints and their shrines. During our conversation, she spoke at length about crafting her identity as a transgendered person, a *khawaja sara*,[5] through her participation in the public culture of Sufi shrines. Almost all the shrines she mentioned as significant for her—Bibi Pak Daman, Madho Lal Hussain, Barri Imam—were already known to me as important centers of *khawaja sara* devotional and cultural life. However, I had not heard of Khwaja Bihari's shrine,

[4] Drawing from Harjit Oberoi's (1994) seminal treatment of popular shrines in Punjab as sites of subaltern lived agency, Snehi presents the expression of beliefs and practices in Sufi shrines in Indian Punjab as a living archive of everyday meanings. Such an archive records the voices and forms of expression that are inaudible for state and bureaucratic archives (Pemberton 2010; Taneja 2018).

[5] *Khawaja sara* are legally recognized as transgender in Pakistan. Those identifying with this nonbinary gender category are members of non-natal kin structures.

which was located near Ghazal's residence. Ghazal explained that it was a "local" shrine and not especially well known among *khawaja sara* circles. She sometimes stopped by it on her way home to say a prayer or to pay a visit to a *khawaja sara malangni*,[6] who was a committed devotee of the saint and often found on his shrine's premises. When I inquired further about Khwaja Bihari, Ghazal offered to take me there and introduce me to the *malangni* as she would be able to give me "authentic knowledge" about this saint.

While our journey to this shrine only lasted a few minutes, it did involve crossing a set of railroad tracks. Mian Mir Pind, where this shrine was located, was on the other side of the tracks from Ghazal's place. Once a historic village, it had now become a very crowded and highly urbanized neighborhood. These tracks acted as a barrier between the two densely populated neighborhoods located on its either side, but the point at which we crossed, they appeared more like a series of porous lines. The fencing of this section of the tracks had fallen apart to the point of complete irrelevance and like many around us, we also leisurely strolled over the tracks and onward to Khwaja Bihari. Though I did not think much of them at the time, I was soon to become aware of the significance of these tracks to this locality.

As we approached the shrine, the narrow lane we were walking along suddenly expanded into a wide road that in turn opened into a sizable square with several large, shady trees that felt like the center of this locality. The tomb of Khwaja Bihari, an elaborate structure, adorned with ornate floral motifs and a large dome in the Moghul style, stood almost at the center of this space. There was a large mosque behind it with a tall minaret jutting from it, a smaller tomb painted a deep green at the base of the stairs leading to Bihari's tomb and a double-storey building on the other side of the stairs. Ghazal led me around the shrine in search of her *malangni* acquaintance, but she was nowhere to be found. While wandering around the double-story building, which had the grave of a female saint,[7] a women's congregation space and a rest area for pilgrims within it, we ran into a small group of men who were lounging in an upstairs hall engaged in a discussion about the job prospects of auto mechanics. Ishaaq, the youngest among them, had just joined this trade a few days ago but was not entirely convinced of its viability, while the others tried to persuade him to stick with it for some time. We were warmly invited to join their small circle and offered cigarettes and tea by way of hospitality. One of the older men, Raja, introduced himself as an avid devotee of Khwaja Bihari and was quite excited to discover that I was interested in learning about his *pir* (spiritual guide). He immediately took me under his wing and offered to share Bihari's numerous stories and miracles. Raja was a local of Mian Mir Pind and his family had lived there for several generations. However, despite having a family home in the area, he was now residing on the premises of this shrine and claimed that he had dedicated his life to serving his saint.

6 *Malangni* or *malang* are antinomian renunciants who reject society to dedicate themselves to serving God. Most of them attach themselves to specific Sufi shrines or wander from one to another.

7 I later discovered that this was the grave of Bibi Jamal Khatun (d. 1057/1647), a sister of Mian Mir, and a Sufi saint in her own right (Ernst 2010).

Our conversation then turned to the biography of Khwaja Bihari. Raja led the way in introducing him but others in the circle also chimed in, including Ghazal who was quiet at first but warmed to the subject. From this collective recounting, I gathered that Khwaja Bihari had lived in the sixteenth and seventeenth centuries. Originally from Bihar, he traveled all the way to Lahore to become a disciple and student of Mian Mir, a preeminent saint of his era who belonged to the Qadiri lineage. Bihari rose among the ranks of Mian Mir's large circle of students and had become one of his most important *khalifas*[8] when he passed away in the early seventeenth century. An indication of his stature was that his tomb was built under the patronage of the Moghul prince Dara Shikoh (also a devotee of Mian Mir), on a similar pattern to that of Mian Mir though smaller in scale. After this brief introduction, the conversation shifted to Bihari's miracles. I was a little surprised when Raja inquired if we had heard about the miracle of the train. Such an event just did not cohere with my own linear, chronological understanding of history in which the railway only arrived in Lahore in the nineteenth century (Glover 2008), at least two centuries after this saint's death. However, no one else in this circle seem to share my concerns as they nodded approvingly at Raja's telling of this story.

The tale began with the coming of the British colonial Raj to Punjab and the laying of an extensive rail network in the region. Lahore was an important hub in this new transportation network but not all residents of the city were happy with this rumbling, noisy intervention into their lives. The residents of Mian Mir Pind were especially perturbed at this intrusion as the trains not only passed perilously close to them, shaking the entire neighborhood, but also bifurcated their locality, disconnecting them from Mian Mir's shrine and other nearby areas that were now on the other side of these tracks. One day, Nathay Shah Deewan, a disciple of Mian Mir, was walking from this neighborhood to Mian Mir's shrine to offer his prayers with a Quran in his hands, when a train sped by almost frightening him to death. On seeing this, Mian Mir was quite incensed and sent a message to Khwaja Bihari to the effect that I have bestowed you with my *jalal* (spiritual rigor, awe-inspiring majesty)[9] and yet my followers are not safe in your territory.

On hearing this complaint from his revered spiritual master, Khwaja Bihari immediately sprang into action. He walked over to the tracks, where another train was approaching in the distance, and simply held out an outstretched palm toward it. The speeding locomotive immediately came to a screeching halt. Despite all the efforts of the driver and railway staff, the train refused to budge an inch. Engineers and technicians from all corners of the British Indian Empire were called over but none could figure out the mysterious paralysis of this train. Finally, an older employee of the Indian Railways figured that since there was no rational explanation some supernatural force must be at work here. On enquiring from the locals about any *baba ji* (spiritual elder) living in the vicinity, he was directed to Khwaja Bihari. He then approached Bihari with some of the senior members of the city's administration to beg for his forgiveness and request

[8] *Khalifa* is the highest rank of a Sufi disciple who are given the authority to represent their teacher and transmit their teachings.

[9] Many Sufi followers that I have come across in Pakistan understand *jalal* as a supernatural power.

him to release the train.[10] Bihari acquiesced but on the condition that the train will no longer disturb the residents of his locality. The representatives of the colonial state readily agreed, and the wheels of the train started turning again. Raja claimed that since that day every train that approached this neighborhood slows down in respect of Khwaja Bihari, and some of the older and knowledgeable drivers even blow their horn to demonstrate reverence to the saint.

Even though Raja and the others telling the story do not consider the historical ascription of this story to be incoherent, it will not pass muster for mainstream history given its chronological crime of making a Moghul-era saint intercept a colonial train. Therefore, a case needs to be made for qualifying this discourse of a saint existing in multiple eras as historical. To do so, I turn to Reinhart Koselleck (2018), who views history as a combination of structures of repetition and novel ruptures from this cycle; discerning the new from the return of the old then becomes the primary task of the student of history. Defining history as the "science of experience" (4), he proposes that at any given moment in time, different layers of historical experience coexist. The gradual accretion of past repetitions creates multiple historical layers or sediments that continuously interact with each other to shape the present.

Such a view of history offers interesting insights into devotees' imagination of Khawaja Bihari. In the stories shared at his shrine, Bihari's persona is based on events that took place at some time in the past, but he is not understood as a figure of some distant past. For many devotees, Sufi saints do not die or leave this world but simply transform their state. For example, Faryaad Saeen recounted to me that his saint, Shah Jamal, never died but simply walked into a tunnel and never reemerged. His tomb in Lahore was not built around his grave but on top of the entrance to this tunnel. For Faryaad and many other devotees, their saints go behind a *purdah* (veil), which renders them invisible, but they continue to be present and can observe and intervene in the goings on in their shrines. They can even reveal themselves and engage with devotees and visitors to their shrines if they wish to do so. This view of Sufi saints as eternal also resonates with a key theological concept in Sufism that places "death before dying" as the goal of the mystical path. Based on a saying attributed to Prophet Muhammad, Sufis seek mystical death, that is the annihilation of the self and its subsumption into the Divine, before physical death (Elias 1998). In embracing this mystical death, Sufi saints escape the restraints of time.

Many devotees understand the eternity of Sufi saints through their shrines, which are a place of memory, a physical reminder, and an entry point into the lives and teachings of the saints. Sufi shrines, however, do not merely commemorate saints but also represent a continuity of their person into the present. They are a physical container for saintly presence in the contemporary moment. In other words, they are a physical form of the saint.[11] Nile Green (2012: 3) describes the spatial process of enshrinement as an "architectural embodiment of collective memory—[that] served

[10] In another version of this story narrated to me in August 2021 by Khalid, another resident of Mian Mir Pind, all the passengers of the train, rather than colonial officials, disembarked and approached Khwaja Bihari for forgiveness.

[11] It should be noted though that this saintly presence is not spread evenly across the physical space of shrines. It is most concentrated in their tomb and radiates outward from it, decreasing in potency the further one goes from it. However, as related to me by Khalid, a devotee of Khwaja Bihari, saints

to bridge the past and present time of his followers." These eternal, timeless saints, existing in the physical form of Sufi shrines, can be understood as a collection of the memories of saints as well as the experiences of their followers and visitors that have been gathered over time. This layered form of Sufi shrines is thus composed of sediments of time that include both repetitions, such as the performance of prayers and other rituals at specific times of the day, week, month, and year, and ruptures, such as Bihari's miraculous intervention in freezing a speeding train. It is the interlinkages between the cyclical structures and the novel events that disrupt them, which define the historicity of storytelling and other acts of imagining Khwaja Bihari that are performed in his shrine.

This understanding of the historicity of a saint is markedly different from the nationalist historiography promoted by the Pakistani state, which presents Sufi saints as founders of the Muslim nation in South Asia. In this linear view of history, Sufis laid the basis for Pakistan by bringing Islam to India and converting Hindus en masse to their religion (Ewing 1983). However, this narrative dismisses the significance of Sufi saints or their shrines in the present because it insists that they have been replaced by the Pakistani state, which is the only legitimate upholder of the Islam introduced by past saints.[12] While this nationalist narrative has been debunked by several historians for its inaccuracies (Eaton 2000, 2009), Faryaad and Raja offer an alternative model for historicizing Sufi saints. For them, their saints exist outside linear time. As we have seen, Khawaja Bihari can be in different time periods and can stitch different slices of time together (Foucault 1986). Such an understanding of Sufi saints allows devotees to inhabit a temporal arrangement in which not only their past and present but also their future is animated by saintly presences that are unbound from the linear progression of calendars and clocks.

Following Koselleck's (2018) insistence on the political importance of history to the present, we can also consider the invocation of history in Khawaja Bihari's miracle as an attempt to offer an alternative reading of the present. This is a present in which railway tracks feature quite prominently in the lives of those living and working in Mian Mir Pind. One of the main railway routes of Pakistan that connects Lahore to Peshawar in the west and to Karachi all the way in the south passes adjacent to this neighborhood. These busy tracks serve as a border for this locality and act as a barrier between it and the shrine of Mian Mir, which is the principal shrine of this part of Lahore. Historically related to Mian Mir, Mian Mir Pind probably emerged because of the economic and religious activity around his shrine.[13] Disconnecting it from the shrine must have dealt a serious blow to the socioeconomic status of its inhabitants. It also severed the spiritual kingdom of Mian Mir and his disciples with the speeding

are able to transform themselves into a lamp or other objects, hence one should treat everything in such sacred spaces with due deference.

12 The Pakistani state takes on the mantle of protecting and promoting Islam through its laws and institutions from the Sufi saints who are no longer required.

13 According to Latif (2005: 178), this village used to be a garden known as Alamganj that was attached to the shrine of Mullah Shah, another *khalifa* of Mian Mir. These gardens were converted into a village in the latter half of the eighteenth century.

trains running between Mian Mir and Khwaja Bihari's shrines loudly proclaiming another power, that of the colonial state.

Recent historiographies of colonial Indian railways have emphasized their role as a social, cultural, and ideological tool of imperial power. Numerous scholars have highlighted their importance to projects of empire- and state-building by demonstrating their role in the uneven production of space in colonial India (Ahuja 2009; Goswami 2010). As Khan (2006) has argued, transport infrastructures are also designed to delineate and transform the relation between the state and its subjects. However, such state projects of shaping subjects' sensibilities also impinge on the territory of Sufi institutions. The commotion created by the passing trains, described as worse than an earthquake by residents of this locality, is clearly disruptive of the otherworldly, devotional dispositions that Sufi shrines are designed to cultivate in their visitors. The train thus serves as both a conceptual and sensorial challenge to the modes of thinking and being that visitors to shrines are encouraged to inhabit. Khwaja Bihari's miraculous intervention neutralizes this threat by transmuting the train's disruption into a single horn of acknowledgment.

To understand the temporality structured by the train and contrast it with that of Bihari's shrine, it is helpful to turn to Bakhtin's (2008) concept of the chronotope, which he uses to understand distinct configurations of time and space in texts. Presenting chronotope as a category of perceiving and understanding things, Bakhtin employs it to distinguish different social settings as well as views of the world (Steinby 2013: 107). As Morson and Emerson (1990: 268) point out, "different social activities are also defined by various kinds of fused time and space: the rhythms and spatial organization of the assembly line, agricultural labor, sexual intercourse, and parlor conversation differ markedly." Constantly moving forward at a rapid speed, the train can be viewed as a representative chronotope for the space-time configuration of modernity. Governed by the precision of the gauge and the clock, it traverses space and time that have been reconceived into discrete and standardized measurements. This requires configuring time as empty, homogenous, standardized (Benjamin 2012), and progressively moving forward—a configuration that is also critical to imagining the modern nation (Anderson 1983).

For the residents of Mian Mir Pind, the schedule-governed and clock-dictated temporality of the train brings a predictability to the experience of time in their everyday lives. The regular appearances of trains according to a predetermined schedule becomes a metronome for marking duration around which daily activities are conducted. However, submitting to the train's schedule can also prove quite deadly as was the case for four local men who were killed by a speeding train in August 2021. These men were hanging out on a train track,[14] the train schedule so ingrained into their habitus that they felt at ease with such proximity to speeding locomotives. Since no train traffic was scheduled to pass on this particular track at this hour, the men ignored the sound and fury of an oncoming train as it was scheduled to run on a parallel track. However, this train had been diverted onto the track where the men

[14] It is a common practice for locals to hang out and socialize on and around these train tracks as they are one of the few open spaces in this highly congested locality.

were sitting but by the time, they realized this, it was already too late for them. Clearly then the temporal order represented by the train is one that remains outside the control of residents, and they have little choice but to submit to its tempo and rhythm.

Passing Things By in the City

Rooted in an entirely different chronotope from the one represented by the train, I have argued that stories of saintly miracles offer an alternative temporality for imagining history and relating it to the present. It is important to reiterate that this historical imagination is spatially moored in the space of Sufi shrines and specifically in the social gatherings around storytelling that take place there. Therefore, I now turn to these gatherings, elaborate the context in which they are embedded and the form they take to demonstrate the ways in which an alternative historical sensibility and disposition flourishes in them. As I have related, Khawaja Bihari's shrine is situated at the center of Mian Mir Pind and serves not just as its spatial nucleus but is also the social headquarters of this neighborhood. Groups of elderly men regularly meet under a large banyan tree on its premises; teams of young boys play cricket and other games at all hours of the day in the open space around the tomb; and groups of younger men frequently convene in one of the rooms or the many open spaces in and around the shrine. Besides its centrality to everyday social life, Bihari's shrine is also a key site for local politics. In fact, influence and standing in the affairs of the shrine is viewed as critical to establishing status and power in this locality. This indicates that it stands as a central symbol of this community and spending money or performing service for it is a gauge of one's commitment to the community. Finally, the largest festival of this locality is Khawaja Bihari's *urs* when the entire neighborhood comes together and contributes resources to celebrate his death anniversary. Clearly then, Khawaja Bihari's shrine lies at the heart of the social, political, and cultural life of this community and is quite critical to its maintenance and continuity.

However, despite such a prominent role in the community, the architecture of Khawaja Bihari's shrine, like many sacred sites across many religions, is designed to shut out external stimulation, to act as a shield against the city and encourage visitors to focus on otherworldly concerns. Many shrines in Pakistan are located within graveyards to promote this sense of detachment but even those, such as Bihari's, that are in the middle of busy neighborhoods or marketplaces share a degree of disconnection from their immediate surroundings. With their dark rooms penetrated by a few beams of light and strategically placed walls, they are designed to focus attention inward and to block out the outside environment visually and sonically. Shrines thus occupy a contrasting position within Lahore's urban milieu. On the one hand, they are very much central to the fabric of urban life and serve important social and political functions in the city, but on the other, they promote a distance from the world. This location allows the emergence of a sociality that is very much a part of the urban fabric but also quite distinctive from other spheres of urban life. While shrines serve as an urban public that invites various groups in the city to enter a dialogue, at the same time these exchanges have an intimate and private character. This contrast explains the appeal of these shrines as well as the socially aware yet contemplative sensibilities and dispositions that can develop from participating in this institution.

Turning to the storytelling gatherings that regularly take place in little-known Sufi shrines, a casual observer may see them as a mechanism to while away the hours with participants having little invested in them. There is certainly a tendency in the sociality of shrines, especially in gatherings for telling stories, to supplement practical, goal-oriented interaction with social exchanges that "pass things by."[15] They drift away from the concerns of everyday reality because they are temporally and spatially removed from the here and now and instead focus on other times and places. They allow participants to step out of their immediate surroundings and reflect and interpret various episodes of their own and others' lives. There is a marked inclination to invoke the past, to slip into a storytelling mode that forces participants to imagine and engage with a variety of characters, settings and events that are located at a distance from the world they usually inhabit.

What makes this social space of storytelling unique is that grand accounts of saintly miracles and supernatural deeds are interwoven with "ordinary" tales of everyday life. In fact, most of the stories shared in this setting are not concerned with Sufi saints or other overtly Islamic themes, but they rather recall and dramatize past events and memories from the lives of the storytellers. Participants tell stories of travel in different parts of the country. Men who have worked in Gulf countries recount tales of run-ins with the police there; a migrant from a village recalls catching fish in a pristine river that has now turned into a polluted sewage channel. Instead of looking to the future, this storytelling encourages reflection on memories and experiences. Rather than speeding to a clearly defined and predetermined destination, life unfolds slowly and without any coherent goal or purpose in these gatherings. The structuring of time in these storytelling gatherings stands in direct contrast to the temporal order established by the trains that speed by Mian Mir Pind. Khwaja Bihari's miracle of halting the train can thus be read as a metaphor for the suspension of the conceptual hegemony of modern linear time. By first stopping it and then slowing it down, he forces the train to conform to the temporality of the gatherings that take place at his shrine.

On the evening of August 27, 2021, I was part of one such gathering in Shahanshah Wali's dera,[16] a small plot of land just across the road from the tomb of Khwaja Bihari. The small group of six men gathered here included Raja, who was now working as a driver for a wealthy businessman's second wife and living in a one-room quarter with his wife and only child in his employer's house in Eden City, a new housing development near Lahore's airport. Despite having to travel around 14 kilometers each way, he still regularly attended gatherings around Bihari's shrine. As we settled on two charpoys, facing each other, our conversation turned to Khwaja Bihari's first meeting with Mian Mir. Terming it the miracle of the *naan* (flat bread) and fish,

15 I borrow this phrase from AbdouMaliq Simone's comments on my presentation of an earlier version of this essay at the Everyday Urbanisms workshop in March, 2018, at LUMS. Also see Simone (2015).

16 Shahanshah Wali was a Sufi saint whose shrine is located near the Walled City of Lahore. This plot served as his *dera* or gathering spot. Some of his friends who were part of his gatherings are buried here.

Raja confidently launched into a historicized description of Khwaja Bihari as a rich ruler of Bihar who was traveling with his army across Punjab many centuries ago.[17] While his army was carrying a lot of treasure, they had run out of food and were desperately looking for something to eat when they came across Mian Mir's *langar khana* (community kitchen) outside Lahore. On being apprised of the situation of the starving army, Mian Mir placed a piece of naan and a piece of fish in a tray, covered it with a cloth, and instructed the head of his *langar khana* to feed the army with it. Considering this little food to be insufficient for a single man, let alone an entire army, the men were astonished to find an unending supply of pieces of naan and fish emerging from Mian Mir's tray. Meanwhile, Khwaja Bihari, who had been observing this miracle unfold from a distance the whole time, was so taken by it that he ordered his younger brother to return to Bihar with his army and to distribute all his wealth among the people there. He had decided to abandon his worldly possessions and title to follow the Sufi path under the discipleship of Mian Mir.

Just as Raja was finishing his story, Haji sahab, an elderly man who worked for a small newspaper publisher, quipped that naan and fish blessed by the hands of Mian Mir was one thing, one cannot even get an authentic bottle of Coca-Cola these days. Even before the laughter at this interjection had subsided, Nadeem, a middle-aged man who was about to start a new job in a restaurant's kitchen, had launched into his own tale of frauds in Lahore. About twenty years ago, while working as a bus conductor, he came across a roadside lemonade vendor, who was notorious for overcharging gullible travelers at his stall outside the Lahore Railway Station. Khalid, who had previously worked as a house painter but was currently unemployed, then chimed in that some fifteen years ago, when he and his friends had just been released from jail, they also got into an altercation with a refreshment vendor who tried to cheat them by not returning the correct change for the amount they had tendered for their drinks. In both stories, our storytellers emerged as heroic actors. Nadeem managed to rescue a poor, old villager from the clutches of the lemonade vendor by using a mix of entreatments and threats that finally forced the vendor to return the old man's money. Khalid delivered physical blows upon the fraudster to make him see the error of his ways and extracted justice by getting his correct change.

While other stories of evil men and the heroic comeuppance delivered to them by the storyteller protagonist continued to be shared in this gathering, there was no further mention of Khwaja Bihari or any other saint after the initial recounting of the naan and fish miracle. Nonetheless, the shadow of the saint hung over this gathering throughout these exchanges. This could be felt in the temporal space that was created by these stories. Besides a few sporadic reminders of the present, such as when tea was being served, this entire evening appeared to take place in other times. The vivid details and the reflective language for analyzing long-ago events, along with the leisurely rhythm and long pauses that characterized our interactions further added to this distance from immediate reality. Inviting participants into collectively forged spaces of imagination and reflection engendered a palpable sense of experiencing different worlds but also of encountering the inner life of each other. I would therefore claim that participating

[17] Notice that this is rather different from the earlier characterization of Khwaja Bihari as a spiritual seeker who had come to Lahore for Mian Mir's tutelage.

in the social practice of exchanging such stories encourages the cultivation of a contemplative sensibility that in turn promotes an alternative disposition to history.

Conclusion

How does the temporal disposition that one finds in everyday storytelling in Sufi shrine connect the past to the present? Approaching this question by linking the subject matter of these "ordinary" stories to the "timeless" miracles of Sufi saints presents a hurdle since they appear far removed from each other. Furthermore, unlike the accounts of saints, they do not challenge the modern conception of temporality and hence cannot be classified as representative of an alternative historical imagination. Nonetheless there are important connections between them that go beyond the fact that they are exchanged in the same social space. Following Benjamin (2012), one can understand storytelling as the exchange of experiences of distant places or distant times. Unlike information, which is understandable in itself, stories do not explain but rather invite their audiences to interpret them in different ways. Storytelling thus retains a certain germinative power to subtly shape the subjectivity of its participants. For the men gathered in Khwaja Bihari's shrine, the weaving together of saints and fraudsters can be seen as a vehicle for articulating their moral vision of society and seeking to imprint it upon others. This is achieved by establishing a series of contrasts between their personal worldly experiences and the milieu of the saints in their storytelling. For example, the generosity of Mian Mir and Khwaja Bihari is contrasted with the profit-at-all-cost mentality of a roadside vendor.

Clearly, the actors participating in Sufi shrine gatherings are not actually dwelling in the past. Rather, their invocation of memory is directed toward staking a claim on the present as well as imagining other possibilities for their futures. By encouraging collective sharing and reflection on experience, storytelling in Sufi shrines offers an interpretive space that is engendered by the presence of saints and takes shape in their shadows. While the actual plot and characters of the stories shared in these gatherings may be ultimately irrelevant for participants, they nonetheless have important social investments in these exchanges. This is revealed in the structure of many of the stories that are performed in these gatherings. There is a marked tendency in them to highlight the storyteller, to showcase their bravery and guts, to project their heroic exploits in standing up to power, to announce their generosity and dedication to saints. They seek to make their reputation and enhance their status in these performances by putting their masculinity, piety, bravado, and wit on display but also link themselves to the moral integrity of the saints. The significance of presenting these memories thus partly lies in investing seemingly distant narratives, events, and actors with the power to define relationships and power dynamics in the present. At the same time, these stories also showcase their narrators' imagination of alternative futures. In her interpretation of the chronotope, Steinby (2013: 122) associates it with "the specific spatio-temporal form of a certain possibility of human action." For men like Raja, Khalid, and Nadeem, who are struggling in dead-end jobs or languishing in unemployment, telling these stories offers a mechanism for reminding themselves and each other about other possibilities for their lives. By invoking the miracles of their saints and interweaving them with tales that showcase their own strength, heroism, and abilities to transform the world, these men hold onto the possibilities of another life.

This essay has suggested that in order to understand people's history in Pakistan, it is not sufficient to just examine the content of subaltern historical discourses but also to pay attention to the social mechanisms and context through which such discourses are constantly produced and reproduced. It has demonstrated that the content of storytelling must be viewed in conjunction with the form of the gatherings in which these stories are shared. Such an approach reveals a distinct chronotope that flourishes in this institution and allows for the emergence of alternative historical imaginations and dispositions. Even though wayside shrines hold little interest for histories of the Pakistani nation and are generally ignored by them, they are quite central to defining the temporal subjectivity of the individuals and communities attached to them. They not only perform important public functions for these communities but also encourage them to turn away from the outside world and cultivate a contemplative sensibility for relating to it. Ignoring immediate concerns and stimulations and instead conjuring up memories and miracles that are presented and represented in their stories allows them to creatively piece together a different history and to imagine other possibilities for their present and future that are not just rooted in the nation. It also allows them to reject the dominant history of their locality and offer an alternative narrative that suspends the state through invoking the spiritual powers of their saints.

Bibliography

Ahuja, Ravi. 2009. *Pathways of Empire: Circulation, Public Works and Social Space in Colonial Orissa, c. 1780–1914*. Hyderabad: Orient Black Swan.

Anderson, Benedict. 1983. *Imagined Communities: Reflections on the Origin and Spread of Nationalism*. London: Verso.

Anjum, Tanvir. 2011. *Chishti Sufis in the Sultanate of Delhi, 1190–1400: From Restrained Indifference to Calculated Defiance*. Karachi: Oxford University Press.

Aquil, Raziuddin. 2012. *Sufism, Culture, and Politics: Afghans and Islam in Medieval North India*. New Delhi: Oxford University Press.

Bacchetta, Paola. 2000. "Sacred Space in Conflict in India: The Babri Masjid Affair." *Growth and Change* 31 (2): 255–84.

Bakhtin, Mikhail. [1981] 2008. "Forms of Time and of the Chronotope in the Novel: Towards a Historical Poetics," in Caryl Emerson and Michael Holquist (trans.), Michael Holquist (ed.), *The Dialogic Imagination*. Austin: University of Texas Press, 84–258.

Bellamy, Carla. 2011. *The Powerful Ephemeral: Everyday Healing in an Ambiguously Islamic Place*. Berkeley: University of California Press.

Benjamin, Walter. 2012. *Illuminations: Essays and Reflections*. New York: Schocken Books.

Bigelow, Anna. 2010. *Sharing the Sacred: Practicing Pluralism in Muslim North India*. New York: Oxford University Press.

Eaton, Richard Maxwell. 2009. "Shrines, Cultivators, and Muslim 'Conversion' in Punjab and Bengal, 1300–1700." *Medieval History Journal* 12 (2): 191–220.

Eaton, Richard Maxwell. 2000. *Essays on Islam and Indian History*. New Delhi: Oxford University Press.
Elias, Jamal J. 1998. *Death before Dying: The Sufi Poems of Sultan Bahu*. Berkeley: University of California Press.
Ernst, Carl W. 2010. "Bībī Jamāl Khātūn," in K. Fleet, G. Krämer, D. Matringe, J. Nawas, and E. Rowson (eds.), *Encyclopedia of Islam, THREE*. Leiden: Brill. http://dx.doi.org/10.1163/1573-3912_ei3_COM_23436. Accessed September 27, 2021.
Ewing, Katherine Pratt. 1983. "The Politics of Sufism: Redefining the Saints of Pakistan." *Journal of Asian Studies* 42 (2): 251–68.
Ewing, Katherine Pratt. 1997. *Arguing Sainthood: Modernity, Psychoanalysis, and Islam*. Durham, NC: Duke University Press.
Flueckiger, Joyce Burkhalter. 2006. *In Amma's Healing Room: Gender and Vernacular Islam in South India*. Bloomington: Indiana University Press.
Foucault, Michel. 1986. "Of Other Spaces," Jay Miskowiec (trans.). *Diacritics* 16 (1): 22–7.
Glover, William J. 2008. *Making Lahore Modern: Constructing and Imagining a Colonial City*. Minneapolis: University of Minnesota Press.
Goswami, Manu. 2010. *Producing India: From Colonial Economy to National Space*. Chicago: University of Chicago Press.
Green, Nile. 2012. *Making Space: Sufis and Settlers in Early Modern India*. New Delhi: Oxford University Press.
Khan, Naveeda. 2006. "Flaws in the Flow: Roads and Their Modernity in Pakistan." *Social Text* 24 (4): 87–113.
Koselleck, Reinhart. 2018. *Sediments of Time: On Possible Histories*. Edited and translated by Sean Franzel and Stefan-Ludwig Hoffmann. Stanford, CA: Stanford University Press.
Latif, Syad Muhammad. 2005. *Lahore: Its History, Architectural Remains and Antiquities*. Lahore: Sang-e-meel.
Mir, Farina. 2010. *The Social Space of Language: Vernacular Culture in British Colonial Punjab*. Berkeley: University of California Press.
Morson, Gary Saul, and Caryl Emerson. 1990. *Mikhail Bakhtin: Creation of a Prosaics*. Stanford: Stanford University Press.
Mohammad, Afsar. 2013. *The Festival of Pirs: Popular Islam and Shared Devotion in South India*. New York: Oxford University Press.
Oberoi, Harjot. 1994. *The Construction of Religious Boundaries: Culture, Identity, and Diversity in the Sikh tradition*. Chicago: University of Chicago Press.
Pemberton, Kelly. 2010. *Women Mystics and Sufi Shrines in India*. New York: Columbia University Press.
Pfleiderer, Beatrix. 2006. *The Red Thread: Healing Possession at a Muslim Shrine in North India*, Malcom R. Green (trans.). Delhi: Aakar Books.
Philippon, Alix. 2014. "A Sublime, yet Disputed, Object of Political Ideology? Sufism in Pakistan at the Crossroads." *Commonwealth and Comparative Politics* 52 (2): 271–92.
Rozehnal, Robert. 2007. *Islamic Sufism Unbound: Politics and Piety in Twenty-First Century Pakistan*. New York: Palgrave Macmillan.
Simone, AbdouMaliq. 2015. "Passing Things Along: (In)completing Infrastructure." *New Diversities* 17 (2): 151–62.
Snehi, Yogesh. 2019. *Spatializing Popular Sufi Shrines in Punjab: Dreams, Memories, Territoriality*. New York: Routledge.

Steinby, Liisa. 2013. "Bakhtin's Concept of the Chronotope: The Viewpoint of an Acting Subject," in Liisa Steinby and Tintti Klapuri (eds.), *Bakhtin and His Others: (Inter) subjectivity, Chronotope, Dialogism*. London: Anthem Press, 105–26.

Steinfels, Amina. 2004. "His Master's Voice: The Genre of Malfūẓāt in South Asian Sufism." *History of Religions* 44 (1): 56–69.

Taneja, Anand Vivek. 2018. *Jinnealogy: Time, Islam, and Ecological Thought in the Medieval Ruins of Delhi*. Stanford, CA: Stanford University Press.

Umashankar, Rachana Rao. 2012. "Defending Sufism, Defining Islam: Asserting Islamic Identity in India." PhD dissertation. University of North Carolina, Chapel Hill.

Werbner, Pnina. 2003. *Pilgrims of Love: The Anthropology of a Global Sufi Cult*. Bloomington: Indiana University Press.

10

Beyond "Forgotten Histories": *Teesri Dhun* (The Third Tune) as Collaborative Performance Research

Claire Pamment

Writing of the liberatory progress of Pakistan's transgender rights, a journalist of the English-language *Daily Times* looks "back" at *vadhai* (alt. *badhai*)—songs, dances, prayers, comic repartee, gesture, touch, intimacies, shock, and/or spectacle—performed by some *khwaja sira* (alt. *khwaja sara*)—*trans* groups:[1] "It *used to* be a regular tradition all across the sub-continent at the birth of a child where Khwaja Saras *used to* celebrate by dancing to welcome the newborn. People *used to* reward them in cash or kind that *used to* be the main source of their livelihood" (my emphasis, Ahsen 2019). Amid an increase of nongovernment organization (NGO) activity, transgender representation, and legal reforms that importantly advocated access to rights and protection for a spectrum of transgender people in contexts of systemic oppression[2]—*vadhai* and other performance lifeworlds are often read as regressive and/or dying traditions, even while they persist.

"Backward" readings of *khwaja sira-hijra-trans* performances are pernicious across South Asia in the last decade of transgender rights and religious and/or neoliberal nationalism, and they carry longer legacies of colonial criminalization, abject othering, fetishization, and classist framings of "art" (Hossain, Pamment, and Roy 2023). Recognizing that these formulations of absence or lack marginalize *khwaja sira-trans*

[1] *Khwaja sira* is a Mughal-era term (lit. "lord of the palace," Abbott 2020: 8; see also Hinchy 2019: 23–4), revived in Pakistan for a spectrum of transfeminine and gender-conforming communities (Khan 2019). The term is often inclusive of various kinship structures and regional variants, such as *hijra, zenana, moorat, faqir* (variant *fakir*), as used particularly in the South (Kasmani 2012; Pamment 2019a: 304), *bugga* in Balochistan (Naqvi and Mujtaba 1997), and *khusra* in the Punjab. With Hossain and Roy (2023), I italicize the prefix "trans" to illuminate its vernacular usage, while not subsuming other identities under its umbrella.

[2] Pakistan's Transgender Persons (Protection of Rights) Act (2018) reiterates that transgender people (whether "intersex or *khunsa*," "eunuch," "transgender man, transgender woman or *khwaja sira*, or any person whose gender identity and/or gender expression differs from the social norms and cultural expectations based on the sex they were assigned at the time of their birth") should have equal access to fundamental rights of national citizenship, as based on an individual's determination of their gender (National Assembly of Pakistan 2018), a legal intervention into prior attempts at biomedical gatekeeping (Redding 2019).

performers and reify hierarchies of heteropatriarchy, class, and nation, prompts alternative epistemologies—ones that might trouble a focus on "forgotten histories." Anjali Arondekar in her work in queer South Asian histories delivers an important critique of archival recovery that has invariably operated through "a search-and-rescue model … where the lost histories of the past were recuperated and reinstated within more liberatory histories of the present" (2015: 215). She instead urges movement "beyond the grammar of failure of loss toward an archival poetics of ordinary surplus" or "abundance" (ibid.: 216; 2021). In this short reflection, I offer an introduction to my engagement with *khwaja sira-trans* performers whose work unsettle the temporalities of "liberatory presents" and "forgotten histories" and their embedded hierarchies—elements that underscore our collaborative devised theater play *Teesri Dhun* (The Third Tune, 2015–)—an attempt to further enact *khwaja sira-trans* performance practices as abundant futurity.

Khwaja sira-Hijra-Trans Performances

Khwaja sira- hijra-trans and other gender nonconforming communities have, and continue to generate, an abundant terrain of performance-making across South Asia. Such performances sprawl across genres, spaces, temporalities, kinship practices, and subjectivities. They include lineage-based practices of *badhai* (Hossain, Pamment, and Roy, 2023); *cholla* (alt. *challa*) or alms collection (Saria 2019); inter/intra community events (Roy 2017); Hindu, Shi'a, Sufi, and Christian forms of religious devotion (Kasmani 2012; Pamment 2019a; Hossain, Pamment, and Roy 2023); circus acts; *nautanki*, *raslila*, *ramlila*, *tamasha*, Punjabi theater and other theater forms (Lothspeich 2021; Pamment 2010; Roy 2015, 2016; Samuel 2015; Vanita and Kidwai 2000); interval acts in film intermissions (Mokhtar 2019); protests (Pamment 2019b); *launda* (Dutta 2022) and various other genres of dance and other types of performance. Anti-*hijra* legislation imposed by the British colonial administration through the Criminal Tribes Act Pt 2 (1871), in areas of North-Western Provinces and the Punjab, sought to contain and eradicate *hijra* subjects. Their panoptic surveillance regimes placed particular emphasis on performance as evidence of "deviance" (castration, kidnapping, "sodomy"):

> Any eunuch so registered who appears, dressed or ornamented like a woman … or who dances or plays music, or takes part in any public exhibition, in a public street or place or for hire in a private house, may be arrested without warrant. (In Hinchy 2019, 108)

Kareem Khubchandani argues that in such colonial and postcolonial contexts where performance has been so bound to public and national regulatory fictions of gender and sexuality—invariably infused by class and/or caste hierarchies (Pamment 2017; Prakash 2019; Roy 2019; and others)—aesthetics offer "a prime site to think about how dissidence is enacted." (Khubchandani 2020: 63–4) While careful not to inscribe emancipatory dissidence on all *khwaja sira-trans* performances, how performers move through scripts that attempt to regulate them are critical to understanding *khwaja sira* agency and futurity. As such, one senior Lahori *guru* proudly flaunts papers dating back to the British colonial government, endorsed with Queen Victoria's head, to evidence her claim on areas where her *chelas* continue to perform. We met in 2019, a few weeks after the aforementioned news article of *vadhai's* disappearance in favor of neoliberal narratives of individual empowerment, heteronormative family structures, and assimilated national citizenship—that have been on the upswing with rights-based discourses and representation. She scoffed at these discourses, and instead showed me videos of a recent event celebrating her promotion in *khwaja sira* kinship lineage while she distributed gold rings embossed with Queen Victoria's head to her *chelas* (including her *khwaja sira* daughters in India)—and of her proudly singing a *vadhai* song on a visit to Amritsar. Beyond the logics of colonial criminalization, nationalist boundaries, and the heteronormative and neoliberal milestones of progressive transgender citizenship, she asserts futurity of her lineage. Lucinda Ramberg, in her work with Dalit religiosities of South Indian *devadasis*, *jogatis*, and *jogappas*, foregrounds the possibilities of queer temporalities when "those deemed backward unsettle the time that has been set for them" (2016: 223). The Lahori *guru* puts in motion such queer temporalities, continuing performances and kinship that exceed "forgotten pasts" and "liberatory presents." Unsettling their regulatory scripts of gender, class, and nation, she renders partial their taxonomies of control. Such acts of creative dissidence, anchored in experiences of resistance, demand methodologies that work beyond recuperative logics, in the service of practitioners, toward continued futurity.

Collaborative Performance Research

Performance as research understands performance as a way of knowing the world, and valorizes proximity and embodiment (Conquergood 2002; Khubchandani 2020; and others); what Diana Taylor advocates as "prioritiz[ing] relational and embodied forms of knowledge production and transmission that take us beyond the colonizing and restrictive epistemic grids that some of our Eurocentric disciplines and practices impose on us" (Taylor 2020: xi). Such impulses motivated *Teesri Dhun* (The Third Tune), which I initiated and codirected (with Iram Sana, Olomopolo Media), working with a core cast of six *khwaja sira* and trans performers (Sunniya Abbasi, Jannat Ali, Naghma Gogi, Lucky Khan, Anaya Rahimi, and Neeli Rana) in Lahore in 2014, over an intense three-month devising workshop and subsequent remakings over seven years of rehearsals and productions.

As a body of cis(ish) women directors and trans and *khwaja sira* performers, across a heterogeneous mix of genders, ages, races, citizenships, religions, kinships: and class and educational backgrounds—we worked in and across difference and privilege (however imperfectly) through collaborative play creation. While theater inheres long histories of coloniality, often prioritizing script-based modes and pushing racialized and classist hierarchies—it has been a space where *khwaja sira-trans* people have found expression and success as performers (past and present), as it has inhered sometimes violently discriminatory representations of *khwaja sira* people (Pamment

Figure 10.1 The *Teesri Dhun* ensemble, 2015. From left to right: Sunniya Abbasi, Naghma Gogi, Anaya Rahimi, Neeli Rana, Jannat Ali, and Lucky Khan. Copyright: Olomopolo Media. Photographer: Khalifa Tayyab Saqib

2022). Valorizing embodied experiences of our performers, we worked collaboratively in sharing, shaping, and weaving material that resonated across the collective. This included personal narratives from the cast, broader fieldwork from *khwaja sira* communities,[3] historical research, news and television footage, and performance modes from the *vadhai* repertoire, intercommunity dance, performances of piety, theater histories past and present, community myths and storytelling, and quotidian acts of *juggats* or comic repartee. Attempting to offer an alternative ethical model and more egalitarian way to approach scholarship—particularly in the contexts of often extractivist practices of academia (Taylor 2020: 7)—the project sought not to speak *for*, but *with khwaja sira-trans* performers and audiences.

As Taylor (2003) notes, embodied performance is a key means through which cultural memory and knowledge are enacted and sustained: performance constitutes community and communities constitute action in the public sphere. This piece generated affected bonds across a broad spectrum of intergenerational audiences, across class and genders, cis-*trans-khwaja sira* in Lahore (2015, 2016, 2022) and abroad. In a co-authored piece with the core devising collaborators, we reflect on the process and challenges of making this piece and its interventions in perpetuating spaces for *khwaja sira-trans* performance, critiques of systemic violence, shifting transgender visibility

[3] Research leading up to this project was conducted in collaboration with Shahnaz Khan (2013–15), and its development was supported by a Social Sciences and Humanities Research Council Grant. *Teesri Dhun* is produced by Olomopolo Media, writing consultant: Sarmad Sehbai.

paradigms, and joyful collaboration (Pamment 2019b; Pamment et al. 2021). In what follows, I offer scene fragments from this full-length play, which gesture—however incompletely in this translation of bodies, dance, music, visuals, and languages (Urdu and Punjabi) to English script—some of our temporal playings, beyond "forgotten pasts" and "liberal presents," toward other futurities.

Scene Fragments from *Teesri Dhun*

Knocking

ANAYA: There was also a time when we had a status!

Back then great people like Baali Jatti would not feel embarrassed to work with us.

Baali Jatti was the lioness of the stage, and we would share the stage to entertain you.

In those days, art was appreciated, not gender.

Vadhai and us became just like chocolate and happiness.

But Mr General Ayub Khan had to put a ban on that also.

So we protested through vadhai to remind him and his respectable mother that we once had done a vadhai to celebrate his birth.

Then came Muhtarma Benazir Bhutto to the shrine of Bari Imam to lay the first chaddar [the sacred cloth laid over the grave]. We stopped her and said, "this is our honour." She immediately stepped back and gave the chaddar to us.

Where has all this gone now? Now, we come to your home and you close the doors on us. At the traffic signals, when we knock on your car windows, you turn your face away.

Human rights, gender empowerment, civil society, plastic smiles, slogans. You have your coffee mornings, kitty parties, marches warchers, enlightened moderation … culture vultures!

Social Change

NEELI	Oh Jannat! You think you are very clever. What did you ask for from the Supreme Court?
JANNAT	I got a proposal Neeli, from the judge.
NEELI	The judge? So what is he giving in dowry? Justice!
JANNAT	Oh Neeli! Change!
NEELI	What was the need to go so far? You could have gone to the nearby shop to get some change.
JANNAT	Neeli! Social change! Social change, Neeli!
NEELI	But I can wash my face, put on my lipstick and silky powder; that's all I need to change.
JANNAT	Oh Neeli! The moorats will get an identity.

Figure 10.2 Anaya Rahimi in *Teesri Dhun*, 2015. Copyright: Olomopolo Media. Photographer: Malcolm Hutcheson

NEELI Who has a bigger identity than me? Everywhere I pass, I clap, and everyone identifies me!

JANNAT Neeli, just think! We will get ID cards, admissions into colleges, and we will get to jobs and become madams. Good morning!

NEELI Chew as much English as you want, study as much as you can, there will be no jobs.

JANNAT Whatever Neeli! Just tell me, could you cast your vote earlier?

NEELI Vote? Or currency note? Why should we care? What do we get? No inheritance, no jobs.

JANNAT Oh Neeli! See how many things are happening here for us! Welfare initiatives, health cards, seminars, transgender firsts, inclusion, diversity, photoshoots! Neeli, this is the real change!

NEELI To hell with this change! Our dance functions got banned, we are almost starving, and you are telling me this is *the* change. It's like you invite a hundred guests to the wedding and only feed one of them! What about the rest of us?

JANNAT Neeli! You should know. Our right, our haq is the might!

NEELI Oh General Ziaaaa-ul-Haq!

JANNAT Oh that is Zia-ul-Haq! And I am not talking about him but our haq! Rights!

NEELI Now I understand, you mean haq mehr, the alimony, it's only 32 rupees! To hell with it! It is not like people will dish out sweets or throw us wedding parties. You think the maulvi will recite our nikah and ask our consent?! 'I accept, I accept, I accept'.

JANNAT Oh Neeli, you are married!

NEELI Oh my God! How?

JANNAT You just said yourself 'I accept, I accept, I accept'.

(Neeli's gaze pans across the audience)

NEELI With all of them?

Regulatory Rhythms and Dancing Elsewheres …

(Jannat, dancing, is interrupted by sirens, barking of dogs, flashlights, gradually the clanging of typewriters. Male voices deliver verbatim text from the Criminal Tribes Act [CT] and Pakistani news channel Abb Takk's crime program Khufia *[Hidden, K1* male voice, K2 female voice*]. Jannat through the scene, listens, and tries to move from the hammering of voices and flashlights that follow her.)*

CT: The Criminal Tribes Act 1871.

K1: Khufia 2013.

K1: The Pakistan that our ancestors made, is this the same holy land?

CT: Faisal Ali, Pathan. Wears his hair like a woman. Suspicious, suspicious.

K1: But we see how men dress up as women just to satiate their sexual desires …

Figure 10.3 Neeli Rana (left) and Jannat Ali (right) in *Teesri Dhun*, 2015. Copyright: Olomopolo Media. Photographer: Malcolm Hutcheson

CT: Any eunuch who appears dressed or ornamented like a woman . . .

CT: Walayat Ali. Draws water and lives with his sister. Suspicious.

CT: In a public street or place, or in any other place with the intention of being seen

K1: They promote the illegal, unethical and immoral activities of dancing and singing

CT: Suspicious!

CT: And may be arrested without a warrant

CT: Suspicious!

K1 Why Hazrat Loot's clan was destroyed?

CT and K: And shall be punished! (*Jannat collapses, under her veil*)

Figure 10.4 Jannat Ali in *Teesri Dhun*, 2015. Copyright: Olomopolo Media. Photographer: Khalifa Tayyab Saqib

(Breaking news sound effects, to a female anchor's voice (Khufia 2). A camera zooms in on Jannat's body, lying crumpled on the floor. Through the scene Jannat tries to avoid the camera, but it continues to capture her face and body—magnified through the on-stage projection.)

K2: Viewers, today we will show you how these khwaja siras live in sin, roaming on our roadsides.
Khwaja sira or men?
What is their agenda?
Today our agenda is to disclose those people who are actually men but pretend to be women, streetwalking!
Their intention is to lure people into their sinful ways, in full open! They make immoral sexual ties.
So come, let us see what is happening here.
Are you a khwaja sira?
Khwaja sira or a male?
If we figure out something fishy, then what?
Male, male?

Oh, so this is a male!
He has accepted that he is a male!
Look here, why are you shying away? There is no need to be frightened.
You guys indulge in sex work!
How many lives have you destroyed?
Do you understand the meaning of gay? What is gay?
Are you a gay?
If you are, just say it once on camera.
Don't explain, just say it once.
Then we will leave you.
Gay? Gay? Gay? He is a gay!
He has finally accepted that he is a gay!
Since how long have you been into this?
It is such a tiny thing, you are a male, you are gay, gay male.
Have you gotten yourself operated?
Did you operate on yourself?-

(Jannat confronts the camera, lifting up her lehenga (skirt), seen in silhouette. *The camera's image turns to static, accompanied by white noise. Blackout.)*

(Anaya enters in spotlight.)

ANAYA: This is what had happened to Mai Nand Murtaza.
She was the first khwaja sira in the courts of the king.
She used to work in the harem.
She was the closest to the king and queen and had access to everything.
One day in the court, they declared a search to prove whether she was a man or a woman.
Well, she was one of us but they could not see it.
The next day, Mai Nand Murtaza was called in for a complete inspection.
The entire night she stood on one leg, crying to Allah.
And Allah was listening.
The next morning, the royal hounds came and ripped her clothes apart.
"Are you a man? Or a woman?"
Mai Nand Murtaza appeared in full woman form!
She came in a woman's form, only to disappear.
She disappeared and was never seen again.
But, we, ladies and gentlemen, we will never disappear! *(sound of ghungroo bells)*
They wanted to make us disappear the day we were born, the moral custodians and religious gatekeepers, we have faced them all.
Ladies and gentlemen, today we will take you out of your cultural barriers.
Today we will remove these misconceptions of yours.
Today we will lift the veil from your eyes. *(The entire cast light up in silhouettes)*

Figure 10.5 *Teesri Dhun* rehearsals, 2022. Copyright: Olomopolo Media. Photographer: Imran Sajid

> Ladies and gentlemen, and my lovely moorats, today we will dance on the third tune …

(Music, Bulleh Shah's Tere Ishq Nachiya Your Love Has Made Me Dance. *The entire cast fills the stage with dance …)*

Futures

Teesri Dhun aims not to "search-and-rescue" marginal voices of "forgotten" performance histories—but instead continues the work of performance, as lived and practiced by the communities it presents, challenging scripts that relegate them "backward." We collectively look back at violence—whether through the classist and neoliberal dismissals of performance ("Knocking"), the inequities of developmentalism and a limited compass of rights ("Change"), to the explicit policing of *khwaja sira-trans* bodies ("Regulatory Rhythms"). Attempts to regulate *khwaja sira-trans* bodies are reproduced across temporalities—demonstrated explicitly in the mirroring of colonial *anti-hijra* legislation and the Khufia crime television program, to the re/tellings of Mai Nandi's dis/appearance. These are not forgotten histories for many *khwaja sira-trans* people—but are experienced in structural violence that continues in the so-called liberatory era of rights. Yet, the performers work abundance into these narratives—dancing, laughing, and storytelling *together* across struggles—through embodied performance they refuse to disappear.

Bibliography

Ahsen, Saud bin. 2019. "Transgenders in Pakistan." *Daily Times*, September 8, 2019. https://dailytimes.com.pk/461958/transgenders-in-pakistan-part-i/. Accessed September 8, 2019.

Arondekar, Anjali. 2021. "Hum Kagaz Nahin Dikhainge: Caste, Sexuality, Protest," UCLA CISA Speaker Series, May 10. https://youtu.be/4u0ZMmVrSBk. Accessed September 1, 2021.

Arondekar, Anjali, et al. 2015. "Queering Archives: A Roundtable Discussion." *Radical History Review* 122: 211–31.

Conquergood, Dwight. 2002. "Performance Studies: Interventions and Radical Research." *TDR* 46 (2): 145–56.

Dutta, Aniruddha. 2022. "The Freedom to Dance: Performance and Impersonation in Lagan," in Harshita Mruthinti Kamath and Pamela Lothspeich (eds.), *Mimetic Desires: Impersonation and Guising across South Asia*. Hawaii: University of Hawaii Press, 127–47.

Hinchy, Jessica. 2019. *Governing Gender and Sexuality in Colonial India : The Hijra, c.1850–1900*. Cambridge: Cambridge University Press.

Hossain, Adnan, Claire Pamment, and Jeff Roy. 2023. *Badhai: Hijra-Khwaja Sira-Trans Performance across Borders in South Asia*. London: Methuen Drama.

Kasmani, Omar. 2012. "Of Discontinuity and Difference: Gender and Embodiment among Fakirs of Sehwan Sharif." *Oriente Modern* 92 (2): 439–57.

Khubchandani, Kareem. 2020. *Ishtyle: Accenting Gay Indian Nightlife*. Ann Arbor: University of Michigan Press.

Lothspiech, Pamela. 2021. "Intersectionally Marginalized Dancers in the Theatre of Ramlila. Working with Vulnerable Communities in South Asian Performance Context." 49th Annual Conference on South Asia, UW-Madison, October 23.

Mokhtar, Sheram. 2019. "Unstable Assemblages: Mediated Discourses and Lived Realities of Hijras in Pakistan." PhD dissertation, University of Oregon. https://www.proquest.com/openview/b84da5a48cdd348af46511697feb6d6e/1?pq-origsite=gscholar&cbl=51922&diss=y. Accessed April 19, 2022.

National Assembly of Pakistan. 2018. *Transgender Persons (Protection of Rights) Act*. www.na.gov.pk/uploads/documents/1526547582_234.pdf. Accessed January 10, 2019.

Pamment, Claire. 2010. "Hijraism: Jostling for a Third Space in Pakistani Politics." *TDR: The Drama Review* 54 (2): 29–50.

Pamment, Claire. 2017. *Comic Performance in Pakistan : The Bhānd*. London: Palgrave Macmillan.

Pamment, Claire. 2019a. "Performing Piety in Pakistan's Transgender Rights Movement." *Transgender Studies Quarterly* 6 (3): 297–314.

Pamment, Claire. 2019b. "The Hijra Clap in Neoliberal Hands: Performing Trans Activism in Pakistan." *TDR: The Drama Review* 63 (1): 141–51.

Pamment, Claire. 2022. "Mediatizing 'Fake' Khwaja Siras: The Limits of Impersonation," in Harshita Mruthinti Kamath and Pamela Lothspeich (eds.), *Mimetic Desires: Impersonation and Guising Across South Asia*. Hawaii: University of Hawaii Press, 148–68.

Pamment, Claire, Iram Sana, Naghma Gogi, Neeli Rana, Jannat Ali, Anaya Sheikh, Lucky Khan, and Sunniya Abbasi. 2021. "A Conversation: The *Third Tune (Teesri*

Dhun," in Tim Prentki and Ananda Breed (eds.), *The Routledge Companion to Applied Performance*. London: Routledge, 215–27.

Prakash, Brahma. 2019. *Cultural Labour: Conceptualizing the "Folk Performance" in India*. New York: Oxford University Press.

Ramberg, Lucinda. 2016. "Backward Futures and Pasts Forward: Queer Time, Sexual Politics, and Dalit Religiosity in South India." *GLQ* 22 (2): 223–48.

Redding, Jeffrey A. 2019. "The Pakistan Transgender Persons (Protection of Rights) Act of 2018 and Its Impact on the Law of Gender in Pakistan." *Australian Journal of Asian Law* 20 (1): 8: 103–13.

Roy, Jeff. 2015. "The 'Dancing Queens': Negotiating Hijra Pehchān from India's Streets onto the Global Stage." *Ethnomusicology Review* 20: 1–23.

Roy, Jeff. 2016. "Translating *Hijra* into Transgender: Performance and *Pehchān* in India's Trans-*Hijra* Communities." *Transgender Studies Quarterly* 3 (3–4): 412–32.

Roy, Jeff. 2017. "From Jalsah to Jalsā: Music, Identity, and (Gender) Transitioning at a Hījṛā Rite of Initiation." *Ethnomusicology* 61 (3): 389–418.

Roy, Jeff. 2019. "Remapping the Voice through Transgender-Hījrā Performance," in Gavin Steingo and Jim Sykes (eds.), *Remapping Sound Studies*. Durham, NC: Duke University Press, 173–82.

Samuel, A. T. 2015. "Performing Thirunangai: Activism, Development, and Normative Citizenship in Tamil Transgender Performances." PhD Dissertation, American University. https://search.proquest.com/docview/1680834346?pq-origsite=primo. Accessed January 8, 2022.

Saria, Vaibhav. 2019. "Begging for Change: Hijras, Law and Nationalism." *Contributions to Indian Sociology* 53 (1): 133–57.

Taylor, Diana. 2003. *The Archive and the Repertoire: Performing Cultural Memory in the Americas*. Durham, NC: Duke University Press.

Taylor, Diana. 2020. *¡Presente!: The Politics of Presence*. Durham, NC: Duke University Press.

Vanita, R., and S. Kidwai. 2000. *Same-Sex Love in India: Readings from Literature*. New York: St. Martin's Press.

Part Four

Politics and "the People"

11

"*Tulba, Mazdoor, aur Kissan*" (Students, Laborers, and Peasants): The Revolution Made Easy

Aasim Sajjad Akhtar

In his magisterial account of revolutionary internationalism in colonial India, Raza (2020: 8) brings alive what he calls "intermediate histories [of] figures who … may not have contributed to Marxist or Communist 'thought' but … were subjects in their own right with an acute sense of their time and place in the history they imagined themselves making"

In charting the lives of these subjects, both in India and during their travels to faraway lands, Raza makes an eloquent case for writing "history from the ground up instead of a history of the party or the intellectuals who dominated it." In this essay, I follow Raza's lead and trace the lives and political struggle of three otherwise nondescript Pakistani revolutionaries between the heady period spanning the late 1960s through to the end of the Cold War.

Raza's work is part of a growing body of scholarship on Pakistan's communist Left which has focused largely on the immediate pre- and post-Partition periods.[1] Separately, the labor, student, and peasant movements of the 1960s and 1970s have also garnered academic attention. Alongside movements and figures from Lahore and the Hashtanagar Valley of Khyber Pakhtunkhwa, Karachi features centrally in most of this burgeoning literature (Ali 2005; Ali 2020; Azhar 2019; Malik 2018; Nelson 2011).

The three men I chronicle in this essay were all active in Left-wing political circles with the labor and student movements in Karachi during the 1970s. The country's biggest city was, by all accounts, a lightning rod for progressive politics and culture, not to mention millions in search of livelihoods. All three of my informants traveled to Karachi from faraway "rural hinterlands." None could be characterized as "elite," but the journey from membership of relatively comfortable, small landholding families to a faraway metropolitan center, where they had few belongings and next of kin, was nevertheless both harrowing and transformative. Like so many of their comrades, these three revolutionaries embodied their political commitments by disowning their "petty bourgeois" upbringings.

My three informants represent, I submit, the prototypical rank-and-file revolutionary of that period. I got to know them long after the heyday of revolutionary

[1] Ali (2015) is most notable in this regard. See also Malik (2013) and Raza (2013).

internationalism had passed; my association with them has now spanned more than two decades, and the information I present here has been gathered over the course of many conversations, formal and informal alike, during our shared struggle.[2] While the political trajectories of these three men in the period under study were far from uniform, they all shared a millenarian belief—inculcated in them by "the party" and "the intellectuals who dominated it"—that they were in the process of becoming genuine revolutionary subjects. This process of becoming was not just limited to their own selves; they were tasked also with inculcating class consciousness in others, the ultimate goal being to foment revolution through the three idealized subjects of *tulba, mazdoor, aur kissan* (student, worker, and peasant).

In his *Prison Notebooks*, Gramsci euphemistically referred to Marxism as the "philosophy of praxis." My informants and many like them may not have mastered the Marxist canon, but nevertheless made revolutionary ideas legible through struggle. As Raza puts succinctly, these individuals became subjects "in the history they imagined themselves making." While my informants' almost unquestioned faith in the inevitability of revolution may not have been rewarded—they subsequently had to come to terms with the sobering reality that the idealized trinity of *tulba, mazdoor, aur kissan* could not conjure up the revolutionary society that they so desperately wanted to see come to fruition—their lives embodied the fluidity of Marxist-inflected political action in practice.

Teleological notions of historical change spearheaded by preordained revolutionary subjects are certainly no longer tenable today. But there is nevertheless something to be said for the otherwise simplified idea of "the people" that my three informants, and their many comrades, constructed from within an otherwise complex and contradictory social mosaic. It is this palpable difference between reified notions of history and revolutionary form on the one hand, and the eclectic political practices that actually constituted history-making, on the other hand, that I draw out in this essay.

Admittedly, this gap between bookish theory and practice was rarely named during the heyday of revolutionary internationalism. This is perhaps why, decades after the fact, my informants lament the difficulty of identifying "enemies" and "friends" in the current conjuncture, which, in their inhabitation of time, began with the traumatic collapse of actually existing socialism in the early 1990s. One of my protagonists spent six months in the Soviet Union as part of an official delegation of the Communist

[2] All three of my informants befriended me after I became politically active in Rawalpindi-Islamabad at the turn of the millennium. I was a very young man, returned from studying abroad and living in an almost mythical revolutionary dreamworld. Zahoor, Munir, and Yamin saw in me, I suspect, their young revolutionary selves, and thereby dedicated their time, energy, and resources to nurturing my person, and also supporting a fledgling political project that went by the name of *Awami Muzhaimat* (translated as People's Rights Movement). It was the generosity with which they received and supported me that, many years later, inspired me to write this short personal and theoretical reflection. Their training as young revolutionaries, as I will document throughout this essay, was decidedly different from the experience we shared in the early 2000s. Yet it was a measure of their openness to changed means and methods of political work—and perhaps how familiar my youthful exuberance must have felt—that they offered often unconditional support for our work, even when they were clearly unsettled by the ideological and practical quandaries that we collectively confronted. A short mission statement for our particular iteration of revolutionary politics in the early 2000s can be found here: http://ghadar.insaf.net/June2004/pdf/peopleright.pdf.

Party of Pakistan (CPP) in 1990–1, and to this day vividly describes his horror at how he observed firsthand the collapse of the world's first socialist state. His experience, to which I return in the conclusion, symbolizes the epochal "defeat" of the Left as a whole, which "ended a century and summarized in itself a cumulative sequence of downfalls that, suddenly gathered and condensed in a symbolic historical turn, appeared as overwhelming and unbearable" (Traverso 2016: 22).

As such, the simple binary of "the people" and "ruling class" that animated the struggles to which my three informants dedicated most of their lives has today been appropriated by the political right, both in the form of religio-political movements as well as ideological-political formations that are sometimes lazily clumped together as "populist." This is not just experienced as traumatic for those who lived out their revolutionary dreams in an era when Left imaginaries of revolution were made easy, but also raises important theoretical and practical questions for Left praxis today.

What Is "the people"?

> *It all used to be so straightforward. It was clear who our allies and adversaries were. Political workers knew their roles and we were all sure that History would bear out our struggle.*
>
> Zahoor Khan

To exhort "the people" always means positing a political unity that bridges any number of divides that pervade actually existing society. The theoretical project that is the construction of this fictional unity always exists in an uncomfortable dialectical contradiction with the practical endeavor of bringing together variegated segments of "the people."

The oral histories that inform this essay focus on the period of revolutionary upheaval that was triggered by the anti-Ayub movement in 1968 and which began to subside in the 1980s. For most of these two decades, "the people" was, in most left-revolutionary circles, generally equated to three idealized social segments, namely students, workers, and peasants. While these three segments were spread out across a highly uneven social formation, Karachi was by some distance the most vibrant gathering place of Pakistani revolutionaries in the heady days of the 1960s and 1970s.

The city's population at the time of India's Partition was approximately 300,000, but within two decades, it had increased tenfold to 3 million. The vast majority of Karachi's incoming residents were upcountry "peasants" surplus to requirements in a fast-mechanizing agrarian economy. Some came to Karachi to populate the burgeoning textile industry as "workers," others gained admission into colleges and universities as "students" aiming to secure upward mobility in white-collar professions. As such, then, those who became associated with Left politics in Karachi embodied the very idealized subjects that they sought to mobilize for revolution.

Zahoor Khan was sixteen years old in 1971 when he left his village near Mansehra in Khyber Pakhtunkhwa to travel to Karachi, where he would soon become involved in Left-wing political work. His small family-owned farm was saturated with household labor, and Zahoor was anything but a conscientious student. In his recollection, he effectively "ran away" from home, the lights and glamor of Karachi almost calling him to them. His elder brother Manzoor was his only point of contact in the city, and also became his "in" to the secretive world of the revolutionary Left. Within a year of arriving in the city, Zahoor joined the iconic National Students Federation (NSF). He was not formally a student but at seventeen years young, the "underground leaders" who ran the NSF decided that it was the organization best suited for him.

Zahoor was instructed to join the NSF-influenced Workers Organizing Committee in the industrial area of Landhi. This was a time of the biggest strikes in Pakistan labor history (Ali 2005). Like all other Left revolutionaries given the task of organizing in the workers movement, Zahoor found work in a factory (hosieries), in which he proceeded to mobilize his fellow workers, first to form a trade union, and then subsequently to deepen the revolutionary zeal of members so as to move them closer to joining The Party (NSF).

The labor movement was peaking around the time that Zahoor became associated with it. He, however, was not to know this, and was in fact experiencing what he calls his "honeymoon period" with the Left. He organized tirelessly, being fired from three different factory jobs in the process, but still managing to induct approximately a dozen workers into the "mother party." In his words: "I was extremely militant, not only in terms of everyday conduct, but also in in terms of my belief that industrial workers were innately more 'revolutionary' than any other segment of society."

Zahoor's time with the Workers Organising Committee and NSF came to a rather abrupt end in 1975 when he was arrested during a routine sit-in, and eventually sentenced to a year of incarceration under the Defence of Pakistan Ordinance that had been passed in 1971, and subsequently was incorporated into the constitutional document finalized by Pakistan's Parliament in 1973. That this draconian legislation—which, in the tradition of colonial statutes, gave the state full reign to arrest and charge citizens under the guise of "national security"—was passed under the tutelage of a government that proclaimed itself to be committed to labor and the Left more generally was not lost on Zahoor.[3] Till this day, Zahoor responds furiously to any suggestion that the Pakistan People's Party (PPP) is a "progressive" entity, his personal experience of twelve months imprisonment testament to the PPP's reactionary nature.

Zahoor's time in prison deepened his political consciousness. He recalls coming across numerous societal misfits who had committed at worse what would be considered petty crimes yet suffered the indignities of extended jail sentences only because of their low class/social status. At least in part because of this exposure, Zahoor became more discerning about the diversity of subjectivities that characterize the "proletarian vanguard."

After serving his time, Zahoor did not rejoin the NSF. In fact, he left Karachi in early 1977 to return to his village, where he stayed for a few months before shifting to Islamabad. He found work in the government-run National Institute of Health (NIH) in 1979 where he became involved in unionizing NIH employees almost immediately,

[3] For a classic formulation of the evolution and contradictions of the PPP and its Left-populist formation, see Ahmad (1978).

getting an association registered with the National Industrial Relations Commission (NIRC) in 1980.

The prototypical NIH worker was very different from that in industrializing Karachi; the latter was a multiethnic hub, and a young "militant" Zahoor was convinced that the metropolitan cauldron of Karachi generated a revolutionary consciousness in what Marxist canon were assumed to be atomized and alienated workers. His experience at the NIH, however, which was itself located in a rural locality of Islamabad (Chak Shahzad), forced him to recalibrate his assumptions about the subjectivities of actually existing workers.

The majority of NIH employees, at least the non-officer cadre with which Zahoor was associated, was from the Potohar plateau of which Islamabad (and its twin city of Rawalpindi) is the hub. They were all heavily integrated into local social networks—patrilineal *biraderi* clans, most notably. NIH union politics, then, was less about an abstract appeal to class as a "universal" category, and more about strategic alliances across *biraderi* factions so as to win electoral votes.

Zahoor is now accepting of the fact that his "militant" years were characterized by a bloody-mindedness to make theory into reality, when in fact "[d]ifference based on political affiliation, region, language, and ethnicity were dividing Pakistan's working class in this period" (Ali 2005: 101). Yet at the same time, he insists that the very idea that a "universal class" could be fomented was what drove the revolutionary upsurge. In other words, irrespective of objective realities, an open-ended imaginary of a revolutionary subject was central to the production of Left-wing politics (Lloretne 2013). For all of the theoretical dogma that prevailed within the Pakistani left in the 1960s and 1970s, a fact that Zahoor himself admits, a deep revolutionary humanism guided the everyday conduct of many of its rank-and-file. It was not by chance that Zahoor was able to successfully mobilize workers in the very different contexts of metropolitan Karachi and rural Islamabad. In both locales, his organizing efforts were certainly inflected with an idiom of inevitable historical change and attendant rhetoric about the essential traits of classes.[4] But upon deep reflection, he acknowledges that both his "militant" young self and his later years were characterized by a great deal of spontaneity in which a variety of methods and ideological anchors were deployed to bring "the people" together.

Scholarly debates and on-ground political realities over the past few decades have put paid to simplistic notions of "transition" from capitalism to socialism via the agency of an idealized industrial proletariat (Therborn 2018). No matter how loyal rank-and-file leftist political workers of a bygone era were to a prosaic theory of politics, their actual political conduct reflected a commitment to transformation—of the self and collective—without any guarantees that the ideal-type revolution would ever come to pass.

[4] Zahoor also acknowledges that considerable time and energy was expended on inculcating antipathy for other left groups. Sectarianism was indeed widespread within left circles, so-called pro-Russian and pro-Chinese groups often dedicated to undermining one another. In the 1980s and beyond, "Trotskyites" also became visible as a separate entity, new sectarian tendencies developing alongside.

Of Exile and "Backwardness"

It is our job to be able to relate to a whole range of people and their experiences, and yet find ways to create an idea of a shared future

Munir Comrade

Munir Virk—known almost universally as Munir Comrade—moved to Karachi from his home town of Kabirwala in southern Punjab after the labor movement had been largely subdued. While the attacks against organized labor and segments of the radical left began under the PPP government, state repression under General Zia-ul-Haq's military regime that deposed Bhutto in 1977 was of an altogether different magnitude.[5]

The Zia dictatorship lasted eleven years, and was resisted heroically by the broader progressive community that included student, labor, and peasant organizers associated with a variety of revolutionary left-wing groups; PPP cadres; professional associations like lawyers, doctors; and a predominantly city-based women's movement. Munir Comrade was, like Zahoor Khan, associated with the NSF in Karachi, which, following the 1977 military coup, had largely shifted its focus from an already weakened labor movement to mobilizing young people and the wider progressive community against the dictatorship. Hailing from a quite comfortable background, his grandfather having inherited a perennially irrigated farm in Kabirwala of approximately 100 acres (4 *morabbas*), Munir Comrade's time in Karachi featured a radical process of de-classing and ideological training. Yet it was when he left the metropole that he truly came of age politically.

In March 1981, the underground organization run by two sons of Zulfikar Ali Bhutto, Al-Zulfikar, hijacked a Pakistan International Airlines (PIA) plane flying from Karachi to Peshawar. Seen as an attempt to avenge Bhutto's death at Zia's hands, the hijacking did force the latter's hand and resulted in the release of over fifty political prisoners, most of them associated with the PPP.[6] However, the longer-term implications of the hijacking were far from unequivocally beneficial for left-progressives. The military junta launched a major crackdown against the PPP and wider progressive circles after the event, with numerous NSF cadres also facing sedition and terrorism cases. Munir Comrade was named in two First Information Reports (FIRs) lodged in Karachi city. He went into hiding and then left the city shortly thereafter, tentatively planning to make his way to Pakistan's easternmost border from where he, along with other comrades, planned to smuggle themselves into India.

Instead, Munir Comrade spent the next two-and-a-half-years in a variety of villages in the Hindu-majority Tharparkar region on Sindh's border with the Indian state of Rajasthan. Given his own farming background, Munir Comrade immersed himself in the region, initially finding refuge with Punjabi settler farmers in a village named

5 State repression against the organized Left can of course be traced back much further than the Bhutto or Zia periods. Most notably the Communist Party of Pakistan (CPP) was formally banned in 1954 in the wake of the so-called Rawalpindi Conspiracy Case. See Ali (2015: 163–205).

6 See https://www.dawn.com/news/1626869. Accessed December 15, 2021.

Guddo, but then eventually integrating himself with Sindhi- and Thari-speaking communities. Here Munir Comrade's somewhat bookish understanding of Marxism and revolution, imbibed during his time in Karachi, underwent a thorough overhaul. He recalls that Karachi's more urbane revolutionaries generally perceived village life to be "backward," even as they propagated the proverbial peasant as part of the revolutionary vanguard. This apparent contradiction was "explained" to younger revolutionaries like Munir Comrade through the mediating force of modern technology. Collectivized and mechanized agriculture would, they were told, help the peasantry transition from relative "backwardness" to both a better standard of living and higher forms of social consciousness.

Given the often condescending manner in which the Pakistani left's high intellectuals imparted Marxist theory to the rank-and-file, it is worth being reminded that toward the end of his life, Marx's studies made him recoil from teleological readings of history so much so that he came to perceive "the communal social forms of the villages of India and Russia … as possible new loci of resistance to capital" (Anderson (2016: 3). Munir Comrade's experience of living in rural Sindh, and that too in one of its most "underdeveloped" peripheries, meant that his understanding of revolutionary transformation developed in a manner not dissimilar to the later Marx.[7]

Not only did the significance of "communal social forms" become apparent to Munir Comrade through the hospitality of his hosts, it was also reflected in shared work ethics that were only fleetingly visible in metropolitan Pakistan. Perhaps most importantly, Munir Comrade's experience in Thar made apparent to him the necessity of a political idiom that resonated with local cultural mores. To this day, Munir Comrade insists that progressives can only challenge retrograde social norms by invoking culturally rooted symbols and examples of reformers and revolutionaries of proverbial sons (and daughters) of the soil.

During his time in Sindh, Munir Comrade learned of figures like Sufi Shah Inayat whose eclectic mix of anti-landlordism and mysticism in seventeenth-century Sindh not only endeared him to the peasantry of his time but also make him a revered national hero to this day (Memon et al. 2013). This provided the impetus for Munir Comrade to verse himself in the legends of other mystics who also challenged tyrants, particularly in his native Punjab. When I met him in the early 2000s, Munir Comrade would reel off couplets and folk stories at will, seamlessly able to relate to working people's spirituality and everyday material struggles. One of his favorite couplets was that of the legendary Baba Farid:

Panj rukn Islam de, te chewan Fareeda tuk
Je na labbe chewan, te panje i jande muk

(Alongside five precepts of Islam, Fareed, the sixth is to subsist
If the sixth is not fulfilled, the five precepts cannot be either)

[7] Large parts of Tharparkar are desert. Rain-fed agriculture is possible in only scattered pockets, while livestock rearing represents the primary source of livelihood. Drought is common, and high levels of risk borne by both cultivators and pastoralists are often shared.

Like Zahoor Khan before him, Munir Comrade refracted his understanding of Marxist ideology and historical change through his very particular experiences. He still claims to be committed to the revolutionary theory he imbibed as a young man in Karachi, even if the means and methods that he subsequently learned betray any formulaic ideas of class, ideology, and social transformation more broadly. In particular, Munir Comrade has throughout the course of his adult life communicated Marxist ideas in an idiom that underscores the religious sensibilities of "the people," inviting comparison with experiments in revolutionary politics in other parts of the world, especially liberation theology in late twentieth-century Latin America. That the Pakistani Left did not hegemonize such an idiom speaks as much to the weaponization of religion by the Pakistani state as subjective shortcomings within revolutionary circles.

In any case, Munir Comrade, like Zahoor Khan, embodied a revolutionary humanism that transcended the intellectual dogmas that for most of the twentieth century overdetermined imaginaries of "the people," revolution, and, indeed, history itself. To fully imbibe practical and theoretical lessons from the past so as to inform Left praxis in the present and future is to give "intermediate histories" like Munir Comrade's their rightful place in the archive. Indeed, for Munir Comrade the explanation for the Left's decline from the 1980s onward has to do with the gradual disappearance of the humble, full-time revolutionary who, like Shah Inayat, gave his entire life to traveling across villages and towns alike to mobilize the masses. Yet what Munir Comrade is unable to explain is why young people today do not exhibit the almost millenarian commitment that drove individuals like himself to give their everything for the cause of revolution. One obvious reason is that the Left can no longer posit a determinate imaginary of revolution and the subject(s) to make it. Today it is the religious right that offers its rank-and-file both ease and certainty about the ends and means of collective and individual struggle. Another important reason, as my last informant's experiences suggest, is Pakistan's tortured tryst with identity.

Of the "National Question"

> *I am not Siraiki. But I have assimilated myself into the land, its culture and its people. That itself embodies a politics that seeks to bridge the divides that the ruling class reproduces, again and again.*
>
> Yamin Rana

Yamin Rana's family migrated to the district of Khushab in West Punjab in 1947 from Patiala. Like many such families coming from adjacent districts across the new border, his family was allotted a plot of agricultural land by the authorities dealing with what became widely known as "evacuee property." Yamin Rana was born shortly after the migration, and he grew up on his small family farm surrounded by both other settler-migrants and the local Siraiki-speaking population.

In comparison to urban Sindh where tensions between Urdu-speaking migrants and local Sindhi-speakers were acute from the time of Partition itself, there was less overt conflict between settler populations and local communities in regions like

Khushab. But tensions existed nonetheless. Yamin narrates that local Siraikis were generally welcoming of migrants in the immediate aftermath of Partition, but that their anxieties became more palpable after the incorporation of the Thal Development Authority (TDA) in 1949. The TDA oversaw the construction of a number of irrigation canals to make cultivable an area of more than 200,000 acres of otherwise arid land. The vast majority of these newly irrigated lands were allotted to Partition "refugees," with locals—both landowners and artisanal castes—often losing out in the process.

Simmering tensions and his own ethnic-linguistic identity aside, Yamin recalls growing up with strong connections to Siraiki-speaking communities. By the age of fifteen, he had developed associations with trade unionists and Left-progressives that were organizing in the handful of agro-processing units around both Jauharabad (Khushab) and Kalurkot (Bhakkar), both of which had emerged as market towns serving newly irrigated agricultural lands. In 1969, the anti-Ayub movement peaked after major trade union federations put in their lot with the students who had triggered it. Yamin Rana's political coming of age was sealed when he joined the National Awami Party (NAP).

Yamin was sent by the party to Karachi in 1970, where he experienced his most defining political moment—the army action in east Pakistan. In his first few months in Karachi, Yamin was taken in by the power of the trade union movement, notwithstanding his recognition that there were ethnic-linguistic fissures within it. He recalls feeling convinced that "the people"—who he had witnessed came to life back home during the anti-Ayub movement—were now even stronger, Karachi's labor movement proving that there could be unity in difference.

This feeling was reinforced by the general election results of December 1970, in which NAP succeeded in winning substantial seats across the country, most notably in the then North-West Frontier Province (NWFP) and Balochistan (where it would later form governmental coalitions). Soon afterward, however, Yamin's youthful idealism was dealt the severest of blows. The Bengali nationalist Awami League had won an absolute majority of seats in the general election, but was denied its mandate by the military government led by General Yahya Khan. In March 1971, all hopes of a democratic and federal Pakistan were crushed when troops were sent to east Pakistan.

Yamin's recollections of the period speak both of the tragic failure of the Pakistani nation-building project as well as the Left's perennial challenge of reconciling class struggle with the national question. He acknowledges that few west Pakistanis, including those associated with the labor and student movements in Karachi, organized against the army action. While NAP's rank-and-file was, in Yamin's account, the largest single political collectivity that called for solidarity with Bengalis facing the wrath of Pakistan's military juggernaut, the party's leadership on the whole took a much more circumspect position. This gives credence to Feroz Ahmed's (1972: 9) claim that "under Chinese influence, the NAP ... shied away from confronting the West Pakistani ruling structure on all substantive issues."

Ali (2015) convincingly demonstrates that the largely Urdu-speaking migrant leadership of the communist Left in the immediate post-Partition period was somewhat out of touch with the concerns of indigenous ethnic-national communities. Yet the CPP and Left intelligentsia more generally did take reasonably clear stands with regard to Pakistan's multinational composition soon after the 1948 Calcutta Congress.

Nevertheless, outmigration of Hindu and Sikh cadres and the nonlocal character of communist left's leadership impeded the task of outreach to the nooks and crannies of Pakistan's multiethnic and unevenly developed society.

In my reading, rank-and-file leftist revolutionaries like Yamin were by no means "out of touch" with their surroundings. They constantly not only tried to connect to grounded material struggles in localized terrain, but also remained extremely conscious of the politics of identity, and did not, as a matter of course, subsume the "national question" within the larger rubric of class struggle. To this day, Yamin argues convincingly both that there is a single ruling class in Pakistan and the fact of ethnic-national cleavages shaping the body-politic. He acknowledges that even a progressive party like the NAP, which historically gave significant priority to the "national question," ultimately could not cater fully to Pakistan's complex social mosaic and articulate a politics to challenge the unitary nation-building project of the Pakistani ruling class. But at the same time he insists that what matters is one's political position vis-à-vis the national question rather than ethnic-linguistic identity per se. He cannot answer for others, but he remains convinced that his role in and around the army action kept alive the best universalist traditions of the Left.

In the post-Cold War world, the "national question" remains as prominent as ever, but class as a political identity, and the labor, student, and peasant movements, have all suffered retreat (Chibber 2006). For Yamin, the Left's task is to continually acknowledge historic forms of exploitation and oppression even while remaining true to a revolutionary humanism that can be universalized across uneven historical-geographical terrain.

Where Are the Women?

If there was one question—and subject—that remained conspicuous by its absence for most of my three informants' political lives, it was that of patriarchy and women. Zahoor notes that one of the first leaders that he looked up to during his time with NSF in Karachi was Lala Rukh Hussain (known to her comrades as Lali); he later named one of his daughters Lala Rukh, even giving her the nickname Lali. Munir and Yamin also recall women in the struggle fondly, yet it was only over the course of many conversations over many years that I was able to get them to accept the imperative of according centrality to the question of patriarchy within leftist canon; they certainly acknowledge that it remained marginal to the Left during their youth.

All three insist that they were part of many, relatively successful attempts to organize among women and girls, and even trans people, But they also acknowledge that the Left was unable—and, in the case of many men in positions of power, unwilling—to accept women at the highest positions within party organizations, let alone consider them part of what Gramsci would call the "professional category" of Left intellectuals.

On a quite different yet arguably even more important plane, younger members of our political circles—particularly women—have challenged Zahoor, Munir, and Yamin over the years about the fact that revolution must begin at home, by dismantling everyday patriarchy. On the whole, all three of them have done much better than most

Pakistani men—and, indeed, leftists—in terms of their relations with, and autonomy of, wives and daughters, but there are some thresholds that their understanding and personal conduct have not transcended.

When All Is Said and Done

> *Everyday you have to fight so that love for humanity can be transformed into concrete deeds, into acts that set an example, that mobilize.*
>
> Che Guevara

The three men that I have chronicled in this essay are neither apologetic about their lifelong struggle nor unwilling to acknowledge how their own ideas about society, class struggle, and revolutionary transformation evolved through the course of their struggle. It was this openness to learning through practice that drew me to them. When I met them at the turn of the millennium, they had scarcely recovered from the trauma of actually existing socialism's demise. But they were still excited to engage to a new generation of budding revolutionaries that wanted to connect to "the people," whatever form the latter took.

We disagreed about many things, including the importance of "the party," how to conceptualize international politics in a post-Cold War world, and, most significantly, whether the classical ideas of a revolutionary vanguard were still relevant. But none of them ever insisted on the righteousness of their conceptions, or offered stiff opposition to political work on the ground, no matter how different it looked to the classical labor, student, and peasant movements with which they were familiar. Indeed, with time they have acknowledged the very big glaring absences in their own political experience. These include, as I noted in the previous section, the question of patriarchy, as well as the ecological implications of industrialism. They now recognize that the specifically Pakistani variant of capitalism will neither conform to the Western prototype, nor is "Progress" simply an end in itself given the realities of global warming and climate change.

As the editors of this volume note in the introduction, a concept of "homogeneous, empty time" undergirded revolutionary imaginaries through much of the twentieth century. This was both cause and consequence of the deterministic notions of historical change that, at least rhetorically, were espoused by my informants, like so many of their peers. Yet I have also demonstrated that, in practice, they sought, as the editor's note, to "reconnect the potentiality of the past, which is never quite dead, to the living." Zahoor, Munir, and Yamin were able and willing to engage with a plethora of "living" subjects, including those who identified themselves in ethnic-national terms, were imbued with faith, or, simply made political choices on the basis of membership of a kinship group.

That Left-revolutionaries took these real subjectivities and articulated them as necessarily consistent with the trinity of *tulba, mazdoor, aur kissan* represented, in my reading, an effort to *make* history, a creative undertaking that all political workers must attempt inasmuch as doing politics is more akin to art than science. Yet politics as art, as history-making, can coexist, in sometimes uncomfortable dialectical contradiction, with the deployment of scientific methods to theorize processes of change in the longue durée.

This is why, even now, as they try and fathom a world far more complex than the one they remember trying to transform in their youth, Zahoor, Munir, and Yamin yearn for an "easy" imaginary of revolution. This yearning, I must admit, bubbles up to the surface ever once so often in myself too.

Perhaps it is this yearning for the idealized revolutionary past that explains why some old adages remain intact for all three of my informants; for instance, they still insist that the party leadership should never be exclusively in "middle-class" hands. It is worth reiterating that the Left's rank-and-file in the heyday of Left politics had a somewhat tortured relationship to the Marxist canon. On the one hand, the classics were eulogized, and, in turn, the intellectual leadership of the Left idolized because most party workers relied on the latter to "read" foundational texts. On the other hand, however, the rank-and-file exercised substantial autonomy when venturing out into society to locate workers, students, and peasants and create collectivities of "the people."

This incipient tension between the paternalism of leaders and the everyday conduct of the rank-and-file came to a head for one of my informants through an epochal historical moment. Zahoor Khan was made a member of the Central Committee of the CPP in 1990, which afforded him the chance to travel to Moscow on an official state visit. In his account, ascent to this leadership position was explained precisely by the fact that many "middle-class" leaders of the party were jumping off what they perceived to be a sinking ship.[8] Zahoor recounts that his time in Moscow reaffirmed his latent suspicion of "middle-class" leadership. The professional-managerial cadres of the Soviet bureaucracy had acquired too much political and economic control of the Bolshevik Revolution, generating apathy among the mass of the people of USSR. This translated into limited resistance to the rapid dissolution of the Soviet federation. For Zahoor, this experience confirmed that any revolutionary organization must remain true to Lenin's classic formula of at least half of the central committee being made up by "working class" members.

At the same time, he somewhat sheepishly acknowledges that, in the thirty years since the demise of actually existing socialism, the "working class" has moved gradually further away from the revolutionary class consciousness that he spent most of his life trying to inculcate. When pressed, he agrees that "the people," like other conceptual constructs, is both internally differentiated and not by any means on a predictable trajectory of social consciousness that corresponds to development of productive forces. As such, then, there are neither guarantees about the conduct of "middle-class" leaders, rank-and-file revolutionaries nor "the people" broadly conceived. The "intermediate" life histories I have briefly documented here illuminate precisely that revolutionary subjectivity can and must be conceptualized intimately—dialectically, in fact. If, on the

[8] Zahoor was very close to Jamal Naqvi, who served as secretary-general of the CPP in the late 1980s and early 1990s. While Naqvi had not "abandoned ship" by the time Zahoor became a member of the Central Committee, his subsequent trajectory bears out at least some of Zahoor's account. See Naqvi (2014).

one hand, this allows for us to distinguish the eclectic political practices of the many that gave their lives to the revolution from the more overly simplistic understandings of history that prevailed in at least some sections of the Left intelligentsia, then it also has significant implications for the present and future of Left organizing.

What drew me to Zahoor, Munir, and Yamin two decades ago was their understated, daily pursuit of revolution. Here I understand revolution to be, following Che Guevara, concrete deeds and acts that, on an everyday basis, inspire and mobilize others to transform themselves and society at large. My three informants certainly aspired to see a mass political uprising that culminated in the acquisition of political power by The Party. Such aspirations also undergirded their sometimes uncritical adherence to a “party line” and attendant theories of historical change.

But, when all is said and done, it is the intimate doses of humanity expressed on a daily basis that most meaningfully reflect commitment to a revolutionary cause. Despite disappointments and even betrayal by erstwhile leaders, Zahoor, Munir, and Yamin remained committed to what was—and is—the daily grind of political organizing. Exercising autonomy as individuals, they always directed their own efforts toward larger organizational goals, innovation, and creativity central tenets of the unending quest to foment a revolutionary subject to enact social transformation.

In the process, they changed themselves, and remain open to doing so till this day. Contemporary revolutionaries have of course not inherited the certainty about a particular revolutionary form like Zahoor, Munir, and Yamin experienced in their youth. In comparison to both Pakistan and the world during the heyday of revolutionary internationalism, objective and subjective conditions for transformative politics in today’s world often appear to be limited. The certainties that are generated by teleological readings of History are now in the past. This is precisely why intermediate histories of revolutionaries like Zahoor, Munir, and Yamin are important to add to the historical archive.

Flawed, but willing to learn—and unlearn—my three informants have to this day remained committed to principles of collective organization so as to work through the uncertainties that actually existing political life has thrown up. Following Raza (2020: 253–4), such life histories invite us to conceptualize in simple terms “alternate ethical subjectivities and possibilities that seem increasingly foreclosed in contemporary South Asia today.” To espouse universal sensibilities, to seek transformation of the self, and to come together as “the people” to both imagine and struggle even in molecular ways for a shared future free of exploitation of all kinds are horizons and practices that, I submit, we must continue to uphold.

Bibliography

Ahmad, A. 1978. “Democracy and Dictatorship in Pakistan.” *Journal of Contemporary Asia* 8 (4): 477–512.

Ahmed, F. 1972. “The Struggle in Bangladesh.” *Bulletin of Concerned Asian* Scholars 4 (1): 2–22.

Ali, K. A. 2005. "The Strength of the Street Meets the Strength of the State: The 1972 Labor Struggle in Karachi." *International Journal of Middle East Studies*, 37 (1): 83–107.

Ali, K. A. 2015. *Surkh Salam: Communist Politics and Class Activism in Pakistan, 1947–1972*. Oxford: Oxford University Press.

Ali, N. G. 2020. "Agrarian Class Struggle and State Formation in Post-colonial Pakistan, 1959–1974: Contingencies of Mazdoor Kisan Raj." *Journal of Agrarian Change* 20 (2): 270–88.

Anderson, K. B. 2016. *Marx at the Margins*. Chicago: University of Chicago Press.

Azhar, A. 2019. *Revolution in Reform: Trade-Unionism in Lahore, c. 1920–70*. Hyderabad: Orient BlackSwan.

Chibber, V. 2006. "On the Decline of Class Analysis in South Asian Studies." *Critical Asian Studies* 38 (4): 357–87.

Llorente, R. 2013. "Marx's Concept of 'Universal Class': A Rehabilitation." *Science & Society* 77 (4): 536–60.

Malik, A. 2013. "Alternative Politics and Dominant Narratives: Communists and the Pakistani State in the Early 1950s." *South Asian History and Culture* 4 (4): 520–37.

Malik, A. 2018. "Public Authority and Local Resistance: Abdur Rehman and the Industrial Workers of Lahore, 1969–1974." *Modern Asian Studies* 52 (3): 815–48.

Memon, Q. B., Z. Yousaf, and A. Shah. 2013. "'I Am a Poet of Workers and Peasants': Working-Class Poets of Pakistan." *World Literature Today* 87 (6): 47–50.

Naqvi, J. 2014. *Leaving the Left Behind*. Karachi: University of Karachi, Pakistan Study Centre.

Nelson, M. J. 2011. "Embracing the Ummah: Student Politics beyond State Power in Pakistan." *Modern Asian Studies* 45 (3): 565–96.

Raza, A. 2013. "An Unfulfilled Dream: The Left in Pakistan *ca*. 1947–50." *South Asian History and Culture* 4 (4): 503–19.

Raza, A. 2020. *Revolutionary Pasts: Communist Internationalism in Colonial India*. Cambridge: Cambridge University Press.

Therborn, G. 2018. *From Marxism to Post-Marxism?*. London: Verso Books.

Traverso, E. 2016. *Left-Wing Melancholia*. New York: Columbia University Press.

12

The People in Their Difference

Humeira Iqtidar

Introduction

In March 2013, a neighborhood with predominantly Christian residents in one of the older sections of Lahore was burnt by a mob. Luckily, there were no deaths. However, more than one hundred families lost their homes as well as assets such as painstakingly collected dowry furniture. More critically, in the context of increased bureaucratization of all spheres of life, the loss of paperwork such as ID cards, educational certificates and degrees, and land ownership deeds meant that those impacted had the daunting task of investing money, time, and social capital in reconstructing their place in the world of "*kaghaz raj*" described so well by Matthew Hull (2012).

The burning of Joseph Colony came to international attention as part of an ongoing discussion regarding the presumed rise of intolerance in Pakistan. The *New York Times* claimed that "the devastation was a testament to the intolerance sweeping across Pakistani society."[1] Within the country commentators called for tolerance, and the incident motivated an outpouring of reflection, anger, and debate, as well as aid for Joseph Colony inhabitants. The initial narrative, and the one that dominates records of the event, was that the burning was undertaken by a mob of Muslims blinded by their anger at the alleged blasphemy committed by a Christian.[2] The dispute between two young men, Muslim Imran and Christian Sawan, one drunken night, transformed into an inter-communal attack. However, as part of a citizen's commission that spent time talking with residents of both the Christian and the Muslim *mohallas* or neighborhoods, the story that subsequently emerged raised doubts about whether there had ever been such a dispute between Imran and Sawan. Regardless of the truth of these accusations, Sawan Masih was imprisoned in March 2013, sentenced to death in 2014, and only acquitted in October 2020. He spent seven years in jail. The 115 accused of participating in the burning were acquitted due to lack of evidence in 2017.

1 Declan Walsh and Waqas Gillani, "Attack on Christians Follows Claim of Blasphemy in Pakistan," *NY Times*, March 9, 2013. http://www.nytimes.com/2013/03/10/world/asia/explosion-rips-through-mosque-in-peshawar-pakistan.html?_r=0.

2 The legal framework for contemporary blasphemy laws in Pakistan is in large part a product of colonial statecraft. See Asad Ahmed (2009).

The citizen's commission, set up with scholars and activists in Lahore, sought to investigate the Joseph Colony burning. I spent several weeks trying to understand how the burning had happened.[3] For all of us, Lahore is the city we call home. Aware of the inequality and brashness that is increasingly coming to define the city, we were also mindful of the longer histories of multiethnic, multireligious cohabitation in this city. We wanted to understand the precise role of multiple pressures that seem to be moving the city away from those histories. Within living memory of many inhabitants the city had had a roughly equal Hindu, Sikh, and Muslim population. While their numbers had been significantly lower, Christians have been a part of the city since the sixteenth century. The expansion of the city's educational institutions under colonial rule also entailed greater social mobility for many of the largely Dalit Hindus who had converted to Christianity during the nineteenth and early twentieth centuries. While Partition violence and religious nationalism explain much in terms of the narrowing of public imagination in Pakistan generally, they do not provide an adequate understanding of the precise moments as well as forms of marginalization practiced in contemporary Lahore.

To highlight not just the specificity of forms of marginalization but also the responses they evoke more starkly I will juxtapose the experience of Joseph Colony inhabitants with that of another group of Lahore's citizens: refugees and migrants from the Federally Administered Tribal Areas (FATA) of Pakistan. The subtle but palpable difference in their treatment linked to and following the Joseph Colony incident, difference now coded through ethnicity and not religion, is important for a consideration of the scope of liberal norms of managing exclusion and difference through the framework of tolerance. Thinking about these two communities within the city also connects Lahore's histories more directly to international political order, more specifically in this case the global war of terror. FATA, home to about four million people, was subjected to US drone attacks and Pakistani army operations from 2004 to 2018. There can be little doubt that the war in Afghanistan had, for the last two decades, brought equal devastation for the denizens of FATA. Pakistani government had encouraged migration into special camps during particularly intensive periods but many also moved to other urban areas using existing networks of contacts and relatives. The refugees from FATA were labeled Internally Displaced Persons (IDPs) but there was little recognition of their rights as Pakistani citizens. A history of legal, social, and political separation from the larger Pakistani polity has meant that the tribals are perceived by themselves internally and by others within Pakistan as inhabiting a liminal place inside the official borders but outside the rule of law of the land as well as its social norms (Embree 1977; Nawaz 2009; Spain 1977; Shaw and Akhte 2011; Tanguay-Renaud 2002). The influx of refugees from FATA as a result of war became particularly pronounced in Lahore from 2008 onward. However, seasonal migrants from tribal areas have a much longer history in Lahore (Nadir 2013).

[3] A short version of our report was published in the *Express Tribune* as "Burning Joseph Colony," September 13, 2013 (tribune.com.pk). The other members of the citizens' commission were Rabia Nadir, Sadaf Aziz, and Ammara Maqsood.

A brief word about the oral histories and ethnographic interviews that form the basis of this analysis:[4] There can be little doubt that collecting oral histories is not an uncomplicated matter of placing a microphone in front of a willing speaker. Its radical potential through centering unknown figures and taking seriously life experiences of the marginalized is unevenly realized due to ambivalence about how best to use the material generated by oral histories without either drowning in minutiae of detail or disregarding the particularities (Abrams 2010; Portelli 2010). Moreover, oral history accounts by the same narrator might shift with time, interviewer, and other audiences. And so, oral history might be helpfully approached as a tool of self-fashioning for the narrator (Scott 1991). Ultimately, collecting oral histories is a messy business; it is full of divergences, interesting asides, and confusing connections. Unlike the neat but perhaps limited narratives contained in texts, human beings carry many surprises and multiple narratives. Why, when and if anybody will share their life's experiences and which aspect they will pick from the multiple ones available to them remains complicated.

However, oral histories are uniquely valuable guides to the discourses and ideological resources available to narrators rather than primarily as a means for gathering data. Moreover, a key benefit of this immensely personal way of understanding history is that the asides open vistas into lives and experiences that a more rigid data-gathering approach might miss. For instance, the deep and yet subtle ways in which state institutions and social norms continue to mark the other becomes apparent from the daily encounters that many endure: from Pashtun rickshaw drivers who talk about the extra aside they must keep for policemen to avoid being locked up as terrorists in case of traffic violation, to students from Tribal Areas in university hostels who are always the first ones to be searched if there is any concern about violence on campus, and to Christian tenants living in precarious circumstances, where they must pay more in rent in certain neighbourhoods. The boundary that is drawn between one group and the other is imagined and enacted in multiple ways that only become apparent through a more open-ended understanding of those experiences. The attempt here is to recognize this open-endedness and rather than establishing a hierarchy of victimhood unravel the contemporary neat packaging of certain peoples as deserving of compassion and others who can only receive "zero tolerance."

A recurrent problem for all people's histories is defining the people. Nationalist and populist visions of the people seem to inevitably require the exclusion of some. Liberalism, particularly liberal nationalism, similarly requires a drawing of boundaries around a particular "people" to whom equal rights are extended. In the past this vision of the people excluded women, working classes, religious minorities, and racialized others. Contemporary exclusions carry the imprint of these earlier ones but in more subtle guises. Liberal polities attempt to mitigate exclusion through the concept of tolerance and the privatization of beliefs. But key questions remain, when and how do

[4] I am grateful to Noor Akbar and Ammara Maqsood for their invaluable research assistance and contributions to the project funded by the European Research Council titled "Tolerance in Contemporary Muslim Polities: Political Theory Beyond the West." The names of all the Pashtun interlocutors have been changed in accordance with their wishes.

certain groups and communities become available as legitimate objects of tolerance? What are the limitations of such liberal strategies of inclusion as they do not question structural exclusions? Drawing on the experience of two marginalized communities in Lahore, I investigate the ways in which their place in the city is linked to international political projects as well as local norms. Foregrounding the experiences of inhabitants of Joseph Colony, burned down in 2013 by a mob, as well as refugees and migrants from the Tribal Areas who faced various forms of marginalization in the city, I highlight the limits of liberal strategies for managing exclusion from the category, people.

Joseph Colony: Christians, Punjabis

It is not clear when the two young men fought with each other, but if at all, the incident would have taken place on Tuesday or Wednesday of March 5 or 6, 2013. It was only on Friday afternoon that a small crowd led by Shafiq, a local laborer and small-time drug dealer—as we found out later[5]—gathered in front of Sawan's house asking the family to hand him over so that he could be punished for committing blasphemy. Shafiq and Imran were both residents of Sheikhabad mohalla, a neighborhood not more than 5 minutes' walk from Joseph colony. Given how close the communities were and that many of these young men had grown up quite literally in each other's homes, some of the older members of Joseph Colony tried to reason with Shafiq, plead with him and also to scold him. Shafiq seemed drunk and a little high.[6]

Police had been alerted and at this point a combination of police and community intervention meant that the crowd dispersed. However, soon after police officers went from house to house to ask residents to leave Joseph Colony immediately as they could not guarantee their safety. In a narrative reminiscent of India–Pakistan Partition experiences, people told us of the panic this created. Many claimed to have left without putting *dupattas* or shoes on properly. Police pressure meant that they were unable to collect their belongings, jewelry, cash, but also the all-important paperwork that has become a necessity of urban life. Even as the residents were leaving—and some chose to stay through the whole ordeal—an orgy of looting started. However, it was only on Saturday afternoon that the colony was burnt. Setting a single house alight, let alone a colony, is not a simple matter. These were concrete houses, often with wooden doors and windows, but without enough combustible material to catch fire just by the throwing of a matchstick. Residents who had dared to stay close to keep an eye on their homes saw bottles of chemicals used for the arson. The burning has been presented in mainstream media as the work of a frenzied crowd, but this was clearly a planned attack.

But who planned and financed this attack? In the early days of our investigation, denizens of Joseph Colony laid more blame on the "*karkhana walas*," the steel mill

5 This was acknowledged also by his relatives. Meeting at Shafiq's house with his mother, April 13, 2013.

6 When one of our older interlocutors who tried to persuade Shafiq mentioned that she smelled alcohol on his breath as she spoke to him that day, others listening to our conversation concurred.

owners whose workshops surround the colony, than members of Sheikhabad mohalla. The method and extent of burnings spoke of finances, planning, and influence with the local police.[7] People asked why did the police not arrest Shafiq on the first day, when he started stirring up trouble? Why did they empty the colony and then wait around while it was looted? And why, most importantly, did they wait around until and while the colony was being burnt one whole day after Shafiq's performance in front of Sawan's house? The alleged motive among the *karkhana walas*, some of whom are also believed to be the only ones in the neighborhood to have any influence on police behavior, was to vacate this property to use it for building bigger warehouses. Joseph Colony certainly occupies prime real estate in the heart of a congested part of the city. The finances, planning, and employment of local roughs, such as Shafiq, suggest that this suspicion may be valid, although it remains to be seen who specifically among the *karkhana* owners was responsible.

As the weeks passed, we noticed a change in discussions about the burning. A narrative of shared ethnicity between Christians and Muslims in the neighborhood became prominent and residents of both Joseph Colony and Sheikhabad began to blame Pathan migrants into the area for the arson. Residents of the two mohallas spoke of their long-running relationships with each other and we began to hear comments like "we buy all our groceries from the Sheikhabad shops" or "we have known these Christian children for years. Our children play together." Some claimed relationships across the two mohallas suggesting that "many of these Sheikhabad Muslims are *Musali*, recently converted from Christianity. X is my sister-in-law's relative." We learnt that Imran, the Muslim man who is said to have accused Sawan and mysteriously disappeared right after, used to bring his mother and sisters to spend their days in the Christian household when they visited from the village.

It seemed that despite the traumatic events there was an attempt at establishing a working relationship again. Perhaps one way to reestablish that working relationship was to shift the blame beyond Sheikhabad. Blaming the Pathans as inherently violent people, certainly willing to undertake violence for a fee, offered in this case by the *karkhanawallas*, seemed to blend in with widely held views about their ferocity and divergent social norms from the Punjabis of both colonies. Ethnicity is an important bond between the Muslims and Christians in the neighborhood. It is virtually impossible to tell the residents of one colony apart from those of the other. As many a Joseph Colony resident pointed out to us,

> There is no way to tell a Christian apart from a Muslim here. Some of us stood in the crowds watching as our houses were being burnt. As long as we didn't protest who could tell?

However, what this comment and others like it also alerted us to was the possibility that many who had participated in the burning were not from Sheikhabad—they

[7] Some have pointed toward local elections in the area and suggested that the blasphemy charge became an election issue. See Omar Warraich, "The Anatomy of an Attack on Christians in Pakistan," *The Times*, March 11, 2013; "Pakistan: What Sparks Mob Attack on Christians," Homes | TIME.com.

did not recognize their Christian neighbors. Some Joseph Colony residents also stated explicitly that while they recognized some residents of Sheikhabad among the attackers, the vast majority were unknown to them. Increasingly, many contended that most of the arsonists were Pathan. A large number of Pashtuns worked for local factories and many had, in fact, replaced Punjabi laborers because of their willingness to work longer hours for less pay. Sheikhabad, whose residents are mostly day laborers, is a poorer neighborhood than Joseph colony whose residents tend to have a higher educational levels and have more stable employment in the municipality or with NGOs.[8] The Pashtuns working in the *karkhanas* live in an even more rundown neighborhood adjoining Sheikhabad. These tensions across minor and major class differences, ethnicity, and religious traditions had been subsumed in the focus on blasphemy laws, but also point toward the difficulty of imagining a ready grouping of the "people" inhabiting the nation-state of Pakistan.

Badami Bagh: Pashtuns, Tribals

We then moved our attention to the neighborhood where the Pashtun attackers had allegedly come from. The councilor for the part of Badami Bagh where many Pakhtun migrants had settled had no compunction conflating Pashtun with tribal, and tribal with Taliban: "These tribal types, Taliban, Pathans are all crazy (*pagal*) as you know too (*aap ko bhi pata hai*). They have no scruples: they will say their prayers and then go sell a sack of heroin. There was no tension (used in English) in our area before these people came here." The association of violence with Pashtuns generally and with people from the Tribal Areas more specifically became an increasing feature of discourses in the urban centers of Pakistan from the mid-2000s onward. It was most pronounced in Karachi where the MQM ran a largely effective campaign for many years to conflate Pathan, tribal, and Taliban into one category.[9]

The local councilor, who we met before meeting any of the Pathan families in that area, kept repeating that the Pathans were all recent migrants, immensely violent and unlikely to meet us. "In fact," he said, standing just outside his gate as we left his home, "you are wasting your time trying to talk to them. I can bet you that you will not even be able to cross the threshold of any Pathan household. It is best for you to turn back now." He spoke with a sense of deep ownership. His family had owned and continued to live in the congested, heavily built over area, which was, as late as the 1950s, part of large fruit gardens. Hence the name Badami Bagh for this area that surrounded the walled city of Lahore and the Mughal fort. These fruit gardens, splendid with blossoms from a wide variety of fruit trees, including almonds, guava,

8 Much of the extant academic literature on Christians in Pakistan is structured around the question of marginalization and exclusion. A recent exception is Ryan Brasher's (2020) study that is attentive to other aspects of Christian life including variations in levels of political engagement and educational attainment.

9 Pamphlets produced by the Muhajir Quami Movement (MQM) between 2008 and 2010 sent to the Centre for South Asian Studies, University of Cambridge, and now with the author.

and mangoes, were quite dramatically transformed into densely packed urban housing after Partition.

The question of how many Pashtun families lived in the locality was a more politically charged one than we had originally realized. The councillor refused to give us a direct answer insisting that the Pashtuns who lived in the area were not settled here. They did not consider Lahore their home, he claimed. He had collected the names of all residents during a campaign to ration out spray to kill mosquitoes carrying dengue in each street. However, there was no official requirement for collecting details of the inhabitants of each house; their ID card number and other details that he showed us neatly catalogued in a register, just to figure out how much spray is needed. As we realized later, the numbers of Pashtun families and their members in the locality were significant enough to tip the balance in elections that were held a month after the Joseph Colony burnings. Pashtuns in the locality tended overwhelmingly to support Imran Khan's Pakistan Tehreek-e-Insaaf at that time due to Khan's vocal critique of drone attacks. In the past this area had been a PML-N stronghold.

The simple story of frenzied crowds and rising intolerance took another turn when we started factoring in the role of the upcoming elections. The ruling party at the provincial level, Muslim League Nawaz group, had responded with extreme speed to the plight of Joseph Colony inhabitants, albeit only after the colony had been burnt. The government announced funds to rebuild houses within a five-week period and to our surprise we saw them being constructed within that time. Plaques thanking the chief minister for supporting the Christian community were put up at the entrance of the older Anglican Church and the newer American evangelical Church in the colony. Both had been damaged by the burning and were restored right away. But more than the gratitude of a few hundred Christians and the bolstering of the government's credentials as a "tolerant" regime, Joseph Colony burnings also afforded the ruling party a chance to criminalize supporters of the then new upstart political party PTI. We found out as we met families in their homes in the Badami Bagh area that many Pakhutun families had been living there for more than twenty years. At the same time, most families also tried to maintain a base in their village. Several families operated a rotational system where siblings and their families would take turns to look after land and the elderly in the village in tribal areas. However, this meant the larger family had retained a home in Lahore for many decades and the children were comfortable in Pashto and Urdu/Punjabi.[10] Yet, given the dynamics of the then upcoming elections, these long settled Pathans were having trouble getting their votes registered.

[10] None of them were recent immigrants, and not all from the tribal areas. Although the Pathans had tended to group together in some streets, they came from a mix of urban, rural, tribal, and "settled" areas. The distinction between settled and tribal regions is a construct of the colonial administration that was in large part driven by administrative concerns (Marsh 2015: 12–34). One family from Mohmand Agency had been living in the area for some thirty years. The extended family of grandparents, four brothers and their families was divided in its support for both PML (N) and PTI, but regardless of this none of the eligible members of family had been able to register their vote. Another family was preparing to move back to Swat when we met them but was planning on retaining the house in Lahore by renting it out to friends from Swat.

While it is entirely conceivable that some Pakhtun laborers from the *karkhanas* could have joined the burning for money or conviction, their criminalization as a group in major urban centers of Pakistan can be seen as a double betrayal of their citizenship. Those worst affected by the violence of the war on terror, at the receiving end of operations carried out by both the Pakistani Army and American drones, bore the brunt of constant blame as a group for the activities of a few among them. Their collective punishment continues beyond the confines of FATA where the British-instituted practice of group incarceration had intensified under the Pakistani state. The notorious Frontiers Crimes Regulation was formally repealed only in 2018, but its legacy of distrust and fear on all sides continues.

The long history of Pashtuns in Lahore city has been sidelined to make room for a vision of the Pashtuns as dangerous and recent intruders. Such a discourse ignores the fact that the walled city of Lahore had many well-known Pashtun families since the time of Mahmud Ghaznavi and that traders from Mohmand, Bajaur, and Waziristan, in particular, have long carried out seasonal migration to Lahore (Nadir 2013: 67–74). Here let us just note that from Rohillas in Mughal Court to Rampur during colonial period, Pakistani military elite to families dominating certain aspects of bureaucracy, from late-nineteenth-century migrants to Australia to contemporary circular migration to the Gulf region (Nichols 2008), FATA "tribals" are much more integrated in regional and transnational history than their construction as isolated peoples can acknowledge, and FATA has been much more entrenched in global markets than the compulsions of the war on terror would allow. In agencies such as Bajaur and Waziristan, my interlocutors claimed that every household has one member who had worked or is working in the UAE and/or Gulf countries.[11] This is not one-time migration, this is circular in the sense that people move back and forth, and there is a flow of ideas, practices, and of course products.

While much attention has focused on drones due the contravention of laws of war that the new technology allows the United States, and the threat this presents to democratic decision making[12] there has been little understanding of the fundamental transformation in the lives of FATA residents because of a long-running war in their region that was not officially recognized for many years. The first time I met Haleem Khan, we sat in a little tea stall, opposite his shoe shop in the walled city of Lahore. I asked him about his experience of moving to Lahore and how his new neighbors had acted toward him and his family. The issue, he replied, was not of unkindness or hostility, but of a lack of acknowledgment of what they had been through. Karim Khan had escaped a war zone, from a war that the state of Pakistan did not officially acknowledge and few in urban Lahore had a clear sense of.

[11] Akbar Ahmed (quoted in Nichols (2008: 174n.33) claimed by 1984 that of the 300,000 total residents of South Waziristan Nichols, 20–30,000 men had migrated to the Gulf. This trend continued and even accelerated through the 1990s and the 2000s.

[12] See, for instance, Humeira Iqtidar, "The Killing of British Citizens without Ddemocratic Oversight Raises Questions Qver the Government's Use of Drones," (lse.ac.uk), October 15, 2015.

> How can we explain our lives to our neighbours here in Lahore … it is so different that (he shrugged) …. The first time that we heard the drones we all ran to bunkers with our children and our animals and spent the whole day sitting in there. But when it came back the next day and the next and just stood there, what could we do? We can't spend all this time in the *khandaq*. We then left our children and animals in the bunkers and went back to our fields. I can't tell you what it feels like to have that thing hovering in the sky above you … Now we have brought our women and children here and they are miserable living in one room.

Haleem Khan's experience expresses eloquently the loneliness that comes not from outright ostracization but from a lack of acknowledgment. He was quick to note that his neighbors in Lahore just had no idea. Nothing in mainstream media representations, in government or civil society statements, in cultural and literary production circulating in the city alerted them to the terror that Haleem Khan and his family had lived through. In fact, despite all the background research I had done before I started the project I too was not able to fully appreciate the layers in his halting narration of that experience until later. He was one of the first people I had met when I started the project. When he narrated his experience, I was unsure if drones really did hover in sight of the villagers. It turns out that they did, and that the US government did use that as a tool of psychological terror.[13]

At the same time, dominant discourses did focus on terror but of a different kind: the type allegedly perpetrated by those who looked and sounded like Haleem Khan. The compulsions of the war on terror meant that an everyday familiarity with the names of some cities was promoted through news reports and commentary at the same time as a sense of immense distance from those regions for inhabitants of Lahore. As a student from Waziristan at the National College of Arts reflecting on his experience in Lahore commented,

> Even here in NCA, a supposedly progressive college, people think that the tribal areas are like a jungle but that is not the case. Our area was also once like this city, but just at a much smaller scale. We had our own culture—and it was not just guns and wars—and we had all kinds of people—like journalists, teachers—but that's all gone now and nobody knows about it.

The continuous repetition of narratives about the tribal areas as beyond civilization and the tribals as people ultimately wedded to an entirely different code of conduct had had a profound effect on public imagination in Lahore, with very real material effects for Pashtuns. What this student meant by singling NCA out as a "supposedly progressive college" was the fact that in many other universities and colleges in Lahore students from the tribal areas felt that they were targets of suspicion from students and faculty. Another student at a different university said:

[13] Saeed Shah, "Deadly Pilotless Aircraft That Have Helped Fuel Anti-American Feeling in Tribal Belt, Al-Qaida," November 24, 2008, *The Guardian. Deadly pilotless aircraft that have helped fuel anti-American feeling in tribal belt | Al-Qaida | The Guardian*. Accessed November 21, 2022.

> Earlier I used to tell people I am from Peshawar because I didn't want to explain where Miranshah was; they didn't know the name. Now I just tell people I am from Peshawar because they think they know too much about Miranshah!

This too vividly imagined Miranshah is encompassed in the construction of FATA residents as primitives; this narrative is important for America's war as well as Pakistani military action. The framing presented drone attacks and later Pakistani army invasion as inevitable: there can be no negotiation, "we" of urban, civilized centers cannot actually go there and thus drones/military action is the only solution. Tribals presented as people outside of history and global circulations became a feature of the urban Pakistani imaginary such that many liberal activists and groups actively urged the Pakistani military to attack the tribal areas. In an open letter to the Government of Pakistan, these civil society actors and human rights activists stated that

> we, representatives of civil society organizations, fully support military operation in North Waziristan launched under the direction of the federal government and assert that the nation must stand behind our military and democratic forces as no country can allow insurgents controlling parts of its territory.[14]

By the time this letter was written in 2014 there was enough evidence to show that some of the most nefarious Taliban groups were those that locals claimed were supported by the Pakistani military. Yet in a strangely twisted argument these civil society activists insisted on the same military carrying out an attack in FATA. There is absolutely no concern expressed for the citizens of the region who were caught between the militants and the military. At no point in the letter do these activists even mention the citizens of the tribal areas. The long-term measures proposed by these groups did not include a single demand for better infrastructure or livelihoods for the citizens of the tribal areas, concerns that a movement in later years led by Pashtun youths, the Pashtun Tahafuz Movement, highlighted consistently. Nor did the open letter express any concern regarding their safety during the operations. There was not a single word about short- or long-term implications of the military operations for the people of FATA, no discussion of what might be needed to support them while their houses are being bombed, and no concern about how they might earn their livelihoods, or rebuild their lives. This was a form of collective punishment worse than the British had ever meted out, as older Pashtun respondents continuously pointed out to me.

[14] The letter was signed on behalf of the following organizations: Human Rights Commission of Pakistan, Aurat Foundation, Citizens-Police Liaison Committee, War Against Rape, Network for Women's Rights, Shirkatgah, Legal Rights' Forum, HANDS, Women Action Forum, Joint Action Committee, Bint-e-Fatima Old Home, Roshni Helpline, Pakistan Institute for Labour Education and Research, ActionAid, Urban Resource Centre, and the Sindh Human Rights Commission. Open Letter available at "Civil society and North Waziristan Operation," June 23, 2014. www.tribune.com.pk/story/725448/civil-society-the-north-waziristan- operation/. See also Shahid Husain. "Civil Society Organizations Back Military Operation," *The News*, June 17, 2014. www.thenews.com.pk/Todays-News-4-256409- Civil-society-organisations-back-military-operation- condemn-terrorism.

Instead, the first priority beyond military operations articulated by the civil society groups was "Teaching to our students and children that all religions preach tolerance and harmony."[15] Their commitment to promoting tolerance in Pakistan betrayed a deep sense of removal and detachment from the citizens of the Tribal Areas. In making such demands these liberal groups were closely aligned with the US demand to the Pakistani government for military operations in the region that had by 2014 been tied to ongoing funding for the Pakistani army.[16] In the two-year-long military operation code named "Zarb-e-Azab," close to a million people were displaced from the tribal areas, villages were flattened through aerial bombing and farmers bankrupted through the razing of ready crops. Predictably, "military assets" such as the militant groups supported by the military managed to escape the worst of these attacks.

Concluding Thoughts

"All we want is *aman* and *insaaf*" is a sentence I have heard countless times during the course of this research among the refugees and migrants from FATA as well as from the inhabitants of Joseph Colony. *Aman* and *insaf*, peace and justice. As different kinds of others and outsiders, as potential objects of tolerance in Lahore, their demand is not for tolerance.

In a subtle analysis that juxtaposes debates about British complicity in the slave trade against those about colonial culpability in the criminalization of homosexuality, Rahul Rao (2020) raises a thoughtful question about the contrasting treatments of these and their relationships with "spectres of colonialism." Thus, Rao notes, that in 2012 as part of a House of Lords debate on "The Treatment of Homosexual Men and Women in the Developing World" Lord Lexden, the Conservative peer articulated a widely supported view within the House that

> we must remember where the laws criminalising homosexuals in many countries came from. They came from Britain, which alone among the European empires of the 19th century possessed a criminal code under which homosexuals faced severe penalties just for expressing their love and physical desire for one another. In In India in the 1820s, Thomas Macaulay, later the greatest of all the Whig historians, devised a legal system which incorporated Britain's then firm and unbending intolerance of homosexuality. The Indian penal code became the model for the legal systems of Britain's colonies in most of Africa and Asia. The love that had freely spoken its name and found expression in their native cultures became,

[15] The other demands were the following: Civil society should have constant engagement with the media to transform its current dangerous and negative rhetoric that compromises national security and glorifies the actions of militants; All mosques, madrassas, and related establishments should be registered and their accounts audited, as per law; The government should undertake a serious crackdown on hate literature and take measures to check the brainwashing of young people; and A code of ethics should be developed for the media.

[16] See for instance, "US Pressure for Operation in Waziristan Mounts," *The News*, June 14, 2014. thenews.com.pk.

> in the definition of their new British-imported law, an unnatural offence.(Rao 2020: 107–8)

Rao contrasts this clear acceptance of responsibility in these debates with the ones in 2007 on the question of slavery. The deputy prime minister, Labour politician John Prescott, set the tone by quoting a line that shrank away from working through the relationship between racism and slavery: "Not every black man was innocent. Not every white man was guilty"(Rao 2020: 119). Others followed by pointing out the involvement of Arab and African slave traders. And still others, such as the Liberal Democrat Vince Cable, pointed out the difficulty of taking responsibility for actions taken by very distant ancestors. Although, as Rao notes, this difficulty does not arise when it is a matter of taking pride in accomplishments of those distant ancestors. Various British prime ministers have refused to apologize for the role of Britain in the slave trade, and until recently the triumphalist narrative reigned of liberal, white activists taking Britain out of the slave trade because of its moral repugnancy. The role that Black activists or the slaves themselves played has only recently started getting some recognition. The larger question that Rao raises for our consideration then is, "What is it about our historical moment that allows for the expression of atonement for the homosexual legacies of colonialism more easily than for its racial ones?" (Rao 2020: 131).

His invitation to consider these differences in responses from those in power and his insistence on recognizing the differential imbrication of each with class in Britain is productive. Locating the parallel plight of Lahore's Pakhtuns and Christians within the specific historical moment of the war of/on terror, we see the mobilization of very different discourses to frame and address them. With Joseph Colony framed as an act of religious violence, questions of economic inequality, political power, *and* their imbrication with religious ideas are brushed aside. At the same time, the inhabitants of Joseph Colony become available as recipients of bourgeois charity and international political support. On the other hand, in the case of the migrants and refugees from the tribal areas, we see the difficulty of containing their concerns within the rubric of tolerance. There is not only an ongoing reluctance on the part of the government and the liberal intelligentsia to acknowledge the concerns of these populations, but suspicion of all "tribals" as potential terrorists also continues to circulate in urban Pakistan.

The emergence of tolerance as a central organizing principle for liberal polities requires more investigation given its contemporaneous career with the wars that an imperial America had waged over the last half century and the increase in inequality at a global level. The war on terror in Pakistan coincided with immense increase in economic inequality. During the Musharaf regime, a military dictatorship supported once again by the United States to wage a proxy war in Afghanistan now against erstwhile collaborators in a previous war, the percentage of Pakistani population living below the poverty line increased from 17 percent to more than 45 percent.[17]

[17] "Poverty Headcount Ratio at National Poverty Lines (% of Population)—Pakistan," Data. worldbank. org.

At the same time as a discourse of increasing tolerance in Pakistani society was being promoted through international funding and resources, the regime actively presented certain groups as enemies of tolerance and others as singularly worthy of it.

At an international level the establishment of regimes of tolerance is presented today as a triumph of liberal governance even though there is little historical evidence to support this claim.[18] The still precarious inclusion of minorities and others in twentieth-century liberal polities is as much a product of Cold War competition where liberal polities began to distinguish themselves through their appreciation of diversity, as any inherent thrust within liberalism as many such as David Scott (2003: 9) and Mark Mazower (2009) have persuasively argued. Pakistan, like many other Third World countries, has been on the receiving end of sermons and funding to instruct citizens into tolerance through workshops and seminars, changes in school curricula, youth programs, and cultural interventions. The implication is that the lack of tolerance is a cultural problem that can be eradicated through the right kind of education. A big donor in what we might call the "tolerance industry" is the United States of America.[19]

Given the compulsions of the war on terror, the concerns of tribals in urban centers such as Lahore were almost impossible to acknowledge. Joseph Colony, however, fits neatly within the framework of liberal tolerance given its historical reliance on religious difference as the key difference to be negotiated. I have argued elsewhere (Iqtidar 2020, 2021) that liberal tolerance is conceptually limited by its deep reliance on European wars of religions as the historical context that sustains its contours. The discourse of liberal tolerance, therefore, is unable to fulfill adequately the role that it is increasingly been required to in the context of demands for social and political equality by those marginalized on the basis of race, ethnicity, gender, or class. This inability is linked not just to the Eurocentric assumptions about the centrality of individual freedom of conscience that are baked into liberal tolerance but to internal contradictions that result from those assumptions. I have parsed out these differences in more detail elsewhere to highlight other non-liberal modes of tolerance. Non-liberal tolerance, the dominant mode of peaceful cohabitation in South Asia even today, I argue, is not dependent upon individualized legal rights nor is it premised on the normative priority of freedom of conscience.

Critically, the gains for inhabitants of Joseph Colony through a discourse of tolerance rather than justice or non-liberal tolerance remain precarious. Within America as well as elsewhere, the focus on liberal tolerance has led to an obscuring of the ways in which difference is produced in the first place and sustained over time. Wendy Brown has argued persuasively that the discursive shift from understanding

[18] What is often ignored in these debates is not just the tenuous and fractured nature of these developments and the many reversals along the way but also that tolerance was often the by-product of other logics. In the case of Jews in Britain Ira Katznelson has discussed how a religiously motivated humanism inspired toleration that preceded liberal tolerance (Katznelson 2010).

[19] For instance, the opening paragraph on the first page of the US Aid website on Pakistan states that "The primary focus of the U.S. civilian-assistance program is to develop a stable, secure and tolerant Pakistan with a vibrant economy." http://www.usaid.gov/pakistan. A review of prominent NGOs and civil society organizations that foreground tolerance in their mission statements found that more than 50 percent had received direct funding from the USAID, United States Institute for Peace (USIP), and the National Endowment for Democracy (NED).

tolerance as linked inextricably to questions of justice and equality to one where tolerance is manifested as a question of personal choice has led to a lack of engagement with the political implications of inequality (Brown 2008). The cracks and fissures in the American context with differential access to resources, for instance, across race and class, continue to exist, she argues, but the space to debate about them is narrowed down through a focus on tolerance rather than inequality.

The term "tolerance" has no direct conceptual translation in Urdu, Punjabi, or Pashto. Public debate in urban Pakistan is structured around the English term "tolerance" even though often what is meant is a much more limited "toleration" (for differences between tolerance and toleration, see Katznelson 2010; Walzer 2007; Zucca 2011). The two terms most frequently used in Urdu were *bardasht* and *aman*. Both *bardasht*, putting up with something, and *aman*, peace, suggest very different points of reference and values regarding the place of religious, ethnic, and other minorities in contemporary Pakistan. More importantly, other concepts such as equality, peace, and justice do find ready equivalents in local languages. What to make of this absence of the term "tolerance"? The absence of a direct translation does not mean, of course, that there are no conceptual tools and lived practices to support tolerance in contemporary Pakistan. Only that other ideas and practices, such as those related to justice, have greater depth, ideological resonance, and potential practical value. In paying greater attention to non-liberal norms of peaceful coexistence in diverse and divided cities, for instance, those that might take difference as a given in social life rather than as a problem that needs regulation as in the case of liberal tolerance, or might recognize the centrality of group belonging to human life rather than individualized legal rights, and/or might find inspiration in religious injunctions for justice, we are more likely to be able to speak directly to the concerns highlighted by the marginalized inhabitants of Lahore.

Rather than apportioning blame or establishing victimhood my interest here has been in demonstrating that in a deeply unequal global and national context, in a country riven by the decision taken by a few to support the "war on terror," very much a site of that war itself, the framework of liberal tolerance seems deeply limited. Moreover, for the purposes of this volume my critique of liberal tolerance highlights how this conception rests on a specific vision of the people: as individuals within civil society who seek to maximize their autonomy through practices of citizenship. Those falling outside of this framework or refusing to abide by its political demands—such as the figure of the "pathan" in the war on terror—become available for state and social violence. Through the reimaging of ties between Joseph Colony and its neighbors, which I discussed above, we also glimpse competing visions of the people, as affiliations formed through shared *and* shifting emphases on ethnicity or religion, profession or locality. This more socially grounded vision of the people is unstable. Its commitments can sometimes pull in opposite directions. It can also sanction violence. Yet I suggest it affords a more solid foundation for establishing a just polity.

In an early article titled, "Two European Images of Non-European Rule," Talal Asad contrasts ideas about Non-European governance in the disciplines of anthropology and Orientalist Islamic studies. In the Orientalist literature Islamic governance is autocratic and authoritarian. In contrast, functionalist anthropological literature, often about the same societies, emphasized the consensual relationship between rulers and the ruled and presented it as unchanged, timeless tradition. Asad (1973: 272) contends that the two disciplines are asking the same questions: "What holds society together? How is order achieved or destroyed?" But they bring different approaches to answering them. Both disciplines are similar in the sense that they take certain ideas as given and omit asking some questions. The difference in their approaches is linked, he argued, to their historical formation in relation to colonialism. Orientalism and Islamic Studies originated at a time when European conquest was not assured, and Christian polemicists sought to defend their claims against the threat of Islam. The discipline carries the imprint of this much more conflictual relationship with Islam and its reliance on juridical texts lends authority to a more limited and rigid reading of Islamic norms of governance. Anthropology as a discipline took shape when colonial rule was already established and rested partially on the claim that local norms of governance had not been disturbed in the imposition of foreign rule. In presenting these arrangements as timeless anthropologists were deliberately ignoring colonial structures and the significant changes in norms of governance within these contexts. Both visions are flawed and Asad is not advocating one over the other. Rather his larger point is that "by refusing to discuss the ways in which bourgeoisie had imposed its power and its own conception of the just political order on African and Islamic peoples, both disciplines were basically reassuring to the colonial ruling classes" (274).

As with the two disciplines and their competing visions that Asad discusses, the different visions of the people I have mentioned have their limitations and remain susceptible to exclusionary practices. However, following Asad's line of reasoning once we assess where they are placed in relation to dominant power structures, today we see that different visions of the people that I have discussed are not equally reassuring to contemporary imperial interests. While liberalism provides the dominant ideational framework for imperial projects today, what I am calling more local and social visions of the people are less easily incorporated within such projects. Attuned to the complexity of life, the importance of association in general but the difficulty of complete affiliation with either class, religion, or ethnic group, this more capacious vision of people exceeds both liberal and nationalist ideas.

Bibliography

Abrams, Lynn. 2010. *Oral History Theory*. London: Routledge.

Ahmed, Asad. 2009. "Specters of Macaulay: Blasphemy, the Indian Penal Code, and Pakistan's Postcolonial Predicament," in Raminder Kaur and William Mazzarella (eds.), *Censorship in South Asia: Cultural Regulation from Sedition to Seduction*. Bloomington: University of Indiana Press, 172–205.

Ali, Kamran Asdar. 2005. "Strength of the State Meets the Strength of the Street: The 1972 Labor Struggle in Karachi." *International Journal of Middle East Studies* 37 (1): 83–107.

Asad, Talal. 1973. "Two European Images of Non-European Rule." *Economy and Society* 2 (3): 263–77.

Asad, Talal. 2020. "Thinking about Religion through Wittgenstein." *Critical Times* 3 (3): 403–42.

Bayat, Asef. 2008. "Cairo Cosmopolitanism: Living Together through the Communal Divide, Almot," in Shail Mayaram (ed.), *The Other Global City*. London: Routledge, 179–201.

Brasher, Ryan. 2020. "Pride and Abstention: National Identity, Uncritical Patriotism and Political Engagement among Christian Students in Pakistan." *South Asia: Journal of South Asian Studies* 43 (1): 84–100.

Brown, Wendy. 2006. *Regulating Aversion: Tolerance and Identity in the Age of Empire*. Princeton, NJ: Princeton University Press.

Embree, Ainslee. 1977. "Pakistan's Imperial Legacy," in A. Embree (ed.), *Pakistan's Western Borderlands: The Transformation of a Political Order*. Delhi: Vikas Publishing House.

Hull, Matthew. 2012. *Government of Paper: The Materiality of Bureaucracy in Urban Pakistan*. Berkeley: University of California Press.

Iqtidar, Humeira. 2020. "Searching for Tolerance in Islamic Thought," in Leigh Jenco, Murad Idris, and Megan Thomas (eds.), *Handbook of Comparative Political Theory*. New York: Oxford University Press, 525–45.

Iqtidar, Humeira. 2021. "Is Tolerance Liberal? Javed Ahmed Ghamidi and the Non-Muslim Minority." *Political Theory* 49 (3): 457–82.

Khan, Abdul Ghaffar Khan. 2014. *Bacha Khan Kī āpbīti*. Quetta: Gosha-e-Adab.

Katznelson, Ira. 2010. "Regarding Toleration and Liberalism: Considerations from the Anglo-Jewish experience," in Ira Katznelson and Gareth Stedman Jones (eds.), *Religion and The Political Imagination*. Cambridge: Cambridge University Press.

Marsh, Brandon. 2015. *Ramparts of Empire: British Imperialism and India's Afghan Frontier, 1918–1948*. London: Palgrave Macmillan.

Mazower, Mark. 2009. *No Enchanted Palace: The End of Empire and the Ideological Origins of the United Nations*. Princeton, NJ: Princeton University Press.

Nadir, Rabia. 2013. "Settlement of Pathan Migrants in Walled City Lahore," MPhil Thesis, Lahore School of Economics.

Nichols, Robert. 2008. *A History of Pashtun Migration: 1775–2006*. Karachi: Oxford University Press.

Nawaz, S. 2009. *Fata—A Most Dangerous Place: Meeting the Challenges of Militancy and Terror in the Federally Administered Tribal Areas of Pakistan*. Washington, DC: Centre for Strategic and International Studies.

Portelli, Alessandro. 2010. *They Say in Harlan County: An Oral History*. New York: Oxford University Press.

Rao, Rahul. 2020. *Out of Time: The Queer Politics of Postcoloniality*. Oxford: Oxford University Press.

Ring, Laura. 2006. *Zenana: Everyday Peace in a Karachi Apartment Building*. Bloomington: Indiana University Press.

Scott, Joan W. 1991. "The Evidence of Experience." *Critical Inquiry* 17 (4): 773–97.

Scott, David. 2003. "Culture in Political Theory." *Political Theory* 31 (1): 92–115.

Shaw, Ian Graham, and Majed Akhter. 2011. "The Unbearable Humanness of Drone Warfare in FATA, Pakistan." *Antipode* 44 (4): 1490–509.

Spain, James. 1977. "Political Problems of a Borderland," in A. Embree (ed.), *Pakistan's Western Borderlands: The Transformation of a Political Order*. Delhi: Vikas Publishing House.

Tanguay-Renaud, F. 2009. "Post Colonial Pluralism, Human Rights and the Administration of Criminal Justice in the Federally Administered Tribal Areas of Pakistan." *Singapore Journal of International and Comparative Law* 6: 541–96.
Walzer, Michael. 1997. *On Toleration*. New Haven, CT: Yale University Press.
Zucca, Lorenzo. 2011. "Tolerance or Toleration? How to Deal with Religious Conflicts in Europe," in Lorenzo Zucca (ed.), *A Secular Europe, Law and Religion in the European Constitutional Landscape*. Oxford: Oxford University Press.

13

Countering the Production of Cultural Hegemony: Reflections on Women's Activism under Zia

Farida Shaheed

The Pakistan's Women's Movement, led by the Women's Action Forum (WAF), with chapters in Lahore, Karachi, and Islamabad, was born in response to General Zia-ul-Haq's martial law regime (1977–88) and its stringent attacks on women, in the form of gender discriminatory laws, directives and policies that pertained to women's sexuality, "honor," and the scales by which they could seek justice.[1] The success and, indeed, the "failure" of the women's movement was, I believe, the consequence of the reactive position we were placed into. Zia was out to create a hegemony—that cut across politics and political alliances—and seeped into society itself. His was an Islamic hegemony. He changed Pakistan's laws, and day-to-day normative culture, while simultaneously shrinking the space available for opposing belief and values. I've been intimately involved with WAF—Pakistan's only national women's activist collective—since the outset.

This essay will examine WAF's work during the Zia years through the lens of Gramsci's central concept of hegemony. I've written about WAF's successes elsewhere. In this essay I'd like to begin, like Gramsci began in his analysis of working-class movements, with an analysis of "failure"—failure in the sense that we did not bring about a revolutionary transformation on questions of gender throughout society. Still, our activism can be seen as what I would term a productive "failure" in that we mobilized an effective resistance, put the women's question permanently on the political agenda, and expanded the question of women's rights and social possibilities in innovative ways, and in unexpected places.

In the initial years, there was a sense of incredulity at what Zia was doing and the speed with which his ideas were gaining support in the public imagination; we were to begin with primarily upper-middle-class women, who were viewed with some suspicion; our numbers were few and the task before us was daunting. For example, we contested Zia's laws with marches on the streets—the first group to do so; investigated

[1] In the initial years, chapters had also opened in Abbottabad and Peshawar but stopped being functional. Subsequently, the Peshawar chapter was revived and new chapters opened in Hyderabad and Quetta as well.

claims of rape and other abuse—with the lawyers among us and allies taking on these cases, often pro bono; we wrote letters to the editors; the journalists amongst us reported on the rising tide of crimes against women. We acted in and staged plays that subtly attacked the Zia regime. And one of our country's leading and internationally known artists spent years of her life designing WAF posters. As we were fighting, we were also documenting. As we were responding to these retrogressive laws and the infringement of women's civil space, we were also trying to address the bigger picture—of systemic patriarchy. Zia's goal was to make women invisible. Ours was to bring women and their voices of protest back to where they belonged—to the sociopolitical realm.[2]

Gramsci's singular most important contribution was to argue for a more complex interlacing of power between and across the formal institutions of the state (political society) and the civic, religious, and social institutions that comprised civil society. In short, he sought to explore the mechanisms, social relations, and circuits of power across the analytically demarcated state-society divide in order to understand how dominant classes were able to create and organize consensus among the dominated social groups and classes. Hegemony, or the social organization of consent to rule, through complex interplays of coercion and consent, is the term Gramsci gives to social, cultural, and political practices through which the subordinated (the dominated) accede to a particular form of rule. Mobilizing consent then was a crucial tool in Zia's cultural hegemony project that is too often overlooked.

General Zia-ul-Haq's regime, which first reneged on the promise of holding elections within ninety days, could never acquire political legitimacy through democratic elections. Consequently, it sought to attain hegemony through a raft of discriminatory policies and pronouncements sanctioned by narrow, restrictive, and regime-serving interpretations of Islam. These were, in particular, directed to conservative and patriarchal aspects of society and culture in order to broaden its appeal. This imperative, to achieve cultural hegemony, was then accentuated by the military's usurpation of formal state power and its pursuit of legitimacy—hereafter I will use the "state" as convenient shorthand for Gramsci's concept of formal political power having made the point that the state, or what he referred to as the "integral state," had expanded its activities into what is in classical liberal theory regarded as the private domain of civil society. Reviewing the hegemonic "Islamization" and "Islamizing" discourse, Saadia Toor concludes that WAF may have affirmed the Islamicists' hegemony by "buying into the terms of the debate set by the Islamicists," but successfully linked up with other anti-martial-law groups to "build up an effective counter-hegemony" by those opposed to the imposition of supposedly religious laws (Toor 1997: 113, 121–2). Counter-hegemony may evoke too binary a dynamic: a unidimensional cultural hegemony of the state to which there is a singular well-articulated response.[3] The reality of both the state's cultural hegemony and struggle against this is far messier—the political landscape is more layered and complex than simple oppositions; the dialectic process

2 Since 2021, the Aurat March, until recently an annual event around March 8, has also gained traction across the country.

3 Strictly speaking, Gramsci did not use the term "counter-hegemony" but it has entered common usage to describe an oppositional and alternate hegemony (Ives 2004: 68).

more complicated. Counter-hegemonic strategies forged in the moment of resistance simultaneously assume many modalities of performance (McLaren et al. 1988) and can use multi-nodal reference points.

Gender was an explicit and privileged component of Zia's cultural hegemony project. Constructs of gender are inherent in all social collectivities simply because, irrespective of all other political, social, or economic factors, all societies have to address three incontrovertible facts of life: birth, death, and the existence of sexes. Consequently, all societies construct gender systems defining the roles, responsibilities, and rights of girls/women and boys/men—the permissible and lauded, the forbidden and penalized (Shaheed 2007).[4] Encased in cultural imperatives and social and physical sanctions, gender constructs are promoted through societal rules governing interactions of everyday life as much as through laws and policies.

As the Zia regime set about reconfiguring the political landscape through both force and popular consent in the creation of cultural normativity, women's resistance articulated opposition by promoting alternative modes of thinking in civil society and concerted efforts to mobilize like-minded groups. A wider mobilization was imperative given that while each city-based chapter of WAF could mobilize a thousand women for specific events, at no point did the core of women activists exceed a few hundred. The search for activists and allies from a wide spectrum of society led to some heated internal debates and disagreements. Resistance was mounted within a deeply patriarchal society further constrained by martial law where people feared speaking out as all political activities were banned. The state had a monopoly over broadcast media and social media had not yet been invented.

Activists did not set out to bring about or set the stage for a revolution. The far less ambitious aim was to prevent a further erosion of rights by mobilizing a maximum number of people to exercise agency to resist the regime's agenda. In the initial years, activism was reactive rather than proactive and yet, in reflecting back, I see a proactive element. This was WAF's conscious determination to create new modus operandi for activism undergirded by feminist thinking, even as feminist understanding was honed and developed further in the dynamics of the theory-praxis nexus. Gramsci's framework of hegemony applies as effectively to active resistance as revolution, both as signifying the discontent of women as subalterns and as conscious effort to oppose Zia's hegemonic project.

The Regime's Cultural Hegemony Project

In March 1978, nine months after usurping power, Zia announced his intention to "Islamize" the country and co-opted two political parties as junior partners. The collaboration of the Pakistan Muslim League (Pagaro group), now known as PML (Functional), was largely irrelevant as it had a very limited presence. However, the co-optation of the Jamaat-i-Islami (JI), a politico-religious party, was an altogether

[4] This binary applies to persons of nonbinary identities too.

different matter. The Jamaat provided the blueprint for the cultural hegemony project as the military "arrogated to itself the task of Islamizing the country's institutions in their entirety" (Khan 1985: 127), and simultaneously set out to alter societal parameters (Shaheed 2010).

Despite inroads in urban centers the JI had always performed poorly at the polls on the rare occasions popular will was allowed to be expressed. Not only did Zia catapult the Jamaat's discourse onto the national stage as a mechanism for the reform of government, but he gave them—and other religious actors—unprecedented reach and power by deploying the state's apparatus to reshape the ideas, beliefs, and moral viewpoints of people. Zia astutely mobilized popular consent through rhetoric that galvanized societal elements as allies in tandem with exercising coercion through directives to enforce compliance and brute force to suppress opposition. Political parties and student unions were banned and politicians incarcerated; several striking unionists in Faisalabad were shot dead; public hangings and floggings displayed ungloved force—all contributing to a brutalizing environment that instilled a fear of speaking out. The ban, however, did not apply to the JI, giving it a state-reinforced pulpit; its student wing, the Islami Jamiat Talaba, was despite the formal ban, nonetheless allowed free reign to impose their will on students and professors alike, including through violence. Religiosity became political currency and the most conservative elements of society were emboldened to take direct action in pursuit of the ideals and values of the hegemonizing discourse. Women and citizens of religious minority groups were easy targets upon which to display so-called Islamic credentials at minimum risk of opposition.

The so-called Islamic laws were as much a means of marshaling consent as imposing coercion, a constitutive part of what is described as "legal ideology" (Tigar and Levy 1977). From the gender perspective, the overriding significance of these new laws, cloaked in religious idiom to appear divine and immutable, was that they legally sanctioned an inferior "half-human" status on all women and non-Muslim men compared to Muslim men. This was most blatant in the Qisas and Diyat law (retribution and compensation/blood money) that stipulated that the life (and limbs) of women and non-Muslim men were only worth half that of Muslim men.[5] Implementation of the monetary compensation was erratic. The *zina* section of the 1979 Hudood Ordinances[6]—making any sex outside marriage a crime against the state, filled the jails mainly with women as the law confounded rape with consensual sex—overturned the principle of being innocent until proved guilty, and allowed anyone to register a case.[7] It was used by former husbands, but also acquaintances and strangers, to punish women.

[5] It was never determined how the "eye for an eye" principle would apply in the case of retribution, for example, the loss of an eye. This part of the law was never implemented because the Pakistan Medical Association had already made clear it would cancel the license of any medical professional found to be associated with the severing of limbs with respect to the Hudood Ordinances.

[6] The Hudood Ordinance covered adultery, fornication, rape, and prostitution.

[7] The *zina* section of the Hudood Ordinance made all intercourse outside marriage a crime against the state. It confused rape and abduction with *zina*, allowed anyone to register a complaint, and overturned the principle of innocence, thereby filling jails with women accused by vengeful ex-husbands, frustrated parents, and random strangers. See Khawar Mumtaz and Farida Shaheed (1987) and Asma Jahangir and Hina Jilani (1990).

In contrast, few cases were registered under the sections on bearing false witness (*qazf*), drinking of alcoholic beverages, and theft. As finally promulgated, the law on Qisas and Diyat[8]—covering murder, bodily assault, and abortion—has largely been used to avoid punishments for so-called honor crimes against women by enabling family members, usually the culprits, to pardon the offender as the deceased's legal heirs.[9] The clauses on abortion remain unused; the 1985 Law of Evidence untested. Reinforcing this legal ideology, Zia promoted various retrogressive preachers in addition to the JI but, as early as 1982, made clear that he, not any particular religious leader, was the authority on Islam (Mumtaz and Shaheed 1987: 84).

Gender was an explicit and central component in this enterprise of cultural hegemony. Amid much paraded discourses on public morality, intensive efforts were made to evict women from the public sphere altogether, impose segregation, and fashion a new "Islamic woman" to replace the notion of a "Pakistani woman." Defined by the proverbial *chador aur char diwari* (shawl and four walls [of a home]), this new "Islamic woman" was to be enveloped in veils and largely confined to the homestead, remain silent and invisible, and only be educated in certain subjects in segregated institutions—sciences were to be excluded and it was suggested girls be taught "domestic math." Women were being reduced to legal minors and social incompetents, to be led like children in all matters, without a say in their own affairs much less the affairs of the state. They were to be confined and hidden away as the source of potential *fitna*, or chaos.[10] Unlike the legal ideology that, excepting the zina ordinance, impacted relatively few women directly, societal measures impacted women across the board and, resonating with a wide spectrum of actors, mobilized and co-opted societal allies in the state's cultural hegemony project. These extensive multifaceted nonlegal pronouncements, measures, and policies tend to be overlooked in the literature and have dimmed in our own recollections. It is worth recalling some key actions.[11]

As early as 1978, the JI's long-standing demand for a separate women's university was approved; in 1979 coeducational extracurricular activities were banned and directives issued to enforce "Islamic" dress, meaning mandatory *chadors* for all female students and faculty in educational institutions, then extended to encompass all state employees. In contrast, men were instructed to wear "national dress." Zia personally presented *chadors* to each woman of his handpicked *Majlis-e-Shura* in 1982 (a consultative body he created to replace Parliament), while handing male members cloth for the national dress, a *shalwar kameez* that would have been equally appropriate for women.[12] Distributing *chadors* became a routinized and publicized state practice. The 1980s saw

[8] Passed by Zia's handpicked Majlis-e-Shura (consultative body standing in for Parliament) in 1984 and presented to the newly elected National Assembly in 1985.

[9] Adult family men—usually fathers and brothers—have often laid the blame on a minor son who is exempt from the death sentence.

[10] On *fitna*, see for example, Fatima Mernissi (1994).

[11] See Mumtaz and Shaheed (1987: chapter 7) for details of legal and nonlegal actions.

[12] This occurred days after a widely reported visit of the highly veiled widow of the former president of Iran who said the state in Iran did not force anyone to wear a *chador* but had created an atmosphere in which the family, neighbors, and people in general ensured compliance. She also said that, properly attired, women should participate fully in collective activities—the latter statement was ignored completely.

a scatter-shot fusillade of initiatives aimed at making women disappear from public view and work. Women athletes' training camps were mysteriously canceled, athletes prevented from going abroad, and in 1982 women were banned from competing in "spectator sports." Women in the Foreign Office were no longer being posted abroad or promoted; nor were women recruited or promoted in government banks—but nothing was given in writing. The Ansari Commission recommended making a husband's permission mandatory for women to contest elections and that too only after the age of forty. Many recommendations made headlines without any further action being taken. The right of women to serve as judges (*qazis*) in the newly established Shariat Courts was challenged by a private citizen in court, arguing that a woman sitting as a judge would contravene the dictates of purdah and if allowed should only be confined to "female concerns." Fortunately this challenge was dismissed.

Optimal use was made of the state's monopoly over broadcast media, especially the increasingly available and popular medium of television, to further normalize the elimination of women from public view. Pakistan Television (PTV) was instructed to exclude women from commercials with "little or no relevance to women" to safeguard against any attempt "to exploit the fair sex for commercial purpose." Then, in 1982, a full-scale anti-obscenity and anti-pornography campaign that was tantamount to equating women's visibility per se with obscenity was unleashed. On television, female models could only appear in commercials for up to 25 percent of the advertisement wearing full-sleeved national dress with a *dupatta* (a lighter scarf than *chadors*), and commercials featuring women were to be suspended during Ramadan. On air women's appearance was conditional on covering their heads, including when shown while sleeping in teleplays, and no teleplay could show women exiting their marriage (seeking or getting a divorce). The print media was instructed to desist from publishing pictures of women unless essential—measures that directly impacted models and entertainers.

Televangelism was introduced and selected preachers given airtime, including a weekly lecture by Dr. Israr Ahmed, a member of the government's Council of Islamic Ideology and Zia's handpicked *Majlis-e-Shura*. Israr had been a prominent member of the JI but parted ways when the party endorsed the first ever female candidate, Fatima Jinnah, in the 1964 presidential elections. Given control over the mosque at Lawrence Gardens, one of the most significant mosques in Lahore, Israr used the pulpit and television to push his version of an Islamic society. He called for working women to be pensioned off and sent home forthwith; women to be secluded in their homes except in emergencies; female patients to only be treated, and cadavers examined, by female doctors. Attempts by the state to eliminate male gynecologists failed but a directive on postmortem examinations was later issued. Most outrageously, he declared that no man could be punished for assaulting or raping a woman until an Islamic society had been created, and urged young men to arm themselves with batons and form vigilante groups to patrol the streets. Particular vitriol was reserved for professional working women who he, and other spokespersons and entertainers, blamed for the disintegration of societal values and happy families on television and other forums.

This agenda to reform culture and society gained traction quite rapidly by successfully mobilizing the most conservative social groups as vocal allies and easily garnered consensus in a patriarchal society. With the public visibility of women and self-judged inappropriate apparel posited as the cause of public immorality, sexual harassment in public spaces spiraled. Men felt authorized to verbally—and sometimes even physically—accost any woman they considered to be improperly dressed in public. Class privileges no longer provided protection, and women were harassed in privileged upmarket shops by individuals; and couples on evening strolls and in parks were stopped by the police demanding proof of marriage—including fathers out with their daughters. Teachers started segregating students and enforcing their own dress codes and ethics, and some refused to teach girls altogether. Harassed and under societal pressure, Parsees and Christians began to abandon skirts and dresses and Punjabi peasants their sarong-like apparel. Working women reported being hassled both at home and at work.

Significantly, the vast majority of working women—peasants and laborers—were not the primary audience for this hegemonizing discourse, although they definitely were the main victims of laws promulgated and the societal fallout. The discourse was aimed at urban working middle- and upper-class women. Tellingly, Israr spoke of pensioning women off—inapplicable for most of Pakistan's working women concentrated in insecure jobs, unregulated employment, and nonformal sectors.[13] Similarly, the hype of segregation saving society conveniently ignored the presence of women agricultural workers where segregation is impossible. Only WAF, noting the discrepancy, quipped that for segregation to be complete, streets and fields should also be segregated: one day allotted for women and the next for men. It seems that proponents of the new cultural hegemony believed, like Maududi, that such women were part of "the foolish and thoughtless … who cannot think and form independent opinions" and so "don't deserve attention and may, therefore, be ignored" (1981: 83). Taking forward Maududi's exhortations, the new hegemony project activated societal allies to promote the new normativity while removing from influence its opponents—in the case of women attempting to remove them entirely from any public presence. This was the contextual crucible in which women's activism emerged.

Countering the Cultural Hegemony Agenda

Gramsci posits that to achieve and maintain cultural hegemony, those in state power include and incorporate some values and interests of subaltern classes so as to attain their consent to the status quo; hence, those opposing this power also need to mobilize allies. The trajectory of WAF activists suggests that the dynamics are much the same when resisting the rescinding of rights as proactively championing a new world vision. To stem the tide of reversals, women needed to organize and activate a variety of social groups and actors within civil society to galvanize popular will in opposition to the state's discourse and actions. To mobilize popular will, this critical counter-discourse must be audible and resonate with at least some sections of the population, find

[13] Paradoxically, the number of women factory workers steadily increased during this period and floor shifts were integrated. PILER, Research report, *Women in the Industrial Labour Force in Pakistan*, unpublished research conducted during 1988–90.

locations and modalities to engage people, and locate and enlist the support of allies for amplification.

Women's activism of the 1980s had to contend with constraints imposed by martial law and was further handicapped by the absence of an existing women's or other social movement from which it could readily draw activists. Avenues for articulating a counter-discourse and demonstrating opposition were highly limited. In the sociopolitical arena, all political activity was banned, public displays of opposition such as demonstrations forbidden, and broadcast media out of reach. The legal arena offered little scope as fundamental rights had been suspended and military courts installed. The occasional isolated voices raised in opposition to the rescinding of women's rights never translated into concerted or collective efforts of societal resistance.[14] That a handful of women managed to challenge the discourse and be heard under the circumstances was remarkable. WAF activists—all urban, preponderantly working, mostly young women—were particular targets of the state's stigmatizing discourse and were frequently disparaged as "short-haired westernized women" (*baal-katey maghrib-zada*) to discredit their voice. The proverbial last straw that sparked activism was the sentencing of a woman and man, respectively, to 100 lashes and death by stoning under the zina ordinance.[15] I should point out that our initial aim was not to start a women's movement but to mobilize a maximum number of people to resist the regime's agenda. That a women's movement emerged was due to the highly misogynist nature of Zia's cultural hegemony agenda and its differentiated impact on women and men.

Anger, prompted by outrage, was palpable at the first meeting in Karachi of some twenty women gathered by Shirkat Gah—Women's Resource Centre in September 1981. The specific case crystallized a sense of shock that such a law had been passed without comment, and confusion regarding its actual content. But the anger had been fueled by the increasing harassment, measures and actions policing women's apparel, comportment and life choices; the further restrictions on women's agency and free will; and the ongoing targeting of women's bodies as the site to produce a religious-inspired sociocultural politics of exclusion. Anger is "an important, necessary, and productive aspect" of consciousness-raising, a key aspect of women's movements of the time (Randolph and Ross-Valliere 1979). In many ways, this first and subsequent WAF meetings were conscious-raising sessions as women shared experiences, developed understanding but also raised unanswered questions. Finding each other broke the sense of isolation and frustration, and gave impetus to an urgently felt compulsion to launch into action to safeguard rights hitherto considered secured and repel efforts to push women back into the *chador* and *char diwari*. Urgency was not confined to Karachi, and within months WAF chapters opened up in Lahore, Islamabad, and Peshawar bringing together individuals and an eclectic group of twenty organizations

[14] In April 1981 a female Islamic scholar, Rayhana Firdaus, wrote a newspaper article arguing that "in the eyes of God and in the eyes of the Qur'an, the personality and status of women in Muslim Society are exactly the same as those of man" and that instances where women appeared to not have equal rights were temporary concessions made in the historical context in which Islam was born (*Dawn*, April 6, 1981 and April 13, 1981).

[15] The lesser punishment of 100 lashes for the woman, Fehmida, was not because she was a woman but because she was considered to be unmarried.

that indicated widespread concern among women. Groups ranged from the most well-established welfare-oriented All Pakistan Women's Association to the socialist Anjuman Jamhooriat Pasand Khawateeen (Democratic Women's Association); from the YWCA (Young Women's Christian Association) to the Business and Professional Women's Club; new and older women lawyers associations[16] and a few more clearly feminist groups.[17] Perhaps because so much of the hegemonic discourse was mapped out on the bodies and rights of women (Shroff 2014), a similar sense of urgency was not felt by the men who were approached. Men's responses were either dismissive (such sentences would never be executed in Pakistan) or defeatist (nothing could be done under martial law). A number of men did support women's activism, but the contrast with women was so vivid that some male relatives and friends of activists joked about being the Men's Inaction Forum.

Activists did "live intellectual life praxiologically, that is, in a state of on-going praxis" (McLaren et al. 1988), learning from our "active participation in practical life" as expounded by Gramsci, and did try consciously to resist the dominant state discourse by presenting a counternarrative to promote alternative modes of thinking. While many were homemakers devoid of any experience of activism, those with either a socialist or a feminist grounding helped steer activism. None were experienced in engaging a confrontational state. Grassroots work was limited and better understanding of issues, such as the vitality of intersectionality—a term that emerged later in the feminist lexicon[18]—grew out of the dialectical interplay of the praxis of trial-and-error activism and theorizing in heated internal debates and endless discussions. An early debate on where to focus energies concluded that, while grassroots work to raise consciousness was essential, the constant barrage of negative laws and policies being promulgated or proposed made it imperative to focus all attention on preventing further retrogressive steps (WAF Convention Report 1982). Praxis was calibrated by the need to ensure collective action and continued agency of highly diverse, oft-times divergent, activists and sympathizers, and find ways to effectively advance their agenda, including by mobilizing allies.

Modalities of Agency and Performance

Women's counter-hegemonic practices of resistance were never violent, did not deploy any fixed singular agency of change, and sought to create modalities and spaces through which to reach the public at large. Modalities ranged from organizing meetings, seminars, and *jalsas* (something between a rally and a meeting with a

[16] Such as the newly formed Punjab Women Lawyers Association, and more established All Pakistan Women Lawyers Association.

[17] In addition to Shirkat Gah that defined itself as a feminist collective, this included Tehrik-i-Niswan, ASR, Simorgh Resource and Publication Centre, Aurat Publication and Information Foundation—the last two created after WAF.

[18] Coined by Kimberlé Williams Crenshaw in her 1989 article, "Demarginalizing the Intersection of Race and Sex: A Black Feminist Critique of Anti-discrimination Doctrine, Feminist Theory and Antiracist Politics."

celebratory element), to conducting research and surveys to producing "position papers" and charters of demand, from producing newsletters, posters, an audiocassette of songs and poems, to inserting the discourse in development forums and running interventions in individual cases. But the quintessential modality that thrust WAF into the public eye was the appropriation of public spaces, both physical and in the print media.

Newspapers were a crucial location for discourse amplification—the principal vehicle both for reaching large numbers of people that activists could not engage with directly, and for focusing the attention of policy-makers. Activists wrote articles and letters to the editor, and in Karachi, activists counted a significant number of journalists who leveraged this connection to ensure the counter-discourse reached their readership. The *Star* newspaper was jokingly called the WAF organ. Coverage was good, in part because the bar on reporting news of politicians left a vacuum for journalists to fill, but the new modality of women's activism piqued interest: the lack of a singular "leader" or spokesperson, the use of infotainment—not yet a term—skits and humor, as well as the occupation of public streets, and the absence of any males at all.

WAF initially caught the media's attention with its first *jalsa* in 1982. Devoid of chief guests, as was and is the norm in Pakistan, it was meant to demonstrate support for the counter-discourse and create a sense of solidarity transcending differences of class, age, and political inclination. Messages were conveyed through songs, and women were regaled with skits lampooning these proposed laws rendering women half human. The hugely successful event left many women, in the overcrowded hall, in tears and was fully covered in the Urdu- and English-language press. As the debate on women heated up, Urdu newspapers started forums pitting WAF activists against conservative religious women, usually associated with the JI. But on February 12, 1983, a WAF-supported demonstration in Lahore, against the proposed law of evidence, catapulted activists into the public eye in an unprecedented and unparalleled way. The intention of the Punjab Women Lawyers Association, that gave the call, was to walk in pairs to deliver a petition to the High Court, maintaining sufficient distance between pairs to circumvent the prohibitions of Section 144 of the Pakistan Penal Code that was in force and that prohibits the gathering of more than five people in public. Delivering the petition proved impossible as the police, who outnumbered the demonstrators, blockaded the women. When, unexpectedly, women managed to break through the cordon this led to pandemonium as the police resorted to violence. The images of women gagging in clouds of teargas; being beaten with *lathis* (truncheons) while battling the mainly male police; the thrashing of the well-known and popular people's poet, Habib Jalib were splashed across the front pages the following day and have subsequently become iconic.[19] Public sympathy was evidenced by shopkeepers raising their shutters to give women refuge and water, one expressed solidarity by sending miniature perfume bottles to the women held in police lockup. The police action shredded the state's much trumpeted discourse of

[19] Male supporters stayed on the side lines until police action and ironically enough Maududi's son was caught on camera trying to protect women demonstrators.

being the "protector of women," while the women found the experience of occupying the Mall Lahore's "high street," and even the fracas, exhilarating.

Internal discussions ensued on the value of public street activism, and possible risks. Riled as they were by the press identifying those jailed as the wife, daughter, or daughter-in-law of prominent men, activists also recognized that the presence of well-connected women had facilitated their release and that it was fortunate that the factory and other women workers, students, and the like present at the demonstration had not been picked up. During this entire period permission was never sought for demonstrations as it would have been denied given that Section 144 had been imposed. Consequently, being a demonstrator entailed dissimilar risks for women of different class backgrounds. As one working-class WAF member eloquently explained at a meeting: "If you [better off activists] get arrested, you will not be raped; we are likely to be. If it becomes known we participated in a demonstration, we will lose our jobs, you will not and if you do, you can afford this, we can't. And, when you return home you will be applauded for your bravery, we are likely to be beaten." She was correct. Some women government employees were issued show-cause notices, others questioned, but as predicted without serious consequences.

The demonstration gave the cause unprecedented visibility and WAF concluded that a failure to show opposition on the streets would be allowing ourselves to be silenced and removed from the public eye. Therefore, in September 1983, Lahore WAF resolved to go back on the street. Unwilling to put women at risk we could not protect, it was decided to picket the governor's house for at least twenty minutes. Breaking any residual fear, seventeen nervous but determined women stood in the picket line for some 30 minutes without incidence, leading to WAF's conscious strategy to continue to disrupt and occupy public spaces. Public protests became the hallmark of Lahore WAF, regardless of which organization gave the call. Activists honed their disruption skills. Discovering that eighty-four women holding outstretched arms could completely block off the Mall, we learnt to disregard promises and accurately predict how many women might turn up to determine tactics at each event, and became adept at deflecting police seeking to disperse activists. Unfamiliar with WAF's collective leadership style, police would ask to speak to the leader or organizer; each activist would deny being the "leader" forcing the police to sequentially engage with different activists in search of a leader—thereby prolonging the duration of public disruption. Not infrequently, police were directed to an elderly activist who younger activists felt could be counted on to confuse them further.[20] Embellishing street action, activists started producing one-pagers explaining the issue and their position that were handed out to anyone passing by in cars, motorcycles, bicycles, or on foot. It was not uncommon for people to give demonstrators the thumbs up, occasionally a few women would actually stop and join when the demonstration concerned a particular case of violence against women.

Women's disruptive presence in the streets was itself a counter-discourse and practice, loudly and visually defying the *chador* and *char diwari* of the state's

[20] This was often Chris Taseer, Aunty Chris, who along with her sister, Alice Faiz, was at all the demonstrations.

discourse—indeed, in a spontaneous act, some activists physically burnt their *chadors* (it was winter) during a demonstration on the Mall to signify the complete rejection of this discourse. Publicly disruptive practices, especially the occupying of public spaces, was clearly political but WAF carefully navigated the ban on political activity by deliberately and tactically employing the argument that "women's rights" were an apolitical issue.[21] Similarly, WAF declared itself nonpolitical and never registered itself to avoid being banned. In this period, demonstrations were all-female affairs and curiously enough, after February 12, the state was careful not to respond violently to women's demonstrations on women's rights, although women's demonstrations made authorities sufficiently nervous that on one occasion the police seeing a newspaper notice of a "cake demonstration" at the YWCA arrived to break it up, only to discover the announcement was for a baking lesson. No such leniency was shown to the same activists when demonstrating for the restoration of democracy and they were unceremoniously jailed. Women activists continued to be picked up occasionally by the police but were never jailed for women's rights activism.

After the first demonstration, the state's societal allies responded with preachers proclaiming that the marriages of all the women demonstrators stood dissolved for their wanton actions (activists joked this was by far the easiest way to obtain a divorce). The JI often verbally attacked and vociferously condemned women activists as nefarious and some as "traitors" in newspapers and their own publications. One fiery JI woman member of the Majlis (Nisar Fatima) regularly demanded action be taken against all "these women" who, she once famously announced in the Majlis, would be met at the gates of hell with hockey-sticks. More than once, the Jamaat said it would physically stop women demonstrators,[22] and at least once, the threat of violence from Jamaat was considered real. The JI male cadre frequently used violence against male opponents. This Left activists, who had never engaged in violence even when subjected to police violence, wondered how to respond. Fortunately, it was never more than a threat.

Some gender-specific constraints to occupying public spaces came to light during a night-time action in which male supporters helped to plaster posters across selected streets and neighborhoods of Lahore to catch the early morning traffic before authorities tore them down. Our all-female team, assigned the Upper Mall with many official buildings but no shops or restaurants, spent the time jumping in and out of the car, fervently trying to stay out of sight and be as inconspicuous as possible. We then watched young male supporters wandering through the bustling commercial area of Lower Mall, casually sauntering through the men milling around, one pasting the glue from his backpack, the other sticking the poster. This would have been impossible for women whose very presence would have attracted far too much attention.

[21] A well-read bureaucrat once laughed out loud when I forwarded this argument, that WAF was nonpolitical, to obtain permission for a venue. However, I stuck to my position and he gave us permission, probably because he was sympathetic to the cause.

[22] They knew about the events because in a time before social media, WAF publicized all public events in the announcements section of newspapers to encourage people to join.

In Search of Allies

As social institutions of large numbers, trade unions were seen as potentially important allies but seemed devoid of any gender perspective. At the first May 1 rally WAF attended, in 1982, men monopolized the stage exclusively addressing their "dear brothers" and ignoring the significant number of women workers present. WAF activists encouraged labor leaders to address the specific problems of women workers and more ambitiously, and with rather less success, attempted to catalyze a rethinking of the labor movement from a singular emphasis on the "worker in the workplace" to encompassing the worker's entire family, for which it organized several events for workers and their families. WAF's direct engagement with women trade union members started in 1984 when a woman leader asked its help to deal with the management's harassment of women in the union. WAF supported the women on this occasion as it was a clear case of sexual harassment, considered a gender issue, but after considerable debate failed to extend support subsequently when workers were dismissed for being union members. The logic forwarded for not supporting the women unionists was that they had been dismissed because of union activity rather than on account of their gender. In retrospect, the logic is puzzling given that non-Muslim women were recognized as facing double discrimination, as women and as minorities, but the unionized women were not. Fortunately, the links endured and continuous engagement brought better understanding among WAF activists of intersectionality; and conversely, a better understanding of gender resulted in some union women forming their own independent organizations such as the Working Women's Organisation. Engagement led some unions and organizations to focus on women workers (such as PILER and the Labour Party), but only with those who shared a general outlook and saw themselves as part of a broader movement for social change. Hence, while WAF extended solidarity, and took up issues raised by associations of women telephone operators and nurses, in particular those of harassment, better remuneration and work conditions, the linkages were temporary and these working women never joined the movement.

In contrast to trade unions, there was considerable discussion over engaging with political parties. A number of activists regularly participated in pro-democracy events, but stressed that they did so as individuals acting on their personal convictions, rather than as members of WAF. Fiercely protective of its independence from any external element—the reason for refusing to accept any money except personal donations—WAF welcomed women political workers, but barred party office-holders from the decision-making Working Committees. Activists were wary of parties that were always keen to mobilize women but whose agenda *for* women was either weak or nonexistent, with women party workers often cordoned off into powerless Women's Wings. Initially, even Benazir Bhutto, when first introduced to WAF members, suggested we meet her Women's Wing. Moreover, political parties had been silent on the Hudood Ordinances and, even in private, ignored the rescinding of women's rights. It did not help that after the famous February 12 demonstration, politicians (as well as intellectuals and union leaders) congratulated activists and then proffered advice on how to become more effective for the "real" and more serious struggle of democracy versus martial law.[23] There was considerable debate, therefore, on whether WAF should support the Movement for Restoration of Democracy (MRD) in 1983, or at least speak out about women injured and/or incarcerated in the movement. By the second MRD wave in 1986, this question had been resolved and solidarity was duly extended to women political workers. By then WAF and women's rights had gained sufficient recognition for some MRD politicians to ask WAF Karachi to help draft a women's section for their manifesto. Instead, WAF chapters opted to collectively draft a general women's manifesto and circulated this to all the MRD parties. At least two parties incorporated a women's section in their manifestos at that time. Eventually all parties, even the JI—which previously did not allow women formal membership—added a section on women's rights in their manifestos. By the end of the Zia era, politicians respected WAF's activism; members were regularly called by Benazir Bhutto's government (1988–90 and 1993–6) while some members went on to join political parties and became full-time politicians.

In search of allies, WAF created the Joint Action Committee (JAC) in 1986 to oppose the Shariat Bill moved by two members of the JI party and subsequently the Ninth Constitutional Amendment bill by the government. Both proposed unbridled powers to overturn any laws deemed to be un-Islamic by a group of "recognized ulema" (Islamic scholars) with no court of appeal.[24] The resultant JAC for People's Rights was a coalition of civic organizations, smaller political parties, and interest groups. Initiated in several cities JAC served as a platform for human rights campaigns and activities bringing together groups with diverse institutional agendas around a common social change goal (now only operative in Lahore). While gender is an integral part of JAC activities, an unintended outcome was the muting of women's distinct voice as a movement.

Framing the Counter-Discourse

In their seminal work, M. Tigar and M. R. Levy point out that "legal rules and principles are justified by resort to sources that are accepted because of their reputed age and authenticity and to principles of social theory that are believed to be self-evidently valid but that in fact express the aspirations of the group which has for the moment achieved dominance" (1977: 283). This principle, I argue, also applies to cultural hegemony agendas. Zia used Islam as the unitary, self-evidently valid basis to justify both the legal and social measures in his pursuit of cultural hegemony but astutely mixed in local patriarchal norms of *chador* and *char diwari*. The ensuing discourse resonated with the general populace as diverse conservative actors picked up, reproduced, and amplified the message. The challenge confronting activists was

[23] A handful of WAF activists once responded to a call by political parties for a women's demonstration only to discover they outnumbered party members.

[24] The only difference between the two was that the government's proposal exempted economic and financial matters from the purview of the group of ulema.

how to formulate a counter-discourse with arguments capable of igniting agency among a sufficient number of activists and allies to stem the tide. In contrast to the state's hegemonic agenda, women activists had no unitary framework. In seeking social and cultural resonance, activists searched for "authenticity," self-evidently valid principles and legitimacy from a number of sources that varied from statements of Mohammad Ali Jinnah, Pakistan's founding father, to general human rights principles and international human rights standards and Pakistan's international commitments, and most controversially from within the broad framework of Islam.[25]

Jinnah became an important reference point to demonstrate how the new agenda contradicted the original vision of Pakistan's founding father. Early on, Najma Sadeque and myself scanned the Dawn Media Group's archives to unearth a now-famous Jinnah quote, now used widely, after Zia's demise, by government representatives and in government publications as well as by a variety of actors other than women activists:

> No nation can rise to the height of glory unless your women are side by side with you, we are victims of evil customs. It is a crime against humanity that our women are shut up in the four walls of the houses as prisoners. There is no sanction anywhere for the deplorable condition in which our women have to live. You should take your women along with you as comrades in every sphere of life.[26]

The quote became the preamble in WAF's charter and appeared on one of WAF's earliest posters, beneath a picture of Jinnah and his sister. Believing, correctly at that time, that it would be difficult for opponents to disrespect and discard the words of the founding father and the actions of his sister as *Madre-e-Millat* (mother of the nation), activists referenced Jinnah in the newspaper debates and elsewhere and forwarded the example of his sister. But such references could only be used to support broad principles of gender equality and were rarely pertinent for specific issues and laws being confronted that purported to be ordained by Islam.

The secular versus religious framework generated intense heated debates among activists until WAF declared itself secular at its tenth anniversary convention (1991). If the initial catalyst for WAF was the zina section of the Hudood Ordinances, and considerable energies were expended on opposing laws that enabled gender discrimination on purportedly Islamic grounds, WAF nevertheless took up nonlegal provisions from the start, including women in state custody, participation in sporting events, restrictions on cultural events (WAF Lahore Newsletter No. 1). Its analyzes always used a feminist lens to examine the issues. On matters such as crimes against women (WAF's terminology for what is now called gender-based violence), workers' rights, women's unpaid labor in the family and economy, and even the separate women's university, arguments were formulated using nonreligious reference points, such as the Constitution of Pakistan, the UN charter, and human rights standards and

[25] Chapters differed in their propensity to use one or the other. Karachi was most inclined to focus on human rights and the UN charter and pronouncements.

[26] Mohammad Ali Jinnah, Address at Aligarh University, 1944.

sociological arguments. These continued after 1991 when the religious references were consciously dropped.

On the question of whether counterarguments to discriminatory laws should be grounded in a secular or religious discourse, it was argued, on the one hand, that we engage in Islamic interpretive work and use the framework of religion to dislodge the idea that the regime's laws were divinely sanctioned. It was contended that arguing on secular grounds alone would be perceived as "a matter of the word of God versus the word of women." This would fail to mobilize agency among potential societal allies, including many women, for whom religion was an integral part of their cultural consciousness (Rubina Saigol 2016). On the other hand, those opposed argued that "the strategic use of Islamic arguments would be self-defeating as women would be 'playing on mullah's wicket,'" thereby putting women at a perpetual disadvantage. Looking back, two things stand out that merit reflection: in the stormy debates at the WAF convention where these two positions were first articulated, non-Muslim women argued it was necessary to use religious idiom. The second is the diametrically opposed reactions to two religious scholars speaking against the government's proposed law of evidence at a Lahore WAF event: many upper-middle-class activists were infuriated by their presence whereas working class and lower-middle-class women were reassured by their talks.

Whether WAF affirmed the Islamicists' hegemony by using "the terms of the debate set by the Islamicists" (Toor 1997) was hotly debated within WAF during these early years and since then by others. Under Zia, WAF did not set out to create an alternative discourse so much as contest the misogynist hegemony being imposed by the state. For this, at its second national convention in 1983, WAF concluded that "it would have to raise people's consciousness and expose the difference between *maulvis* and Islam as a first step, and between progressive and conservative Islam as a second" before asserting itself on purely secular grounds (Mumtaz and Shaheed 1987: 159). WAF's contestation of the dominant discourse did open up the space for subaltern women and allies to join it and take up women's rights through independent actions.

Concluding Thoughts

Movements arise at particular historical junctures and are shaped as much by the specific circumstances and configurations of power, particularly the character of the state, as by the ideals, volition, actions, identity, and resources of its activists. WAF-led women's activism until Zia's demise in 1988, was state-oriented and reactive, adversarial, and confrontational. Confronting hugely asymmetrical power dynamics, activists crafted new modalities to articulate resistance: disrupting and occupying public spaces, multiplying voices, and seeking allies all while striving to maintain unity among a highly diverse group of women. In a historical juncture in which women, their bodies, visibility, and presence became hyper-politicized sites, women activists not only articulated but also embodied adversarial models of gender appropriateness to the state's hegemonic agenda, one also promoted by independent societal actors. If the foremost focus of activism was countering discriminatory laws and policies, the praxis of women's activism in and of itself, of occupying physical and discursive public spaces, was perhaps as (or more) successful in countering the production of cultural hegemony. This disruptive public presence successfully countered normative expectations of women's roles. It may not have transformed the debate but it kept it alive and open.

Thinking back, it feels as if the radicalness of this disruptive modality may explain how such a small number of women with such a small reservoir of economic and political power managed to elicit concessions from the state, insert women's rights permanently on the radar of all political parties; ensure labor unions and groups paid far greater attention to women's issues, and gave an impetus to working women's own voices. While it would take women's activism another eighteen years to knock the teeth out of the zina ordinance,[27] WAF's outcry stopped the public flogging of a woman in Islamabad, and soon thereafter the flogging of women altogether. After the February 12 demonstration, Zia suddenly started addressing women in speeches and specially appealed to women to take part in his referendum; state-controlled television made a show of covering women receiving awards and participating in government events. Activism even started to influence JI women. In those years, I was particularly struck by one press statement by the JI's women's wing, which could have been issued by WAF, were it not for one line on maintaining gender segregation. On another occasion, in Karachi JI women joined WAF activists protesting a case of rape. WAF broke the silence around violence against women—an issue that galvanized women across the political spectrum. Decades later, Samiya Rahil Qazi, an active JI member told me she followed what we were doing in Shirkat Gah very closely and took up the issues, such as the gendered division of labor, appropriating and refashioning WAF's discourse into an Islamic idiom.

WAF's framework of articulation was contested, sometimes conflictual and often fragmentary, as it responded to the relentless unfolding of events. As Gita Sen stresses, in the "messy world outside academe," confusion is ever present, and "the excitement of reflection, self-reflexivity, analysis, and conceptualization jostles for space with the challenges."[28] Under Zia the challenges were daunting and a coherent theoretical basis for desired social change and what needed to be overthrown or radically changed was never fully elaborated. This was not altogether surprising given the disparity of activists WAF brought together. Yet, despite the lack of clarity, WAF formulation of an alternative viewpoint and what was to be rejected was sufficient for it to become a beacon for women's rights, eliciting what in retrospect is a surprising degree of faith among so many that it could be counted on to take up any women's issue. Having broken the silence around violence against women, WAF became the immediate go-to for this with a surprising number of women trusting WAF sufficiently to ask for help in personal cases of domestic violence and sexual harassment. Activists were approached

[27] This was effected in 2006 with the Protection of Women (Criminal Laws Amendment) Act that was passed in the National Assembly under the rule of yet another general, Pervez Musharraf.

[28] https://dawnnet.org/wp-content/uploads/2018/04/Tambe-and-Trotz-Historical-Reflections-on-DAWN-An-Interview-with-Gita-Sen-2010-Comparative-Studies-of-South-Asia-Africa-and-the-Middle-East-2010-30_2-214-217.pdf.

by diverse actors with a variety of issues, such as working women's groups, but also sympathetic (male) journalists sharing new atrocities and proposals they learnt of, for WAF to take up.

Never a mass movement, WAF-led activism generated wells of tacit support among women well beyond its activists—perhaps articulating in public what many felt in private, especially among working women. How widespread such tacit support was can never be ascertained, but anecdotal evidence indicates it existed. Conducting fieldwork in those years, women working both in urban centers and remote towns would often ask whether I was part of WAF and unexpectedly (and sometimes covertly) give a thumbs-up. Running down the Mall during the February 12 demonstration, when my companion stopped to tell the policewoman running toward us not to touch us physically, her response was "keep running, I'll run along with you." Even my politically uninvolved homemaker mother-in-law would happily inform visitors that her new daughter-in-law was to be found either on the Mall (meaning at a demonstration) or at the Lahore High Court. Support was evident in renowned artists repeatedly performing for free; Habib Jalib writing a poem dedicated to WAF; the Karachi Press Club offering its premises when other venues were closed; independent cartoonists taking up the issues.

Women's activism in its totality—its theoretical productions of alternative positioning, practical public engagement and presence—generated considerable political frisson, opening possibilities and providing an impetus to women across the social spectrum and across social stratification. Reflecting back, it seems clear that women's activism and resistance of that time presented a critical nodal point through which women's roles in private and public could be rethought, including by unlikely actors, such as the JI women to argue for greater rights despite their differing in some key respects with the predominant liberalism that informed WAF. Activism did not change structural power bases that remain as asymmetrical as ever; the construction of alternative models of consciousness in political and cultural arenas was fragmented at best and support confined to pockets. A permanent place on the national agenda has not ensured a change in praxis and activists still grapple with how to leverage the redistributive potentialities of state power. Such fundamental changes demand a broader prolonged struggle, beyond the potential of such a small number of women in such a short time.

While Zia's discriminatory laws, policies, and rhetoric had multiple deleterious practical effects on women, they nonetheless had the unintended consequence of creating the conditions for women's activism, and for more sustained reflections on questions of gender and power, on feminism in postcolonial conditions, than otherwise may have been the case. Zia's regime generated various kinds of possible reflections—on the one hand, the fact that it was a dictatorship that enacted gender inequality impelled a straightforward response within liberal democratic terms, that is, it was illiberal, unequal, and discriminatory and also undemocratic. Had the laws been overturned and the status quo ante restored, this might not have provoked such intense reflections. Its hegemonic dimension, however, meant it forced the women's movement to think about the social and cultural aspects of patriarchy outside of a modernization narrative. The social and political struggle to enlist allies meant dialogue, rethinking, and engagement and this, in tandem with the consequential discursive proliferation of women's concerns across society, led even those on the religious right to expand their perspective on women's rights.

While it remains a common refrain that the women's movement was restricted and had a small base—it is also the case that these long years of activism leveraged the social and political importance of women's issues across the social and political spectrum in ways that had not happened before. In short, activism created forms of thinking and action, praxis, which exceeded the liberal problematic of a restoration of a status quo ante. The liberal emphasis on state and society as distinct, and of power located solely in the formal state apparatus is inadequate to both Gramscian and feminist thinking.

Bibliography

Crenshaw, Kimberlé Williams. 1989. "Demarginalizing the Intersection of Race and Sex: A Black Feminist Critique of Antidiscrimination Doctrine, Feminist Theory and Antiracist Politics," *University of Chicago Legal Forum* 1989 (1), Article 8, 139–67. http://chicagounbound.uchicago.edu/uclf/vol1989/iss1/8.

Ives, Peter. 2004. *Language and Hegemony in Gramsci*. London: Pluto Press.

Khan, Omar Asghar. 1985. *Political and Islamic Aspects of Islamisation in Islam, Politics, and the State: The Pakistan Experience*. Edited by Mohammad Asghar Khan. London: Zed Books, 127–63.

Maududi, S. Abul A'la Al. 1981. *Purdah and the Status of Women in Islam*, sixth edn. Lahore: Islamic Publications (First published 1939 in Urdu and translated in English in 1972).

Mernissi, Fatima. 1994. *Dreams of Trespass: Tales of a Harem Girlhood*. Cambridge, MA: Perseus Books.

McLaren, P., G. Fischman, S. Serra, and E. Antelo. 1988. "The Specters of Gramsci: Revolutionary Praxis and the Committed Intellectual." *Journal of Thought* 33 (3): 9–41.

Mumtaz, Khawar, and Farida Shaheed. 1987. *Two Steps Forward, One Step Back*. London: Zed Books.

Randolph, Bonnie Moore, and Clydene Ross-Valliere. 1979. "Consciousness Raising Groups." *American Journal of Nursing* 79 (5): 922–4. https://doi.org/10.2307/3462300.

Saigol, Rubina. 2016. *Feminism and the Women's Movement in Pakistan: Actors, Debates and Strategies*. Islamabad: Friedrich Ebert Foundation.

Shaheed, Farida. 2007. "Citizenship and the Nuanced Belonging of Women," in Jennifer Bennett (ed.), *Scratching the Surface: Democracy, Traditions, Gender*. Lahore: Heinrich Böll Foundation, 23–38.

Shaheed, Farida. 2010. "Contested Identities: Gendered Politics, Gendered Religion in Pakistan," in "The Unhappy Marriage of Religion and Politics: Problems and Pitfalls for Gender Equality," Special Issue. *Third World Quarterly* 31 (6): 851–67.

Shroff, Sara. 2014. "Politics of State Feminism in Pakistan: Diffusion of Gender Machineries." Political Economy and Public Policy Analysis II Professor Rachel Meltzer Final Paper May 19.

Tambe, Ashwini. 2010. "Introduction: Feminist State Theory." *Comparative Studies of South Asia, Africa and the Middle East* 30 (2): 161–3.

Tigar, M., and M. R Levy. 1977. *Law and the Rise of Capitalism*. New York: Monthly Review Press.

Toor, Saadia. 1997. "The State, Fundamentalism and Civil Society," in Neelum Hussain, Samiya Mumtaz, and Rubina Saigol (eds.), *Engendering the Nation-State*, vol. 1. Lahore: Simorgh, 111–46.

14

Political Emotion and Bodily Politics: Zulfikar Ali Bhutto and "the People"

Asad Ali

"*Bhutto zinda hai*" (Bhutto is alive), "*Bhutto humaray dilon mein hai*" (Bhutto is in our hearts), "*Mein bhi Bhutto*" (I too am Bhutto). These, and other similar refrains, are common among diehard Pakistan People's Party (PPP) supporters, workers, and activists, who, in Urdu, are collated into the umbrella term, *jiyalay* (singular: *jiyala)*. The heightened emotion exemplified by these refrains is viewed as characteristic of a "*jiyala* mentality," a mentality that is said to be so partisan that it cannot brook criticism of Zulifikar Ali Bhutto, the PPP's founder. It is also seen as emblematic of a politics that now no longer exists in Pakistan, a politics of egalitarianism that galvanized the poor and the working class and was, despite all the mistakes that were made, radical in its potential and its implications.

In this essay I seek to explore the political emotion of the first *jiyalay*—the generation who were mobilized by Zulfikar Ali Bhutto.[1] The PPP's promise of every man and woman having access to *roti, kapra, aur makan* (food, clothes, and a house), may, on one level, seem pragmatic—a socialist idea of an end to scarcity, but what Bhutto, in his words and in his actions, indeed, in his performance of politics, enabled was something far deeper than merely material gains. The emotion that linked Bhutto to the *jiyala* was genuinely political, one rooted in emancipatory possibilities—the desire for equality. It was central to the forging of an agentive people's politics and the formation of a self-conception of "the people" as a political entity and collectivity. This essay then seeks to relocate the place of political emotion in the politics of the oppressed.

My thanks to Anita Mir, Sohail Akbar Warraich, and Haris Gazdar for their comments and suggestions on this essay, and to Ameem Lutfi for his diligent field research.

[1] Although the term "*jiyala*" may only have been coined, or came to prominence, in the mid-eighties (Haris Gazdar, pers. comm., November 25, 2021), it expresses the characteristics of the ideal PPP worker from inception. Both supporters and opponents accept that the "*jiyala*" stands for an emotionally committed PPP supporter but differ in their assessment of the value and meaning of this commitment. PPP supporters see a *jiyala* as someone who is selfless, courageous, and intensely loyal. Opponents use the term in a derogatory manner to signify someone, usually from the poor, who lacks reason, exhibits excessive emotions, and is blinded by his/her personal devotion to Bhutto.

The success of Zulfikar Ali Bhutto's PPP in the 1970 elections in West Pakistan was often described, by supporters and opponents alike, in metaphors—as a *tufaan* (typhoon), a *zalzalla* (earthquake), a *salaab* (flood).[2] This resort to naturalistic language expressed the realization of how Bhutto and the PPP, in the first elections under direct universal adult franchise, had, by winning 81/138 seats in West Pakistan, effected a political revolution (Lodhi 1980: 108).[3] At the same time, it suggests the social transformation that accompanied this political success had, as yet, not been comprehended.

The PPP had routed establishment political parties through a relentless campaign of equating "the poor" (*gharib*) with "the people" (*awam*) and putting the oppressed and exploited at the center of politics, a politics they argued, that had been captured and co-opted by landlord and capitalist elites. Drawing from socialist discourse, the PPP emphasized equality, and Bhutto, in particular, communicated in a highly emotive language and style. Through speech and bodily acts he signaled empathy, respect, and a promise of social recognition and political inclusion for the poor. Bhutto showed that he grasped the systemic coercion and exploitation they endured, the ongoing everyday indignities of social inequality and the vulnerability of their lives.

Nazir Ahmed, aka Baba Jeera, a staunch PPP worker and lifelong Bhuttoist *(jiyala)*, who came from a deeply impoverished background, while reflecting on his political awakening over forty years ago, highlighted Bhutto's emotional empathy, and said that Bhutto was a "*gharibon ka saati*" and "*gharibon ka hamdard*" (gloss: emotional solidarity with and compassion for the poor). It was this quality in Bhutto that opened Baba Jeera to the PPP's message of empowerment, liberation, and, above all, equality. This was a political message that catalyzed an imaginative horizon in which "the people" (*awam*) could envisage their lives as independent, free, and meaningful. As Baba Jeera noted, appropriating a Persian phrase, "He gave us that sense of worth to live" (*jeenay ka sharf bakshna*).[4]

While this framing of "elites" against "the people" is characteristic of populist politics, what was unusual and striking in the Pakistani context was that "the people" had been mobilized by one of the largest landlords in the country. Bhutto was not just from one of the major Sindhi landlord families but had been educated at Berkeley and Oxford. He became a cabinet minister from 1958 and served the military dictator General Ayub Khan (1958–69), most prominently as Pakistan's cosmopolitan, and immaculately tailored, foreign minister (1963–6) before breaking with Ayub and maneuvering to position himself at the forefront of the anti-Ayub movement for democracy. At one end of this new political relation, a "charismatic" elite leader; at

2 For a summary review of the political background and types of elections prior to 1970, see Talbot (2009: part 2). For a detailed history of PPP and 1970 elections, see Lodhi (1980: chapter 3) and with a specific focus on the Punjab, see P. E. Jones (2003), especially chapters 7 and 8.

3 This essay's focus on the PPP, and hence on West Pakistan, entails exclusion of the wider political context of Mujeeb ur Rahman's Awami League's electoral victory, the refusal of the West Pakistani establishment to transfer power to the Awami League, the subsequent murderous military actions in the East and the eventual independence of Bangladesh.

4 Interviewed April 21, 2010, by Ameem Lutfi.

the other end, the emotionally invested and diehard PPP worker, the *jiyala*, who was usually, but not exclusively, drawn from the underclasses.

Field research for this essay, of PPP activists and workers in Okara, an urban town in central Punjab, repeatedly highlighted their emotional attachment to Bhutto, the force of his personality and *karishma* (charisma).[5] In particular, they valued Bhutto's emotional sensibility and style, which distinguished him not just from establishment politicians but also from other PPP leaders, for he touched them at an emotive level, and his behavior and social interactions made abstract political ideas of equality and emancipation socially and politically real and relevant to them. The concern of this essay then is political emotion. I seek to understand its place, the manner of its constitution, and its effects in the context of the PPP's emergence.

How was a political relation, one of intense attachment, often described in the idioms of "love," between an elite leader and those socially and politically marginalized and excluded, produced? What implications does this have for our understanding of the politics and history of the period? In this essay I focus on the idiom and style of the PPP, and of Bhutto in particular, in order to highlight the centrality of emotion in the making of political attachments and constitution of a new political subjectivity (Ahmed 2003; Blom and Lama-Rewal 2020; Mouffe 2002, 2005; Pernau 2019, 2021).

Emotion, Politics, and Populism

In mainstream political science emotion has long been, and widely continues to be regarded, as illegitimate. Politics, as it has conventionally been thought of, is centered on policies and interests, on reason and deliberation, rather than emotion and sentiment. Thus support for the PPP from the underclasses is explained through the parties' socialist and democratic program that was explicitly aimed at their interests—and this was undeniably a crucial factor in their success (Jones 2003; Lodhi 1980; Syed 1992). The PPP appropriated and benefited from a long history of Left organization and activism, but this still does not explain why the PPP was so much more successful, in a fraction of the time, than other leftist parties. That the Left had long been a target of state stigmatization, suppression, and violence was a contributory factor in the PPP's success (Asdar Ali 2015; Toor 2011; essay 2, this volume). Further, unlike most other socialist parties, the PPP, by conjoining Islam with democracy and socialism, effectively blunted the charges made by religious groups, of atheism and anti-Islam. While scholarship has been important in mapping out the ideological and socioeconomic bases for PPP support, it has, unsurprisingly, rarely attended to the emotional

[5] Field research for this project was undertaken in 2009 and 2010 by a research assistant Ameem Lutfi, who spent about three consecutive months in both years. He conducted twenty semi-structured interviews, usually with a repeat interview in the second year. He also made numerous additional notes of unstructured interviews and interactions with many more interlocutors. All interviews referenced in this essay were conducted, under my guidance and supervision, by Lutfi. Research was funded by grants from Harvard University's South Asia Initiative and Weatherhead Center for International Affairs, for a study entitled "The Dialogics of Populist Politics: A study of the cultural politics of the Pakistan People's Party."

attachment and affective intensities between Bhutto and PPP supporters. Emotional expressions and attachments are often glossed over as indicative of a personalistic and populist politics, characteristic of "immature" and authoritarian manipulation and regarded as a necessary "transitional" phase between the erosion of traditional authority and the development of a rule governed parliamentary democracy.

This question of attachment, of emotion and passion, for Bhutto should not, however, be regarded as aberrant. Insofar as it is explained, it is often through resort to the Weberian concept of charisma, an explanation commonly given by the interviewees, but also by Bhutto's contemporaries. It is also evident in the genre of political biographies and popular scholarship (Quddus 1993; Wolpert 1993).

Weber's conceptualization of charisma is best understood in relation to his account of the increasingly pervasive processes of rationalization characteristic of modern life, processes that reduced the scope of individual action, creativity, and autonomy. Developed within the typology of the various forms of authority (*herrschaft*—forms of rulership), charismatic authority, deriving from an individual's extraordinary and exceptional qualities, sharply contrasted with modern forms of rational legal authority, typified by a system of rules in legal and bureaucratic institutions. While the ideal typic example of one endowed with charisma is a religious prophet, Weber also held, and hoped, that democratic politics allowed for the possibility of extraordinary and revolutionary leaders who could revitalize the polity with new values and norms and stem the inexorable processes of rationalization and disenchantment (Reiter and Wellmon 2020; Riesebrodt 1999; Schnepel 1987; Weber 1978: 241–5).[6] Weber's conceptualization of charisma would seem, then, to have analytical purchase as it sought to describe the role of emotion in enabling both religious and political authority. However, as both sympathetic commentators and critics have pointed out, Weber's emphasis on charisma as an individual, albeit socially recognized, quality is analytically and sociologically weak as he effectively psychologizes and naturalizes charisma (Bourdieu 1987; Csordas 1997; Worsley 1968). The assertion of charisma, as explanation, then leaves "emotion," if one may say this without confusing the matter, as merely "emotional"—that is both an excess, as mere intensity, and as a reduction, of social emotions to naturalized feelings such as love and passion. In short, charisma as an explanation of the constitution of political emotion is inadequate as it takes *politics* out of emotions.

"Charisma" renders the *jiyala's* political attachments as individuated love and passion, so that the *jiyala* is reduced to a "devotee." This, I suggest, works to erase the history and actions of those *jiyalay* in the co-production of a new political subjectivity and movement. A double exclusion. It is not just that they are politically marginalized but that the modality of their participation is rendered as irrational, pre-political, or illegitimate. The concept of charisma then is less an explanation or analysis than a recognition of emotion in the constitution of authority, but as such, it involves

6 The predominant contribution of Weber's sociology has been to entrench the modern dichotomy of reason and emotion, of rationality and irrationality, while at times reversing this evaluation so that charisma is figured as a creative force (Emirbayer 2005).

an erasure of the political and substitutes a mystical attachment to an exceptional individual.[7]

Instead of explanations based on individuated actors and their personal or psychological dispositions, an analysis focused on the interrelation of the social and the political is required to see how these were crucial to the emergence of political emotions and sentiments, a political collectivity (the people), and a political subjectivity (democratic equality glossed as socialist). But one cannot escape Bhutto, the individual and social person, for he has come to stand for a political aspiration and collectivity, one that magnifies his personality and charisma as it were and thereby simultaneously diminishes the activities of PPP workers and supporters. One then, in a sense, cannot escape Bhutto and the *jiyala* but one has to "put them in their place." By this I mean Bhuttoism, as a co-produced political subjectivity expressive of democratic equality, that emerged in this period of the election campaign (1969–70) has to be understood within an analysis of collective populist politics rather than as within an individually led charismatic movement (Jalal 1995).

But populism, like emotion, has also presented a problem for mainstream political thought. Commentators have noted how it is vague, indeterminate, and protean, escaping definition (Canovan 2005; Taggart 2000). Often, it is ideologically "thin" or fluid, composed of multiple and often conflicting demands (Mudde and Kaltwesser 2017). As such, it lacks a coherent political rationality and consequently, emotions and sentiment centered on key slogans and symbols, and particularly, the leader, play a crucial role. This combination of charismatic leaders, emotional intensity, ideological fluidity, and the rhetorical invocation of "the people" and of an antagonist, the "enemy of the people," has led many to regard populism as irrational and dangerous to liberal democracy (Rosanvallon 2008; Urbanati 2014). Unable to define or adequately theorize this phenomenon, scholars have tended to describe instances of populism and classify its types and varieties (Canovan 1981). The Argentinian post-Marxist social theorist, Ernesto Laclau, however, developed a framework that takes these very aspects of populism—which make it seemingly aberrant—as the starting point of theorization (Laclau 2005). Drawing on aspects of poststructuralist theory, psychoanalysis, and post-Marxism, he resituates populism as an essentially democratic political phenomena and delineates the manner in which a "leader" can become the symbol of popular aspirations and affective identification. Laclau's theorization is complex and sophisticated. Substance, as well as nuance, is necessarily lost in my summary below.[8]

Populism, Laclau argued, is best understood as a democratic "political logic," one that is particularly salient when existing political institutions and infrastructures are unable or incapable of addressing social and political demands. As such, it is especially evident at times of political crises where a plethora of varied claims and demands from excluded, marginalized, and heterogenous social groups—demands that remain unaddressed—link together to form a broader based social and political movement. The heterogeneity of such a broad-based movement makes it difficult for a coherent

[7] For an account of why and how charisma became the conceptual means to explain political leadership especially in the newly decolonizing states, see Derman (2012).

[8] For a useful introduction to Laclau, see Howarth (2015).

political ideology to address multiple concerns, and irreducible tensions are therefore continuously present. Laclau argues that certain demands increasingly become positive symbolic expressions in that they link, articulate, and come to stand for all the other demands. That is, there is a process of simplification and equivalization around key slogans and symbols. But as these symbols become more generalized, increasingly divested of their particular content in order to stand for the totality, they become "empty signifiers."[9] As such, these symbols are able to link, organize, and represent an otherwise heterogeneous collectivity into a self-conscious social formation—"the people." These signifiers, then do not merely express but performatively constitute, the unity of this incipient collectivity.

Laclau further argues that a signifier which is entirely nominalistic, such as a name, for example, that of a leader, is even more suited to serve such a unifying function. The leader, in his account, through a process of "affective identification" comes to symbolize key collective aspirations. That is, the leader's name is understood as an overdetermined sign, one invested with desires and aspirations that emerge from multiple ongoing social and political struggles. This enables us to think of the relationship of leader and follower as constructed through semiotic and material processes and practices, and as such, to relocate attention away from the leader and his individual will, to reciprocal and interactional processes through which the leader comes to stand in for, and to signify, collective aspirations. Laclau's psychoanalytically and linguistically derived conception of affect explains the process of identification between leader and the people at the level of representation. However, the manner through which emotions are socially generated, circulated, and create attachments remains underdeveloped in his account.[10] In Bhutto's case, I suggest, that Bhuttoism primarily stood for equality (*musawaat*) both as a signifier, as in Laclau's telling, *and* as an embodied and enacted social practice.[11] As such, "equality" reflected the logic of modern democracy, of equal individuals expressing their collective will in political sovereignty. For this to occur, however, required social processes whereby the leader not only represented existing aspirations and desires but also embodied and exemplified this abstract notion of equality in concrete social practices or conduct.

[9] As Laclau notes, an "empty signifier" is something of a paradox but one he uses to express that which comes to represent the absent but desired fullness in a political community (Laclau [1994] 2015: 66–74). As Howarth explains, "empty signifiers" have two related aspects: (1) they are the symbolic means to represent essentially incomplete orders and (2) as their signification/meaning is indeterminate and struggled over they can function to hold together multiple and even contradictory demands in a precarious unity (Howarth 2015: 11–12).

[10] Laclau's use and understanding of affect, from psychoanalytical and linguistic theory, where language and affect are intimately connected, is very different from recent theorizations of affect, which eschews language and representation and emphasize the pre-social biological body. It is, however, beyond the scope or capacity of this essay to disentangle the complex and expanding literature on affect, emotions, and feelings. On language and affect, see Riley (2005), and on the emphasis on the body in "the affective turn," see G. J. Seligworth and M. Gregg's introduction to the *Affect Theory Reader* (2010), Teresa Brennan's "Introduction" in *The Transmission of Affect* (2004) and Daniel White (2017). For critiques of affect, see Leys (2011) and Mazzarella (2009). Plamper (2015) provides a useful and thoughtful review in his introductory chapter.

[11] Although Laclau argues that his conception of discourse is not just linguistic but extra-linguistic and material, in that signification is inherent to social practice, he nonetheless privileges the logic of representation in his analysis.

It was through this interplay of social practices and abstract political values that a new political subjectivity was forged. That is, the leader's name is both constitutive of, as well as expressive of, a political subjectivity and political sovereignty. In order to understand how this political subjectivity (equality) and collectivity (Bhuttoism) was effected we must attend not just to Bhutto's speech, or the content of what he says, but to his bodily practices. We have, in short, to take into account the total communicative act that implies not just the speaking subject but also the wider audience and speech community and further the typical ways of speaking, doing, behaving, and evaluating that are indicative of a habitus. I use Bourdieu's terminology of "habitus" in order to highlight not just language but the body, how power relations, through emotions, aesthetics, and sociocultural practices are constitutive of bodily dispositions and orientations in everyday social practices while acknowledging that these can change, that any particular configuration of social practices encoding and expressive of power relations is at best, hegemonic, and, as such, under contestation and liable to change (Bourdieu 1977; Hanks 1996: chapter 10; Abu-Lughod and Lutz 1990).[12] Bourdieu's emphasis on embodied social practices and semiotic processes, on acts as well as signs, is in my assessment a helpful addition to Laclau's emphasis on signification—when trying to account for the relationship forged between Bhutto and "the people."

Land and Habitus

Given the reproduction of economic and political power in highly discriminatory social practices it is not surprising that claims to equality became the principal signifier that united diverse social and political groups in Pakistan during the 1960s. Demands for political equality came to the fore in the anti-Ayub movement for democracy; demands for land redistribution and labor rights crystallized into arguments for greater economic equality and the continuing forms of social hierarchy made the claim of social equality especially palpable. Power and rights were embedded in land ownership,[13] so it is quite remarkable that Bhutto, possibly the largest landowner in the country, came to represent and embody equality.

In the immediate decades after independence, land ownership and the relations of agricultural production, as it had under colonial rule, continued to structure a social economy of power and authority. The landlord's political and symbolic power, at the apex of this predominately agrarian society, was reproduced and mediated through a range of social and cultural practices, a habitus. These gradations of social hierarchy were maintained and signaled through repertoires of social and bodily practices, including styles of dress, forms and tone of speech, bodily comportment, social distancing, rules of commensality all with the purpose of maintaining social

[12] This is not the usual understanding of Bourdieu where many critics have argued that his model emphasizes social reproduction and does not adequately account for change. Hanks, however, argues that there is a generative dimension to "habitus" that allows for both continuity and change (Hanks 1996: 239).

[13] For quite some time, property ownership gave one access to various entitlements under administrative and legal rules. If one did not have property one was excluded from these benefits.

distinction and differentiation. These social, cultural, and political entitlements linked to land ownership are summed up in the cultural meaning of being an owner (*malik)* as opposed to a non-owner (*be/ghair malik*) where the latter is understood as being a "nobody." Land, then, conferred power, respect, distinction, and autonomy, whereas non-landowners—whether tenants, sharecroppers, or agricultural laborers—were in varying relations of deference, dependence, and precarity.

Even in urban areas, with the possible exception of large industrial and metropolitan areas such as Karachi, land continued to remain the key marker of social distinction and power. This was also the case for Okara, one of the most industrialized towns in the canal colony districts, and the surrounding rural area. However, the rural areas of the canal colonies were characterized by less inequality in the size of land-holdings as compared to other regions in Pakistan. Following Partition, Okara and its environs experienced considerable migration from across the new Punjab border that also led to relatively greater equality and mobility.[14] Home to one of the largest cotton mills in the country, Okara was a venue for Left politics, equality, and egalitarianism—a theme in both urban and rural society. Okara was selected for this study because of its long and varied history of Left activism and also because it had, as Philip Jones noted in his study of the PPPs emergence and initial electoral success, "The best organized urban PPP unit" (2003: 291).

Semi-structured interviews were conducted by a research assistant primarily with two groups. The first group comprised PPP activists and workers (*karkun*) from Okara who had joined the party after its formation in December 1967 and participated through the election campaign of 1970. Socioeconomically and occupationally, this was a diverse sample that included middle-class lawyers, laborers, petty traders, shopkeepers, artisans, informal sector workers, and small-scale entrepreneurs. The second group were located in adjacent rural villages, principally chak 40//3 and 54/2 and comprised landowners, sharecroppers, freehold tenants, and independent peasant cultivators.

The research project sought to understand what it was about the PPP/Bhutto's political discourse, one that borrowed from the Left, that contributed to its success, whereas the Left's appeal continued to be limited. What, in short, made the PPP so popular? While considerations of space do not allow for a full elaboration of the argument in this essay, the aspiration of equality (*musawaat*), whether social, political, or economic, was of singular importance. *Musawaat* was central to the PPP's messaging, to the extent that this is what the party newspaper was named. In Laclau's terms, we can understand *musawaat* as one of the key signifiers that enabled the articulation of diverse groups into "the people."

The PPP's slogan "Islam is our faith; democracy is our polity; socialism is our economy," signaled the importance of equality across three key dimensions: faith, politics, and economics. Islam signified a community of equals (*musawaat e muhammadi*), democracy signaled political participation predicated on equality, and socialism stood for greater economic equality. Thus "equality" was both

[14] On the colonization and construction of the canal colonies, see Imran Ali (1989).

a simplification and a generalization that articulated aspects of these three traditions. Attempted commensuration across these traditions, such as, "Islamic socialism," was a scandal to those who understood the relations of religion, economy, and politics quite differently—in particular the Jamaat-e-Islami—who became the clearest ideological and political opponents of the PPP. These commitments were popularized through slogans such as, to take the most prominent examples, "*Roti, kapra, aur makan, mang raha hai har insaan*" (Bread, clothes, and shelter are the demands of each person) and "*Taqat ka sarchasma awam hai*" (the people are the source of all power). While at an ideological level these commitments to socioeconomic equality and political legitimacy were inspiring, nonetheless, I suggest that at the lived level, equality, in this time, by and large, existed as an imaginative aspiration rather than in social practices. Apart from temporary realizations, such as through the performance of Muslim ritual practice, as in public prayer, social relations across status difference were marked by practices of speech, dress, bodily stance, tone, and touch that inscribed hierarchy and inequality. Bhutto, I suggest, through his personality, social conduct, and political performances was key in translating abstract aspirations of equality from a political imaginary into a social and political reality.

Drawing from the interviews, I am going to argue that Bhutto, his person, body, and name were central in three ways to the forging of a highly personalized but nonetheless coproduced political emotion: First, the value accorded to empathy and compassion. Second, through a body politics that performed equality by transgressing social practices of distinction. And third, rhetorical techniques and gestures in speeches that negated his personhood and enabled the co-construction of a political collectivity, an imagined body politic, under the nominal sign of Bhutto/Bhuttoism. It was through this interplay between personal characteristics, social conduct, and political representation that an abiding emotional attachment between leader and supporters, especially with those who became political activists, was formed.

I will therefore delineate three aspects of these *jiyalas*' understanding of and encounters with Bhutto. The first is their perception and attribution of emotional empathy and compassion. The second involves interactions or close encounters they had with Bhutto, in less formal or informal settings, often just before, after, or between formal political events. In these socially proximate exchanges what many of the *jiyalay* remember and speak of is of how Bhutto "mixed with them," that he did not seem to bother with maintaining social distinction or imposing hierarchies, despite his social status and standing. I argue that Bhutto's transgressive body politics enabled social intimacy and enacted social equality. Third, I draw upon the interviewee's recollections of Bhutto's public political speeches at mass rallies and records of these or similar speeches to analyze how a collective political personae (Bhuttoism) was constructed. In this, a process of political equality and identification occurred in which Bhutto was both a representative and a sign of popular political sovereignty—and an embodied representative of the people, that is, a metonym for the body politic. Given that Bhutto, through socially transgressive practices, becomes the principal signifier of political equality, and is therefore central to this analysis I am aware that I could be misread, that is, through the analytical focus on Bhutto as leader, I am in danger of overemphasizing his importance. However, I argue that while it is impossible to ignore Bhutto as an individual, I will focus on how he is a personification, medium, and sign of social and political desires, aspirations, and struggles.

Empathetic Politics, Body Politics, and the Body Politic

Bhutto described himself and was described as someone who had compassion for the poor (*gharibon ka hamdard*). This attribute was widely commented on in the interviews. As Rana Azhar, a middle-class lawyer, who had attended the PPP inaugural meeting in Lahore and was one of the founding members of the PPP in Okara, put it, "If he was talking to some poor person he would speak with a lot of sympathy, as if he was himself moved. And that could move you, too. And it's not as if he was acting. He could feel other people's pain."[15] I take this as but one illustration of Abu-Lughod and Lutz's observation that "We should view emotional discourse as a form of social action that creates effects in the world, effects that are read in culturally informed ways by the audience for emotion talk" (Abu-Lughod and Lutz 1990: 12).

Mohammed Arshad was a young man, a laborer, in his early twenties at the time of the election campaign and, prior to the election campaign, largely uninterested in politics. He attended one of Bhutto's first rallies in the area, in nearby Sahiwal, a rally, he said was sparsely attended, with the majority of the audience being, like him, laborers. He had earlier attended rallies by the National Awami Party (NAP) and heard Maulana Bashani speak and Habib Jalib perform his poetry. But it was the PPP and Bhutto who, Arshad said, with their "fiery slogans" that captured his attention and ignited his youthful enthusiasm. Slogans such as "*Roti, kapra, aur makan*" spoke with an immediacy to people's vulnerability—hunger was a persistent concern. *Roti*, or rather the lack of it, expressed for many the consequences of struggles over exploitation in terms of pay and rights—where inability to collectively bargain meant one was at the whim of individual employers. Hunger was a physical harm, a social hurt, and expressed a collective condition. PPP slogans articulated a recognition of his socioeconomic condition, gave expression of its cause (elite exploitation), and promised redressal. This was a potent combination for it made sense of the unjust present and called for a different future. Mohammed Arshad recalled how in that first speech he heard Bhutto's slogan that "*Taqaat ka sarchasma awam hai*" (that the people are the source of all power). This made a forceful impression upon him. It was the beginning of his political education for he began to realize that through concerted political action and solidarity he could count as a political actor. He became a lifelong political activist, initially with the PPP with whom he remained until Bhutto's death, but later as the analysis of class struggle became more salient to his worldview, he joined the communist Mazdoor Kisan Party (Labourer and Peasant Party). Reflecting on his varied experiences of political campaigning, he noted that it was crucial to speak in the *lehja* (tone) of one's audience and that when speaking with the poor it was this language of hurt, pain, and suffering that articulated their condition. This was after all what he had heard from the PPP and

[15] Interviewed May 6, 2010.

Bhutto in that first speech, and was why he had joined the PPP: "I was a poor man and when someone spoke to our pain and suffering we thought finally we might get some relief and that we would get our rights."[16] At that first sparsely attended rally he had heard a man who seemingly recognized the pain and suffering of what it meant to be poor and who energetically promised to transform their condition.

Until Bhutto, said Mohammed Arshad, no politician had understood the experience of daily inequality. For him, Bhutto and the PPP recognized and gave expression to their legitimate grievances, which were simmering but suppressed within a social economy of elite power. Once out in the world, and given new words and a language popularized in slogans, disseminated through meetings, discussed in homes, shops, and newly politicized public spaces and with social solidarity practiced in mass rallies and smaller numerous gatherings and processions, a new collective, of the *gharib* as the *awam* became palpable and visible. Mirza Afzal Baig, who was a teenager at the time, recalled the enthusiasm. His father, a boiler engineer in the Indian railways, who had migrated at Partition, had been impressed by Bhutto and joined the PPP at its inception. Recollecting the excitement he said:

> We were told that the founder of the PPP, Zulfikar Ali Bhutto, understands the pain and suffering of the poor man, so cast your votes for him and the PPP only. Since he possesses "*dard-e-dil*"(a heart that feels pain and suffering of others) we have to help them win.[17]

Dard-e-dil expresses that quality of sympathy, of one who can feel the suffering of the poor. Bhutto was, as Nazir Ahmad, aka Baba Jeera, said, understood as the "friend of the poor" and as compassionate to the poor. Baba Jeera, as he was affectionately known, was a lifelong *jiyala* and had, in those early heady days, been given the task of carrying the PPP flag at rallies. Landless, he came from an impoverished rural background. Over his lifetime he engaged in a variety of work from small-scale cattle trading, agricultural labor, and assorted odd jobs while his wife and daughters did occasional tailoring and laundering in order to sustain the household. For Baba Jeera, like others interviewed, this fact of being landless and poor was the defining feature of their social existence. To be landless meant that one was always in bonds of service and servitude, of dependence and deference, instead of independence and respect—to be at the beck and call of social "superiors" rather than to have freedom from their claims and commands. To be without land (*be maliki*) meant that one was effectively a nobody. Even his assertion to a social identity, such as being from the Bhatti *zat* (caste),[18] was precarious in that this was often contested and ridiculed and regarded as an illegitimate claim to a higher social status. Instead, he would be marked as a *kammi* (low-level occupational caste), and the obligations and social reciprocities linked to a socially recognized and valued identity were then often denied. Unsurprisingly, caste

[16] Interviewed May 12, 2009.
[17] Interviewed April 22, 2010.
[18] Bhattis are often considered a martial caste, so his claim was ridiculed as he was considered to be from the low occupational castes (*kammis*).

and kinship seemed of little or no value if one was poor, for it was poverty that largely determined one's social relations:

> Only the poor associate with the poor. If someone comes into money then they stop associating with the poor, even if they are your close relatives, if they somehow become wealthy then they don't accept you, they'll consider you as poor ... one would have to work to earn a living as a barber, washerman ... but they would just call us poor. So we have no caste. There is only one caste, the children of Adam.[19]

In this world where land and social value were long sedimented, Baba Jeera then attempted to resignify the meaning of landlord. While describing how his paternal grandmother had loaned money to Sikh neighbors who were fleeing their homes during Partition, and who in return had offered some of the land they were leaving behind, he indicated that one does not benefit from the plight of those with whom one has social relations. For "the person who has compassion in the heart, understand them as a landlord, as leader. The one who helps and stands with the poor, the one who cares for them, that is a landlord."[20] Baba Jeera attempts to make an equivalence between the value of compassion and the landlord, that figure who is at the apex of value in the rural social economy. It was, for him, this quality of compassion, this emotional outreach that existed beyond social ties and obligations, that enabled friendship and solidarity as well as attachment and love. Whether it was Bhutto's example, as landlord and as compassionate, that inspired this attempt at resignification one cannot say for sure, but it was clear that for him Bhutto, one might say, involved a transvaluation of landlord from a figure of social and political authority to a moral and social register of compassion and equality.

Power and hierarchy, distance and difference, as well as closeness and intimacy are generated, inscribed, and reproduced through social practices, such as where one sits, how one talks (tone), with whom on eats, one's physical orientation to the other (proprioception), the etiquettes of touch and tactility (the haptic). In short, one's deportment is crucial to creating emotional states, whether of fear, respect, resentment, or attachment. Bhutto's apparent disregard for the social conventions that maintained hierarchy and distinction, his easygoing affability and empathy across social status, summed up as his capacity for *milna julna* (mixing) was frequently commented upon.

Abdus Sattar Pardesi was in his late teens during the election campaign of 1970. Although unable to vote in those elections he became and remained a Bhuttoist, an attachment and identification that endured a lifetime, despite his subsequent disgruntlement with the PPP as a political party. This bond was one that he shared with other PPP *jiyalay* in that it went beyond Bhutto's life, and was summed up by a commonly expressed desire to be buried at Bhutto's ancestral graveyard in Larkana.[21] Pardesi's father, a small trader and shopkeeper, had been impressed by Bhutto's

[19] Interviewed April 21, 2010.

[20] Ibid.

[21] Where Zulfikar Ali Bhutto and other members of the Bhutto family are buried.

nationalism and performance as foreign minister, and Sattar Pardesi saw Bhutto a number of times when he visited Okara in both social and political settings. He attended Bhutto's campaign speeches and later travelled to Lahore to be present at the public speeches at the Organisation of Islamic Cooperation (OIC) conference in February 1974. By the time he was interviewed he was in his mid- to late fifties and had become a religious man, of Barelwi persuasion, and when he spoke of Bhutto he did so using language drawn from Sufism, a lexicon of love and attachment.

Pardesi describes how as a young man he was struck by Bhutto who, like a Sufi pir, "Would immerse himself in the people. I personally saw him at a wedding ceremony. He did not sit at the table and have food, but sat on the ground and ate with the workers. There are very few people like that."[22] Of another occasion he said,

> By birth Bhutto was a landlord but the way he lived was like a Sufi (*sufiyaana*). He would even sit on the ground. I once saw him at Jinnah Park sitting on the grass … although he was wearing a three-piece suit … Then he just lay down and put his head on a worker's lap. Just ask that worker how proud he must have felt that Bhutto *sahib* put his head on his lap. That is the *awami* (people's) style.[23]

Bhutto's clothes, especially his expensively tailored foreign suits, were as often spoken of as his easy going familiarity and conviviality.[24] Instances of Bhutto letting his suit get dirty, or carelessly discarding his jacket crop up anecdotally in many conversations. In Pakistani society, clothes are one of the primary visual means of signifying social distinction. Clothes are obsessively "read" and "interpreted," and cleanliness and starched white linen signify status, social respect, and moral rectitude. Bhutto's wanton "dirtying" of his clothes was understood as a radical act in which he, like an ascetic Sufi, disregarded material things and social conventions.

Although Pardesi drew upon Sufism, he also sought to differentiate the kind of attachments to a political leader from the kind of requirements and love inspired within Sufism. While the love of a *mureed* (disciple) for his Sufi master, in its intense devotion, appears similar to the *jiyala*'s love for Bhutto, the former involves a process of losing one's "self/ego," initially through mimesis—with a Sufi master, but eventually in the divine. The love for Bhutto, by contrast, was a deep-seated attachment, one borne not from a loss of the self or ego but a recognition of the self—a self that was worthy of equality and respect. In this sense it was political recognition and a political identity and identification, rather than mimesis. Within the transcendental concerns of Sufism, love for the other (master/divine) is the necessary means to discipline one's self/ego. In the temporal world of politics, love for the other (Bhutto) was a means/medium through which one could love one's self, a recognition necessary to emerge as a social and political equal. Nonetheless, Sufism with its idiom of love from disciple to master and its ascetic disregard for social conventions can be considered as one

[22] Interviewed April 23, 2010.

[23] Ibid.

[24] Bhutto had a varied sartorial politics often wearing an ordinary *shalwar kameez* to communicate his link to the people and Mao caps and suits to signify his leftist, especially Chinese, affiliation.

conceptual means through which many could locate Bhutto and themselves in this newly emerging political fabric.

In the examples cited by Pardesi, Bhutto breaks other social conventions that maintain hierarchy by milling and eating with workers at a wedding rather than sitting at the high table along with the bride and groom. Perhaps most radically, he breaks taboos on touch and intimacy by lying on the ground with his head in a worker's lap. Other interviewees spoke of how, despite the magnitude of their social differences, Bhutto would interact with them as equals, and this was expressed in the manner and tone of his voice, his physical proximity, and behavior. Moreover, he was, they said, attentive and sympathetic.

Saeed Majhiana, born in a village on the outskirts of Okara where his father was a menial household employee (*mulazim*), escaped poverty and the structures of servitude in the rural economy through education. He would go on to become a lawyer. Around forty at the time of the election campaign, he was enthused by Bhutto and the PPP's message of greater social and economic equality. For him, it was the PPP's message of respect, irrespective of social position, that was especially appealing. As a young man he had been influenced by the Khaksar movement which emphasized equality, humility, and autonomy—as had a number of other interviewees. More than anything, he appreciated Bhutto's personal disregard for social conventions:

> Once the party workers of my district, Sahiwal, were meeting, so Bhutto came and joined us. We were sitting around on the ground, on the grass. And so, like us, he too sat on the grass with us and he listened to what the workers had to say … We thought that he would make an excellent representative.[25]

In this anecdote we see how Bhutto's empathy and social familiarity consolidated ideas of political equality and democratic representation.

Mohammed Abdullah came from a somewhat less impoverished and more educated background than Majhiana—from a family of independent peasant cultivators whose land was adjacent to extensive military-owned farms.[26] His father had been a man of considerable religious learning and Abdullah continued this tradition. In addition to small-scale farming he became a mosque Imam in the military farms. His direct interactions with military personnel and the experience of their authoritarian, high-handed, and exploitative relations with their tenants (*mazaray*/sharecroppers) made him receptive to Bhutto's vocal critique of Ayub's dictatorship and pro-democracy message. He was in his late thirties when the PPP was established, joining immediately and becoming a lifelong *jiyala*. Describing how he conveyed what this abstract term "democracy" meant while campaigning as an activist, he explained how in a democracy people sat together equally, without fear, hearing each other's suggestions and coming up with a compromise that was agreeable to all. By contrast, dictatorship was marked by fear and a single authority. In his view, landlords were politically inclined toward

[25] Interviewed in May 5, 2010.

[26] Abdullah had been involved in organizing the sharecroppers/tenants in mid-1970s vis-à-vis the military owners.

dictatorship in that land ownership entrenched hierarchy and social inequality. Equality and co-participation were anathema to them. These attitudes toward democracy and equality, and dictatorship and command, were expressed through how social standing and power were reproduced in the seating arrangements in the landlords *deray* (meeting-place) and houses.

> Before Zulfikar Ali Bhutto came into power, in the houses of *waderas* and *zamindars* there were three kinds of division. For the *waderas* there were chairs. For, people of one rank below there were *charpais*. For the rank below that there were stools (*mooray*). As for the poor, they sat on the floor. This was the difference. It was this kind of distinction that Bhutto finished.[27]

Democracy then was not just about political equality but about social transformation; it allowed individuals to assert social equality and develop a sense of self-respect (*izzat-e-nafs*).

These seemingly unimportant anecdotes of Bhutto's behavior in ordinary everyday social interactions, transgressing the social practices that structure, and are constitutive of a habitus, were, I suggest, of considerable importance in consolidating and transforming ideological affinities into emotional attachments. Such anecdotes were narrated, transmitted, and widely circulated, and they indicated how Bhutto performed a body politics, one which socially enacted the PPP's wider message of equality.[28] In this performance of social equality Bhutto transgressively traverses a terrain of carefully calibrated social hierarchies that maintained status, distinction, and difference. However, unlike those Sufis who embrace asceticism as a step in a fundamental process of self-transformation, Bhutto's gesture was performatively transgressive, that is, directed toward social consequences rather than inner dispositions. Its efficacy was partly generated by the fact that he was the exemplar of the elite, so his mixing and milling with social inferiors was, like the dirtying and shedding of his suit, seemingly radical but transient. He would reclothe in the same apparel, return to his social world only to later sally forth and repeat the same disregard for social conventions, and sully yet another suit. Bhutto's performative transgression derived its efficacy from the differential of his social status, as such, his actions—personal motivations notwithstanding—were a powerful assertion of social and political equality.

I have suggested, thus far, that compassion, as a highly valued sentiment, enabled a political relationship that contributed to the emotional bond between leader and supporters. I have also argued that transgressive behavior, where Bhutto enacted equality, generated social and political intimacy and was another constituent in the forging of emotional and affective bonds. Finally, I briefly highlight some aspects of Bhutto's oratory and rhetoric where he negates his individual self and privileges the people's will thereby effecting a political identity through the logic of popular

[27] Interviewed April 22, 2010. While "waderas" and "zamindars" both mean landlords the former term suggests large landholders with a distinctively "feudal" style.

[28] The 1970 elections were delayed and the campaign extended for over eleven months. Bhutto was an energetic and tireless campaigner (Burki 1988: 54).

sovereignty. At other moments, he evokes a different kind of negation, of his bodily vulnerability and mortality. This interplay between his physical body and a political body enables identifications and transitions between Bhutto and his audience, at both a phenomenological and political level, transitions that effect an imagined body politic.[29]

In his campaign speeches Bhutto often related how, in the struggle for democracy, he was under constant harassment, intimidation and the threat of imprisonment, violence, and possible death at the hands of Ayub's regime. This resonated with those whose social existence, laborers and peasants, was always potentially subject to violence at the hands of capitalists, landlords, and their henchmen. That Bhutto put himself at risk for them meant he seemingly shared a key aspect of their social ontology—precarity and vulnerability at the hands of authoritarian power. The political struggle for democracy paralleled their struggle to overcome the hierarchy and authoritarianism that structured their social existence, and became an existential matter of life and death. Consequently, Bhutto's performance of courage and defiance in the face of adversity and authoritarianism was thrilling and inspiring.

The theme of vulnerability, death, and political identity becomes more pronounced in the wake of an attack by gunmen at one of Bhutto's campaign rallies at Sanghar in late March of 1970 from which he narrowly escaped and in which one of his supporters was killed:

> The PPP is the party of the masses. It is your party and it represents your feelings. There is no difference between you and me. My voice is your voice … If one Bhutto is assassinated a thousand Bhuttos will arise. If I am killed the people of Pakistan will carry on this democratic struggle. (Speech at Gabole Park, Karachi, April 12, 1970)[30]

Bhutto's non-self, or rather the possibility of his death, marks the reduction of his self to a site of collective harm or injury, his individual nonexistence allows for his continued political existence. Increasingly he portrays himself as the personification of the people's aspirations and will:

> It is not the person of Bhutto they want to defeat because there is no personal enmity between us; they want to defeat the people of Pakistan … our enemies are enemies of the people. (November 3, 1970 Speech at Lahore)[31]

The logic of the dictatorship/democracy opposition maps onto their own social position in an authoritarian and hierarchical social polity. Thus, the vulnerable social body is

[29] It is beyond the scope of this essay to undertake a study of Bhutto's rhetorical techniques. Such a study would require audio or audiovisual recordings that capture the dynamic interplay between speaker and audience. While audio recordings of his campaign speeches were collected and published in a volume by Hamid Jalal and Khaled Ahmed (*Politics of the People, vol. 3. Marching Towards Democracy* (Karachi: Pakistan Publications, n.d.)), these were not traceable at the time of writing. One has therefore to make do with their written record but these focus on the referential content of Bhutto's speeches. One suspects that all the humor, jokes, satire, and repartee with the crowds, that interviewees suggest made such speeches so engaging, have been edited out.

[30] Jalal and Ahmad, *Politics of the People*, 47.

[31] Ibid., 147.

politically identifiable and locatable in Bhutto. He is both physically and politically the embodied representative of the people.[32] The logic of popular sovereignty, of democracy, allows for the emergence of a political imaginary of populist politics, of Bhuttoism, of a man of the people, and of an imaginary of a body politic, of the people in their multiplicity as Bhuttos. This interrelationship is perhaps most clearly, or at least most famously, stated in a public speech he gave at Liaqat Bagh in Rawalpindi in December 1973, where he said:

> I will never hide anything from you. You are my brothers. There is not one Zulfikar Ali Bhutto, there are two. There is one who is physically standing here, and the second is you (collectively), each one of you in you all (collective). For this reason it is not just me talking, this is not just my speech, it is not just me giving a speech, these are your words, this is your speech, your aspirations. The suffering you experience, that is also mine. Why? Because as I have just said, "I am two." I am not one. One is here, in this (living) body, in this blood, existing and the other is in your spirit, in your body, animating your body.[33]

This speech was recalled by a number of interviewees, no doubt made all the more poignant, powerful and enduring as a consequence of Bhutto's judicially delivered execution at the hands of General Zia-ul-Haq in 1979.[34] Sattar Pardesi recalled the passion with which Bhutto said these words, how his hands gesticulated and knocked into the microphones, and how the words summed up Bhutto's political ideology and legacy so that the project of democracy, through popular sovereignty, effected this populist collectivity, of the political identification of Bhutto and the people:

> Through his rule, Bhutto proved that he is from us and we are from him … Democracy is our politics. He spread this in the public in such a way that every man used to think it is not Bhutto who is sitting there, but that it was oneself who was sitting there.[35]

Another PPP stalwart recalled this explicit identification whilst describing how the PPP, only because of its workers commitment, continued to remain a political force:

> Bhutto had a slogan "I am one Bhutto here, you are also Bhutto. Your spirit is in me, my spirit (*ruh*) is in you. We go with that slogan. As long as we are alive we are Bhutto's soldiers (*sipahis*)."[36]

Here, *ruh* (spirit) can be understood as both an ethos, what Bhuttoism stood for, and also as a force, an energy transmissible from one body to another.

[32] As the embodiment of people's sovereignty, Bhutto also often acted with the high-handedness, authoritarianism, and violence of a traditional sovereign.

[33] See 55.24–56.07 of https://www.youtube.com/watch?v=qniOzdmz7xk. Speech on December 20, 1973, at Liaqat Bagh, Rawalpindi. See *Pakistan Times*, Lahore, December 21, 1973.

[34] Syed notes that he twice heard Bhutto make similar statements in the fall of 1973 (1992: 70–1).

[35] Interviewed on April 21, 2009.

[36] Rana Amim, interviewed April 21, 2009.

Embodied Politics

Compassion, as an empathetic emotional orientation, I have suggested, signaled and enabled a political relationship with those outside the immediate bonds of family and kin group while Bhutto's transgressive conduct, his body politics, performed equality and produced political intimacy. Finally his oratory and rhetoric effected an imaginary of a body politic, of Bhuttoism/the people, of leader and follower, as interchangeable. Together, these varied dimensions generated political emotions that were, I suggest, crucial to the making of a new political subjectivity, one that was democratic, egalitarian, increasingly assertive, and autonomous. This was especially so among the rural and urban poor, the vast majority of whom had no sense of themselves as political beings, as actors in the shaping of a collective history. These values of compassion, equality, recognition, and respect effected individual transformations and were manifest in behavior and practices—an embodied politics.

It was not just the poor who saw some value in the PPP message, but political opponents too. Hajji Rao Akhtar was from a long-settled and influential landlord family with lands in Chak 40/3. He was politically affiliated with the Muslim League.[37] An economist by training and modernist in outlook, he was critical of how Bhutto's nationalization of industries had reduced economic efficiency, incentives for work, and of the general transformation in attitudes of workers and peasants to those in authority. The "*joshelay naraas*" (emotive slogans) of the PPP that seemed to promise land appropriation such as "*jeera waaway ohi khawy*" (he who sows shall eat) had, he said, led to excessive enthusiasm. On his own lands he was struck by how, seemingly overnight, the tenants attitude, posture, and stance radically changed. They no longer showed traditional forms of deference, but spoke to him in louder voices and, he thought, in a more abrasive way; they were in general more "bold" and challenged existing work arrangements and shares of produce over land and labor. While differing with the PPP's redistributive economic policies he acknowledged that the poor should be socially and politically treated as equals, and receive their dues—and in this sense, the changes brought about by the PPP were, he thought, both legitimate and profound.

> He (Bhutto) became the voice of the poor. Before that they were just an invisible population who were not given any kind of respect. They were not given their basic rights and their needs and wants were completely ignored … one thing is for sure though—Bhutto established that there was no difference between men. No man should be treated like an animal; it doesn't matter how poor a man is.

The ever present threat of physical intimidation along with coercive exploitation was precisely why Baba Jeera was so invested by promises of redistribution, especially with respect to land. They seemed to augur a new era of social, economic, and political transformation in that they would allow for independence and autonomy from the

[37] Interviewed May 7, 2010. He was in late eighties at the time of interview and therefore would have been in late forties at the time of election.

authority and coercion of landlords to whom they had, hitherto been in thrall. As he explained the various forms of intimidation and coercion through which landlords extracted unpaid labor and how the PPP had given them the courage to stand up for their rights, his brother-in-law interrupted to comment:

> Bhutto taught the poor how to speak up: Push your chest out when you speak (*seena taan ker bolain gai*), look them straight in the eye (*logon ko ankh mein ankh mila ker dehkna).*What was the meaning/purpose of the PPP? It was to look at everyone with the same eye (i.e. non-discriminatory) ... Before, when a poor man went to speak with a landlord, he would look at the ground when speaking. Bhutto said: Look at them straight in the eye when speaking and ask for your rights. This was Bhutto's manifesto.[38]

A manifesto that entailed embodiment. These are not then, just metaphors, but literal bodily modifications (Connerton 1989). Equality and nondiscrimination required changes in tone, stance, and gaze as one moved from a deportment inscribing social inequality toward a comportment of equals. As the basis of recognizing political claims these may seem trifling as compared to the usual events of conventional historiography, of regime changes and crises, of protests, social movements and repression, of wars and revolutions. But in relation to an existing sociopolitical habitus these small changes in bodily orientations, in interactions, and gestures was not lost on any one. It bespoke of a change in attitudes and the transformation of existing social relations, a continuous re-negotiation and struggle over power relations that were embedded in the everyday minutiae of social practices. Here, politics, as well as aesthetics, as Rancière has argued, is a disruptive activity that can bring about a "redistribution of the sensible," that is, the ways of perceiving, being, and acting in the world (Rancière 2004, 2010). This new sense of empowerment and assertion was widespread and for Baba Jeera, and many others, evident in the transformations of the machinery of the state, of bureaucracy, and especially the police. Baba Jeera marveled at how the state, after a slew of legislation in first couple of years of PPP rule, now sought to extend rights and protection to poor people like him. Nor were they any longer afraid of the police, who in the rural economy were long regarded as the rough hands of landlord power. Now with the party and Bhutto behind them they could, without fear of being ignored or maltreated, take their complaints of injustices to the police station. Baba Jeera hyperbolically recalled this new sense of visceral empowerment:

> During Bhutto's time we would open the SP and DSP's office/door (Superintendent of Police and Deputy Superintendent of Police); we would "kick" it open. That's how much courage we had.[39]

Mohammed Abdullah recalled how the Punjab police had attempted to go on strike during the PPP government because, in his assessment, they had been made "public

[38] Interviewed on April 21, 2010.
[39] Ibid.

servants of the people and that any (common) man can just walk up to the SHO (Station House Officer) and demand his rights." That is, the authority and superiority that came from being public officials had been transmuted into public *servants*, a humiliation, that he thought was for them too great to bear.[40]

This coalescing of the body and politics as a form of empowerment was articulated by almost all, across the social divide, as how "Bhutto gave voice to the poor." In the more common telling, as with Hajji Rao Akhtar, this described how the political power of the Bhutto/PPP government enabled the poor to find their voice and speak up—to make claims and contest existing socioeconomic arrangements that perpetuated inequality, oppression, and exclusion. But the expression captures the double sense of giving voice, that is, Bhutto gave expression to already existing voices—the discourses of the Left, of the poor, of historical movements for greater equality that he, along with the PPP, disseminated and popularized. Language and communicative practice is always a dialogical and dialectical process (Bakhtin 1981; Voloshinov 1986). PPP activists and workers vernacularized the PPP's message of greater social, political, and economic equality in and through their communicative practices. Further, through their actions and collective political practices—of organizing, arranging and holding public meetings, chanting slogans, demonstrating, marching in processions, engaging, and persuading others—these individual and collective activities inspired and produced emotions as well as giving, distributing, and fortifying courage. It was this strength in numbers, a developing solidarity and mutual respect and an ideological commitment to equality of persons, of democratic political participation that were instrumental to the formation of a political collectivity. This did not mean that class and hierarchy within the party vanished; they continued to manifest in party hierarchy and after the election success became more pronounced as political elites joined, much to the distress of leftists and working-class urban and rural activists. Nonetheless, the commitment to equality, while unable to eliminate or radically diminish perduring structures of class and hierarchy, was sufficient to transform a social ethos of deference to one of self-respect and dignity, and at times, defiance—that is, the formation of a new political subjectivity among the poor.

Concluding Thoughts

One must, therefore, while recognizing the force and qualities of Bhutto's personality, move away from the mystifications of charisma and recognize this was a coproduced political subjectivity—one in which Bhutto may have been at the center, but in important ways, was not as central as he seems. He was at the center in that he symbolized and manifested important cultural qualities of compassion and courage; as a landlord he exemplified the social relation of power, which he subverted through his bodily practices; as leader he was the nodal point of political demands for equality.

[40] While the reasons for the police strike were multiple and varied, including demands for improved wages and conditions, Bhutto had criticized the police for being the instruments of an oppressive state rather than acting in the service of the people.

However, he was not central in that these desires, aspirations, practices, and politics already existed in a multitude of sociopolitical struggles that came to coalesce, as Laclau's theorization suggests, under the sign "Bhutto." The name "Bhutto," does not just refer to a historical and socially locatable individual but to wider currents and desires for equality, respect, freedom, and independence. "Bhutto" here is merely the instantiation and exemplar, of these desires and struggles. The radical potentiality of the sign "Bhutto," however, always existed in tensions with the actual person, the pragmatic politician, who in life and government, could never resolve the multiple and contesting claims and interests that made up a broad-based and heterogeneous democratic political movement. In efforts to maintain political power, and engaging in the everyday practice of a contingent and pragmatic politics, he more often than not sought to control, curb, and even confront this radicalism (Ahmad 1978; Ali 2010).

In opposition, and especially after his death, however, Bhutto's name becomes a disembodied sign, an empty signifier unencumbered from the contingencies, compromises, and disappointments of everyday politics. In death Bhutto was forgiven for his many trespasses and his name came to stand for a political subjectivity and radical potentiality. To put Bhutto and the *jiyalay* in their place is not then just to recognize the politics in emotion but to reverse the topology of charisma that prioritizes emotions over politics. It is also to understand the intensification of this emotion, of this emotional attachment to the sign "Bhutto"—not as an excess of emotion but as a repository of an emancipatory and socially just politics, one that can be conceived in millenarian terms, a politics that is sustained as it is thwarted by forces of revanchism. This affective identification with Bhutto as indicative of a continuing politics of the oppressed was summed up by Abdus Sattar Pardesi as he recited a PPP-inflected popular verse on life-and-death struggles:

> *yeh baazi khoon ki baazi hai,*
> *yeh baazi tum hi haaro gai,*
> *har ghar se Bhutto niklay ga,*
> *tum kitnay Bhutto maro gay?*
>
> (This struggle is one of life and blood
> This struggle is one you will lose
> From each house a Bhutto will emerge
> How many Bhuttos can you kill?)

Another long-serving PPP activist, Abrar ul Haq Farooqi, while saying, "They can't remove Bhutto from our hearts," insisted, "If the PPP is still a force today it is because of us bare foot workers, if it were upto the leaders, it would have ended with Bhutto."[41] As a force of a possible politics "Bhutto" lives on, embodied as a political subjectivity, constitutive of a political collectivity and as a sign of continued struggle.

[41] Interviewed on April 21, 2009.

Bibliography

Abu-Lughod, Lila, and Catherine Lutz. 1990. "Introduction: Emotion, Discourse and the Politics of Everyday Life," in L. Abu-Lughod and C. A. Lutz (eds.), *Language and the Politics of Emotion*. Cambridge: Cambridge University Press, 1–23.

Ahmad, Aijaz. 1978. "Democracy and dictatorship in Pakistan." *Journal of Contemporary Asia* 8 (4): 477–512.

Ahmed, Sara. 2003. *The Cultural Politics of Emotion*. New York: Routledge.

Ali, Kamran Asdar. 2010. "Strength of the State Meets Strength of the Street: The 1972 Labour Struggle in Karachi," in Naveeda Khan (ed.), *Beyond Crisis: Re-evaluating Pakistan*. London: Routledge, 210–44.

Ali, Kamran Asdar. 2015. *Communism in Pakistan: Politics and Class Activism 1947–1972*. London: Bloomsbury.

Ali, Imran. 1989. *The Punjab under Imperialism 1885–1947*. Princeton, NJ: Princeton University Press.

Bakhtin, Mikhail. 1981. *The Dialogic Imagination*. Austin: University of Texas Press.

Blom, Amélie, and Stéphanie Tawa Lama-Rewal (eds.), 2020. *Emotions, Mobilisations and South Asian Politics*. New York: Routledge.

Bourdieu, Pierre. 1977. *Outline of a Theory of Practice*. Cambridge: Cambridge University Press.

Bourdieu, Pierre. 1987. "Legitimation and Structured Interests in Weber's Sociology of Religion," in Scott Lash and Sam Whimster (eds.), *Max Weber, Rationality and Modernity*. London: Allen and Unwin, 119–36.

Brennan, Teresa. 2004. *The Transmission of Affect*. Ithaca, NY: Cornell University Press.

Burki, Shahid Javed. 1988. *Pakistan under Bhutto, 1971–77*. London: Macmillan Press.

Canovan, Margaret. 2005. *The People*. Cambridge: Polity Press.

Carter, Peter. 2010. "Maulana Bashani and the Transition to Secular Politics in East Bengal." *Indian Economic and Social History Review* 47 (2): 231–59.

Connerton, Paul. 1989. *How Societies Remember*. Cambridge: Cambridge University Press.

Csordas, Thomas. 1997. *Language, Charisma and Creativity: The Ritual Life of a Religious Movement*. Berkeley: University of California Press.

Derman, Joshua. 2012. *Max Weber in Politics and Social Thought: From Charisma to Canonization*. Cambridge: Cambridge University Press.

Emirbayer, Mustafa. 2005. "Beyond Weber Action Theory," in C. Camic, Philip. S. Gorski, and David M. Trubek (eds.), *Max Weber's "Economy and Society": A Critical Companion*. Stanford, CA: Stanford University Press, 185–203.

Gregg, Melissa, and Gregory J. Seigworth (eds.), 2010. *The Affect Theory* Reader. Durham, NC: Duke University Press.

Hanks, William. F. 1996. *Language and Communicative Practices*. Boulder, CO: Westview Press.

Howarth, David (ed.). 2015. *Ernesto Laclau: Post Marxism, Populism and Critique*. New York: Routledge.

Jalal, Ayesha. 1995. *Democracy and Authoritarianism in South Asia: A Comparative and Historical Perspective*. Cambridge: Cambridge University Press.

Jalal, Hamid, and Khaled Ahmed (eds.), n.d. *Politics of the People, Vol 3. Marching Towards Democracy*. Karachi: Pakistan Publications.

Jones, Philip E. 2003. *The Pakistan People's Party: Rise to Power*. Karachi: Oxford University Press.

Laclau, Ernesto. 2005. *On Populist Reason*. London: Verso.

Laclau, Ernesto. 2015. "Why Do Empty Signifiers Matter to Politics," in David Howarth (ed.), *Ernesto Laclau: Post Marxism, Populism and Critique*. New York: Routledge, 66–74.

Leys, Ruth. 2011. "The Turn to Affect: A Critique." *Critical Inquiry* 37 (3): 434–72.

Lodhi, Maleeha. 1980. "Bhutto: The Pakistan Peoples' Party and Political Development in Pakistan 1967–77." Unpublished PhD dissertation, London School of Economics and Political Science, University of London.

Mazzarella, William. 2009. "Affect: What Is It Good For?," in Saurabh Daube (ed.), *Enchantments of Modernity*. New Delhi: Routledge.

Mouffe, Chantal. 2002. "Politics and Passion: Introduction." *Philosophy and Social Criticism* 28 (6): 615–16.

Mouffe, Chantal. 2005. *On the Political*. London: Routledge.

Mudde, Cas, and Cristobal R. Kaltwasser. 2017. *Populism: A Very Short Introduction*. New York: Oxford University Press.

Pernau, Margrit. 2019. "Feeling Communities: Introduction." In Special Issue Feeling Communities, *Indian Economic and Social History Review* 54 (1): 1–20.

Pernau, Margrit. 2020. "Studying Emotions in South Asia." *South Asian History and Culture* 12 (2–3): 111–28.

Pernau, Margrit. 2021. *Emotions and Modernity in Colonial India: From Balance to Fervor*. New Delhi: Oxford University Press.

Plamper, Jan. 2015. *The History of Emotions: An Introduction*. Oxford: Oxford University Press.

Quddus, Syed. A. 1993. *Zulfikar Ali Bhutto: Politics of Charisma*. Lahore: Progressive Publishers.

Rancière, Jacques. 2004. *The Politics of Aesthetics: The Distribution of the Sensible*. London: Continuum.

Rancière, Jacques. 2010. *Dissensus: On Politics and Aesthetics*. London: Continuum.

Reiter, Paul, and Chad Wellmon. 2020. *Charisma and Disenchantment: The Vocation Lectures*. New York: New York Review Books.

Riesebrodt, Martin. 1999. "Charisma in Max Weber's Sociology of Religion." *Religion* 29 (1): 1–14.

Riley, Denise. 2005. *Impersonal Passion: Language as Affect*. Durham, NC: Duke University Press.

Rosanvallon, Pierre. 2008. *Counter-Democracy: Politics in an Age of Distrust*. Cambridge: Cambridge University Press.

Schnepel, Burkhardt. 1987. "Max Weber's Theory of Charisma and Its Applicability to Anthropological Research." *Journal of the Royal Anthropological Society of Oxford* 18 (1): 26–48.

Syed, Anwar H. 1992. *The Discourse and Politics of Zulfikar Ali Bhutto*. New York: St. Martin's Press.

Taggart, Paul. 2000. *Populism*. Buckingham: Open University Press.

Talbot, Ian. 2009. *Pakistan: A Modern History*. London: Hurst.

Taseer, Salman. 1979. *Bhutto: A Political Biography*. London: Ithaca Press.

Toor, Saadia. 2011. *The State of Islam: Culture and Cold War Politics in Pakistan*. London: Pluto Press.

Urbanati, Nadia. 2014. *Democracy Disfigured: Opinion, Truth and the People*. Cambridge, MA: Harvard University Press.

Voloshinov, Valentin N. 1986. *Marxism and the Philosophy of Language*. Cambridge, MA: Harvard University Press.
Weber, Max. 1978. *Economy and Society*, Roth Guenther and Claus Wittich (eds.), Berkeley. University of California Press.
White, Daniel. 2017. "Affect: An Introduction." *Cultural Anthropology* 32 (2): 175–80.
Wolpert, Stanley. 1993. *Zulfi Bhutto of Pakistan: His Life and Times*. Oxford: Oxford University Press.
Worsley, Peter. 1968. *The Trumpet Shall Sound: A Study of "Cargo" Cults in Melanesia*. New York: Schocken Books.

Contributors

Mahvish Ahmad studies state violence and the intellectual and the political labor of movements targeted in repression. Movements produce analyzes, critiques, and alternatives to violent states, for example, in underground pamphlets. As part of this work, she co-founded *Revolutionary Papers* and is a UK-based Trustee of the South Asian Resource and Research Centre. She is also Assistant Professor in Human Rights and Politics at the Department of Sociology, London School of Economics, the co-founder of the Left-wing magazine *Tanqeed* (online), and a co-convener of the research collective, Archives of the Disappeared.

Aasim Sajjad Akhtar is Associate Professor of Political Economy at the National Institute of Pakistan Studies, the University of Quaid-i-Azam. He works on diverse subjects such as state theory, digitalization, class formation, colonial history, and social movements. He has published widely in journals such as *Third World Quarterly*, *Journal of Contemporary Asia*, *Journal of Peasant Studies*, and *Critical Asian Studies*. He is also the author of four books, most recently *The Struggle for Hegemony in Pakistan: Fear, Desire and Revolutionary Horizons* (2022). He also writes a syndicated column for Pakistan's newspaper-of-record, *DAWN*, and has also been closely involved with progressive politics in Pakistan for more than two decades.

Asad Ali is a sociocultural anthropologist who has taught at the Pratt Institute, and at Rutgers University and the University of Harvard. His principal work examines the intersection of language, emotions, and politics as mediated by law and religion in colonial, and postcolonial, Pakistan. He is also interested in the relationship of aesthetics and politics and is the co-editor of *Love, War and Other Longings: Essays on Cinema in Pakistan* (2020).

Kamran Asdar Ali is Professor of Anthropology at the University of Texas, Austin. He is the author of *Planning the Family in Egypt: New Bodies, New Selves* (2002) and *Communism in Pakistan: Politics and Class Activism 1947–1972* (2015). He is the co-editor of *Gendering Urban Space in the Middle East, South Asia and Africa* (2008), *Comparing Cities: Middle East and South Asia* (2009), and *Gender, Politics, and Performance in South Asia* (2015). He has published several articles on issues of health and gender in Egypt and on ethnicity, class politics, sexuality, and popular culture in Pakistan. He is currently co-authoring a book with Iftikhar Dadi on Pakistani Cinema.

Humeira Iqtidar is Professor of Politics in the Department of Political Economy at King's College London. Her research brings together postcolonial theory, comparative political theory, and Islamic thought with a focus on modern South Asia. Thematically, her research has been concerned with questions of justice and tolerance, the place of religion in contemporary political imagination, and the ideational and institutional legacies of colonialism. Methodologically, she has argued for cross-disciplinary research.

Amen Jaffer is Assistant Professor of Sociology at the Lahore University of Management Sciences. His research is located at the intersection of religion and urban studies with a particular focus on sociality, community, and infrastructure in neighborhoods, markets, and Islamic institutions. His first monograph, which is currently under preparation, is provisionally titled *Making Islam Real: The Social Space of Sufi Shrines in Urban Pakistan* and examines the coming together of Islam and the city in Pakistan's Sufi shrines. He is the co-editor of *State and Subject Formation in South Asia* (2022).

Hassan Javid works on dynastic politics and the historical roots of social inequality and caste-based politics, mainly focusing on the Pakistani Punjab. Formerly an Associate Professor at the Lahore University of Management Sciences in Lahore, Pakistan, he is currently a Faculty member in the Sociology Department at the University of Fraser Valley in British Columbia, Canada.

Omar Kasmani is Postdoctoral Research Associate in Social and Cultural Anthropology at the Collaborative Research Center 1171 Affective Societies at Freie Universität, Berlin. His research practice is situated across the study of contemporary Islamic life-worlds, queer and affect theory and queries critical notions of intimacy and post-migrant be/longing. He is the author of *Queer Companions: Religion, Public Intimacy and Saintly Affects in Pakistan* (2022). His current book project turns to autotheory and brings personal memoir to bear on an affective geography of Berlin.

Naila Mahmood is a Karachi-based visual artist, writer, and documentary photographer. Her lens-based works investigate the complexities of urban spaces and human rights issues. She often examines the social and spatial inequality of hidden gendered spaces. Her artwork has been exhibited in solo and group shows nationally and internationally, and she has been a speaker at various universities. She is an educator and visiting Faculty at the Indus Valley School of Art and Architecture. She has also been a visiting Faculty at University of Karachi and Habib University, Karachi. She served as the director of Vasl Artists' Association (2008–22) and is editor of the volume *Between Quarantine and Quest*, a bilingual anthology of art, poetry, and writings.

Anushay Malik is a labor historian who researches progressive movements. Her earlier work focused mainly on the city of Lahore. Her current research has segued into public history, tracing the story of South Asian labor activists in British Columbia. She was formerly an Assistant Professor at the Lahore University of Management Sciences and is currently a Lecturer at Simon Fraser University in British Columbia, Canada.

Nayanika Mookherjee is Professor of Political Anthropology at Durham University and Co-director of the Institute of Advanced Studies. Based on her book *The Spectral*

Wound: Sexual Violence, Public Memories and the Bangladesh War of 1971 (2015), in 2019 she co-authored a graphic novel and animation film *Birangona: Towards Ethical Testimonies of Sexual Violence during Conflict* (www.ethical-testimonies-svc.org.uk) and received the 2019 Praxis Award. She has published extensively on the anthropology of violence, ethics, and aesthetics, and she researches on gendered violence during wars, debates on reconciliation, and transnational adoption. She has recently published the 2022 *JRAI* (*Journal of Royal Anthropological Institute*) special issue on Irreconciliation.

Claire Pamment is Associate Professor of World Theatre and Gender, Sexuality, and Women's Studies, and Director of the GSWS Program at William & Mary, Virginia. She works in areas of Pakistani theater and performance, foregrounding practices marginalized at the intersections of class, gender, sexuality, and/or religion. Her collaborative work with *khwaja sira—trans* communities—includes the devised theater *Teesri Dhun* and the short film *Vadhai*. She is the author of *Comic Performance in Pakistan: The Bhānd* (2017) and *Badhai: Hijra-Khwaja Sira-Trans Performances across Borders in South Asia* (2023), collaboratively authored with Adnan Hossain and Jeff Roy.

Hashim bin Rashid studies social movements and popular culture in South Asia. He is completing his doctorate at the School of Oriental and African Studies, London, on the development of the peasant movement in Punjab, Pakistan. He is one of the co-organizers of the Emancipatory Rural Politics Initiative (EPRI) South Asia Collective, and has worked as an activist and journalist in Pakistan.

Ahmad Salim is a Pakistani poet, journalist, translator, historian, and archivist currently living in Pakistan. He is the editor and author of around a hundred books including those on the history of the Pakistani Left and on Punjabi literature, as well as research reports on education, labor, gender, the Partition of 1947, the tragedy of 1971, and religious minorities in Pakistan and South Asia. He is the founder and custodian of the South Asian Resource and Research Centre (SARRC), which holds over 40,000 documents and materials of Pakistan's progressive history (www.sarrc.org.pk).

Farida Shaheed is a founding member of Pakistan's national lobby, Women's Action Forum (WAF), created in 1981 to resist the systematic rescinding of women's rights under Zia, and is currently the executive director of Shirkat Gah-Women's Resource Centre that catalyzed WAF. A gender-equality and justice advocate, activism informs her scholastic work and vice versa. She has published widely on the interface of women, identity, state-citizenship, and rights. Recipient of numerous awards, she served as the first UN Independent Expert & Special Rapporteur for cultural rights (November 2009–October 2015) and is currently the Special Rapporteur for education.

Dina M. Siddiqi is Clinical Associate Professor in Liberal Studies at New York University. Her research, grounded in the study of Bangladesh, joins critical development studies, transnational feminist theory, and the anthropology of Islam and human rights. She has published extensively on supply chain capitalism and the garment industry, the politics of representing Muslim women, and forms of cultural nationalism. Her publications are available at https://www.researchgate.net/profile/Dina-Siddiqi. Professor Siddiqi is on the advisory board of *Dialectical Anthropology*, *Contemporary South Asia*, and the *Journal of Bangladesh Studies*. She also serves on the editorial board of Routledge's Women in Asia Publication Series. She sits on the Executive Committee of the American Institute of Bangladesh Studies (AIBS). She is a board member of *Sakhi for South Asian Women*, and on the advisory council of the South Asian feminist network, *Sangat*.

Adeem Suhail is Assistant Professor of Anthropology at Franklin and Marshall College. His research addresses issues in the anthropology of violence, social theory, and urban studies. His current project, *Machines of Violent Desire,* interrogates how non-state violence and transnational kinship networks contribute to order-making in urban South Asia. He is concurrently working on another co-authored book project titled *Sacropolitics*, which addresses how human communities confront emergent ecological and political crises across the globe through a politics of repair and rejuvenation.

Index